VICHY
POLITICAL
DILEMMA

VICHY
POLITICAL
DILEMMA

by Paul Farmer

COLUMBIA UNIVERSITY PRESS

New York 1955

PREFACE

THE ASTUTE READER will want to know at the outset what were the circumstances that induced the author to undertake this study of the Vichy regime. At the time of the events which provide the substance of this book, the author followed the news of France appearing in the newspaper press with the same general interest as other Americans and with a more particular concern arising out of his vocation as a student and teacher specializing in the history of modern France. He had no other, more personal, involvement in what was transpiring in France. At that time and for some years afterward, moreover, his studies in the history of France centered in the period between the Revolution of 1789 and the First World War, so that his interest in the current news of France was no different from that of others in America who were concerned with the world-wide problems of public affairs in our time.

In the fall of 1950 the author was invited to spend a semester in research at the Institute of Advanced Study in Princeton, New Jersey. During these months he took part in a seminar, under the chairmanship of the late Professor Edward Meade Earle, dealing with problems of France since 1918. In this seminar also participated a number of other American, British, and French scholars concerned with modern France.

In the course of the discussions in this seminar, the author came to the conviction that it would be worthwhile to reexamine the experience of France under the German occupation, to discover what new light this might throw on both the history of France in the period 1918–1939 and on the course of affairs since 1944. At the conclusion of the meetings of the seminar, he proceeded to France, where he spent the remainder of the academic year 1950–1951 and the summer of 1951 in research on this topic. The work continued to engage his attention for another two years after his return to America to resume his duties as a member of the Department of History of the University of Wisconsin.

For the research on which this study is based, the author received grants of financial assistance from the Institute for Advanced Study, the Social Science Research Council, and the University of Wisconsin. He is also under a debt to members of the staff of the General Library of the University of Wisconsin, who have been generous in honoring his requests for the purchase of materials relating to this problem and have been helpful beyond the call of duty in locating fugitive items.

In expressing his thanks, however, the author is in conscience bound to make plain that he alone is accountable for his opinions. None of the institutions which have given him assistance in his research is responsible for the views expressed in this book.

PAUL FARMER

Portland, Maine
November, 1954

CONTENTS

VICHY
POLITICAL
DILEMMA

I

PROLOGUE

THIS IS A STUDY of the government, maintaining its seat in the town of Vichy, that assumed the rule of France on July 10, 1940 and retained its rule, at least in name, until August 20, 1944. Taking as its protagonists the men who participated in or gave their active support to this government, it seeks to throw light on the circumstances that brought them into positions of leadership or prominence, the problems they encountered and the solutions they proposed in their endeavor to meet the issues of a period of deep national crisis, and the ideas upon which they purported to base their actions.

The story of the men of Vichy is charged with the most intense political passions. In the view of some, it is a chronicle of the vilest treason; the dark record of the triumph—fortunately, only temporary—of a long-premeditated conspiracy to deliver France to her hereditary enemy; the story of men who betrayed their country either for a crass personal profit or for motives of a narrow class or partisan interest.

In the view of others, on the contrary, Vichy represents the Calvary of a small band of high-minded patriots who chose not to shirk the responsibility of governing their nation under the most painful circumstances and who risked their lives and honor in a desperate struggle to preserve the interests of their countrymen—all this only to incur the abuse of exiles who fled their homeland in its time of crisis and later to suffer the ingratitude of the populace for whose welfare the men of Vichy had labored.

Those who were involved in the struggle that divided France into two hostile camps as soon as her government withdrew from the war—whether they took their stand with Vichy or with its adversaries—were sure that History would vindicate their position. "God and posterity will make answer to your judgment of me," declared Marshal Pétain when his enemies brought him to trial. And the presiding magistrate of the High Court that condemned him acknowledged that "though today we sit in judgment, on a day to come History will judge the judges."

Perhaps in some distant time the disembodied spirit of History will speak on the issues involved in judging the men of Vichy. We cannot have high hopes of hearing its ultimate verdict, however, since even now we can scarcely catch the whispered judgment of History upon issues as far removed from the present as those that rent France during the Revolution of 1789. At any event, the ordinary historian in our time will find it virtually impossible to render perfect justice. Few Frenchmen of our generation can review the evidence without having prejudged the debate. No one abroad, lacking intimate knowledge of the circumstances of each case, can hope to distinguish between those men who served Vichy solely from low motives and those who served with an honorable intent.

For certainly there were patriots who chose to serve under Marshal Pétain in Vichy—as there were also men of selfless heroism who joined General de Gaulle in London or the "Resistance" in France, at the very moment when the Axis seemed to have gained sure mastery of France and reached the threshold of world dominion. And unquestionably there were scoundrels of the worst sort who ultimately gained leading positions in the Vichy regime—just as there were men who joined the opposition abroad or at home, particularly as the day of liberation drew near, simply from motives of personal opportunism. It will not be a major purpose of this study, however, to assess praise or blame among individuals, although inevitably it will imply some kind of estimation of the dozen or so leading personalities of the regime.

Not only would it be presumptuous to divide the men of Vichy into patriots and traitors—it would be fatuous. For most of these men were neither heroes nor villains. Like their adversaries, they were, rather, men who acted from a mixture of high and low motives, in search of both public and private interest.

Therein lies the fascination in the study of Vichy. For this brief episode in the history of France provides a microcosm in which are to be observed nearly all the nuances of human behavior in a time of deep political and moral crisis. To be sure, the story of Vichy does not include the whole range of the human drama. It gives no illustration of the kind of heroism that lends moral grandeur to the saga of the "Resistance." Nor does it furnish comic relief. The issues of the times were much too dire to permit even bitter laughter. Yet it does include what, under happier circumstances, would have seemed farcical buffoonery and the ludicrous posturing of timeservers who today explain away all that yesterday they proclaimed as eternal high principle. And at moments it reveals the stoic dignity of men who did what had to be done, no matter how much they loathed the task.

Yet the most striking impression the observer garners in the study of Vichy is one of tragedy—not quite classic, but embodying something of that inexorable doom within the man which the Greek tragedists sought to portray. For the most characteristic of the various kinds of men who figured in the Vichy regime was not the blackguard who sold his countrymen for his own gain, quite without pretense of principle, nor the patriot who steeled himself to loathsome deeds because the interests of the nation required them. Rather, it was the man of ordinary good will who at the outset recognized that collaboration with the enemy was a painful necessity, as indeed it was, but who thereafter became the prisoner of this initial decision and continued in the course of service to the enemy even after this no longer was the path of the national or of his personal interest. The man of this sort was a tragic victim of his own logic, dragged on to his doom as though by an evil genius.

Regardless of such human interest, some observers regard the serious study of Vichy as a vain endeavor, for the reason that that regime was essentially a function of the momentary hegemony of Nazi Germany. In this view, the men of Vichy were merely the puppets of a monster whose birth and death occurred outside the bounds of France. Hence, they have no history of their own. Certainly there is an element of truth in this view.

Nevertheless, the Vichy regime has real historical importance because of the light it throws on the history of France between the two World Wars. It is sometimes described as the triumph of all those elements that had failed to find expression in the political life of France under the Third Republic. This is an apt observation. Sooner or later, the adherents of Vichy included both the old monarchist opposition to the Third Republic and the newer fascist and protofascist opposition—indeed, virtually all the critics of the liberal republican tradition save the Communists.

At the same time, it is no less valid to regard Vichy as an extension of the Third Republic. Not only was this regime instituted by the vote of the overwhelming majority of the elected representatives of the nation, under the procedure prescribed by the Constitution of 1875: but subsequently it revealed the same crosscurrents of political opinion and the same pattern of intrigue within the governing circle—involving opportunistic alliances among men who detested one another and an unremitting struggle among men who professed the same allegiance—as had been characteristic of the previous republican regime. In the ill-assorted band that proclaimed its devotion to Marshal Pétain one can discern both authoritarians and parliamentarians, fascists heralding the "New Order" of Hitler and royalists lauding the golden age of the Bourbons, socialists who hailed the age of the common man and business magnates who rejoiced in becoming once more "masters in their own homes"—in short, quite the same adversaries who had fought one another so bitterly under the Third Republic.

Yet the "National Revolution" of Marshal Pétain defined as its special mission the task of ridding France of the evil heritage of the Third Republic and reestablishing the life of the nation on a new foundation. Noting the stubborn persistence of the old order, despite the intentions of the new regime, the observer cannot help but gain a new appreciation of how durable was the pattern of political life that France had developed under the Third Republic.

In much the same manner, Vichy illuminates the Fourth Republic. The National Revolution which Vichy proclaimed was but the first of two attempts, in close succession, to wipe the slate clean and devise new social and political institutions for France. The second such venture began in the millennial atmosphere at the close of the war, when the provisional government that succeeded Vichy undertook once more to regenerate the nation. Yet within a short time it became apparent that the Fourth Republic was not so much different from the Third. The adversaries of Marshal Pétain, who succeeded him in power, had little more success than he and his henchmen in solving the problems that bedeviled France. Thus Vichy and its sequel, taken together, give striking indication of those characteristics of French life in the middle of the twentieth century which seem immutable. For the customs and institutions that have withstood both Pétain and De Gaulle are deep-rooted indeed.

Moreover, the Vichy regime affords a new perspective on the position of France in European international relations. This is significant, not merely, nor even mainly, for what it reveals concerning the problem of the relations between France and Germany. Rather, it is notable for what it suggests as to the readiness of the French to accept their exclusion from a leading rank among world powers. Even in the aftermath of the First World War, some Frenchmen were dimly aware that France was unequal to the task of maintaining a position of diplomatic preeminence, but not until the epoch of Vichy did a French government frankly accept a position in the second rank of powers. Only then did Frenchmen begin to speak of France as though she were one of the nations of lesser might in a world torn by struggle between greater antagonists. At the close of the Second World War, new rivals became the adversaries in the titanic contest for mastery of the world—Soviet Russia and the United States superseding Britain and Germany. But the basic situation, as it bore upon France, was to remain the same. And a large segment of French opinion under the Fourth Republic was to continue to think of France, as had some of the men of Vichy, as of a satellite of one or the other of these mightier antagonists, or else as of an arbiter between them.

Indeed, the more we study the men of Vichy, the more we incline to look beyond the men themselves to the problems they faced. These men have interest and importance mainly because they labored to solve a number of problems that had beset France before their rise to prominence and that were to prove no less vexatious after their downfall. Hence, in any broad view of France in the twentieth century, Vichy must take its place as one phase in the continuous inner crisis of modern France. It must appear as one of the chapters in the uninterrupted course of French history.

The story of Vichy also has a broader interest, as a portion of the history of Europe in the period of the Nazi dominance. Indeed, France under Vichy provides perhaps the best place in which to examine the Nazi rule in Europe. The reason is that the Nazis did not rate the French, as a people, either at the top of their scale or at the bottom. Clearly, France did not belong among the partners in the Axis, along with Spain and Italy. Nor did she rank among the privileged "Nordic" satellites. But neither were the French classified with the "semicivilized" or even "subhuman" Slavic peoples.

Perhaps because the Nazis had neither a wholly favorable nor a wholly unfavorable view of the French nation, they showed an ambivalence in their relations with Vichy that probably pervaded their entire policy toward Europe, though it never became so clearly manifest in their relations with other countries. For the Nazis never quite made up their minds whether to deal with conquered France simply by exploiting their military victory on the hallowed principle of *vae victis* or to make France their starting point in an attempt to reorganize Europe on the basis of a "New Order," in which the Germans would retain leadership of Europe but would renounce their opportunity to reduce other nations to servitude, and in which therefore the peoples of Europe would live and prosper together in peace. Because they did not consistently pursue either course, their government never harvested the advantage which it hoped to realize from the triumph of the German armies. Yet a government is seldom indecisive merely because of a weakness of character. Usually it hesitates because it is obliged to choose between alternatives neither of which gives a surer promise of advantage. Thus the study of Vichy suggests that Germany under the Nazis, no less than France under Pétain, was caught in a dilemma.

But the experience of France under German domination holds a meaning that transcends its relevance to the history of the Second World War. For in the middle of the twentieth century a situation of military occupation is by no means exceptional or transitory. One may almost say that in the Europe of our time an alien domination backed by military power is as normal as was the phenomenon of revolution throughout the Europe of the generation of 1848. Virtually every country in continental Europe underwent military occupation at some time in the period 1939–45. At the conclusion of the war, many countries merely passed from one regime of foreign rule to another.

Now, there is a basic problem common to countries in such a situation—the problem of carrying on an inescapable collaboration with the superior power without sacrificing more than the irreducible minimum of the national interest and without losing their sense and pride of nationhood. Unhappily, the study of Vichy therefore has a living interest, because of the light it throws on the problem of other countries that are still in a similar situation. As a case study, it has the more value for the reason that Vichy has now passed into history. Its experience therefore can be reappraised from beginning to end.

The story of Vichy has relatively clear and narrow bounds. It deals with a government that began on July 10, 1940, when the two houses of the French Parliament, meeting together as a National Assembly, voted virtually unlimited powers to Marshal Pétain. It disappeared on August 20, 1944, when the Germans carried away the "Victor of Verdun" as their prisoner. Yet the problem it involves exceeds these bounds. We must look back at least to the close of the First World War in order to explore its background, as we must wait many years more before we can perceive its furthest consequences.

II

THE DILEMMA EMERGES

THE FRENCH look back upon the period between about 1900 and 1914 as a kind of golden age. Like most golden ages, this seems more blessed in retrospect than it did to the men of the times. In this era of reputed bliss, the historian can now perceive omens of the doom that was soon to descend upon the land. Yet the French have much reason to remember the epoch before 1914 with nostalgia. For in that time of childhood memories and the legends of the elders, France seemed to have solved her problems. She had attained a larger economic advance than she had ever known before—and one that she has perhaps never since surpassed. She had maintained her proud rank in the vanguard of European culture—the whole world recognized Paris as the haven of the arts and the home of gracious and elegant living. In the vexed world of domestic politics, her republican regime had proved itself. In the outcome of the Dreyfus affair, the Third Republic had emerged victorious over its enemies on the Extreme Right, while the labor movement on the Extreme Left, though still professing the Marxian doctrines of proletarian revolution, had taken its stand with the embattled partisans of parliamentarism. In the broader arena of world politics, the Third Republic had won a colonial empire second only to the British. By virtue of her alliance with tsarist Russia and her *Entente Cordiale* with Britain, France had apparently gained strength enough to challenge German might. To be sure, no one in France could read the omens of an impending general European war without some deep sense of misgiving. Yet so large was the sense of well-being in that archaic age that the French soldiers could mount the trains taking them to battle, when at last the storm broke in the summer of 1914, with an assurance that seemed lighthearted.

The First World War marked the dawn of a grim new age throughout Europe, and France never regained even the spurious luster of her "golden age" before 1914. Not only did France bear more than her proportionate share of the pain and devastation of the war. But in its sequel, despite the victory she bought at a nearly ruinous price, she found it impossible ever to escape the shadow of a new war or to make herself secure against its menace. For France, the "postwar" period led without an intermission into a new "prewar" period.

Because they were so continuously preoccupied with the problems of war, the French in a sense deluded themselves. Throughout the 1920s and 1930s, the nation looked across the Rhine, rather than at home, for the source of its woes. To be sure, the French were not oblivious of problems within their own borders. Some of them were loud in their criticism of one or another source of civic corruption, and loud in their praises of this or that panacea. In the main, however, France cherished a smug conviction of the excellence of her way of life. And in this view, indeed, much of the outside world concurred.

The French were not wholly wrong in regarding their institutions as adequate to their needs. Despite numerous serious deficiencies, the social, economic, and political institutions of France under the Third Republic satisfied the demands the French themselves put upon them. Though France was lagging behind her neighbors in economic progress, the French did not want to pay the price of greater economic efficiency. Doubtless the Third Republic was a cumbrous and slow-moving political mechanism, but the French knew how to make it work. It had the virtue, as well as the vice, of being responsive to the pressure of a citizen with a personal grievance. It would perhaps have continued to give the same satisfaction as in the blessed era before 1914—provided that France could have lived at peace.

However, in the 1920s and 1930s France could not withdraw from involvement in the issues of world politics, as America did. Facing always the threat of a German resurgence, she could not maintain a secure and self-imposed isolation, even though the French might have been willing to choose this course. Nor, because of circumstances over which they had little or no control, could they organize a system of defenses that would ensure them against a new German attack. Under the stresses which the threat of war imposed upon it, the Third Republic began to weaken and sag even before the deluge struck it in 1940.

Viewed in the perspective of the 1920s and 1930s, the catastrophe that descended upon France in the spring and summer of 1940 was no surprise. Rather, it signalized the moment when a diplomatic and domestic crisis that had been developing throughout the interbellum period reached the point of explosion. At that time, American observers did not recognize or acknowledge this. They refused to admit that the Vichy regime had any genuine connection with the Third Republic—save insofar as it represented the triumph of a conspiratorial alliance between French monarchists and fascists, who had made use of German power to accomplish a revolution they were unable to carry out by themselves.

But the French knew better. No matter how much they disagreed otherwise, in 1940 virtually all Frenchmen saw in their defeat the proof that France lacked the means of withstanding German might. Thus at last they acknowledged a bitter truth which they had sensed for more than twenty years without ever frankly admitting it. And as the nation began its anguished search for a new guidance, Frenchmen of all kinds shared the same recognition that France must reconcile herself to dependence upon one or another stronger nation. This was the view of those who placed their hopes in an Anglo-American deliverance of France as well as of those who urged Franco-German collaboration as the inevitable choice. At the same time, nearly everyone saw in the collapse of the Third Republic the clear evidence of weaknesses in their domestic institutions. Those who supported the National Revolution of Marshal Pétain and those who scorned it shared the same deep conviction that France must make a fresh start.

Hence, in order to understand the state of mind in France which the Vichy regime both expressed and exploited, we must examine the problems that France faced or failed to face in the interval between the two World Wars. The two decades may be divided naturally, though without a sharp break, into two periods. The "postwar" period comprises the 1920s and the beginning of the next decade, and a new "prewar" period begins when the resurgence of German might became no longer a potential but an actual menace. This distinction between the two periods marks a progression within France as well as in international politics. Though the basic problems of France remained much the same, the attitude of the French underwent a profound change.

In the 1920s, despite an ill-defined but widespread uneasiness, no substantial portion of the populace paid serious heed to the voices on the Extreme Right and the Extreme Left that urged the need of a new departure. In the next decade, public opinion passed into quite another mood. No longer did the partisans of the *status quo,* who had monopolized the role of national leadership in the 1920s, evoke the accustomed popular response. In the new era, none save advocates of extreme solutions seemed to speak to the temper of the times. This new mood of desperation and bold venture seemed, at the time, a response to the new pressures of the 1930s, summed up in the depression and the threat of war. In retrospect, however, we can now see in this evolution a sign that the French were beginning to recognize a crisis in their national life, the origins of which had passed unheeded in the previous decade.

At the beginning of the postwar period, France was still a relatively happy land. It had an advantageous inheritance, as we have noted, since the Third Republic had done much, in its epoch of brilliance before 1914, to raise France to new heights. Then, in the course of the four interminable years of the First World War, the republican regime had proved capable of winning a place for France among the victors at the conclusion of one of the greatest struggles the world had ever known. In this test, moreover, the French had shown an amazing solidarity in the face of the enemy.

The war, to be sure, imposed an immense burden upon France in both blood and treasure, and it wrought immeasurable damage in the shock and stress it inflicted upon men's minds and souls. In dead and wounded, France suffered heavier losses, in proportion to her population, than any other large nation. Her death toll mounted to more than one million, in a population just under 40,000,000. Experts never satisfactorily reckoned the cost in money, but it is sufficient to note that France bore upon her soil nearly the whole devastation of warfare on the Western Front, and that warfare laid waste a region which included much of her industrial economy and some of her best agricultural land.

Yet France recovered with remarkable resilience. Inevitably her population showed signs of the bloodletting, in the diminished proportion of adult males in the total population. Nevertheless, the total population declined by only a relatively small percentage, and most families that suffered casualties, while mourning their dead, eventually resumed a more or less normal pattern of life. Within a few years, the land that had been laid waste in the war was brought back under cultivation, the damaged buildings, roads, and bridges were repaired, and devastated mines and factories were put back into operation.

In some measure, France was more fortunate than other nations that took part in the First World War. She escaped some of the dislocations that shook other countries in the postwar period, or experienced but a milder shock. For instance, she kept her colonial empire intact and continued to gain advantage from it, whereas the Germans had to relinquish their dreams of such a resource. Though France had to cope with new resistance to her rule among the Moslem natives of North Africa and in the Near East, she faced no such huge problem of colonial nationalism as did Britain. Moreover, though she experienced a serious inflation, which reduced the franc to one-fifth of its previous value, she did not undergo such an utter collapse of her monetary system as did Germany.

In the postwar period, France even seemed to rise to a new level of preeminence. While Vienna, Berlin, and St. Petersburg passed into eclipse, Paris stood unchallenged as the metropolis of culture and the pleasure resort of Europe. Tourists from Britain and America thronged her streets, engulfed her cafés, crowded her theaters, and swarmed over her historic sites. Latin Americans, after but a hurried obeisance to Madrid, rushed on to *la ville lumière,* there to pay homage alongside the Europeanized upper classes of Islam. In the shops of Paris, the cosmopolitan élite of other European nations rubbed shoulders with these exotic pilgrims before passing on to their round of summer and winter resorts in the French provinces. These now took rank as lesser courts, where the whole world rendered tribute to the unrivaled charm of France.

Meantime France seemed to have discovered new economic vigor. Not only did the suppliers of the traditional French luxuries—women's fashion wear, high-grade textiles, wines, and the like—press their wares upon the world market with a shrewd business sense no less keen than that of the most aggressive American huckster: even in realms involving large-scale manufacture and up-to-the-minute technical skill, the French gained a position of prominence. So well did they exploit their pioneer interest in the automobile that they gained a leading rank among the European producers of cars and trucks. Nor in the 1920s did France lag behind her neighbors in experimentation with the airplane. Likewise she insisted upon demonstrating the prowess of her shipbuilders and her seamen, by launching luxurious North Atlantic steamers, such as the "Île de France," to challenge the worthiest products of British and German ship design.

Despite such evidence of well-being, postwar France began to experience at least a relative decline. The French themselves were aware that something was amiss in their land, and innumerable Frenchmen sought to diagnose the trouble and prescribe a cure. Not even the tourist, intoxicated by the very air of Paris, was unaware that there were serious maladies in France.

In a narrow sense, the problem was diplomatic, and it was as simple to define as it was hard to solve. The crux of the matter was that France was obliged to make herself secure against the inevitable German resurgence, although, if it came to a test of strength between the two countries, she would be unequal to her neighbor. In terms of either population or the economic and technological bases of military power, France by herself did not have the resources needed to enable her to measure up to Germany. Such had been the situation ever since 1870, when Bismarck had at last united the German nation and had smashed the armies of Napoleon III.

From the morrow of their defeat in 1870–1871, the French recognized their inferiority of power. Never thereafter did they attempt to challenge Germany without first gaining the help of strong allies. Throughout the 1870s and 1880s, while they lacked such help, they made no move to avenge their humiliation at Sedan. Not until the 1890s, after she concluded her alliance with Russia, did France begin to venture again upon an active role in European diplomatic affairs. Not until after the *Entente Cordiale* of 1904, when the British gave sign of their readiness to stand with them, did the French dare to offer a serious challenge to the Hohenzollern Reich. And even with the aid of Britain and Russia, and ultimately that of the United States, France had mustered barely strength enough to match the German might.

At the conclusion of the First World War, the French were quite aware of their long-range disadvantage in relation to the Germans. As before, they looked for outside help as the only means of redressing the balance. As an ideal solution, they would have wished for a restoration of their alliance with Russia and their *entente* with Britain, as well as for an assurance of the continued support of the United States. But in the postwar world such a coalition was quite impossible. First, France could no longer hope for the help of Russia. Not only were the French unwilling in the 1920s to accept the Soviet regime as an ally, but Russia was reduced to such an utter chaos that she could barely defend her own borders.

As an irreducible minimum, the French believed they must have a firm assurance of British and American military assistance. Yet, even before the peace conference concluded its labors in 1919, the United States made evident its unwillingness to pursue any active role in European affairs. Soon the British made it clear that they now viewed the French preponderance on the Continent as a disturbance of the balance of power in Europe. Presently the French discovered that, far from giving them help, their erstwhile comrades in arms were now disposed to champion Germany as a makeweight against France.

In lieu of the Anglo-American guarantee that they regarded as their only adequate assurance of security, the French undertook to develop a system of alliances and quasi alliances with some of the nations of Central and Eastern Europe. They began in 1921 by signing a military alliance with Poland. Subsequently they negotiated diplomatic agreements, amounting to alliances, with each of the states of the "Little Entente"—Czechoslovakia, Rumania, and Yugoslavia. With this support, France could feel reasonably safe as long as Germany remained partially disarmed. In the day to come, however, when Germany would repudiate the limitations of the Treaty of Versailles and measure up to her full potential of power, France could not depend upon Poland and the Little Entente to make up her own want of strength. No Frenchman could misjudge this. Plainly, Poland and the Little Entente together did not promise aid equivalent to that which Britain, Russia, and America had contributed during the First World War.

As to a longer-range answer to their problem, the French were divided in their counsels. Many of them thought that the best course was for France to prolong her temporary ascendancy over Germany as far into the future as possible. To do so, she should rigorously enforce those provisions of the peace settlement of 1919 that disarmed Germany and saddled her with an immense burden of reparations. Further, she should utilize the League of Nations as a means of involving other nations in the enforcement of these measures. This policy we may call, for convenience, the "hard" policy toward Germany. It strongly appealed to the French because it corresponded to their long-standing view of Germany as the hereditary enemy. It hearkened back to the time-hallowed French diplomatic tradition of exploiting every opportunity to render Germany weak and helpless. In the postwar period, this "hard" policy was endorsed generally by the French political parties of the Right, although it was also supported by some elements of the Left. Among its principal advocates were Clemenceau, Poincaré, and Tardieu.

On the other hand, a considerable number of the French favored another approach to the problem. They urged a policy of conciliating the Germans by gradually easing those provisions of the peace settlement which especially galled them. Thus they hoped to establish some measure of Franco-German friendship. This policy we may call, again for convenience, the "soft" policy. In the 1920s, British and American observers tended to think of the French as eternally united in their fierce hatred of the *boche* and wholly committed to the "hard" policy. But actually the "soft" policy commanded much popular sympathy.

By no means had the French always shown a single mind in their attitude toward the Germans. Since at least the time of the First Empire, they had shown some signs of recognizing that the principle of national self-determination, which they themselves proclaimed in the Revolution of 1789, implied the unity of Germany. Napoleon I had done much—more, indeed, than he intended—to prepare the way for German political unification. Then, during the epoch of the constitutional monarchies of 1815–1848, the republican minority in France had been enchanted by a rapturous vision of the coming age of the brotherhood of free peoples, when all nations, including the German and the French, would clasp hands in eternal peace.

The Second Empire revived the Bonapartist tradition of French support for the principle of nationality. In the crisis of 1864–1866, as Bismarck took the decisive steps toward German union, Napoleon III made no move. To be sure, the French emperor was not quick to perceive the seriousness of the crisis. But he was also in some measure a prisoner of his own commitment to the doctrine of national self-determination. When the Second Empire perished as a consequence of its policy toward Germany, the French saw fresh proof that weakness toward Germany must inevitably lead to their own ruin. Yet, for more than a generation after the inception of the Third Republic, a considerable portion of the French showed little sign of a desire to avenge the defeat of 1870–71. Under the impulse of Marxian principles, as well as the older dream of a brotherhood of nations, the socialist movement, which rose to prominence in the 1890s, proclaimed the common bonds between the French and German peoples. In the decade before 1914, the Socialist leader Jean Jaurès gained the reputation of a traitor to the French nation because of his devotion to the idea of Franco-German reconciliation. Some individuals in the more moderate parties of the Left also continued to think in terms of a Franco-German *rapprochement,* even down to the outbreak of the First World War. Notable among these was Joseph Caillaux, whose attitude toward Germany remained so dubious that he was accused of having had contact with the enemy during the war. One of his protégés, Pierre Laval, was later to win an even larger renown as an apostle of Franco-German collaboration.

In the 1920s, the "soft" policy won new support. This came in part from a widespread pacifist revulsion from the horror and apparent futility of the war. This sentiment gained much ground in veterans' organizations and generally among the common people. It also drew nourishment from the new vogue of Wilsonian idealism. Despite the skeptical attitude of French politicians, the idea of the League of Nations reawakened the liberal dreams of the age of 1848. The notion behind the Parliament of Nations did not center in only Franco-German reconciliation, but it seemed to sanction a "soft" policy toward Germany as well as more grandiose proposals for universal disarmament and the arbitration of all international disputes. In the 1920s, the "soft" policy won political support mainly from the parties of the Left. The acknowledged leader of those advocating Franco-German reconciliation at this time was Aristide Briand.

In the immediate aftermath of the war, the advocates of the "hard" policy occupied the positions of political leadership in France. This was partly because the war itself had fanned French hatred of the *boche,* partly because, for reasons of domestic politics, the parties of the Right gained the upper hand. In conformity with the views of the champions of the "hard" policy, the French government insisted throughout the peace conference of 1919 upon reducing the borders of Germany, saddling her with a bill for reparations that would mean economic ruin, and imposing severe limitations upon her army and navy. In the same spirit, the French delegates in the Reparations Commission continued to work to wring the utmost tribute from the former foe. Likewise, when Germany fell behind in her payments, France seized the opportunity to occupy the Ruhr in 1923.

After 1924, the parties advocating the "hard" policy lost ground. They suffered a setback when the failure of the French occupation of the Ruhr became apparent. Thereafter advocates of the "soft" policy began more largely to influence French diplomacy. By this time, indeed, the French had little choice but to adopt the "soft" approach, since the British were now openly supporting the Germans. Moreover, the Germans made it easier for them to revise their orientation. For moderates such as Stresemann, who came into prominence at this time, gave at least the outward signs of a readiness to establish more amicable relations between the two countries. At the Locarno conference in 1925, France registered her desire for reconciliation, when she agreed to Germany's admittance into the League of Nations. Thereafter the French also gave ground on the issue of reparations. In the Young Plan of 1929, the German indebtedness on this score was reduced to a sum which the Germans could pay without unreasonable hardship. Likewise, France agreed in 1930 to the temporary suspension, and in 1931 to the virtual termination of reparations payments, and likewise, she acquiesced in the open rearmament of Germany in 1934 and the remilitarization of the Rhineland in 1936.

It was partly because of their vacillation between the "hard" policy and the "soft" that the French in the postwar period had poor success in dealing with the German problem. They did not attain the objective of the "hard" policy, for Germany was permitted to rise out of her pariah status and eventually to undertake large-scale rearmament. Nor did they attain the objective of the "soft" policy, for they insisted so long upon enforcing the vexing provisions of the Treaty of Versailles, and hesitated so much in their gestures of friendship, that the Germans had little reason to trust their talk of reconciliation. Yet the French were not wholly to blame for their diplomatic failure. Throughout the 1920s, they were obliged to deal with Germany under conditions which they regarded as impossible. For, without British and American backing, they were in no position either to enforce a harsh peace or to trust to the risky venture of winning German good will.

In a broader view, however, the diplomatic problem was not basic. The weakness of France was not due to circumstances outside her borders. Rather, her diplomatic dilemma was indicative of a weakness somewhere within France herself. Even in the postwar decade, the French were not unaware of this, and many of them saw their trouble as due to the problem of population. In this view, France was unable to make herself secure because her population was less than 40,000,000, whereas Germany had more than 60,000,000. Hence Frenchmen without number in the 1920s sought to discover the cause and cure of the low French birth rate, and vainly exhorted their countrymen to raise larger families.

Unquestionably France did have a low birth rate. Undoubtedly she suffered a serious disadvantage in military power because of her lesser number of adult males available for service in the army. But outsiders never took the problem of population as seriously as did the French. In recent times, population does not determine the military strength of a nation, although naturally it sets a maximum limit to its potential power. This depends more upon the horsepower and the firepower

available to the military, and these, in turn, reflect economic and technological factors.

Even before 1914, France barely ranked with the leading industrial
nations, and in the postwar period she fell farther and farther behind
such nations as Britain, Germany, and the United States. As size is
reckoned by twentieth-century standards, France has never developed
large-scale business operations, even in those branches of her economy,
such as the production of wines, where she has shown special economic
vigor. Rather, the French economy reveals nearly everywhere the persistence of small, family enterprises. Generally, firms of this kind are
short of capital, use a labor force of seldom more than a few score men
in a single establishment, with a minimum of power machinery, depend
upon time-worn methods of marketing, are often quite innocent of
bookkeeping, and rarely make even a gesture at cost accounting.[1] Nor
is French agriculture more progressive. In some areas, to be sure, France
supports large-scale farming, and in other areas, her peasants sometimes
achieve wonders of intensive cultivation on their minuscule holdings.
On the whole, however, the general level of French agriculture is no
higher than that of her manufactures and commerce.

In itself, this economic retardation is perhaps not critical. The French
themselves apparently do not want their economy organized on a large
scale. They do not have rapacious economic appetites. They attach perhaps more importance to personal security and independence than to
higher economic returns, at the price of greater risk and a more exacting
discipline of work. Moreover, the French economy has some advantages
that are bound up with its "backwardness." France is more secure against
the vicissitudes of the business cycle than Britain, Germany, and the
United States. She is also less subject to such disturbances as technological unemployment and the rapid obsolescence of plant investment, which
are some of the costs of a more dynamic economy.

[1] Though retardation, as evidenced by a slow rate of expansion, dependence on traditional
methods of production, and small-scale enterprise, is a general characteristic, there are some
branches of the French economy that have shown remarkable readiness to accommodate themselves to new practices and technics. For example, in the marketing of wines and liquors under
the label of the producer or wholesaler, or under appelations controlled by the government, the
French were among the pioneers in brand-name merchandising. And France was far from
backward, we have noted, in comparison with other countries on the Continent, in developing
an automobile industry. The phenomenon of economic backwardness in France is by no means
universal, nor is the problem of its causes simple.

Nevertheless, the resistance of the French economy to expansion has become a national problem because France is inescapably involved in a diplomatic situation where war is a chronic likelihood. She can keep a small-scale, stable economy only at the expense of her military strength. What causes this relative stagnation of her economy, no one can say with assurance. Indeed, we shall never fully answer the question as it bears upon France until we discover the prime factors causing economic expansion generally in the modern world.

In numerous respects, France is exceptionally well endowed. She has good access to both the Atlantic and the Mediterranean, a terrain that presents no serious hindrance to inland transportation, a large area of fertile farm land, a mild and diversified climate, fair deposits of coal and iron ore, excellent resources of bauxite for the production of aluminum, and an adequate potential of hydroelectric power. Moreover, her colonial empire, which includes tropical and semitropical lands, supplies many of her wants that cannot be satisfied at home. Despite these advantages, however, France suffers from some serious economic handicaps. Her coal resources are not ample, nor of the best quality for industrial uses. Furthermore, the principal deposits of coal are in the north, near the Belgian border and the Channel coast, but the main deposits of iron ore are in the east, in and around Lorraine. So the region rich in iron ore lacks the coal needed for smelting and working the iron.

Matters of historic custom, particularly the traditional preeminence of France as a producer and exporter of luxury wares, have been perhaps more important factors in checking the growth of large-scale enterprise. Since the age of the Bourbon kings, France has been chiefly renowned for such costly specialities as silks, lace, wines, and, latterly, women's high fashion. Over the span of generations, the market for such items has been relatively stable and generally profitable. But it has always been a rather small market, never allowing much room for expansion, and this kind of business does not lend itself to the use of modern techniques of mass production. Instead, it puts a premium upon the labor of skilled artisans, among whom vintners may be numbered, and a kind of business management that reveres tradition as the gauge of its success.

Because of this and other causes, French business depends largely upon small family firms, comprising father and sons or brothers and their sons. These family firms can function satisfactorily in some luxury trades, where the name and reputation of the family are valuable assets and the need for capital is not great, but they are ill suited to businesses that seek to exploit a broad mass market and therefore require a huge investment in plant, machinery, and inventory. Nevertheless, the family firm predominates in most branches of the French economy, not only in those luxury trades in which it is not inappropriate. One reason for its prevalence is that it responds to the deep French sense of family solidarity. For the French temper their characteristic individualism mainly by clannishness rather than by regard for a broad and impersonal public interest. Ordinarily a French businessman prefers not to share the management and income of his business with an outsider.

Moreover, many a family firm, making little distinction between the household purse and business capital, could hardly function on a wider basis. Its primitive methods of bookkeeping would not be adequate to the task of dividing the profits among several partners or a number of shareholders. And businessmen are well aware that if they were to keep fuller business records, so as to render an accounting to stockholders, they would also have to make a fuller accounting to the tax collector.

Perhaps France shows this predilection for small enterprises also because of a distinctive attitude toward business—a temper that is hostile or antithetical to venture, innovation, and expansion. Perhaps French economic life is "backward" because of the lack of a dynamic, modern business psychology. For French business shows a marked preference for time-proven methods as against possible improvement. Its characteristic orientation is toward operations based on a small volume of business with a large margin of profit, which assures an income of known limits. A smaller margin on a larger volume offers greater possibilities of return but involves more speculative risk. The American observer cannot escape the impression that French business seems to show the mind of the peasant, preferring the clear, limited advantage in the short run. It seldom reveals the sanguine optimism of the pioneer, risking the calculable but limited present for a bold gamble on the future.

This economic stagnation was related to the social problems that engaged the attention of France in the interbellum period. These social

problems were far from new, for no nation has a longer record of ran-
corous strife between the bourgeoisie and the proletariat than has France.
Nor were these problems a distinctive concern. Throughout Europe, demands for the betterment of the condition of the common people gained
new vehemence after the First World War. But in France more than
elsewhere in Western Europe, the problems of social melioration were
enmeshed in the problem of economic retardation.

As in other countries in Western Europe, the urban working class
was the prime mover in the drive for democratic or equalitarian social
reform. But in France, the urban labor movement did not have such
obvious reasons for assuming this leadership as might seem. First, the
industrial proletariat, in a rigorous definition of the term, was a relatively
small class, because large-scale industry was not characteristic of France.
Then, too, the urban working class of France was not conspicuously
oppressed in the postwar period. The French urban worker had perhaps less protection in the form of social legislation than did his German
or British comrade, but he had no less protection in the form of trade-
unionism. Moreover, by virtue of rent-control laws introduced during
the First World War and never really relaxed thereafter, he had to pay
only a nominal rent. Hence he could spend most of his wages on other
necessities than shelter. Furthermore, because of the stability of the
French economy, he was relatively secure against either technological
or cyclical unemployment. And, in an economic situation where small
shops predominated, he still had some hope of rising out of the working
class.

Nevertheless, the French worker had grievances. Though he might
dream of having a shop of his own, the average workingman had little
chance of getting more than his daily bread and wine, little hope of a
secure old age, and little likelihood of providing a better prospect for
his son. From these bleak though not wretched realities, the proletariat
of postwar France derived some of its stimulus for a renewed offensive
against the bourgeoisie. Even more, however, it drew inspiration from
its long tradition of class struggle. For out of the romantic legends running back to the Paris Commune of 1871, the "June Days" of 1848, and
the reign of the Jacobins in 1793, the urban populace of France gained
a sharp sense of class consciousness and a unique militance of spirit.

Because of this heritage, French workingmen are normally more vigorous in the assertion of their grievances than the British or the German proletariat.

In the Socialist Party and the Communist Party, the French working class found the political expression of its demands. However, neither party in the 1920s developed more than the rudiments of a program for succoring the masses. Both supported trade unions, invariably sided with workers who were on strike, regularly protested any intervention by the government against strikers, and favored higher wages and lower prices. But beyond such a blanket endorsement of the immediate demands of the urban workers, neither party had much to propose. The Communists saw no real improvement for the proletariat save through a revolution on the Bolshevik model. By way of a program for France, they pointed to the example of Soviet Russia. For their long-range program, the Socialists paid lip service to the principles of Marxism. But ever since the period of the Dreyfus affair, their leaders had been committed to an active role in Parliament in alliance with nonsocialist parties. In practice, they devoted their attention mainly to the routine intrigues of the French parliamentary system.

In the 1920s, neither the Socialists nor the Communists accomplished much toward satisfying the demands of the proletariat for social reform. In the immediate aftermath of the war, the parties of the Right gained the upper hand in Parliament. The representatives of the conservative upper bourgeoisie retained strength enough in Parliament to block any measure of social legislation that threatened to impose a serious burden on the rich in order to relieve the poor. In such a situation, the Socialists were reduced to an unrewarding endeavor to maintain an alliance with the Radical-Socialists, while the latter shifted back and forth from Right to Left, without making a firm commitment to either side. Meantime the Communists held only a negligible representation in Parliament and made practically no use of the few seats they controlled, save as a means of propaganda.

In some measure, the proletarian parties owed their ineffectiveness to their own weakness. Because the labor movement was split between the Socialists and the Communists, neither party could mobilize the whole strength of the urban working class. But even if either party had vanquished its rival, a single party of the labor movement would not have commanded overwhelming strength, because the industrial working class comprised only a relatively small proportion of the entire population. And both the Communists and the Socialists were so wedded to the proletariat that neither could win over the broad lower strata of the urban middle class or the rural populace.

But in some measure, too, the Marxian parties owed their check to the stubborn resistance of the business classes. For the French bourgeoisie proved much slower than the British or the German industrialists in accepting the principle of social legislation. In their practices of business management, moreover, they showed little or no evolution toward an "enlightened" capitalism. Being committed to the old system of high margins of profit on a small turnover, they did little to give the mass of the people the advantage of mass production by providing the necessities of life at a lower cost, thus raising the standard of living within the framework of a regime of laisser-faire.

Yet the French bourgeoisie was not simply the heir to Bourbon and aristocratic selfishness and shortsightedness. It, too, had some reasonable grievances. As long as the urban working class accepted the leadership of Socialists and Communists, whose program consisted of little more than a dogmatic endorsement of demands for higher wages and vague dreams of a proletarian millennium, businessmen could hardly give a sympathetic ear to the wishes of the labor movement. Nor did the moderate parties in Parliament, such as the Radical-Socialists, offer guidance; for the leaders of these parties showed little interest in discovering a basis for reconciliation between business and labor.

At bottom, the social problem was a reflection of the national economic problem. For without the aid of modern machine technics for mass production, the French worker simply could not produce as much wealth as the German or the British. The businessman therefore could not afford to give him a higher real income, whether voluntarily or under the compulsion of social legislation. In a narrow sense, the businessman was to blame, since he, not the worker, was responsible for economic management. But in a broader view, the business classes were not wholly accountable for their failure. It would have been a work of superhuman proportions to undo the complex of customs inhibiting modern industrialism in France.

Besides the classic conflict between business interests and labor, another kind of social problem arose as between the rural and the urban populace. One aspect of this problem was the antagonism which the urban labor movement felt toward the peasants. Both the parties of the Right and the moderate parties, such as the Radical-Socialists, owed much of their strength in Parliament to rural constituencies. This aroused the ill will of the urban workers toward the village population, since the peasants thus provided strength to the parties identified with a conservative point of view on social issues.

Yet the peasants had some reason to feel themselves the forgotten men of France. Notwithstanding the politicians' declarations of solicitude for him, the peasant was well aware that the townsmen, whatever their class, looked down upon him. In France, ambition leads to the town. Though this attraction is not peculiar to France, it is perhaps more pronounced and of longer standing there than in other countries. For his part, the peasant feels a deep resentment and suspicion of the world outside his village.

Here, again, the social problem is bound up with the basic economic problem. The cleavage between the town and the village was not, at bottom, due to the political preponderance of the rural voters, nor to the economic exploitation of the village by the city. Rather, it was due to the slow and limited penetration of modern economic technics in France, which did less to revolutionize the village than the town. Hence, the village remained, as in the preindustrial era, at a lower cultural level than the town.

In the 1920s, the French more commonly conceived of their national problems in terms of politics than in terms of social and economic issues. The relative economic decline of France attracted little or no attention in the postwar decade, and social issues did not attain prime importance until the 1930s. But since time out of mind, matters of government had been a normal preoccupation of French public opinion.

In respect to her political institutions, postwar France seemed singularly fortunate. Long before the other nations of continental Europe, she had developed a viable republican regime, such as now seemed the norm toward which Europe as a whole was striving. To be sure, the Third Republic had been set up in the 1870s by men who would have preferred a constitutional monarchy, and throughout the 1880s and 1890s it had been subjected to royalist attack. So sharply had the nation been divided over constitutional issues that foreigners spoke of France as comprising two separate nations. One of these accepted democratic republicanism as the logical outcome of the Revolution of 1789, while the other repudiated the entire individualistic outlook on the world which the Revolution expressed. In the immediate aftermath of the war, however, these "Two Frances" seemed reconciled. The Right had rallied behind republican leadership when the crisis struck in 1914, and the Left had proven itself no less deserving of the gratitude of the nation.

Nevertheless, everyone could see that the practice of representative government in France produced a number of problems. Most of these seemed to arise because her republican regime was too responsive to the sovereign people. The French Parliament had long since gained complete control over the executive. The President of the Republic had been reduced to a mere figurehead, and the President of the Council of Ministers—the Premier, as outsiders call him—had become simply the chairman of a committee of influential deputies and senators.

One of the numerous circumstances that brought this about was the proliferation of political parties. The Premier owed his position to a temporary coalition of perhaps a half-dozen parties rather than to the preponderance of his own party. Consequently he lacked a secure control over the majority in the legislature. Another notable reason for the weakness of the executive was the custom that made it impossible for the Premier to dissolve a hostile Parliament and order new elections. This meant that the Premier lacked the means of holding Parliament in check by the threat of requiring unruly members to risk their seats in a campaign for reelection. Nor could he appeal to the voters over the heads of their representatives for endorsement of his legislative program.

Because he was in so insecure a position, the Premier was obliged to develop his policy primarily with a view to reconciling the diverse opinions and interests of the deputies on whose votes he depended. Seldom was he successful, even in this limited endeavor, for a period of more than a few months. And whenever Parliament voted against the Premier, the entire Council of Ministers was obliged to resign. In the whole span of the Third Republic, between 1871 and 1940, there were 101 successive cabinets. Only nine of these lasted more than two years, and none for as long as three years.

To be sure, no one attached much importance to the fall of one cabinet and the formation of another. Ordinarily a new cabinet included many members of the previous one, sometimes even the previous Premier. Often it carried on much the same policies. There were only a small number of men in Parliament recognized as *ministrables,* that is, as men considered eligible for appointment to a ministerial office. New men were only slowly admitted into this circle, and never men of extreme political views or "difficult" temperament, since such persons did not easily fit into a coalition. Moreover, the civil service carried on much of the work of the government without regard to the changes in the cabinet. Indeed, the Conseil d'État, the supreme administrative council, comprising the high functionaries of the civil service, had nearly as much practical influence as the Council of Ministers.

This regime had its good side. The voter who had a complaint against an administrative ruling, or a pressure group that had a legislative interest of large importance, could appeal to a member of Parliament who in turn could count upon getting the Premier or the appropriate minister to give attention to the grievance. Indeed, the Premier seldom had so secure a majority that he could afford to turn a deaf ear to even a single deputy. This kind of regime gave France a needed protection against too strong an executive: for French political institutions are so centralized that if a single person or a small group were to have a free hand in managing the government, this man or this faction would have power enough to dominate the nation.

However, the French parliamentary system unquestionably put too strong a check upon the executive. The Premier was scarcely ever in a secure enough position of political leadership to be able to diagnose one of the several national problems, develop a long-range program for its solution, and then carry the program through to completion. Neither in the postwar period nor in the prewar decade of the 1930s did France suffer as much from the consequences of wrong policy as from the absence of any consistent policy.

Under this system, the men most apt to secure the office of Premier or other ministerial positions were those adept at intrigue in the lobbies of Parliament and in shrewd tactical maneuvers on the floor, rather than men distinguished by their ability to analyze the broad problems of the nation and propose a remedy. Because the politicians of the Third Republic seldom showed distinction as statesmen, some foreign observers used to belittle them as mediocrities, as did the French themselves. But this was not an accurate appraisal of the situation. The French politician was an exceptionally skilled practitioner of a rigorous vocation. A man who held office in one coalition after another—cooperating at one time with colleagues pledged to laisser-faire, at another time with avowed Marxians, and sometimes with both at once—was by no means without competence. As long as France lived under the kind of parliamentary regime characteristic of the Third Republic, the political life of the nation depended upon the specialized talent of men such as these.

Because its members were fellow practitioners of an esoteric skill, the French Parliament took on the character of a guild or fraternal association. No matter what principles he professed, a deputy was primarily a man committed to winning and holding office. He had a fellow feeling with any other man who made his livelihood in the same strange way. The citizen did not always take a charitable view of this comradeship among deputies. Indeed, it had an unattractive side, as is the case in most guilds. Whenever a member of Parliament got in trouble because of a devious or even corrupt use of the power of his office, some of his colleagues would rally to his side. They would help him cover up because they knew they might themselves need such fraternal assistance some other time. So notorious was this solidarity that a large proportion of the French people looked upon the average deputy as one of a gang engaged in a gigantic swindle, the members of which invariably stood together against an outsider.

Consequently, a good many Frenchmen thought that there was something in their political life that needed changing. In the 1920s, only a relatively small faction on the Extreme Right, and the Communists on the Extreme Left, went so far as to question the intrinsic worth of Parliament as an institution, and only a few voices were raised among republican politicians in favor of measures of reform. Nevertheless, the criticism of Parliament in the 1920s bespoke an attitude that was to persist and gain more vigor in the 1930s. Still later, it was to have importance in the Vichy interlude.

In the postwar period, the *Action Française* had a virtual monopoly of the criticism of Parliament from the Extreme Right. The *Action Française* was a newspaper of opinion, which had begun as a biweekly magazine in 1898 but had become a daily in 1908. Throughout its career, its leading light was Charles Maurras, who served as editor and wrote a column of comment in each issue. Léon Daudet, son of the famous novelist, was a frequent contributor. Latterly, Maurice Pujo took over much of the routine management of the paper. Associated with these was Jacques Bainville. From time to time he wrote essays for the paper, though he won a larger renown for his books on the history of France and of the Third Republic. These and other personalities whose contributions appeared in the *Action Française* were men of much intellectual brilliance. Their writings attracted wide attention in the richer bourgeois and aristocratic circles.

The *Action Française* also sponsored a loose political association, known as the Camelots du Roi. This comprised mainly university students of well-to-do conservative families, who frequently organized noisy demonstrations in the streets of Paris and on the premises of the Sorbonne. In the main, however, the *Action Française* expressed an intellectual position rather than a political movement. The directors of the newspaper, who were primarily men of letters, took little or no interest in establishing a political party to give voice to their views in Parliament.

By its own profession, the *Action Française* was royalist, denouncing the Third Republic and demanding the restoration of a king. In accordance with the traditions of French royalism, it also proclaimed its staunch devotion to the Catholic Church. However, its doctrines were not a mere continuation of the traditions of earlier French conservatism. Indeed, it incurred the condemnation of both the Church and the spokesmen of the older monarchist movement in France.

During the nineteenth century, French royalists had generally accepted the principle of parliamentary supremacy. Moreover, because of their allegiance to the Catholic Church, at a time when Rome was at odds with the new principle of nationalism, the conservatives of the nineteenth century had been committed to a cosmopolitan outlook rather than a narrow preoccupation with the interests of France alone.

But the *Action Française* voiced an unequivocal opposition to the institution of Parliament. It demanded an authoritarian government that would "integrate" the French nation. The king must give France a single, strong leadership. He must break with the liberal tradition of giving rein to individual self-interest and of trusting to a miracle to transform the aggregate of selfishness into the common good. To square their aristocratic predilections with a democratic recognition of the masses, the theorists of this new school of royalism espoused an intense, chauvinistic exaltation of French nationalism.

The *Action Française* also adopted the creed of anti-Semitism. These doctrines had gained new vogue in France, as elsewhere, in the 1880s and 1890s, winning disciples on the Left as well as the Right. In the crisis of the Dreyfus affair, however, the Left had taken a decisive stand against anti-Semitism. In the anti-Dreyfusard camp, which became the rallying ground of all enemies of liberalism, hatred of the Jews became a cardinal principle. In the sequel to the Dreyfus affair, the publicists of the *Action Française* had carried on the crusade against the Jews and by the time of the First World War they had become its chief propagandists. This campaign they continued throughout the 1920s. In much the same vein, the partisans of the *Action Française* took over the old conservative hatred of the Free Masons. Indeed, they lumped together Free Masons, Jews, liberals, and socialists, denouncing them all indiscriminately as members of a single, long-standing conspiracy to destroy the French nation.

During the 1920s, British and American observers of France were fascinated by the *Action Française*. Generally, they paid it more attention than its influence at that time warranted. The French themselves were not disposed to take its views seriously. The newspaper never had a large circulation, and its staunch partisans were even less numerous than its readers.

Yet the *Action Française* was not without importance. Probably it made a considerable mark insofar as it spread the ideas of anti-Semitism, gave them a kind of respectability, and helped fix them in the minds of men of the conservative upper classes. And doubtless it did much to transmit to a new generation some of the tradition of the France of the counterrevolution, which otherwise might have died with the survivors of the last generation that had reached mature years in the nineteenth century.

Some of the conservative criticism of the parliamentary system led to an interest in corporatism. To be sure, these doctrines ran counter to some of the hallowed postulates of French thought concerning social and political problems. Since the Revolution of 1789, France had become accustomed to the principle that society should recognize the equality of men as axiomatic. This equality would be vouchsafed, not by reducing the obvious disparities between the rich and the poor, but by defining men primarily as members of the political community, or citizens, and by recognizing no distinction among citizens in respect to their legal obligations and privileges. Hence, the state should not recognize social classes or any other kind of grouping of citizens.

In the late nineteenth century, however, various voices had been raised in France that urged a public recognition of the natural associations among men. Foremost of these is the family. No less important are the larger vocational or professional communities, uniting men who gain their livelihood in the same pursuit. This interest had arisen mainly among Catholic social theorists and reformers. They wished to develop a positive approach to social and political problems, in accord with Catholic religious doctrines, as an alternative to the liberalism and socialism which the Church had condemned. Notable among these pioneers, and representative of some scores of others, were Frédéric Le Play, Count Albert de Mun, and René de La Tour du Pin.

In the view of the Catholic advocates of corporatism, the recognition of "corporative" associations, that is, some kind of organization binding workingmen and businessmen together and stressing the dependence of each upon the other, was an indispensable prerequisite to a harmonious social order. Only thus would society make answer to the vicious and un-Christian principle of egoism, which is implicit in liberalism. At the same time, it would make answer to Marxism, which endorsed class warfare. In the 1890s, this Catholic corporatism gained endorsement in the pronouncements of Pope Leo XIII. Soon it became the slogan of all those who professed to approach social and political problems according to the principles of the Catholic Church.

In the postwar period, the idea of corporatism continued to gain ground. The *Action Française* made corporatism one of the planks in its platform, even though this principle ill accorded with its espousal of an authoritarian dictatorship. French conservatives also became more aware of the corporatist approach through their interest in Italian Fascism, which in the 1920s made much profession of corporatist principles.

Not all the interest in corporatism was conservative. Some of the pioneer Catholic corporatists had been more interested in bettering the condition of the masses than in defending the interests of the rich. And in the decade before the First World War, some elements in the Marxian labor movement had toyed with syndicalism, which proposed to make use of the trade unions in the construction of a socialist new order. These notions ran parallel to the corporatist emphasis on vocational communities as the basis of the social organization. In the 1920s, some individuals identified with the labor movement, as well as conservatives, had become interested in Italian Fascism. Notable among these was Hubert Lagardelle, who had gained some renown before the First World War as a militant Marxist. For the most part, however, corporatism remained identified with conservatism in the 1920s. And, like the royalism of the *Action Française,* it was a topic of table talk rather than of serious political debate.

The Left voiced less criticism of political institutions in the postwar period than did the Right. This was natural enough, since the Left was traditionally the champion of the parliamentary system. The Socialists had long since become reconciled to the collaboration of classes which capitalism implies. Their deputies were as deeply involved in the game of parliamentary maneuver, and as avid for office, as those of the other parties in Parliament.

The Communists were more stubborn in their insistence upon a rigorous interpretation of Marxism, and they made little attempt to disguise their scorn of Parliament. They placed their faith in a Soviet regime on the Russian model, rather than in a Parliament purporting to represent both bourgeois and proletarian interests. But the Communists did not meet with much success in the 1920s. Not until the 1930s did they win a large following in France, and then only after they shifted over to a more favorable view of Parliament.

No less notable was the growing recognition, among those who endorsed the republican regime, of the need for some measures of reform that would render the parliamentary system more effective. For knowledge of the shortcomings of the political institutions of the nation was by no means a monopoly of those who avowed their opposition to the Third Republic.

Various alternative courses gained advocates among those who wished to strengthen the republican regime. One of these would have been to give a larger role to the President of the Republic. In principle, this would have been a reasonable line of constitutional development, since the President of the Republic was the titular head of the state. Being elected to office for a term of seven years, he was not subject to the ceaseless shifts of alignment among the parties in Parliament. Hence, he was presumably in a position to rise above partisan interest and exercise an influence in favor of consistent, long-range policies. Indeed, some such role had been intended for the President of the Republic at the time when the constitution of the Third Republic was devised.

In practice, however, this intention had never been realized. One reason was that, during the 1870s, the royalists had hoped to transform the office of the President of the Republic into that of a king whenever they should succeed in reestablishing a constitutional monarchy. Consequently the republicans had stoutly resisted any move to give real influence to the nominal head of the state. Another reason was that the republicans never forgot the use that both Napoleon I and Napoleon III had made of their position as chief executive in a republican government: they regarded any move to strengthen the hand of the President as a symptom of Bonapartism. Still another factor was chronic personal jealousy, which was characteristic of republican politicians under the Third Republic. Invariably they would unite against any of their own number who seemed about to rise above his peers. Thus the tradition developed that only political nonentities were eligible for the office of President of the Republic. Once elected, the chief of state was to confine his exertions principally to ceremonial functions.

In the constitutional practice of the Third Republic, the President had a single prerogative of importance—the right, whenever a cabinet resigned, to select the man who would attempt to organize a new one. Since there were often a half-dozen men who might accomplish this, if invited to make the attempt, the President of the Republic might have a chance to exercise a personal influence. However, he could never go far in this direction. For the new Premier would have to gain a majority in Parliament, and if the President of the Republic should make too bold a use of his right to nominate the Premier, Parliament would certainly vote the new cabinet down.

Shortly before the First World War, a notable attempt was made to challenge the tradition which reduced the President of the Republic to so slight a role. Raymond Poincaré, who held the office from 1913 to 1920, was a man of more strength of character and conviction than most of his predecessors, and he was bold enough to make use of his position in behalf of the policies and personalities he favored. He provoked bitter opposition, however, and ultimately he found himself compelled to give up his quest for personal influence and to accept the usual, narrow definition of his role. Despite the lesson of Poincaré's venture, Alexandre Millerand, who won election as President of the Republic in 1920, made a similar bid for personal influence. But in his turn, he met with so determined an opposition in Parliament that he had to resign in 1924, before completing his term of office. None of his successors made another such attempt.

Another possible means of providing more stable leadership would have been to strengthen the position of the Premier, or President of the Council of Ministers. An obvious means would have been to give him the right to dissolve Parliament in the event of a vote against his government. Then members of Parliament would think twice before voting to overthrow the cabinet, since their vote might well mean that they would have to run the risk of a new election to regain their seats.

Such a procedure would not have been a new departure. The constitution of the Third Republic included provision for the dissolution of the Chamber of Deputies, on the initiative of the President of the Republic and with the consent of the Senate. However, this device was inoperative. Only once, in 1876, had a President of the Republic ever made use of it. On that occasion he had provoked so hostile a reaction that shortly afterwards he had to resign. During the 1920s and 1930s, a number of republican politicians, including André Tardieu and Gaston Doumergue, proposed to revive the procedure of dissolution, perhaps with some modification so as to put the initiative in the hands of the Premier. But no Premier made a move in this direction. So it remained a matter of idle talk.

Still another approach would have involved a modification in the method of electing members of Parliament, so as to give more importance to political parties and less to individual candidates. The usual method of election under the Third Republic provided for small constituencies, each having a single deputy. Commonly the deputy was able to build up so strong a personal following in his constituency that he was sure of his reelection, whether or not he had the help of a national party organization. Hence he was under little practical compulsion, once he reached Parliament, to submit to the dictates of a party in determining whether to vote for or against the government. As a result, political parties were numerous, small, and ill-disciplined, and the "majority" in the Chamber of Deputies was never made up of a single party. Rather, it represented a temporary coalition of a half-dozen or more parties. Any single party that withdrew from this coalition might cause the downfall of the cabinet.

In the postwar decade, an attempt was made to substitute larger electoral districts, each having a number of deputies, for the traditional single-member constituencies. The presumption was that a deputy, finding it hard to develop a personal political machine in a large district, would have to depend to a greater degree upon the endorsement and help of his party and would, presumably, be more willing to take orders from his party leaders.

Such an electoral procedure had been tried before, between 1885 and 1889, but had been abandoned. The new venture, which became operative in 1919, fared no better. It naturally produced resentment among the deputies, who saw their independence curbed. It also drew criticism because it was coupled with a cumbersome scheme for proportional representation. Moreover, experience seemed to demonstrate that, while the new method of election brought about somewhat more cohesion within each political party at the time of elections, it did not substantially reduce the number of parties represented in Parliament. Nor did it produce stronger alliances among them in support of the cabinet. The experiment was given up in 1927.

Another innovation, also intended to bolster the executive, proved more acceptable. This was the use of decree-law. In the course of the First World War, France, like other countries, had met with an inexorable demand for more decisive political leadership. Parliament had responded to this need by granting the cabinet the temporary right to issue decrees having the force of law, subject to the sanction of Parliament at the expiration of a specified period of time. In the postwar decade, Parliament resumed this practice, for the purpose of helping the government to take action to check the depreciation of the franc. Thus France became accustomed to the virtual abdication of Parliament, even in time of peace, in the face of critical problems. In the 1930s, various governments were to make further use of decree-law, and on the outbreak of the Second World War Parliament was wholly to renounce its legislative role in favor of the cabinet. Subsequently, Vichy was to mark the ultimate in this line of constitutional evolution, when Parliament voluntarily handed over unlimited power to the Premier, including the right to revise the constitution, and then disappeared from the scene.

In the situation of France in the 1920s, as it appears in retrospect, we can now readily discern the emerging visage of Vichy. Lagging behind her neighbors across the Rhine in both population and economic vigor, without the hope of Russian aid or the assurance of British and American help, France was already beginning to despair of making herself secure against the German threat. She was beginning to think, instead, in terms of some kind of reconciliation with her former foe. And dimly she was beginning to sense that somehow her diplomatic dilemma gave evidence of some kind of weakness within herself. We are tempted to conclude that the lessons of the postwar decade were in themselves sufficient to explain what was to happen in the area of Vichy, without refer-

over, the depression was never so severe in France as in some other countries, such as Britain and the United States, where the economic crisis had much milder political consequences. But in France the depression helped widen the gap between the Extreme Right and Left. At the same time, it undermined the parties of the middle ground.

At the outset of the depression, France seemed relatively secure against an economic collapse. Because her industry did not generally depend upon large-scale methods of production, it was not quickly vulnerable to the shrinkage of a mass market. And because her agriculture produced mainly for home consumption, it was not wholly at the mercy of a sudden drop in prices on the world market. So France was in a favorable position to withstand the initial shock of the depression. On the world scene, this came in the fall of 1929, with a bank panic in Vienna and the stockmarket crash in New York, which soon led to a general constriction in business. In Britain, Germany, and the United States, the downward movement proceeded without interruption until the winter of 1932–33. France, however, showed but little sign of depression throughout 1929 and 1930. Not until 1931 did a drop in economic indices become pronounced, and not until 1932 was the distress acute.

Once the depression reached France, however, it proved more stubborn than elsewhere. No appreciable improvement began until the middle of 1936, and there was only a slow and partial recovery in 1937–38.[1] During this prolonged slump, industrial production declined more than 20 percent, the number of unemployed exceeded 400,000, and the general level of employment, taking into account those who worked less than the normal number of hours as well as those quite without work, dropped about 40 percent.

At worst, to be sure, the situation was not dire. The drop in production was severe in those branches of manufacture which made use of machine methods of manufacture. But mass production was not characteristic of France. The depression was much less severe in the artisan trades, which are the backbone of French business. Furthermore, the wage rates of skilled workers did not decline as much as living costs.

[1] Statistical data on the economic crisis in France, together with a comparison of its course with that in other countries, is available in État Français, Ministère des Finances, Statistique Générale et Institut de Conjoncture, *Mouvement économique en France de 1929 à 1939* (Paris: Imprimerie Nationale, 1941).

These circumstances afforded some measure of protection to those artisans who remained at work, even on short time. Farm prices dropped somewhat more than the prices of manufactures, as in other countries, but this worked hardship mainly upon the larger agricultural producers. It did not cause as much distress to those peasant-proprietors, comprising a considerable share of the rural populace, who produced primarily for their own consumption.

Despite these cushions, the economic crisis imposed a real burden upon other elements. It worked real hardship upon unskilled labor in the cities, wage workers in agriculture, and those peasants whose livelihood depended upon the sale of crops and livestock in urban markets. For the entire nation, moreover, the stress became serious because the crisis lasted so long.

At the outset, the government took little or no action in response to the depression. It put its reliance in the curative powers of laisser-faire. This course proved attractive to Parliament because it corresponded to the orthodox doctrines of liberal economics, but also because it suited the reluctance of professional politicians to take vigorous, positive action. In its reliance upon laisser-faire, the French government was not unique. At the onset of the depression, most other governments, notably the British and American, adopted much the same attitude. They hoped that the economic problem would solve itself, as in previous periods of "panic," simply by the passage of time. However, the crisis of the 1930s did not respond to this simple kind of treatment. The governments of other countries, where the depression had had a more sudden and severe impact, came to realize this sooner than did the French.

While the government thus muddled along and the stresses of the depression became more and more severe, French political life began to show new signs of movement outside Parliament. In the previous decade, the nation as a whole had been content to choose among the moderate republican parties of the Right or the Left, which shared much the same predilection for compromise and repugnance for decisive action. In the 1930s, on the other hand, the French seemed to lose patience with this kind of political leadership. Meanwhile the moderate parties, which had earlier appeared to represent the quintessence of the French temperament in politics, now passed to the defensive.

One manifestation of this polarization in French politics was the new surge of strength evident in the political movements of the Extreme Right, which were hostile to the parliamentary system and favorable to a dictatorship. Most of these were frank in acknowledging their kinship to the fascist movements of Germany and Italy.

In the new decade, other organizations rose to a prominence rivaling that of the *Action Française.* Some of these took their start in this period; others, founded in the 1920s but hitherto small in size and little noticed, now took on a larger stature.

Foremost of these was the Croix de Feu, under the leadership of Colonel François de la Rocque. This association had been organized in 1927 as a league of war veterans. At the start, its membership had been limited to men who bore decorations won in combat. Though its leader spoke in broad and vague terms of the need for a national regeneration, the Croix de Feu had not begun as a political movement, and because its members were men of acknowledged valor and patriotism, it had won a considerable measure of public respect. As time passed, however, Colonel de la Rocque had become more outspoken in urging the need for a strong, authoritarian government, in terms reminiscent of the *Action Française* and suggestive of Italian Fascism. Gradually, too, its membership was broadened. First, it opened membership to veterans of service in the front lines, then to sons of veterans and to others with a more remote claim to distinction. Finally, it took virtually anyone who accepted the ideas Colonel de la Rocque advocated. Ultimately, the Croix de Feu came to be regarded simply as a fascist or quasi-fascist political movement.

Notable among the other political leagues that rose to prominence on the Extreme Right were the Jeunesses Patriotes, which had been organized in 1924 under the sponsorship of a business magnate, Pierre Taittinger. Another was the Solidarité Française, which was founded in 1933 by the perfume manufacturer François Coty. After the death of Coty in 1934, its leadership passed to Jean Renaud. Of curious interest, though of lesser importance, was Francisme, under the leadership of Marcel Bucard. As their insigne, the Francistes used a double-headed axe, which was later to appear in the heraldry of Vichy.

These various movements, old and new, became a serious menace to the republican regime in the winter of 1933-34. Their membership, to be sure, did not reach the proportions of a mass movement. Their strength was mainly in Paris. Even there, much of it was made up of mercenaries, hired for a pittance among the rabble of the capital to take part in street demonstrations. Though the Croix de Feu boasted, at this time, some 30,000 adherents, none of the other "leagues," as the French called these movements of the Extreme Right, approached this size. None of their leaders was distinguished either for political acumen or personal magnetism, and each was unwilling to cooperate with the others.

These critics of Parliament gained an immense tactical advantage, however, when news leaked out of a scandal involving politicians prominent in the moderate republican parties. This began with a swindle perpetrated by Alexandre Stavisky, a naturalized Russian émigré. Stavisky had gained control of the municipally owned pawnshop of Bayonne, then had issued bonds against the credit of this pawnshop to the value of a fantastic sum. By devious means, he had succeeded in marketing the bonds with a huge profit for himself. As news of this swindle began to leak out in the winter of 1933-34, it became apparent that Stavisky had escaped prosecution because of his connections with influential politicians. Then, when a prosecution was belatedly set in motion, Stavisky died under circumstances which made it seem probable that he was murdered by the police in order to prevent his implicating persons of prominence.

The zealots of the Extreme Right seized this chance to denounce Parliament as a nest of thieves. The *Action Française* took the initiative in arranging a demonstration against the government. With a rare degree of cooperation, the Croix de Feu, the Solidarité Française, and the Jeunesses Patriotes agreed to take part. In the late afternoon of February 6, 1934, several thousand demonstrators converged along the avenues leading to the Palais Bourbon, where the Chamber of Deputies held its sessions, while others gathered in the Place de la Concorde across the Seine. The police promptly established a protective cordon around the palace. But the crowd swelled in size, drawing into its midst, besides those who assembled on the prearranged plan, other thousands of curious spectators and irate citizens.

By evening, as the deputies assembled in the Palais Bourbon for their regular session, the police were hard pressed. The mob in the Place de la Concorde was beginning to press back the barrier on the bridge leading across the river to the Palais Bourbon. The more timorous deputies became alarmed lest the crowd break in upon them, thrust them aside, and proclaim the overthrow of the government. However, the police proved equal to their task. Though eventually obliged to fire into the crowd, at last they broke up the demonstration. The casualties numbered six dead and more than four hundred wounded or injured.

The riot of February 6, 1934, did not lead to a new attack upon the republican regime. Even at the height of the demonstration, the rioters had had no clear intention of precipitating an insurrection. Nor had they gained the upper hand over the police, who were hard-pressed only so long as they were under orders not to shoot into the crowd. Tension persisted in Paris a week or more, with minor outbreaks of disorder in some quarters of the city, then subsided.

Yet this crisis had a sequel of decisive importance. For the riot revealed the potential menace of the "leagues." Having gained such considerable success with an impromptu demonstration, the "leagues" might well decide to repeat the venture, with better preparation and a more serious purpose. Another time, they might well accomplish a coup d'état. The lesson was not lost upon the parties of the Left, which now began to draw together for common action against the Extreme Right. Thus the demonstration of February 6, 1934, served to precipitate the emergence of the political alliance that was to be known as the Popular Front.

Gestures toward such an alliance had been made even earlier, though without success. The three principal parties of the Left began in the spring of 1934 to open negotiations in the hope of reconciling their differences. The Socialists took the initiative in an appeal to the Communists, and presently the leaders of these two parties together approached the Radical-Socialists. The discussions dragged on through the remainder of 1934 and into 1935, for the leaders of each of the three parties proved slow to slough off their mutual suspicions. Moreover, the Communists seemed undecided as to their position. Jacques Doriot, at that time one of their leaders, was a vigorous partisan of the new orientation.

But he became embroiled in an intramural dispute, in the outcome of which he was expelled from his party. However, Moscow eventually gave its sanction to the new policy, and ultimately the Communists became strenuous advocates of the Popular Front.

The outcome of this gradual rapprochement among the parties of the Left was their acceptance of a common legislative program. The more notable items in the program proposed measures to restrict the activities of the "leagues" of the Extreme Right, to relieve the economic pressure upon the popular classes by raising wages and shortening the working week, and to raise the price of grain, for the benefit of the peasants. The manifesto also pointed to the need for action to meet the problem of German and Italian aggression on the world scene.

The national elections of 1936, held on April 26 and May 3, resulted in a decisive victory for the "Popular Front," as the alliance among the Communists, Socialists, and Radical-Socialists was known. In the new Chamber of Deputies, the Communists held 72 seats, the Socialists 146, and the Radical-Socialists 116. The three parties together commanded a clear majority, with about a score of votes to spare. In the upper house, to be sure, the Popular Front did not have a similar preponderance. However, the Senate seldom ventured upon outright opposition to a government having the clear support of the Chamber. So the Popular Front gave promise of a more concerted and effective leadership in Parliament than France had known for a generation or more.

On the morrow of the elections, a new government took office. Léon Blum, the head of the Socialist Party, became Premier, with a cabinet comprising Socialists and Radical-Socialists. The Communist Party declined to accept ministerial positions, though agreeing to give active support to the new cabinet.

This government of the Popular Front which Léon Blum inaugurated on June 4, 1936, represented a new departure. It began its career with a legislative program that had been drawn up in advance and had been endorsed by the electorate. Previous governments had customarily developed their program only after taking office, by an empirical process of negotiation and compromise on the floor and in the lobbies of Parliament. The Blum government was also remarkable in that it represented a more pronounced orientation toward the Left than any previous government. It had its base in the Socialist Party rather than the Radical-Socialist, and it depended upon the support of the Communists, who now held more seats in the Chamber than ever before. Hence the new government was largely proletarian in outlook and strongly tinged with the Marxian doctrines which the Communists and Socialists both professed.

As soon as it took over, the new cabinet met with a serious crisis outside Parliament. In the weeks between the elections and the investiture of the Blum government, a wave of sit-down strikes had spread through Paris and its suburbs. Workers barricaded themselves in the plants and refused to leave until their demands were met. A large number of industrial plants had ceased to operate. In the view of the more timorous among the upper classes, these strikes seemed a portent of proletarian revolution. In reality, the movement had no such ominous implication. Nevertheless, the strikes constituted a serious problem. The Blum government could not permit the sit-downs to continue, yet it dared not use force to drive the workers out of the factories. The government therefore intervened in negotiations between the unions and the management, throwing its weight on the side of the workers, and brought about a settlement on terms advantageous to the strikers.

Forthwith the government proceeded to enact its legislative program. The principal items of interest to urban labor were measures establishing a forty-hour working week, requiring collective bargaining between management and labor, making the arbitration of disputes virtually compulsory, and prescribing two weeks of paid vacation for nearly all employees. For the rural populace, the Popular Front had less to propose. Its principal accomplishment was to create an Office du Blé, or Wheat Administration, which would determine a fair price for wheat. The government would then purchase the crop at the stipulated price, if this proved to be more than the open-market price.

The Popular Front also took steps toward the nationalization of a number of business enterprises. One of these measures established a larger degree of public control over the Banque de France. The other major reforms of this kind provided for state ownership of the railroads and, ultimately, the state monopoly of the manufacture of airplanes and armaments.

So far as concerned political reform, the Blum government proved less venturesome. Its one notable move in this direction was to dissolve the "leagues" of the Extreme Right, but most of them soon reemerged in the guise of ordinary political parties.

These various measures, enacted or decreed in the interval between June, 1936, and June, 1937, constituted a more systematic and extensive body of reforms than any government had accomplished in a comparable period for more than thirty years before.

The more excited critics of the Popular Front assailed its work as a Marxian assault upon capitalism, designed to serve the proletariat in utter disregard of the other classes in the nation. More moderate critics argued that the forty-hour week—the "week with two Sundays"—lowered national productivity, as did the attempts at the nationalization of the railroads, airplane manufacture, and armaments industry. This, they charged, worked hardship upon the whole nation, without even giving real benefit to the working class. Moreover, critics pointed out that the Popular Front not only showed prejudice in favor of the laboring classes as against the middle classes and the rich, but it showed much less concern for the rural populace than for the urban working-men.

Much of this criticism was unwarranted. Certainly the Popular Front did not represent the beginning of a socialist regime in France. Measures such as the forty-hour week and the support of farm prices had been introduced in a number of countries besides France, without bringing ruin upon business enterprise. In their savage attacks upon these reforms, the business classes of France gave less evidence of a disastrous hardship imposed upon them than of their own lack of social conscience.

Yet, though the enemies of the Popular Front doubtless overstated their case, its champions were not much more persuasive. Insofar as the Popular Front represented a political alliance for the purpose of defending the republican regime against the menace of the Extreme Right, it won but a dubious success. By dissolving the "leagues," it eliminated the likelihood of a popular insurrection under the leadership of the Extreme Right. But this likelihood had never been large. Nowadays an uprising in the streets has little chance against a government that commands the immense modern resources of political repression. Since the close of the classic age of popular revolutions in 1848, virtually no European government has ever been overthrown unless it has first been defeated in a foreign war, or else the revolutionaries have been aided by henchmen within the government.

Within four years after Léon Blum became Premier, these conditions were to be met. With the emergence of Vichy, in the wake of the defeat of 1940, the partisans of the Extreme Right were to accomplish their coup d'état. Perhaps, by temporarily occupying the positions of command in the government, the Blum cabinet briefly postponed the downfall of the republican regime. But manifestly it proved unable either to eliminate the pressure of the Extreme Right or to build a secure bulwark against it.

The Popular Front achieved no clearer success in its endeavor to improve the material welfare of the popular classes. Though the economic crisis eased a little in the fall of 1936, the depression lingered on until 1938, when the approach of war ensured a general boom. Perhaps the Popular Front won a durable advantage for the proletariat by establishing the principle of the forty-hour week and annual paid vacations, by giving stronger public sanction to collective bargaining, and in a broader and vaguer sense, by committing the government to a larger solicitude for urban labor. Yet the Blum government made no serious attempt to solve the basic problem of the economic retardation of France, although there is no other way to cure poverty but to increase the production of wealth.

Even at the time, the partisans of the Popular Front seemed aware that they were unable to solve the domestic problems besetting France. By June, 1937, the Popular Front had enacted virtually all the measures it had inscribed in its program, and Blum himself announced that the time had come for a "pause" in domestic reform. Though no one doubted that serious maladies still afflicted the nation, the Left had nothing more to propose by way of their solution. In this sense, it acknowledged its inadequacy.

The Communists, indeed, had never expected the Popular Front to solve the basic problems of the nation. They had viewed its program as no more than a palliative. Nor had the Radical-Socialists had much more confidence. They had never really approved the mingling of political issues with proposals for social and economic reform, nor had they given up their trust in laisser-faire. Even the Socialists had remained divided in their attitude toward the Popular Front. On the one hand, they had begun to modify their conception of proletarian revolution into a preference for a "directed" economy within the framework of political democracy. On the other hand, they had never renounced the principles of Marxism, which allowed no room for class collaboration. Hence they never quite made up their mind as to whether they viewed the Popular Front, like the Communists, as a tactic in the class struggle of the proletariat or, like the Radical-Socialists, as merely a maneuver by which their party might succeed in attaining the normal ambition of any political party, namely, a large share of ministerial portfolios. Considering these various doubts and hesitations among the parties that made up the alliance, it is little wonder that the government of the Popular Front accomplished no more.

Meantime the opposition of the Extreme Right did not abate. The ban which the government soon imposed upon the "leagues" made it harder for them to conduct street demonstrations, but it did not mean their disappearance.

The Croix de Feu, to be sure, suffered a decline. At its peak, in the interval between the riots in the Place de la Concorde in 1934 and the national elections of 1936, it had mustered perhaps 100,000 adherents. It had thus ranked as the largest of the "leagues." But it had proved quite ineffective in the national elections of 1936. Though Colonel de la Rocque pretended to have some dozens of henchmen among the deputies in the new Parliament, he could not disguise his defeat. In the aftermath of the elections, when the Blum government decreed the dissolution of the "leagues," the leadership of the Croix de Feu reorganized the movement as a political party, under the name of the Parti Social Français. In its new incarnation, however, the movement seemed to lose vigor, and the P.S.F. never loomed as large as had the Croix de Feu.

Following the elections of 1936, a new political organization rose to prominence on the Extreme Right. This was the Parti Populaire Français, under the direction of Jacques Doriot, a renegade Communist. Doriot had been a member of the Communist Party since its inception in 1920, and had risen to a position in the national leadership. In 1933–34, he had been outspoken in urging cooperation between the Communists and the Socialists. However, he had been expelled from his party in 1934. One reason for this was that the party at that time still maintained its stand that the Socialists were traitors to the working class—although the Communists, two years later, were to enter into alliance with both the Socialists and the Radical-Socialists. Another reason for his expulsion was that Doriot did not advocate union between the Socialists and the Communists as a means of combatting the threat of fascism, but rather as the first step toward developing a national program of socialism, which virtually amounted to fascism.

Despite his expulsion from the Communist Party, Doriot kept an enthusiastic personal following among the workers in the suburbs of Paris, and he won election to Parliament in 1936. Forthwith, in June of 1936, he organized the P.P.F. as a new totalitarian movement, with a program demanding the establishment of a dictatorship on the German and Italian model, diplomatic reconciliation with Germany, and a break of relations with Soviet Russia. Though Doriot was quite without distinction as either a thinker or a tactician, he was a capable rabble rouser. He soon succeeded in building the P.P.F. into a movement of considerable size.

Another venture of much the same kind was the neosocialist movement, among the sponsors of which were Marcel Déat and Adrien Marquet. A student at the École Normale Supérieure, then a professor of philosophy who, like many French professors, sought a career in politics, Déat had won election to Parliament in 1928 and, though subsequently failing to gain reelection, had risen to the position of administrative secretary in the national organization of the Socialist Party. In the early years of the depression, he had begun a campaign to induce the party to renounce Marxism and develop a program of socialism on a national basis. In this campaign, he won the support of a number of the rising young men in the party, including Adrien Marquet, who was himself gaining renown as mayor of Bordeaux. However, the stalwarts of the party, Léon Blum among them, denounced this proposed new orientation as an ill-disguised form of fascism.

In the upshot, Déat, Marquet, and a number of others seceded from the Socialist Party in the winter of 1933-34. Thereupon Déat undertook to organize a new party, in conformity with the ideas he propounded. This did not materialize. Nevertheless, Déat continued to develop his ideas in articles which he contributed to one or another newspaper. He continued to have an influence upon a number of lesser personalities in the Socialist Party, many of whom were subsequently to rally behind his leadership in the Vichy era.

In the period of the Popular Front, the *Action Française* passed into an eclipse. It was the senior among the various movements on the Extreme Right that demanded an authoritarian regime, for it had propounded the merits of such a dictatorship as far back as 1899, and the Camelots du Roi, its strong-arm branch, had assumed a leading role among the "leagues" at the time of the demonstration in the Place de la Concorde in 1934. Yet the *Action Française* remained somewhat archaic. Its leaders, Charles Maurras and Léon Daudet, were men whose careers dated back to the time of the Dreyfus affair. Even Maurice Pujo, who represented the newer blood, was a man past sixty. The newspaper retained a loyal clientèle, but as a political movement, the *Action Française* showed little new vigor.

More notable was the *Cagoule*. This was a secret political association which arose out of a secession from the *Action Française* in 1937, when some of the members of the Camelots du Roi, despairing of their lethargic leaders, set up a new organization known as the Comité Secret d'Action Révolutionnaire (C.S.A.R.). Eugène Deloncle was known as the head of the organization. However, it never became clear whether he was its guiding genius or a mere liaison agent among more august personages behind the scenes who preferred to remain unknown to the public. The *Action Française,* which took a dim view of the secession, nicknamed its members *les cagoulards*—the Hooded Men. The name stuck, although in actuality they never wore hoods nor made public appearances at all. Apparently the organization hoped to accomplish a coup d'état with the help of the army, and it had connections with a number of high army officers, many of whom had long been sympathetic to the ideas of the *Action Française*. The *Cagoulards* kept their secrets well, so no one knows how extensive was their network of members and friends. From the meager evidence available, it appears that the organization loomed larger as a legend in the public press than as a threat to the Republic. However, it seems quite probable that its role might have been important, because of its links with the military, had the zealots of the Extreme Right ever attempted a forcible seizure of power.

Though most of the apostles of totalitarianism made Paris their base, one of the numerous organizations of the Extreme Right directed its appeal to the peasants. This was the Front Paysan, of which Henri Dorgères was the head. Dorgères launched his movement in the summer of 1935, at a time when the decline in farm prices was producing serious distress in the provinces and the rural populace was giving signs of an unwonted restiveness. He soon demonstrated remarkable acumen as a demagogue, working up the peasants to a high pitch of resentment against the townsmen and exhorting them to pay no more taxes until the government should recognize their grievances and relieve their distress. Dorgères was more than a spokesman of agrarian unrest, however. He was a bitter critic of Parliament, and in his attempts to organize his partisans into bands of "Green Shirts," he gave clear enough indication of his orientation toward fascism. In the summer and fall of 1935, the Front Paysan won a prompt and warm response in the rural regions. Thereafter, as farm prices began to rise and the situation of the peasants showed signs of improvement, its appeal dwindled, and the movement disappeared as suddenly as it had arisen. There is no way of knowing how serious was the protest at the republican regime which it momentarily seemed to express. Perhaps the movement represented no more than a widespread feeling among the peasants that they were the "forgotten men" of France. Perhaps it expressed a more serious disillusionment with the parliamentary system. At any event, it drew attention to an unrest in the countryside which the Popular Front was never wholly to allay, and which Vichy was subsequently to turn to its uses.

The Extreme Right waged its campaign against the republican regime not only through its political parties and other organized political movements but also through the columns of numerous newspapers and magazines. Most of the leading Paris newspapers of general circulation, such as *Le Matin* and *Le Jour,* though not openly identified with any party, attacked the government of the Popular Front with unbridled violence.

They proclaimed the need of a strong, authoritarian regime to protect conservative interests in much the same terms as did the avowed advocates of fascism. In addition, these zealots had command of several newspapers of their own, some of which gained wide circulation. Among them were the *Action Française,* of course, the pioneer among the protagonists of "integral nationalism"; *L'Ami du Peuple,* which was associated with Solidarité Française and the Jeunesses Patriotes until the dissolution of these "leagues" in 1936; *La Liberté,* which became the voice of Doriot's Parti Populaire Français; and *Le Petit Journal,* which passed under the direction of the Parti Social Français of Colonel de la Rocque. Notable also were the weeklies *Gringoire* and *Je Suis Partout,* which became notorious for their virulent anti-Semitism, and *Candide,* which was close to the *Action Française* in its viewpoint. Also linked with the *Action Française* in doctrine, though perhaps more austere in tone, was the bimonthly *Revue Universelle,* among the contributors to which were several writers who were later to appear as personal advisers to Marshal Pétain in the Vichy regime.

It is impossible to determine the relative importance of the particular political movements that espoused fascist or near-fascist ideas in the period of the Popular Front or to measure the strength of the Extreme Right as a whole, since there was no general election in France after 1936 until the close of the Second World War. But it is manifest that, despite the apparent triumph of the Popular Front in 1936, the Extreme Right retained its hold upon a considerable portion of public opinion. It is quite possible that this support even increased, at the expense of the more moderate parties.

However, the partisans of the Extreme Right developed their propaganda, after 1936, principally in terms of foreign-policy issues. They put less emphasis on their program for domestic reform. The reason for this was that their adversaries were securely entrenched in Parliament. Hence there was no hope of establishing a dictatorship save by coup d'état. But no matter how divided were the parties of the Popular Front on other issues, they were firmly united in their determination to resist any forcible attack upon the republican regime.

In matters of foreign policy, on the other hand, the parties of the Left were seriously divided among themselves. This disunion afforded their adversaries a new opportunity. By concentrating upon foreign affairs, the strategists of the Extreme Right could hope to widen the cleavages within the Popular Front so much as to cause its breakup, which would permit a new political alliance, comprising moderates and conservatives, to take command of Parliament. A new cabinet, based upon such a coalition, might assure the partisans of dictatorship a more favorable environment in which to undertake a coup d'état.

But before we pass on to the fateful issues of foreign relations, we must pause to take note of some features of the domestic politics of the 1930s that help illuminate the later Vichy regime. First, we must remark upon the sudden decline of the moderate parties, which was one of the pivotal happenings of the decade. For fifty years or more, the government of the Third Republic had remained in the hands of one or another combination among a number of political parties that shared much the same outlook. For their support, moreover, the governing parties had all made their appeal to the same elements in the population—the urban middle classes and the rural populace—and they had consistently gained a sufficient measure of popular endorsement to assure them a clear preponderance in Parliament. On the grounds of principle and interest alike, they had remained firmly committed to the doctrine of laisser-faire. Only slowly, hesitantly, and grudgingly did they accept the principle of social legislation at the expense of the propertied classes, for the advantage of the urban laboring classes.

Then, in a sudden shift of mood in the decade of the 1930s, France seemed to lose patience with the leadership of these moderate parties. The entire nation seemed eager for some bold new course. Unmistakably, the moderate parties were now on the defensive, while their adversaries on either side were gaining new vigor.

Momentarily, this new mood promised to benefit the Marxian parties. But their seeming success proved far from conclusive. Rather, their temporary victory served only to prolong the crisis of indecision and to provoke a violent reaction among the propertied classes. As observers at the time were quick to report, a considerable portion of the upper bourgeoisie was prepared to pay any price in order to destroy the Popular Front—even going so far, if need be, as to hand France over to Nazi dominance. In this sense, the government of Léon Blum proved but the prelude to that of Marshal Pétain—which marked the triumph of those whose motto was "better Hitler than Blum."

But in another sense, too, the experiment of the Popular Front prepared the way for the "National Revolution" of Vichy. Quite as ominous as the envenomed bitterness of the conservatives was the widespread sense of disappointment at the failure of the parties of the Left to provide the nation with new guidance. For most of France—not merely the stalwarts of the Extreme Left and their opponents on the Extreme Right —was vainly hoping for fresh leadership. In the sequel, this sense of frustration was to work to the advantage of the Vichy regime, which was to take its start in 1940 with the acclaim of those who reveled in their revenge upon Léon Blum as well as those who awaited the new leadership Blum had failed to furnish.

Finally, we can perceive signs of those weaknesses in the leadership of the Extreme Right that were to prove its undoing in 1940. Notable among these was the absence of agreement among the enemies of the republican regime as to a practical program for their proposed alternative. In broad, vague, and negative terms, all the partisans of the Extreme Right joined in demanding a dictatorship to overcome the "weakness" and "corruption" of Parliament, in urging the need to resolve the class struggle in the interest of the nation as a whole, and in blaming the ills of France upon the Jews, Free Masons, Marxists, and liberals. However, the critics of the parliamentary system had no clear idea as to what should be the relationship between the dictator and Parliament; what kind of device, corporative or other, should be instituted in order to reconcile the interests of business and labor; what should be done to provide for the peasants; or, indeed, as to the solution of any other problem of this order. While the old guard of the *Action Française* sang the praises of a golden age in the past, prior to the Revolution of 1789, the newer evangels of fascism heralded a golden age still to come, when a new Messiah would appear to redeem the nation.

No less portentous than their want of program was their lack of agreement on a candidate for their dictatorship. In all its many years, the *Action Française* never ventured a nomination, save to pledge its troth to the monarchist pretender to the throne. The newer recruits to the cause proved less hesitant. Both Colonel de la Rocque and Jacques Doriot headed parties pledged to their own candidacies. Likewise, Marcel Déat made public announcement of his personal mission. None of these was willing to defer to the others, nor able to outdistance them. Meantime a dozen other advocates of single-minded national leadership proceeded to build up minuscule movements of their own, some of which amounted to little more than a committee of three would-be *Fuehrers,* armed with a bale of printed letterheads. Virtually no one proposed the name of the venerable old soldier Pétain, who was eventually to prove the only man capable of gaining a personal rule.[2] A shrewd observer would have had ample reason to predict that, should France ever pass under an authoritarian government of the Extreme Right, it would require a miracle to make it monolithic.

Throughout the 1920s, the illusion persisted that all would be well with France, provided only that she could solve the problem of her relations with Germany. The bitter social and political strife that broke out within France in the 1930s dispelled this smug confidence. Meanwhile, the menace of a German resurgence, hitherto no more than an ominous cloud on the horizon, became terrifying reality. Though ultimately these two crises, domestic and diplomatic, merged into a single, stark disaster, in the early 1930s, they began quite separately. Issues of social politics began to dominate the attention of France in 1933 and 1934, and the domestic crisis reached a climax in the interval between February 6, 1934, when the "leagues" gave evidence of their new strength in their demonstration in the Place de la Concorde, and May 3, 1936, when the parties of the Popular Front emerged victorious in the national elections. In this same interval, Hitler was consolidating the hold of the Nazi Party on Germany and making ready his challenge to the *Erbfeind.* Yet in these years, France seemed to have won a respite from her preoccupation with diplomatic problems.

Certainly France had no occasion to take immediate action in re-

[2] The adversaries of Pétain during the war indulged in much loose talk of a plot, the origins of which were in the 1930s, to make Pétain dictator. A representative statement of this charge is André Schwob, *L'Affaire Pétain: faits et documents* (New York: Éditions de la Maison Française, 1944). The one notable item of evidence is a brochure published by Gustave Hervé, an old-time Socialist turned fascist, which bore the title *C'est Pétain qu'il nous faut* (Paris: Éditions de la Victoire, 1935). No one has shown, however, that this tract was noticed at the time, or that its author spoke for others besides himself.

sponse to Hitler's accession to the German chancellorship in January of 1933. From the outset, French observers were aware that the Nazi program boded ill for France. Nevertheless, there was nothing that a foreign government could do to bar Hitler from taking office. For some time, moreover, there was reasonable doubt whether the Nazis would make good their seizure of power. It was not until after the "blood purge" of June, 1934, that Hitler achieved his goal of complete dictatorship. Not until 1935, when he began the open rearmament of Germany, did he take a step which gave foreign governments a good opportunity to lodge a diplomatic protest. And at this point, France was forestalled from taking forthright action by Britain, which gave its sanction to German rearmament, and by Italy, which raised a more open and immediate threat to international peace when she embarked upon the conquest of Ethiopia.

Mussolini's attack upon Ethiopia in the fall of 1935 was a sinister omen, since it revealed that Britain and France were no longer in command of the European diplomatic scene. But its meaning was obscure. France had little reason to recognize this crisis as the portent of another world war on the model of 1914, since she was accustomed to viewing German aggression with alarm, but not Italian. Moreover, this move of Mussolini seemed to represent a venture in old-fashioned colonial expansion rather than a disturbance of the *status quo* in Europe.

Under a mild pressure of public opinion, the British and French governments agreed to have the League of Nations impose a limited embargo upon trade with Italy, as a deterrent or punitive measure. Neither government had much enthusiasm for this policy, however, and they refused to permit the League of Nations to strengthen its embargo to the point where it would become a serious threat to Italy. So Mussolini proceeded to complete his conquest of Ethiopia.

Meantime, Hitler was also becoming bolder. In March of 1936, he ordered German troops to march into the Rhineland, in open violation of the Treaty of Versailles and the Treaty of Locarno. Though no one could mistake the portent, the French government took no action. The Sarraut government, which held office at the moment, was in no position to assume such a risk. For this government had but a dubious mandate. It had taken office in January, 1936, with the mission of managing the election of a new Parliament, and it had little reason to presume that the new Parliament would renew its tenure or that the succeeding government would underwrite a policy of firmness on the issue of the Rhineland.

Moreover, it is likely that the British would have looked with disfavor upon a French occupation of the Rhineland in 1936, as they had in 1924. Quite probably, therefore, the French would have been obliged to withdraw again, sooner or later, as they had in the outcome of their previous venture. Hence they would presumably have accomplished little by a show of firmness, save to postpone the issue. Thus, in the last analysis, we again encounter the dilemma confronting all French governments in the interbellum period, which were unable either to make a single-handed resistance to the German menace or to obtain dependable help.

Hard upon the German march into the Rhineland came the outbreak of the Civil War in Spain in the summer of 1936. The issues in the emerging crisis took on sharper outline. From the outset, it was obvious that this struggle represented a revolt on the part of champions of authoritarian conservatism against a democratic regime. Unlike the Italian invasion of Ethiopia, the rebellion did not bear the guise of a venture in colonial expansion, such as most "liberal" governments had themselves undertaken at one time or another. Nor did it appear, as had the German move into the Rhineland, as a protest against the obsolescent Treaty of Versailles. The crux of the matter was an unequivocal clash of political ideas.

Moreover, the help which Hitler and Mussolini gave Franco bore witness to the new solidarity between the German and Italian dictatorships. For the first time, it became obvious that fascism was a force in international politics, directed against the principle of liberalism wherever it prevailed, not merely an affair of German and Italian domestic politics. Since Germany and Italy were both committed to the cause of the Spanish rebels, France had to view her policy toward Spain in relation to her policy toward Germany, which always remained her principal concern. Hitherto, in the issues involved in the question of relations with Germany, the Right had generally upheld what we have called a "hard" policy, whereas the parties of the Left had commonly championed a "soft" policy. Now, however, the Right began to urge a new kind of "soft" policy, while the Left became identified with a fresh version of the "hard" policy.

The Popular Front did not find it easy to make this turnabout. Throughout the 1920s, the parties of the Left had stood for international peace and reconciliation. The Socialists and the Radical-Socialists had supported the League of Nations as the instrument for the settlement of international disputes, made gestures toward disarmament, sought to reduce the period of compulsory military service, and, on some occasions, acquiesced in extreme expressions of pacifism. Even the Communists, though in principle opposed to pacifism and hostile to the League of Nations, had denounced the harsh treatment of Germany under the Treaty of Versailles, particularly after Soviet Russia became friendly toward the Weimar Republic.

Yet in 1935, these three parties had banded together on the basis of a common resistance to the threat of fascism. By logical implication, the program of the Popular Front meant resistance to fascist aggression on the world scene as well as opposition to the "leagues" at home. The Communists accepted this logic, since Soviet Russia took the lead among European governments in advocating "collective security." Accordingly, after 1935, the French Communists championed a common stand by France, Britain, and Russia against the expansionist moves of Germany and Italy.

The Socialists, however, did not so readily support this demand. Although the left wing of the party, under the leadership of Léon Blum, endorsed the policy of "collective security," the right wing, under the leadership of Paul Faure, held firm to pacifism. The left wing controlled the national executive committee of the party, but the right wing had the larger representation among the Socialist deputies in Parliament.

For their part, the Radical-Socialists proved even more reluctant to relinquish hope of peaceful compromise of international disputes, including those arising between liberal and totalitarian governments. Under the pressure of the Communists and the left-wing Socialists, the Popular Front adopted an official position that condemned fascist aggression. But in practice, the Left never held together in support of this stand.

Like the Left, the Right also began to repudiate its previous position. Since before the First World War, the *Action Française,* which spoke for the Extreme Right, had whipped up hatred of the *boches* as the hereditary enemy. Even the moderate parties of the Right had identified themselves with the policy of crippling Germany. By 1936, however, the Extreme Right as a whole, as well as some among the moderate parties of the Right, began to oppose any measure that would challenge German or Italian aggression. The extremists of the Right took this new stand, in part, because of their ideological sympathy for fascism, abroad as well as at home. Some of the enthusiasts of this persuasion went so far as to pretend that Germany and Italy were really desirous of friendship with France.

Yet the moderate politicians of the Right did not share this zeal for fascism as a political principle, much less the illusion that Hitler and Mussolini were well disposed toward France. Probably even the extremists of the Right did not wholly believe their own propaganda. In large part, the Right espoused "appeasement" simply as a tactic which would help break up the Popular Front, thus enabling the conservatives to regain power in France. By challenging the policy of "collective security," the Right could play upon the division within the Popular Front between the old-school pacifists and the champions of the newer policy of firmness toward Germany and Italy. At the same time, they could hope to discredit the Left. For the mass of the nation dreaded the prospect of a new war above all else and therefore distrusted any move involving the risk of bloodshed.

Not quite all the men of the Right made this about-face. The *Action Française* developed but scarcely any more enthusiasm for Germany under Hitler than under the Weimar Republic. It remained skeptical of any policy that would subordinate the security of France to the interests of fascism as an international movement. Henri de Kérillis, who was regarded as the spokesman of the *Action Française* in Parliament, became conspicuous for his opposition to "appeasement." Likewise Louis Marin, the leader of the Fédération Républicaine, the principal republican party on the Right, spoke out against the dangers of the "soft" policy in its new guise. But such men were exceptions. In the main, the men of the Right made their reversal of position with better grace, and in better order, than did their opponents on the Left.

In the realm of theory, another policy was conceivable as an alternative to both "appeasement" and "collective security." Such a policy was sketchily propounded by some moderate politicians in Parliament. Notable among them were Pierre-Étienne Flandin, Camille Chautemps, and Pierre Laval. These moderates were unwilling to join with the partisans of "collective security" in opposing fascism wherever it might crop up, but unlike the apostles of "appeasement," they were also unwilling to see German might increased. They thought in terms of a policy which would offset the German threat, without involving an ideological war upon fascism as a form of government. As one means to this end, they contemplated maintaining diplomatic cooperation with Britain, which seemed the indispensable first condition of French security. Further, they urged the strengthening of the French alliances in Central and Eastern Europe, perhaps to include Russia as well as Poland and the Little Entente. In addition, they talked of improving relations with some of the fascist or profascist powers, as a counterbalance to Nazi Germany. Some of them contemplated a "Latin Bloc," which would comprise France, Italy, and perhaps Franco Spain. Others spoke of a "Catholic Bloc," which would also include Austria.

This intermediate position between "appeasement" and "collective security" never gained enough support to challenge the policies urged by the Extreme Right and the Extreme Left. In part, this was doubtless due to the circumstance that the moderates did not have command of Parliament after 1936. Hence, they did not have the primary responsibility for foreign policy. Moderate republican politicians seldom undertook to urge any kind of policy before assuming charge of the government. In part, the weakness of the middle ground was also due to the characteristic preference of the moderates for opportunistic devices. Instinctively they shied away from systematic programs, either at home or abroad, even when such a program represented a systematic compromise. Perhaps the reason for the weakness of the middle ground was still simpler—perhaps it meant only that the diplomatic problem facing France was virtually insoluble.

The reorientation of opinion on issues of foreign affairs became apparent in the summer of 1936, as soon as the Popular Front had to meet the problem of the Civil War in Spain. At the outbreak of the war, it seemed obvious that the Blum government would give support to the embattled Spanish Republic. However, it also became evident that Paris was not free to take the obvious course of action. First, the British government made it clear that it preferred a position of formal neutrality between the two warring camps in Spain, shutting off aid to either side. Of course, Blum might have gone ahead to help the Spanish republicans without waiting for British approval. But as a matter of practical politics, he was unable to take such a decision. Neither the Radical-Socialists nor the right wing of his own Socialist Party would support this policy. Without their backing, the Blum government would lose its majority in Parliament.

Blum might have forced the issue, taking the chance that his government would be unseated and trusting that shortly he would regain office. But he had reason to hesitate. For if he were compelled to resign in the summer of 1936 over the issue of aid to Spain, the coalition of the parties of the Left would be broken, and the domestic program of the Popular Front would probably not be enacted. Moreover, the Radical-Socialists would be tempted to close ranks with the republican parties of the Right in forming a new government. Such a move toward the Right, at a moment when the advocates of fascism were gaining more prominence, would involve risks to the entire republican regime in France. In view of such considerations, Blum made up his mind to abandon the policy of firmness in foreign affairs. Bowing to the British pressure, he agreed to give no aid to the Spanish republicans, even though Hitler and Mussolini were providing considerable help to Franco.

Having made this decision in favor of "appeasement" in the summer of 1936, France stood idly by while the Spanish Nationalists slowly drove back the republican armies. Nor did she make a move in 1937, when the Japanese launched their war upon China, nor in the spring of 1938, when Hitler incorporated Austria into the Nazi Reich. But she could not avoid facing the issue again when, in the summer of 1938, Hitler made evident his desire to annex the Sudetenland, and thus render Czechoslovakia helpless to resist him. For this move, unless thwarted, would destroy the whole system of alliances in Central and Eastern Europe upon which France depended for support in the event of a new European war.

At first glance, France seemed to have no choice but to support the Czechs against the Germans. If the French were to permit Hitler to seize the Sudetenland, they might as well tear up their treaties with Poland and their Balkan satellites. Moreover, Soviet Russia made it known that she would help defend Czechoslovakia, provided that France should do as much. Thus Russia underlined the moral and political responsibility of the French.

Nevertheless, France was in a position where it was about as hard to take a stand against German aggression as to capitulate. Once more, Britain made clear her disposition to "appease" Hitler. Denied British backing, France could not lightly take the risk of unloosing a war with Germany. To be sure, she could perhaps consider the Russian pledge of help a compensation for the want of British aid. But, on close examination, she could not put much faith in this promise. Russia had no common border with Czechoslovakia, and neither Poland nor Hungary would give the Red Army passage across their borders in order to reach Czechoslovakia.

Perhaps, in the balance of factors, France would have done better to take a stand against the Germans in 1938, even at the risk of war, than to capitulate once more. Looking back with the knowledge of what was soon to transpire, we can scarcely imagine how France would have fared worse if she had gone to war in 1938, with the Czechs and the Russians beside her, than in 1939, when she had only the Poles for allies in the East. Yet no one foresaw, in 1938, how much worse the situation of France was to become in the next two years. Nor did anyone in France dare to propose that France give the signal for a general European war, even if this were virtually inevitable, so strong and widespread was the dread of a new bloodletting. Even the most vociferous advocates of resistance to the Axis had always to plead their case upon the unproven premise that Germany would back down in the face of firm opposition.

Ultimately the French government made its decision in favor of further "appeasement," and scarcely any save the Communists raised voice against this decision. Thereupon the alliance of the parties of the Left completely dissolved. For more than a year, since Blum stepped down in June, 1937, the Popular Front had been in process of dissolution, and Daladier, who had taken over the premiership in April, 1938, had been working toward a new alliance between the moderate parties and the Right. In the aftermath of Munich, this reorientation was completed. The Communists, who had supported the government with increasing reluctance, now passed into the opposition. The Socialists, riven by the cleavage between the right and left wings of their party, ceased to have a policy of any kind. The Daladier government, depending now upon the Radical-Socialists and the republican parties of the Right, made no more pretense of representing the Popular Front.

Yet "Munich" did not solve the diplomatic problem. Within six months, Hitler annexed all Bohemia and Moravia. Forthwith he designated Poland as his next victim. Once more, France seemed destined to humiliation, on the model of "Munich." For the same logic that had led to the surrender of Czechoslovakia in 1938 appeared to require the surrender of Poland in 1939. To be sure, public opinion now registered a minimum of enthusiasm for the course of "appeasement," inasmuch as the sacrifice of Czechoslovakia had evidently only whetted the Nazi appetite. And both the French and the British governments, seeming to share this disillusionment, made gestures toward consultation with the Soviet government as to means of common action in defense of Poland.

In the next chapter, we shall consider in some detail the course of these negotiations. At the moment, we need only note that the consultations between Paris, London, and Moscow in the spring and summer of 1939 served only to demonstrate to the satisfaction of the British and the French that there was no possible means of achieving a common action with the Russians.

Then on August 23, 1939, the bombshell burst—the Germans and the Russians signed their Nonaggression Pact. Thus France found herself face to face with a Germany stronger than ever before, which now could count upon the benevolence of Russia, while France had no backing but that of Britain and Poland. Neither was a source of comfort. Britain was in no position to provide more than a token force for operations in Europe, and Poland, far from promising help, represented a military and political liability. Such was the unhappy plight of the France that, only twenty years before, had seemed so tranquil at home and so secure against her hereditary enemy.

In the chain of circumstances that led to this diplomatic catastrophe, we can perceive much that helps explain the later Vichy experience. At first glance, we can recognize the triumph of the Extreme Right in its campaign to utilize the Nazi menace for its own purposes in French domestic politics. Through their unscrupulous exploitation of the French dread of another war, the French apologists of fascism accomplished their aim of breaking the alliance among the parties of the Left and of restoring a conservative preponderance in the government.

As the sequel was to show, they achieved their success at the price of rendering France helpless against German might. Some among the extremists of the Right did not think the price too high. As they acknowledged at the time, they preferred Hitler to Blum. In 1940, when they found France under the rule of Hitler, they showed no sign of regret. But many of those who played along with the partisans of fascism in this scheme did not mean to go so far as to deliver their country into the hands of the enemy. Though some of the advocates of "appeasement" richly earned the name of traitors, others deserve only the lesser reproach of criminal irresponsibility.

But the Right did not have a monopoly on folly. Indeed, the partisans of "appeasement" perhaps earned more than their fair share of opprobrium because they succeeded in making their policy prevail, so that its consequences became evident. The men of the Left never had a chance to put their policy of "collective security" to the test of practice. But are we sure that France would have fared better if she had made her stand with Czechoslovakia in 1938 rather than with Poland in 1939? Would she have long postponed a decisive struggle with Germany, or entered it upon more equal terms, if she had broken with Britain in 1936 or 1937 and given aid to the Spanish Republic? We shall never know.

Yet we must recognize that the course of "collective security" involved a highly unpredictable venture. Though the outcome could scarcely have been worse than the sequel to "appeasement," it might have been much the same. Without question, many of those who refused to allow France to take the risks of a firm stand against the Axis were knowingly guilty of treason. But probably some of those who promised that the Axis would halt its drive, the fascist regimes collapse, and peace descend upon Europe once more, provided only that France should threaten war, were no less demagogic than those who proclaimed that "appeasement" would surely bring "peace in our time."

In retrospect, we can see that French diplomacy in the 1930s did not break down simply because "appeasement" prevailed over "collective security." Neither policy gave assurance of solving the French dilemma. For without powerful allies, France could not cope with Germany, whether by a "soft" or a "hard" policy. Yet France had no assurance of such help. Certainly she could not look to the United States. Time and again, Britain made clear her unwillingness to support France, and even a disposition to befriend Germany. Seemingly, France could hope for the aid of Russia, after the conclusion of the Franco-Soviet alliance of 1935. But even if her people had been united in their readiness to make good this alliance—and manifestly, they were not—France could not have regarded Russian help as sufficient. Moreover, she could develop her alliance with Russia only at the price of worsening her cleavage with Britain. In sum, France was unable to deal with Germany by herself, and powerless to influence the nations upon whose help she must depend.

Hence, virtually all the diverse political factions that in 1940 identified themselves with Vichy were able to find "proof" of their wisdom somewhere in the experience of France during the 1920s and 1930s. Those who argued that France had no choice but to accept the hegemony of Germany could urge that France was powerless to prevent the German resurgence. Others could argue that Soviet Russia had done her best to embroil France with Germany, then had betrayed her at the last moment before the war broke out. Those who inveighed against Britain for pushing France into the path of the Nazi juggernaut could develop an imposing indictment of British perfidy. And those who ridiculed the hopes of American help to France had little need to exaggerate the open record of American isolationism throughout the period between the wars.

Vichy also drew upon the experience of the 1920s and 1930s in a broader sense than as an arsenal of propagandistic arguments. For the motley crew that surrounded Marshal Pétain in 1940 included others besides the fanatics of the Extreme Right who sought to make France into a province in a Europe permanently organized under German hegemony, and perhaps some who never despaired of the ultimate deliverance of their country through Anglo-American intervention. It also included a faction which saw the role of France as that of a hardbeset neutral between mightier rivals.

Men such as these saw in the interbellum period the lesson that France could not serve her interests by a firm commitment to either side in such a contest, but only by playing one against the other. During the period of Vichy, this view was to be known as *attentisme,* and it was to imply that France would disserve her interests by pinning her hopes on either the Axis or the Anglo-American bloc. Much the same view was to persist after the close of the war, when it was to be known as *neutralisme* and was to imply neutrality between Russia and the United States.

We cannot say that this position of neutrality was the characteristic policy of Vichy. Nor do we have grounds on which to regard this approach to the French diplomatic problem as the proper course of French interest. Yet we can see in this attitude a link between the France of the interbellum period and the France of the period after the Second World War. Thus we can begin to recognize the Vichy interlude as not only an aspect of the history of Europe under Nazi dominance but also as an integral part of the history of modern France.

IV

FROM PEACE TO WAR

IN THE DISASTROUS PARTICIPATION of France in the initial phase of the Second World War, the tragic drama of the Third Republic reached its denouement, and the Vichy regime had its unblessed beginning.

This ultimate crisis of the Third Republic involves a number of vexed problems. Virtually everyone agrees that France made a fatal error at some point between September, 1938, and September, 1939, but opinion divides as to the nature of the mistake. In the view of some, the error was in that France should have decided to resist the Axis in September, 1938, if not earlier. Blame lies upon those advocates of "appeasement" and apologists for fascism who subsequently became partisans of Marshal Pétain. Generally, this view prevailed among those who eventually aligned themselves in opposition to Vichy. It became the common American opinion in the course of the war.

In the view of others, the error was in that France should have continued longer in the course of "appeasement," since manifestly she lacked the strength to resist the Axis in 1939. The onus of criminal irresponsibility therefore lies upon those who chose to plunge France into a war she was not prepared to win, nor even to contest upon equal terms. Such was naturally the view of the extremists of the Right, who had been the consistent advocates of "appeasement" before the war. However, it was also upheld by the more moderate elements that aligned themselves with Marshal Pétain in 1940, and apparently it was widely held among the mass of the French nation that took little or no active role in politics. It is notable that in the immediate aftermath of the war, even though the wave of exultation that welled up at the time of the Liberation seemed to vindicate those who had earlier committed themselves to the course of resistance to the Axis, public opinion in France continued to view with some suspicion those men who had held positions in the government in September, 1939. Indeed, most of them were unable to regain their previous positions of political leadership.

We cannot hope at present to resolve this difference of views—nor can we even presume that the dispute is conciliable. Yet we cannot gain the needed perspective upon the Vichy experience unless we reexamine the chain of circumstances that stretches from the diplomatic capitulation of France in the summer of 1938 to her military surrender in the spring of 1940.

At the outset of this inquiry, we encounter an unanswerable question of prime importance: When and why did the French government decide upon resistance to the Axis? Obviously, the decision came within the interval between the Munich settlement and the outbreak of hostilities. But no one can say at what point within these twelve months, nor explain satisfactorily the considerations inducing the government to reverse its earlier course.

France seemed at the time of "Munich" to have made a decision for more than the moment. Once and for all, she seemed to have settled the debate between the partisans of "appeasement" and of "collective security" by a clear choice in favor of the former. In the fall and winter of 1938–39, the Extreme Right gained a still larger influence in the government, while the Communists, who represented the main proponents of resistance to the Axis, were driven into utter rout. The Socialists, riven by the intramural dispute between those who condemned war and those who denounced the Axis, were reduced to helpless inaction.

Nevertheless, France did not proceed in the path to which "Munich" pointed. Never again did the advocates of "appeasement" muster as much strength as in the summer of 1938. And as soon as the Nazis raised the issue of Poland, the French government made a public declaration of its intention to support the Poles. Whatever its unrevealed intentions or reservations, at no time did the cabinet ever give an open sign that it was even considering a breach of its word or putting pressure on the Poles to give ground.

But Poland did not become a critical diplomatic problem until the spring of 1939. In the meantime, France seemed to have attained equilibrium both at home and abroad. The government now gained its support among the moderates and the republican parties of the Right, while the Communists and the Socialists passed into opposition. On the basis of this new alignment, Édouard Daladier, who had taken over the premiership in April, 1938, and had presided over the government at the time of "Munich," seemed to have a secure command of Parliament.

On November, 1938, the Communists undertook a rear-guard action, in an attempt to check the march toward the Right. Having no hope of reconstituting the Popular Front and challenging Daladier within Parliament, they sought to put pressure upon his government by means of a general strike. The government took prompt action to break the strike, however, and the Socialists refused to lend their support to the demonstration. So the general strike failed of its purpose. Far from causing the government fear, it served only to reveal the impotence of the Extreme Left.

As the winter wore on, the Axis registered new gains. In Spain, the armies of Generalissimo Franco captured Madrid in March and thus put an end to republican resistance. Meantime Hitler broke up the remainder of Czechoslovakia that had survived after the settlement at Munich in the previous fall and annexed Bohemia and Moravia. In April, Mussolini invaded and annexed Albania.

Then Poland came to the fore. In the winter of 1938–39, the Nazis began to raise demands upon the Poles, in the course of discussions in Warsaw and Berlin. At the outset, the Germans expressed their demands in modest terms, ostensibly seeking only a revision of the status of Danzig. But the Poles steadfastly refused to make concessions, suspecting that these would only lead to new and broader demands.

Forthwith the Nazis stiffened their stand. Moreover, at the end of March, Hitler made public the German demands, thus transforming the issue from a matter of bilateral negotiations between Berlin and Warsaw into a problem of general diplomatic concern. Britain and France immediately responded by public declarations of their support of the Poles.

From the nature of the situation, the British and the French could not back up their promise of aid to Poland without inducing Russia to make a similar engagement. Accordingly, on April 15 the British government formally invited the Soviet government to make a unilateral pledge of assistance to Poland—and also to Rumania, against which the Nazis were raising a lesser threat—parallel to the declarations of the British and the French. Moscow made answer on April 17, proposing a general defensive alliance among Britain, France, and Russia, and a common guarantee by these three powers to all the states bordering Russia, between the Baltic and the Black Sea.

Upon receiving the Soviet counterproposal, the British at first balked. Instead, they again asked Russia to make a unilateral pledge to Poland and Rumania. Once more the Russians refused, again proposing a tripartite alliance. Eventually, on May 27, London gave ground to the extent of agreeing to discuss the possibility of such an agreement. On this basis, conversations began in Moscow between the British and French ambassadors and the Soviet Ministry of Foreign Affairs.

In this interval, the British and French apparently put no pressure upon the Poles to back down. However, they made plain their desire to avoid war and their willingness to discuss German demands. Moreover, men of prominence in both Paris and London continued to talk in terms of a new "appeasement" on the model of "Munich."

Because the Germans might well choose to settle the crisis by a sudden attack upon Poland, the Soviet government proposed on July 23 that the British and French governments should immediately send military missions to Moscow to discuss plans for common action in the event the Nazis should resort to arms. London and Paris agreed, and the missions reached Moscow on August 11. Yet it proved no easier to reach an agreement on military action than to define the basis for a treaty of alliance. The Russians insisted upon having the right to send their troops into Poland to assist the Polish army in withstanding a German invasion, but the Polish government, dreading the presence of the Red Army on Polish soil no less than a German invasion, refused to grant this permission. The British and French chose to support the Poles in this stand. Hence the military conversations in Moscow made no progress.

Behind the scenes, the Russians were now engaged in secret negotiations with the Germans, the ultimate outcome of which was the Nonaggression Pact between the two countries. On August 20 public announcement was made of an economic agreement between the German and Russian governments. At midnight on August 21, Berlin announced that the German Foreign Minister, Ribbentrop, was leaving for Moscow to sign a nonaggression treaty. On August 23, the two governments revealed the public text of this accord. By the terms of a protocol not made public at the time, the two governments marked out spheres of influence, which in substance provided for the partition of Poland between them.

The news of this turn of events caused profound shock in both Paris and London. The ultimate significance of the pact remained obscure, but its immediate bearing was obvious. In the new situation, the British and French could not possibly forestall an invasion of Poland. They could make good their promise of help only by declaring war upon Germany and striving to restore Polish independence at the conclusion of a protracted struggle.

Such was the course that Britain and France chose. Perhaps the two governments continued to hope for a new agreement with Hitler, such as that reached at Munich in the previous fall. But such a hope was doomed. On the morning of September 1, German troops began to invade Poland, and German airplanes started to bomb Polish cities.

At 5 o'clock that afternoon, the British ambassador in Berlin delivered a message to the German Foreign Office, indicating that unless the Germans halted their invasion, the British government would come to the aid of the Poles. On the evening of the same day, the French ambassador delivered an identical message. On the following morning, the two ambassadors separately called upon Ribbentrop, who gave a negative answer to each. Thereupon each informed him that Britain and France would regard themselves at war with Germany as from the next day, September 3. Thus, within a year after their purchase of "peace in our time" at Munich, the British and French found themselves once more at war with the Germans, on conditions much less favorable than in 1914.

Since that momentous hour of decision, a plethora of interpretations have been advanced to explain the considerations leading Britain and

France upon the road to war. In the mass of charges, countercharges, and apologetics, we can discern three principal lines of argument. One of these represents the quasi-official interpretation, defending the action of the two governments. Another corresponds to the views of the Extreme Left, and the third expresses the views of the Extreme Right. Though we cannot settle the issues in the debate, we must take note of these arguments, because each, in some degree, throws light upon the background of Vichy.

The quasi-official explanation holds that the British and French governments were sincere in their public professions. In the period of "appeasement," they honestly believed that they would secure a durable peace by conciliating the Nazis. Moreover, they felt that the Germans had some measure of legitimate grievance in their demands for a revision of the diplomatic *status quo*.

However, this argument goes on, the British and French began to see their mistake in the spring of 1939, when Hitler violated the agreement he had made at Munich by annexing Bohemia and Moravia. At this point, it became clear for the first time that Hitler harbored aggressive designs upon the independence of neighboring countries, not merely a desire to unite all peoples of the German tongue under a single, strong German state. Thereupon, in the spring of 1939, London and Paris had given their pledges of aid to the Poles and invited Moscow to share in this pledge. At no time thereafter did the British or the French waver in their stand.

This interpretation has apparent confirmation in that it conforms to the repeated declarations of the British and French governments and supplies a plausible motive for their actions. Yet it remains hard to believe that these two governments had such naive trust in the readiness of Hitler to forego further aggression after his success at Munich. Indeed, this argument saves the good faith of Britain and France only by attributing gross ineptitude to their governments.

The interpretation which the partisans of the Extreme Left urged at the time exonerates the British and French governments of the charge of naive incompetence by charging them instead with colossal duplicity. According to this argument, the British and French recognized the immense dynamism of the Nazi regime long before the Czech crisis in 1938. But their governments hoped to cope with the problem by encouraging Hitler to turn his aggression toward Eastern Europe. Some of the advocates of "appeasement" hoped that Hitler would thus launch a crusade against Bolshevism, in which the British and French would sooner or later join. Others, the Extreme Left argued, urged this course of "appeasement" with a less venturesome perspective: they hoped to see the Nazis exhaust themselves as well as the Russians in a violent but indecisive struggle in the East. This would leave Britain and France secure and at peace in the West. Hence, according to this interpretation, London and Paris surrendered the Czech Republic in 1938 not because of a desire to prevent war but because of a wish to see war come about between Germany and Russia. For the same reason, the British and French made no more than verbal protests in the spring of 1939, when Hitler annexed Bohemia and Moravia. And when they gave their pledges to Poland shortly thereafter, they never meant to live up to their promises.

However, the argument goes on, the policy of "appeasement" eventually broke down because Hitler ultimately saw that Britain and France were weaker adversaries than Russia. Consequently, he chose to make peace with the Russians, so as to turn his expansion in the opposite direction. Once the Nazis made overtures for a reconciliation with Moscow, the Russians had no choice but to accept the offer. They well knew that the British and French, far from desiring an alliance with them, hoped only to see them embroiled in war with the Nazis. In sum, then, the British and French did not decide upon resistance to Hitler until after the news of the Nonaggression Pact broke on August 23, 1939, and only because Hitler was unwilling to continue his *Drang nach Osten* as far as Russia.

This interpretation, as well as the other, adduces credible motives to explain the actions of the British and French governments, both in pursuing and in renouncing "appeasement." Moreover, it gains corroboration from the fact that a considerable number of men of political importance in both London and Paris gave voice to their hopes of a Russo-German war. However, this thesis requires us to set aside, as deliberate prevarication, the professions of the British and French governments that they sought only to secure peace within the bounds of international reconciliation. It likewise requires us to regard their repeated assurances to Poland as wholly spurious. But we have no conclusive evidence that will permit us to establish that men in responsible positions in Paris and London meant other than what they publicly declared.

A third interpretation is worthy of special note because it gained much vogue in France under Vichy sponsorship. This argument alleges that the French government took no decision on its own initiative throughout the successive crises leading up to the war. Rather, it acquiesced in whatever the British decided. Generally the British were reluctant to take a stand against the Nazis because they feared this would mean a new world war, and they well knew that such a war would impose a ruinous strain upon Britain. On the other hand, because of the insular nature of their homeland, they had much less reason than the French to fear the rise of German might within the bounds of continental Europe. Indeed, they even favored a strong Germany as a makeweight to France.

Eventually the British gave up the policy of "appeasement" when they perceived that German power had become so great as to menace the world-wide interests of Britain, and not merely the security of France. In the summer of 1939, therefore, the British determined to draw the line at Poland, and to go to war if Hitler refused to halt. In this new policy of firmness, as in the previous regime of capitulation, the French government once more tagged along behind the British.

But therein, according to this argument, the French government made a criminal error. Put in bluntest terms, this thesis charges that the men who administered the French government committed the double folly of first permitting the Germans to build up their military power, then embarking upon war with them when the time was too late, simply because of a senseless determination to preserve a Franco-British *entente* at any cost. Instead, France should have broken with Britain, established amicable relations with the Germans, and let the British cope with their own problems.

This argument is not to be dismissed simply because it was put forth in the period of Vichy by some of the more notorious advocates of "collaboration." Certainly the French, throughout the 1920s and 1930s, were unwilling to take any action involving the risk of war without British backing. But for their part, the British were much less concerned with preventing Germany from regaining preeminence in continental Europe than with preserving the delicate structure of their own imperial relations, which could ill support the strain of a new world-wide war. Hence the British were much more inclined toward conciliation with Germany in the 1920s than were the French. We cannot avoid the impression that it was also the British who took the initiative in "appeasement" during the 1930s, while the French uneasily acquiesced. Likewise, we may reasonably surmise that the final decision to embark upon war in the summer of 1939 was made in London rather than Paris.

On the other hand, we cannot accept the proposition that the British knowingly pursued a policy which would lead to the German conquest of France. We have no evidence whatever that the British had any better knowledge than the French of how the war would turn out. Nor can we accept the implication that the French would have done better to seek "collaboration" with Germany in 1939 and leave the British to their own devices. We have no occasion to believe that France would have fared better as a satellite of Germany if she had chosen that role in 1939 than when she had it forced upon her in 1940.

Various though they are, probably each of these three interpretations has some measure of validity. We have no occasion here to establish which is the soundest. But, whatever the reason, we cannot but acknowledge that the French government made a rash decision in embarking upon war in September, 1939, for France was in no position to win, nor even to contest the war on equal terms.

Furthermore, we must note that the decision was primarily the responsibility of the moderate parties. The partisans of the Extreme Right were too deeply committed to a pro-Nazi orientation to welcome the outbreak of war with Germany, no matter what the circumstances. On the Extreme Left, the Communist Party reversed its stand as soon as Russia signed the Nonaggression Pact and openly proclaimed its opposition to the war. Hence, the blame for the decision to embark upon the war fell principally upon those parties traditionally regarded as the bulwarks of the Third Republic. This, in turn, was to strengthen the hands of those who, in the era of Vichy, strove to exploit the defeat

of 1940 as a means of discrediting and supplanting the republican regime.

Finally, we must note that the circumstances under which France
entered the war were not such as to buttress public morale. Throughout
the anguished months of crisis in the summer of 1939 both the French
and the British governments insisted upon their determination to defend
Poland. But they also kept speaking of their hope of finding some
solution without resort to war. Remembering the outcome of the similar
Czech crisis in 1938, the nation at large had reason to believe that a
settlement on the model of "Munich" was as probable as a declaration
of war.

Even after the government took an irrevocable decision for war, it
did not make it clear why it had made this choice. The cabinet concluded its deliberations behind closed doors, and Parliament gave its
approval without debate. Hence the public had reason to regard the
issues as obscure and the decision for war as tentative. No one can measure to what extent the doubts and reservations in the public mind
weakened the French resistance in the test of strength that came in the
following spring. But we may presume that, once France had lost the
struggle, the obscurities surrounding the declaration of war made it
easier for public opinion to repudiate the regime that had led the nation
to its doom.

France entered upon a state of war with Germany on the afternoon
of September 3, some hours after the United Kingdom. Within a week,
Canada, Australia, and New Zealand also declared themselves at war.

So far as involves offensive action, the opening phase of the war was
confined to Poland, and its course was brief. German armies began to
invade Poland on the morning of September 1, while German planes
began to bomb Polish cities. Within a week, the German armored divisions, spearheading the attack, shattered the Polish armies and threw
them back in a disorganized retreat. On the 17th, the Red Army crossed
the Russian border and swept over the eastern plains of Poland. Beset
on both sides, the Polish armies crumbled. On the 28th, the Soviet and
Nazi governments signed a treaty establishing a common border, and
Poland once more became a victim of partition. Thus the campaigns

beginning the Second World War reached their conclusion within a month.

Throughout September, as this doom descended upon Poland, the British and French forces remained motionless upon the Western Front. Nor did the Germans launch an offensive of their own in the West. So began that curious interlude, known variously as the "phony war," the *drôle de guerre,* and the *Sitzkrieg,* in which some millions of armed men remained stationed on either side of the Franco-German border, officially at war, but apparently as much at peace as though on maneuvers. For nine months, only occasional salvoes of artillery disturbed the quiet, while from time to time flights of planes passed over the lines on cautious missions of reconnaissance.

In France, apart from the *départements* along the border, where the troops were concentrated, life proceeded much as before. To be sure, the mobilization withdrew millions of men from their usual pursuits, and neither they nor their families could regard their situation as more really one of peace than of war. However, a substantial portion of the industrial proletariat remained at work in war industries, and likewise a portion of the male population engaged in agriculture. Paris had reason for misgivings, since even a war without bloodshed boded ill for those who made their livelihood from catering to cosmopolitan sightseers and pleasure seekers. Yet the capital had her share of war industries, and she took on new animation as the nerve center of the nation in arms, while her restaurants and theaters had business enough, that winter of 1939-40, to tax their decimated staffs.

Meantime an unwonted quiet descended upon the world of domestic politics. On August 24 the government instituted a strict censorship. Consequently the press, normally partisan to a degree of venomous passion, became monotonously single-voiced. All papers printed the same news, in much the same words, not daring to depart from the official releases. Though the sophisticated might read between the lines, the public at large could scarcely tell one paper from another.

On September 13 Daladier reorganized his cabinet in order to give it a broader base, including representatives of all parties from the Socialists to the republican parties of the Right. Thereafter, political debate took place almost exclusively within the cabinet. None of these discussions reached the public. The sessions of Parliament soon ceased to command attention, since the two chambers in December empowered the government to issue decree-laws at its discretion. Thenceforth Parliament met only to transact routine business and, at rare intervals, to hear reports behind closed doors on the course of the war.

Thus the political life of the nation was entrusted to the charge of perhaps two score political leaders, who decided policy as they chose, issuing brief official reports and permitting no public discussion or criticism of their actions. And thus the mass of the nation became accustomed, nearly a year before the Vichy regime took over, to a passive acceptance of the rule of a government which issued laws on its own counsel and required mute obedience.

In another respect, too, the Daladier government set a precedent in this period which the Vichy regime was to follow. For the cabinet determined to turn the occasion of the war to good advantage by striking a decisive blow at the Communist Party. At the moment, public opinion was generally favorable to a move against the Communists. In their sudden swing from advocating "collective security" to urging neutrality in the war, they had exposed themselves as subservient to the vagaries of Russian foreign policy and had laid themselves open to the charge of a disloyalty to the nation that verged on treason. So, on September 26, the cabinet ordered the dissolution of the Communist Party and its affiliated organizations. All the other parties in Parliament, including the Socialists, endorsed this action. The next step was to expel the Communist members of Parliament, who continued to hold their seats. This proved a slower process, but eventually the Chamber voted the expulsion, on February 20, 1940, and the Senate on February 29.

On the international scene, the *Sitzkrieg* continued, while Russia seized the initiative. In September and October, 1939, Moscow opened discussions with the governments of Estonia, Latvia, and Lithuania, ostensibly aiming at the negotiation of nonaggression treaties. Under pressure, the Baltic states concluded agreements which permitted Russia to maintain military installations within their borders. Then on October 5, Russia began negotiations with Finland, in the course of which the Soviet government eventually demanded modifications of the border. Upon the refusal of the Finns, the Red Army on November 30 began an invasion of Finland.

No sooner did this Russo-Finnish war break out than speculation began to develop as to the possibilities of British and French intervention on the side of the Finns. Both London and Paris gave prompt expression of their sympathy for the Finns. Voices rose up urging bold moves, on the ground that Russia and Germany were practically allies, and Russia could be attacked more readily than Germany. Perhaps, as some observers suggested at the time, those who urged such a course were still hoping to open a crusade against Bolshevism, in which Germany would ultimately side with Britain and France. At any event, by the end of December the British and French governments were considering means of sending military aid to Finland. But the scheme came to naught, for early in March, the Finns sued for peace. On the 12th, they signed a treaty with the Russians terminating the war.

A minor political crisis ensued in France when the Finnish war thus came to an end without Allied intervention. Even though Parliament had granted him virtually unlimited power, Daladier had conspicuously failed to gain any success in the war so far. He therefore found it expedient to hand over the premiership to Paul Reynaud, while remaining in the government as Minister of War.

In Britain, too, there were murmurings against the inaction of the government. In response to the pressure of criticism, plans were made for an offensive operation in Norway. The ostensible purpose was to stop the Germans from sending ships, within the shelter of neutral Norwegian coastal waters, to the port of Narvik, where they obtained cargoes of iron ore brought by railroad from Swedish mines. The plan matured to the point where the British were prepared to begin sowing mines in Norwegian waters on April 9, in violation of Norwegian neutrality and despite formal protests from Oslo.

This never came to pass, however. On April 9 the Nazis launched a well-planned and well-executed operation in which their troops invaded Denmark and Norway simultaneously. The Danes put up no resistance. While the Norwegians were striving to stem the Nazi invasion, the British and French undertook to send an expeditionary force to their assistance. On April 15 Allied troops began to land near Narvik and at other seaports. But the expedition proved unequal to its task, and within ten days the Allies began to withdraw. Within a few weeks the Germans held mastery of Norway, although resistance continued in scattered localities.

The setback in Norway brought the downfall of Chamberlain in Britain, as the termination of the Russo-Finnish war had earlier discredited Daladier. On May 13 Churchill succeeded him as Prime Minister.

Meantime the *Sitzkrieg* exploded in a violent eruption. On May 10 Nazi armored divisions spearheaded a broad attack across the borders of Belgium, Luxembourg, and the Netherlands. The attack won quick success in the Netherlands. On May 14 the Dutch commander ordered his armies to surrender, while Queen Wilhelmina and the cabinet escaped to London. The Belgians put up a more stubborn resistance, and the British and French dispatched a force to support them. This force was soon cut off, however, by German armored divisions which broke through the French line near Sedan, then swept westward to the Channel coast. On May 27, the King of the Belgians ordered an end of Belgian resistance. Meantime the French and British troops that had been cut off in Belgium fell back to the French port of Dunkirk and on May 28 began to evacuate by sea.

No sooner was their conquest of the Low Countries assured than the Germans threw their whole weight against the main body of the Allied forces in France. The German armored divisions shattered the French line with rapid thrusts, opening gaps through which their regular divisions could penetrate, and drove their adversaries into a disorganized retreat that verged on rout. Thus the Germans began an advance which had as its objective the capture of Paris and the destruction of French resistance. So began the stage in the struggle in the West that was dubbed the "Battle of France."

From the start, the outcome was obvious. The French armies could do no more than strive to slow down the German onrush. At no time did they succeed in withstanding the pressure long enough to give hope that a stable front could be established before Paris.

We shall leave to the next chapter our consideration of the course and conclusion of the Battle of France. The question of interest in it was not whether France would make an eleventh-hour stand, but how France would face up to her defeat. But at this point, taking the outcome of the struggle as already settled when the Battle of France began, we must pause to note some aspects of the campaign in the West in May and June of 1940 that had special consequence in the period of Vichy.

The unavoidable question that arises at the outset is: Why did France prove unable to defend herself successfully? We cannot hope as yet, if ever, to make a satisfactory answer. Perhaps we shall never do better than respond by noting once more that France was caught in a hopeless dilemma, since she was obliged to wage war in order to resist the German attack without ever being able to meet the Germans on equal terms.

From the start the French themselves were not unaware of their inferiority of power. Accordingly, they planned to attempt no more than defend their homeland. They renounced hope of taking the offensive and winning a sweeping victory. In this they acted reasonably. France lacked both the manpower and the industrial resources needed to support an army equal to the German, once the Germans utilized their potential to the utmost. Recognizing her own weakness, she had good grounds to believe that if her army would remain entrenched behind strong fortifications, it could inflict murderous casualties upon an attacking force. Presumably, the war would ultimately be settled by the exhaustion of one side or the other. In such a war of attrition, she would have a large advantage, since Britain's command of the seas would give her access to the resources of lands across the ocean.

In view of these considerations, the role of the French in the *Sitzkrieg* is quite understandable. It is not necessary to assume that the French promise of aid to Poland was a deliberate hoax, nor that the French government was planning an alliance with the Nazis against Soviet Russia. The French were thinking in terms of maintaining the defensive, so as to make the Germans pay the price of the aggression upon which they had embarked. They counted on winning the ultimate victory by steadfastly refusing to attack. And in this ultimate victory, not by a Quixotic sally at the start, France would restore Poland to her independence.

The French did not suffer defeat in 1940 simply because they thought in terms of defense instead of attack. Rather, their mistake was that they did not anticipate the new methods of warfare which the Germans utilized in their Blitzkrieg. For their failure to anticipate the new tactics, the French do not deserve intemperate blame. They were not wholly oblivious of the potentialities of the airplane and of mechanized warfare. In the 1920s, they had developed a large air force, in comparison with others at the time. Their army had also made ample provision for tanks. But the French did not appreciate the importance of these new weapons. Hence they permitted their air force to decline in relative strength during the 1930s, while the army kept up its apparent strength in tanks largely by retaining obsolete models.

By no means were the French alone in this error of judgment. Certainly the British and Americans did not make significantly larger provision for airplanes and tanks. Quite probably the Russians in 1940 had the same weakness. Yet it is only a mitigation of the blame, not an excuse, to argue that the leaders of other nations were also unprepared.

As to precisely where within France the blame lies, we cannot presently hope to determine. Nor are we under an obligation to concern ourselves with this problem. However, we must recognize that this problem loomed large in the French mind at the moment when the Vichy regime took over. As the disaster developed in May and June of 1940, the entire nation, shocked and outraged, became convinced that someone had perpetrated treason.

Let it be noted that rather few Frenchmen thought in terms of a Nazi "Fifth Column," as did some of the more excitable American reporters at the time. Nor did the French generally believe that the collapse of their army was due to a weakness of national character, expressed in desertion or cowardice. So far as the evidence shows, they were right about this.

They felt this sense of betrayal, not only because they thought that theirs was a matchless army, but also because knowledge of the catastrophe came to them without warning. Throughout the Battle of France, the censorship prevented news of the military reverses from reaching the public. The men in the army knew, of course, the extent of the rout around them. But they had no way of knowing how general it was, and the civilian population had little more than an inkling of the magnitude of the disaster until German tanks hove into sight. Hence the whole nation shared a deep conviction that persons in high position had concealed the truth from the people. Later, when Marshal Pétain was to inveigh against "the lies they have told you," he was to address his words to a widespread sense of indignation.

Though the government of Marshal Pétain exploited this sentiment, it certainly did not create it. Any government that assumed office in the summer of 1940 would have had to find a scapegoat. And it was not hard to find a scapegoat, since the blame was so diffuse that it could be laid upon nearly anyone.

Obviously, a principal question was whether to put the burden upon the civilian authorities or the military command. The Vichy government chose to direct the wrath of the populace toward the politicians of the Third Republic. One reason was that military men had large influence in the new government and wished to protect their caste. Another was that elements sympathetic to facism wished to discredit the parliamentary regime. We must not mistake the partisan interests in this propaganda. But neither must we assume that the men of Vichy sought to indict the Third Republic, merely as a device of demagogy.

The débâcle left another heritage to the Vichy regime insofar as it produced a widespread distrust of Britain. Apart from any criticism of British diplomacy before the war, there were circumstances in the course of the fighting in 1940 that readily led to an anti-British sentiment in France. In the first place, the British never put a large force into action on the Western Front. At most, they contributed no more than about ten percent of the troops in France. In the second place, they evacuated their troops at Dunkirk with remarkable dispatch. The decision to withdraw was probably necessary and wise. Certainly it was approved by the French command. Nevertheless, it gave grounds for a suspicion among the French that their allies were as quick to leave the battle as they were slow to enter it.

Furthermore, the British made a prompt decision, at the time of their evacuation at Dunkirk, to give no more than a token aid to the French in the Battle of France, which was then beginning. As a gesture, they sent back two divisions to share the agony of the French army. But they steadfastly refused to provide planes for air support. Again, this was probably a wise decision, since the Battle of France was hopeless, and Britain needed her men and planes for her own defense. Yet this decision, too, did little to allay the suspicion of the French that the British were ruthless in deserting their stricken ally. After the armistice, some elements in the Vichy regime were to capitalize upon this sentiment in order to defend the diplomatic break with Britain, and some of the partisans of "collaboration" with the Axis were to give voice to scurrilous accusations of British perfidy.

To a lesser degree, the defeat also nurtured anti-Russian sentiment in France. To be sure, the Soviet government gave the Germans no positive assistance in the course of the campaigns of 1940. Nevertheless, the French could not help but view the Russians as hostile neutrals. Such a position was perhaps better, perhaps worse, than that of a perfidious ally. But it certainly was not a role of friendship.

Finally, the circumstances of the war provided the basis for a view that France was foolish to have fought at all, regardless of the issues at stake. In the painful months that followed the *Blitzkrieg,* the French were faced with the knowledge that only they and the Poles had striven to their utmost to hold back the Nazi armored divisions, while the Danes and the Norwegians, the Dutch and the Belgians, had all admitted their defeat before it was complete. And the French could take little or no comfort from their more stubborn resistance. Instead of the consoling knowledge that they had waged an heroic fight against a stronger foe, they had garnered only the humiliation of seeing their armies shattered to bits and swept aside, without giving pause to the enemy or requiring him to pay in blood for his victory. This, too, was a dark heritage which Vichy was to put to its own uses.

V

FROM WAR TO PEACE

THE GERMAN ATTACK in the West proceeded at such a whirlwind pace that in the previous chapter we were caught up in the sweep of events and carried on to the beginning of the Battle of France; and the start of that battle foretold the conclusion of the war in France. After the evacuation at Dunkirk (May 28–June 4), the matter of prime interest was no longer the course of the military struggle but the political problem involved in the question as to how the French government would respond to its defeat. In order to examine these problems as a whole, we must turn back to March 21, 1940, when Paul Reynaud succeeded Édouard Daladier as Premier, since it was the Reynaud cabinet that had to cope with the problems arising from the defeat.

Reynaud assumed charge of the government at a moment when all was still quiet on the Western Front. He owed his rise to the dissatisfaction that had developed because the Daladier cabinet had accomplished nothing whatever in nine months so far as concerned the prosecution of the war. However, Daladier's resignation was in the nature of a strategic maneuver, rather than a surrender. He kept a seat in the new government as Minister of National Defense. Moreover, he had about as much influence in the new cabinet as did Reynaud. For Daladier had held the premiership, with only a brief intermission, ever since 1937. As head of the government throughout the critical period of 1938–39, he had set the course that led France into war. Because of his role in liquidating the Popular Front and smashing the Communist Party, he had won the special favor of business interests.

Reynaud had never served as Premier, nor had he loomed large in the politics of Parliament. He was known principally as a staunch advocate of diplomatic cooperation with Britain, and he had gained an undeserved reputation of being vigorous and decisive. Because of this reputation, he appeared a logical successor to Daladier. Yet he found it impossible to exclude his predecessor from the cabinet, even though he disliked Daladier personally and resented him as an obstacle to his own ambition and self-esteem.

Besides these two, the new government comprised thirty-three others, ranging in political complexion from Socialists to members of the republican parties of the Right. Ostensibly, it was a government of "national union." That is, it included representatives of all parties in Parliament rather than a coalition of some parties to the exclusion of others. But in actuality, it was under the control of the conservative republicans. Neither the Socialists nor the Radical-Socialists had a decisive influence in its deliberations.

The more notable members, other than Reynaud and Daladier, were Camille Chautemps, the Vice-Premier, who was known as a partisan of "appeasement" during the Munich crisis, and Georges Mandel, who had once been *chef de cabinet* to Clemenceau and ever since had waged a vain struggle to gain recognition as the political heir to the "Tiger." Since the government was too large to meet and deliberate as a whole, save to pass on routine matters of domestic administration, policies concerning the war were decided in the Comité de Guerre, comprising the President of the Republic, the Premier, the Vice-Premier, the ministers in charge of the three armed services, and the commanding officers of each of these services.

From the start, the Premier was far from master of the policies of his government. He took office with the slimmest possible margin of support, since Parliament voted its approval by only 268 votes against 156, with 111 abstentions. To be sure, Reynaud did not long have need to trouble himself on this score, inasmuch as Parliament had proved unable to keep a close rein upon the government. But in the Comité de Guerre, where the basic issues involved in the disaster were debated, Reynaud had to cope with Daladier, who never disguised his sullen distaste for the new Premier. Moreover, Daladier soon entered into a kind of alliance with General Gamelin, who as Chief of Staff of the Army was a member of the Comité de Guerre.

Nor was the French government free to prosecute the war as it saw fit. Early in the war, the French and British governments had agreed to set up a single command, under the general direction of a Supreme War Council comprising representatives of the two governments. Under this arrangement, the British assumed the primary responsibility for naval operations. In return, the French assumed over-all direction of both British and French troops in Europe. Nevertheless, the French government was constrained to seek the approval of London before making any major decision on military policy.

Then, on March 28, 1940, a week after Reynaud became Premier, the two governments went still further. Both agreed never to negotiate with the enemy, or conclude a separate peace, without the permission of the other. At the time, the declaration ruling out a separate peace seemed to have no large practical importance, since neither government was contemplating a withdrawal from the war. But within two months it was to become the crux of acrimonious debate.

Far from fearing the possible implications of such an involvement, Reynaud welcomed a close partnership between France and Britain. With his approval, the two governments proceeded to draw up their plan for sowing mines off the coast of Norway. When the Nazis forestalled this operation by their sudden invasion of Denmark and Norway, beginning on April 9, a wave of popular indignation brought down the Chamberlain government. Much the same sentiment welled up in France. Thereupon Reynaud determined to make a scapegoat of General Gamelin, the French Chief of Staff. However, Daladier spoke up in Gamelin's support and prevented his dismissal. Angered at this opposition, Reynaud contemplated resigning as Premier. But before he finally made up his mind to resign, the Germans launched their assault on the Low Countries on May 9–10. Once this attack had begun, Reynaud found it quite impossible to step down, since this would leave France virtually without a government while in the midst of a crisis in military operations.

Instead of resigning, Reynaud contented himself with a minor renovation of the cabinet on May 10, in which he brought into the government Louis Marin and Yves Ybarnegaray. Marin, the aged and venerable head of the Fédération Républicaine, was known as the leader of one of the most conservative of the republican parties, but he was also known as a consistent advocate of resistance to the Axis, having urged such a course at the time of "Munich." He proved a source of strength to Reynaud. Ybarnegaray was a more dubious addition, however, since he had been identified as a spokesman in Parliament for Colonel de la Rocque as well as the *Action Française*. Thus he had been associated with the protofascist and fascist movements of the 1930s.

Within a week, the German invasion of the Low Countries developed into a major reverse for the Allies. On May 14 the Nazis broke through the main French defenses at Sedan and began to spread out through northern France. This marked the moment, as we now can see, when France lost the war.

As soon as the news of the Nazi breakthrough at Sedan reached Paris, the French command recognized the dire omen. On the 15th, General Gamelin made clear to Daladier, his immediate superior as Minister of National Defense, that the French armies were on the verge of destruction. This report was handed on to the other members of the government. On the 16th, General Héring, in command of the defenses of Paris, sent a formal communication to the Premier, advising him that the road to Paris lay open to the advance of the enemy. He therefore urged the government to move its seat elsewhere. Already the Foreign Office was making ready to evacuate, and the staff was hard at work ransacking the archives, removing whatever documents might prove of value to the Germans upon their entrance into Paris, and burning these papers in open fires on the lawn outside the Ministry. However, fearing the effects upon public morale, the government determined not to quit the capital as yet. Meantime the censorship forbade the press to give any warning of the imminence of disaster.

On the afternoon of May 16, Churchill arrived in Paris to take stock of the situation. Surprised at the state of alarm he discovered in his conferences with the French, he gave them assurance that the British would redouble their contribution to the common struggle. With refulgent rhetoric, he painted word pictures of the dread retribution that would ultimately be visited upon the Nazis. "Until one o'clock in the morning, he soared astride this apocalyptic vision," according to one of the members of the French government who was present at the meetings. "From the depths of Canada, across the rubble of a bombed-out England and the cold ruins of France," he promised, would come swarms of planes to match the new might of the Axis. For the moment, this tonic seemed to steady the shattered nerves of Reynaud. But the conferences broke up with no practical decision as to how to meet the immediate crisis.

During the following week, Reynaud made desperate efforts to inspire new resistance. On May 18 he persuaded the cabinet at last, despite the opposition of Daladier, to sanction the dismissal of General Gamelin. He himself replaced Daladier as Minister of National Defense, giving his rival, instead, the portfolio of Foreign Affairs. To succeed Gamelin he named General Weygand, who had earlier been recalled from retirement and put in charge of the inactive theater of operations in the Near East.

No one in the government had reason to believe that this enigmatic septuagenarian could work the miracle of stemming the Nazi onslaught. But Weygand had been Foch's right-hand man in the First World War, and he had thus passed into the legends of French military glory. Reynaud hoped that his presence in Paris, reviving memories of the previous war, would at least improve public morale. With the same idea in mind, he elevated Georges Mandel, the minuscule heir of Clemenceau, from the minor post of Minister of Colonies to the crucial role of Minister of the Interior, trusting that the shadow of the redoubtable "Tiger of France" would strike terror into the hearts of "defeatists." Then, as a climax in this campaign to recapture the grandeur of an earlier crisis, Reynaud brought Marshal Pétain into the cabinet as Vice-Premier.

Regardless of the ultimate consequences of his decision, Reynaud had good reason to call upon Marshal Pétain. As the lone survivor of the three men who had gained the marshal's baton for their services in the War of 1914, Pétain was unquestionably the venerable old soldier of France. Whatever the merits of his disputed claim to the title, he was widely regarded as the man who had won the Battle of Verdun. In the interbellum period, Pétain had studiously cultivated this reputation. He had gained a decisive advantage over his rivals for fame, Marshals Joffre and Foch, by his success in outliving them. Moreover, he had kept himself in public view without becoming embroiled in public debate, save to defend his reputation as the "Victor of Verdun."

Pétain had retained an active role in the administration of the army into the decade of the 1930s, and in 1934 he had made his sole venture into politics as Minister of War. He had made no conspicuous enemies while in the cabinet, however, and soon thereafter he had passed into a semi-retirement until 1939, when he was appointed ambassador to Spain at the time when France recognized the Franco regime. He was still at this post when Reynaud summoned him back to Paris, on May 18, to enter the cabinet. Though rumors, which seem to have little basis, linked his name with the *Cagoulards,* republican politicians had a good opinion of him at this time, and even Léon Blum had praised him as a humanitarian and a republican.

On his entrance into the Reynaud government, Marshal Pétain assumed primarily a decorative role. At the age of eighty-five, he was regarded as too old to undertake the active direction of military operations. General Weygand, who accepted the supreme military command at the same time that Pétain entered the cabinet as Vice-Premier, was not disposed to seek Pétain's counsel. The two old soldiers were not personal friends, and in the past they had belonged in rival camps in the intramural rivalries of the upper echelons of the army. So at no time, down to the eve of the armistice, did Pétain have an active part in either the direction of military operations or the political deliberations of the cabinet. But his presence in the government was warmly hailed in the French press and favorably noted in Britain and America. It had the effect, as Reynaud hoped, of inspiring a momentary surge of new confidence.

From the moment when he assumed command, General Weygand did not dissemble his pessimism. Upon his arrival in Paris on May 19, returning from Syria to take over his new position, he made clear to Reynaud that he would neither promise nor hold out hope of victory. Immediately he set out to make a personal inspection of the front. The disorder which he discovered, verging on rout, gave him no reason to improve his estimate of the desperate plight of the Allied armies.

On May 25 he made a comprehensive report to the Comité de Guerre, summarizing the situation in detail and analyzing the various possible plans for stabilizing the line. But he concluded his report with the pronouncement that there was no realistic hope of stemming the German advance. Unhappily for France, he simply spoke the truth.[1] From May 25, the French government had only to consider the problem of how to respond to the defeat of the Allied armies.

The problem was complex to the utmost degree. In broad outline, to be sure, there seemed but two alternatives—either to appeal to the Germans for an armistice or else to abandon France to German military occupation and continue the struggle from somewhere abroad. But both alternatives involved a multitude of consequences, most of which were quite unpredictable. So the choice between them was far from simple.

For a time, Reynaud sought to avoid a choice by proposing a third course. This would involve withdrawing what could be salvaged of the Allied armies into the peninsula of Brittany. Dug in behind this "Breton Redoubt," the French might continue their struggle in alliance with the British, and on the soil of the homeland.

However, it was extremely doubtful that even a token resistance could be sustained within this "Breton Redoubt." The troops pinned in there would have to be supplied with food and munitions from Britain by sea and air. It was problematic how long the British and French navies could maintain the flow of supplies, and it was manifest that the British could ill afford a drain upon the slim resources needed for their own defense.

The government could not seriously consider continuing its resistance save by withdrawing to North Africa. Yet such a course would have grave disadvantages. It would mean abandoning the whole of the homeland to German occupation. Thus the mass of the nation would be given over to the mercy of the Nazis. Probably the Nazis would set up a puppet French government, the members of which would be recruited among French fascists. This puppet government would label

[1] The epithet "defeatist" has been applied to General Weygand, without the term being defined, presumably because of his pessimistic view of the military situation. It is true that he held out but little hope of success at any time after he took command. However, there is no evidence that he exaggerated the seriousness of the Allied reverses or the imminence of a complete collapse, nor is there reason to believe, contrary to his view, that there was a real possibility of stabilizing a defensive position.

the refugee government, established in North Africa or elsewhere outside the homeland, a pseudo government and would denounce its members as men who had deserted the nation in its hour of need. This puppet regime might endure for a long time, since the hour of the ultimate defeat of the Nazis seemed far off indeed. Holding power for perhaps a decade or more, a pro-Nazi government might well accomplish such a deep transformation of France, involving numberless proscriptions, immense spoliations of property, and profound alterations in the moral outlook of the nation that its traces might never be wholly expunged.

Even if the legal government were to accept these probable consequences of its emigration, it could not be sure of maintaining an effective struggle from abroad. Apparently there was no possibility of evacuating any sizable portion of the French army to North Africa. Hence the government would have to depend for its defense, once it reached North Africa, upon the military resources presently available in the African colonies. These amounted to no more than about seven divisions, mostly native troops, with no modern matériel.

To be sure, the Germans would not find it easy to cross the Mediterranean and carry on their attack in North Africa, since the French and British navies would block the passage of German troops by sea. But the Germans might undertake an airborne invasion. Or they might induce Franco to grant them transit through Spain to Spanish Morocco, whence they could drive eastward through French Morocco, Algeria, and Tunisia. There would be little or no chance of the seven French divisions withstanding this attack or gaining appreciable reinforcements from the hard-pressed British.

Of course, the refugee government would not have to make its last stand in North Africa. It could withdraw again, if need be, into the remoter stronghold of Equatorial Africa, or to one of the French colonies overseas. Gaining haven in some such outpost, the government might then give material help to the British by sending the French navy to join theirs. Yet a refugee government could do little more. Inevitably it would have to trust to the British to bring the war to a victorious conclusion.

But in the spring of 1940, such a prospect seemed utopian. Unquestionably, Britain would feel the full shock of the German attack as soon as France was conquered. At the time, to be sure, American opinion did not regard the defeat of Britain as probable, much less as certain, nor apparently did the British ever really think themselves on the brink of doom. Nevertheless, as the French watched their own proud army, once conceded in all quarters to be the mightiest in the world, disappear into powder under the blows of German tanks and planes, they had reason to take a less sanguine view of Britain's chances. And even the dauntless Churchill was warning his people of the prospect of German hordes sweeping in from the beaches and dropping from the skies, of hand-to-hand fighting in the streets and fields, of the government fleeing to one of the Dominions to await the eventual entry of America into the lists.

In such a prospect, there was little to encourage the French government. Surely it would not make a considerable contribution to the outcome of the struggle by seeking a haven in the inaccessible wilds of Equatorial Africa, sharing the wanderings of a refugee British government in Canada or Australia, while biding the far-off and uncertain time when America should see fit to cross the Atlantic and do battle in Europe.

The other of the two broad alternatives—to terminate hostilities with Germany on the basis of an armistice—seemed no happier. Such a course would require France to abandon the policy of solidarity with Britain, which her government had so long cherished as the best guarantee of her security. Furthermore, France would certainly have to pay the Nazis a heavy price for an armistice. In all probability, Hitler would sooner or later require the retrocession of Alsace and Lorraine. Doubtless he would also pillage the French colonial empire, either to form the nucleus of a new German dominion overseas or to reward his partners in the Axis. Unquestionably he would even the old score of reparations. Finally, France would have to accept the status of a satellite to Germany in the Nazi "New Order." No one could say to what extent she might have to transform her political institutions and laws to conform to Nazi principles of race, "leadership," and regimentation.

Though the choice between these alternatives subsequently became a matter of long and empassioned debate both within France and abroad, the implications of each were never systematically explored at the time the decision was made. The nation as a whole had no share in the discussion. The censorship did not permit the press or radio to acquaint the public with the seriousness of the situation, nor did it permit public discussion of any kind involving the issues of the war. So the argument for and against the armistice was conducted wholly within the government.

Even among the members of the government, the considerations in favor of each course were never fully analyzed. The discussions were rambling, reiterative, and vague. Indeed, as we piece together the account of the debate, which began on May 25 and did not close until June 16, we cannot help but regard the men who controlled the decision as muddleheaded and vacillating.

In some measure, they merit this blame. Few of them were men of strong character. This is quite understandable. The pattern of French political life under the Third Republic, as we have noted in a previous chapter, was such as to bring into prominence men who were disposed to compromise and easy adaptation, while penalizing men of stubborn conviction. The same circumstances also made the political leaders of the nation view issues largely in terms of how their decisions from moment to moment would affect their future career. In the issues before them in the crisis of the spring of 1940, it was especially difficult for politicians to take a stand, since they would incur an indelible stigma, no matter what they decided. For if they should choose to remain in France and make peace with the Nazis, they would become the agents of a humiliating surrender. But if they should choose to leave the homeland and continue the war from abroad, they would open themselves to the charge of having deserted their posts of duty.

Yet we must not ascribe their hesitation solely to personal opportunism. We must bear in mind that these men were deliberating upon an issue of the utmost importance, in circumstances that did not conduce to calm thinking or easy decision. The Nazi invasion proceeded with such demonic speed that no one could know at any moment the true proportions of the disaster. Nor could men longer trust even the simplest assumptions of common sense. After the true nightmare of the *Blitzkrieg,* no one could know what devilish miracle lay beyond the power of the Nazi horde. Perhaps we should not think best of those men who took a clear position, whether for peace or surrender, simply because at least they made up their minds. For the truth was that no course open to the French government was satisfactory—either surrender or resistance involved predictable hardships but only unsure hopes of improvement. Perhaps the men who promptly made their choice of one alternative or the other displayed merely a readier disposition to gamble rather than a shrewder quality of mind or a sounder trait of character.

The problem was perhaps made simpler because the decision lay with only a few men—perhaps forty—who could count upon making their choice prevail. From a legalistic standpoint, to be sure, Parliament remained the ultimate authority in the land. In practice, however, Parliament passed into eclipse as soon as the German attack began. The two chambers did not meet again, after May 17, until the armistice was signed. At most, the cabinet would have to gain the approval of its decision by the President of the Republic, the President of the Chamber of Deputies, and the President of the Senate, the latter two representing Parliament as a corporative institution.

On the other hand, the task was rendered more difficult because a decision of the cabinet should be unanimous. According to the traditions of the French parliamentary system, whenever a member of the cabinet was unwilling to endorse a decision of the cabinet on an issue of prime importance, he must resign. And whenever a considerable number of members chose to withdraw in protest, the whole cabinet had to step down. In this hour of crisis, however, France could scarcely afford to have her government resign, since no one knew how or when a new cabinet could be organized. In practice, therefore, the cabinet was under a strong moral pressure to reach a unanimous agreement. Hence, the members on either side in the debate shrank back from pressing for a final decision, seeking instead to leave time for their adversaries to come around to their view and underwrite the ultimate choice.

Throughout the deliberations, two antagonists dominated the debate. From the start, Reynaud argued in favor of continuing the struggle, while General Weygand insisted upon the termination of hostilities. Marshal Pétain consistently supported General Weygand, although he only infrequently spoke up in the argument. Thus, by an ironical turn of events, Reynaud found himself pitted against the two men whom he had summoned to his side at the outset of the crisis, in the hope that they would inspire a desperate resistance.

In urging his position, Reynaud quite probably did not believe there was any realistic hope of stemming the German advance within France, even by a withdrawal into the "Breton Redoubt." Nor, we may reasonably presume, did he believe that the French government could give decisive aid to the British and help determine the outcome of the war, even if his government were to move to North Africa. However, he was convinced that the long-range interest of France required her close association with Britain and America, and that she would lose the sympathy of these nations if she broke her word by making a separate peace with the Nazis. Nor would she gain a worth-while advantage in the short run, since the Nazis would probably treat her as badly under an armistice as under an outright military occupation.

On the other hand, provided that her government honored its pledge to make no separate peace, France would gain an immense advantage for the future. For Reynaud remained unshaken in his confidence that eventually Britain and America would prevail over the Axis. At the conclusion of the war, the French government, having refused to make a peace without the permission of the British, could then likewise require the British never to make peace on terms which the French would not approve. In short, France would retain a seat in the peace conference, with a veto power.

For his part, General Weygand made his estimate of the problem within a narrower perspective. He insisted that there was no hope of the French maintaining an effective resistance either in the homeland or in North Africa. Moreover, he expected that the British would be obliged to sue for peace within a matter of weeks after the Germans completed their conquest of France. He therefore saw no point in establishing a moral lien upon Britain or America.

Since Weygand deemed it inevitable that France must terminate hostilities with the Nazis, he was primarily interested in accomplishing this under conditions that would preserve what he regarded as the honor of the army. In his conception, this meant that France must make peace while her army was intact and before disorder could break out. It would be shameful beyond words, he judged, if the Germans should simply pulverize the French army and sweep it aside like rubble, or if they could boast that France had disintegrated to the point where her government could no longer maintain public order.[2]

Hence General Weygand was in a race against time. He was desperately anxious to have the cabinet sanction an armistice before the French army was utterly destroyed. Reynaud, on the contrary, had everything to gain from prolonging the debate and postponing a decision. He sensed that a large number in the cabinet leaned toward the choice of an armistice, so he certainly could not hope for a prompt vote in his favor. But he might well improve his position by dragging out the discussion until the Germans had overrun so much of France that they would see no point in granting an armistice on any terms.

On May 25, the French government for the first time faced the issue of how to respond to the probable collapse of its armies. The discussion began in a meeting of the Comité de Guerre, rather than the cabinet as a whole, when General Weygand presented his report on the military situation as it then stood. In this report, he indicated that the Germans were continuing their advance in the Low Countries and exploiting their penetration of the Allied lines at Sedan. Though he made clear that the French forces were still presenting an organized resistance, he gave warning that the time was near when this might prove no longer possible.

At the conclusion of his report, President Lebrun took the cue to raise for consideration the problem of what the government should do in such an unhappy eventuality, pointing out that France was bound not to seek a separate peace. In response, General Weygand acknowledged that the problem was interallied, rather than one for the French alone to decide, but he suggested that it was none too soon to sound out the British on what would be their attitude when the French could no longer continue the struggle. Marshal Pétain then intervened to argue

---

[2] Those hostile to General Weygand have alleged that he was largely motivated in his insistence upon an armistice by an exaggerated fear that the Communists were about to attempt a coup d'état in Paris. There is no doubt but that, on several occasions, General Weygand expressed fears of the outbreak of disorder and urged the need of preserving the army from utter destruction in order to cope with this danger. But there is no indication that this was his main concern or that the thought of an uprising was patently absurd.

that France was under obligation to Britain in proportion to the aid the British provided. Since the British were furnishing only ten divisions as compared with eighty French divisions, he implied that France was under no large obligation. No one pursued this argument, nor spoke against it. But a consensus emerged in favor of an immediate consultation with the British. Reynaud agreed to broach the problem the next day, the 26th, when he was to meet with Churchill in London.

However, Reynaud had no desire to secure British permission to seek an armistice. So he chose not to raise the question with Churchill while in London. Instead, he and Churchill devoted their attention to means of averting the entry of Italy into the war, which now seemed imminent. Nor did the discussion resume at once upon the return of Reynaud to Paris. Attention was absorbed by news from the front, where the military situation was rapidly worsening. On the 27th, King Leopold ordered the surrender of the Belgian armies, thus putting the whole German pressure upon the French and British troops that had been dispatched into the Low Countries. On the 28th, these troops began their evacuation at Dunkirk.

As the evacuation proceeded at Dunkirk, the debate between Reynaud and General Weygand resumed. On May 29, General Weygand again gave warning, this time in a written memorandum to the Premier, that the hour was approaching when the French armies would no longer be capable of effective resistance. Again he urged consultation with the British as to their attitude toward a French surrender.

Reynaud countered by proposing that General Weygand develop plans for establishing a defensive position in the "Breton Redoubt." This proposal was discussed at length on the morning of the 29th, at the regular daily conference which Reynaud held with Marshal Pétain, General Weygand, and Admiral Darlan. At this conference, General Weygand seemed not unreceptive to the suggestion. Both Marshal Pétain and Admiral Darlan likewise indicated their approval of the plan. At the close of the conference, Reynaud expressed pleasure with the reception of his suggestion.

The next morning, however, General Weygand proved far from optimistic, and on the succeeding morning he dismissed the whole idea as impractical and shut off further talk of the "Breton Redoubt" as amounting to "two words, and nothing more."

The same afternoon, May 31, a British delegation, including Churchill and Clement Attlee, arrived in Paris for a meeting of the interallied Supreme War Council. The French representatives included Reynaud, Marshal Pétain, General Weygand, and Paul Baudouin, who served as aide to the Premier. At the start of the conference, the two governments approved a British plan for the removal of the remnants of the Allied expeditionary force in Norway. Then Churchill reported on the progress of the evacuation at Dunkirk. The discussion then passed on to the problem of what might be done to meet the threat of Italian entry into the war. Plans were made for naval and air action in reprisal.

At the conclusion of the meeting, Churchill proceeded to some more general observations. In the course of these remarks, he gave the first sign of the British attitude toward the prospective French collapse. At the beginning of a circuitous statement, he expressed optimism as to the ultimate outcome of the struggle. The Nazis might overrun Western Europe, he acknowledged, and might even accomplish an invasion of Britain. But the British would defend their island in hand-to-hand fighting, he averred, should their army be overpowered, and the invasion would fail. In the long run, America would take her place in the war, and British and American resources would prove superior to Nazi might.

In this prospect, he recognized, much hardship might be in store for France. But with unconcealed emotion, he vowed that Britain and France would remain allies, no matter what might happen. "If one of the two comrades should fall in the fight," he wound up, "the other shall not lay down his arms until after he has raised up his stricken mate."

Thus Churchill seemed to indicate that the British were no longer expecting the French to continue the struggle, nor disposed to regard the collapse of their resistance as a breach of faith. Apparently Churchill meant this declaration as a generous gesture. However, his statement was to prove an embarrassment to Reynaud, who was striving to keep his colleagues in the French government from demanding an armistice.

For Churchill now seemed to give the French tacit permission to abandon the fight.

For nearly a week after the meeting of the Supreme War Council on May 31, no new debate occurred on the problem within the French government. But on June 5, the issue arose once more, this time in more urgent terms. For as soon as the evacuation at Dunkirk was completed, the whole weight of the German offensive bore upon the main French line of defense. On the morning of the 5th, Reynaud held his usual conference with Marshal Pétain, General Weygand, and Admiral Darlan. At the outset of the meeting, General Spears, who was the British officer designated for liaison on military matters with the French government, made an appearance to deliver a message from Churchill. In this communication, the British government formally indicated that it would give the French no further air support beyond the three R.A.F. squadrons presently operating with their air force. It would provide reinforcement of the one British division still in France only to the extent of another division, which would embark within about a week, plus two more at some unspecified date in the future.

Reynaud and Weygand both protested that this was tantamount to denying any effective aid until after the outcome of the Battle of France was decided. Reynaud then prepared a message urging Churchill to reconsider.

As soon as General Spears took his leave, Reynaud and the others began to discuss what course to take. Once more, Reynaud proposed a withdrawal into the "Breton Redoubt." Again General Weygand dismissed this scheme as chimeric. The sole order to be given the French army now, he declared, was to fight where it stood, without thought of further retreat. Since this resistance could lead to no other outcome than the destruction of the army, he insisted that the government must face its duty and sue for terms. Once again, Reynaud dropped the discussion without a decision.

Though unwilling to force a decision on the basic issue, Reynaud now screwed up his nerve to dismiss Daladier from the cabinet. Accordingly he summoned a meeting of the cabinet on the afternoon of the 5th and requested the members to sign the usual letter of collective resignation. The Premier accepted the resignation of Daladier, made some other changes of minor importance, then reconstituted his government. He himself took over the portfolio of Foreign Affairs, which Daladier gave up, since Marshal Pétain, to whom Reynaud offered the post, declined the appointment.

From the 5th to the 10th, as the German drive proceeded unchecked across the breadth of northern France, the argument went on at each morning conference between Reynaud and Weygand, with no decision or new proposal on either side. By the 10th, the Germans were so near Paris that the departure of the government could no longer be put off. Consequently the order was given for the ministries to withdraw to Tours. On the same day, Italy at last declared war upon France, raising the problem of invasion from another quarter. Thus a new stage in the crisis began.

In the interval while the ministries were moving to Tours, Reynaud requested Churchill to come to France for another conference. The British Prime Minister arrived at Briare, where the G.H.Q. of the French army was then established, late in the afternoon of June 11. That evening, in the château of Briare, he met with Reynaud, Marshal Pétain, General Weygand, and some others. Churchill did his best to inspirit the French, whose low ebb was a surprise to him. He reminded Pétain of the bold determination France had shown in the crisis of 1918, summoned up the memory of Clemenceau, and urged the French to defend every inch of Paris.

In response, Marshal Pétain pointed out that in 1918 the French had had a mobile reserve of sixty divisions, whereas now they had none, and that in 1918 sixty British divisions were engaged in the line, whereas now there were none. Thereupon General Weygand appealed to Churchill to provide every available R.A.F. squadron for service in support of the French. Churchill unequivocally refused.

The interchange revealed an unhappy irony, since Churchill, who had just asked the French to wage a house-to-house battle in Paris that would reduce their capital to rubble, now tacitly admitted that he regarded the Battle of France as hopeless. But Pétain and Weygand, who quite shared this view, had nonetheless asked the British to make a vain sacrifice of their whole air force.

As the discussion went on with no sign of a meeting of minds, Gen-

eral Weygand took it upon himself to indicate that the French might
have to ask for an armistice. Reynaud quickly reprimanded him, pointing out that that was a political issue, and therefore outside his province.
Nevertheless, Churchill made answer, in much the same vein as at the
Supreme War Council on May 31, by saying, "If it is thought best for
France in her agony that her army should capitulate, let there be no
hesitation on our account, because whatever you may do, we shall fight
on, forever and ever and ever." Thus once more he seemed to give the
French a release from their pledge, though without using the word
"armistice." On the morning of the 12th, Churchill returned to London,
where he reported to the War Cabinet that the French resistance was
nearing its close.

As the French government reassembled in Tours, the debate resumed. Hitherto the argument had gone on within the Comité de
Guerre or, latterly, in the informal meetings each morning between
Reynaud, Weygand, and Pétain. Henceforth the issue was considered
in the cabinet as a whole.

The new stage in the discussion opened at a meeting of the cabinet
in the evening of June 12, in the château of Cange, near Tours, in the
midst of the region of the Loire, so rich in the monuments of an earlier
age of French greatness, which afforded a poignant contrast to the
present time of sorrow and humiliation.

From the start of this meeting, the issue was defined in sharp alternatives. General Weygand began by summarizing the military situation,
which left no room for hope. In his view, the problem was simple—the
government had ordered the army to wage war; the army had now to
report that the war was lost; the government must therefore terminate
the hostilities. Otherwise the army would have to fight on, in obedience to its orders, until it was utterly destroyed.

Pausing, then speaking more rapidly so as to contain his emotions, he
then concluded: "Gentlemen, I have read the terms of the armistice
which was imposed upon the Germans by Marshal Foch and the victorious Allies on November 11, 1918. The moment which I now foresee
is the most painful of my life. The moment of another armistice has
arrived. This time, it is we who have to ask terms."

Reynaud then took the floor. He thanked General Weygand for his statement, acknowledging that he spoke like a soldier. But he rejected his conclusion, on the ground that the problem was not simply military. "Don't imagine that you're dealing with the Germany of William I," he continued. "William I was a gentleman. Hitler—is Genghis Khan." The crux, he argued, was to preserve the French alignment with Britain and America, and this meant that France must remain at war. The government must strive to organize resistance in the "Breton Redoubt"; that failing, it must withdraw to Algiers, to Dakar, to the West Indies, but never make peace.

The discussion then became general, with various members of the cabinet speaking on either side, while the larger number spoke on both sides or else remained silent. Shortly the meeting degenerated into a hubbub. But when Reynaud announced that he was going to see Churchill again the next day, the cabinet decided to take no action until the Premier had had a chance to report on his new conference.

The next day, June 13, Churchill arrived in Tours about noon. Such was the chaos that no one met him at the airport, so that he and his party had to drive through the town in search of Reynaud. After some hours, a meeting was arranged in the local prefecture. The British representation comprised Churchill, Lord Halifax, Lord Beaverbrook, and General Spears; Reynaud was attended only by Paul Baudouin.

Reynaud opened by summarizing the discussion in the French cabinet the previous day and by reporting that General Weygand was insisting upon an armistice. In a move of desperation, Reynaud announced that he had sent an urgent appeal for help to President Roosevelt, and he was going to send another, in stronger terms. Yet, he continued, he knew he could not have large confidence that the response to these appeals would materially alter the situation. He was therefore obliged to ask what attitude the British would take if the French were to seek a separate peace.

Churchill replied that the French should take no action before receiving the answer of President Roosevelt. But whatever course the French might choose, the British would make no vain recriminations, and would restore her to her former grandeur at the conclusion of the war. Then he withdrew to consult with his colleagues. Returning in about half an hour, he announced that they endorsed his statement.

After some discussion of the terms in which Reynaud should make his new appeal to Washington, Churchill took his leave and returned to London.

No sooner had Churchill left than Reynaud and Baudouin hastened to the château of Cange, where the cabinet was impatiently waiting to hear the report of the Premier. A sharp protest went up when Reynaud indicated that he had not asked Churchill to come in person to the meeting of the cabinet, and an even sharper protest when he declared that he had told Churchill the French cabinet was opposed to an armistice. This was a misrepresentation, inasmuch as the cabinet had taken no decision on the question, nor had Reynaud so reported to Churchill. However, he well knew that he would give aid to his adversaries if he were to reveal Churchill's ambiguous attitude toward a separate peace.

Once more the argument went round and round, with little new coming forth save a pronouncement by Marshal Pétain. For his part, he declared, he not only favored an armistice but was determined never to leave France, no matter what course the others might choose. At length, the discussion terminated with a decision to take no action until an answer should be received from President Roosevelt.

So the issue remained in abeyance while Reynaud dispatched his last, despairing message to Washington, warning that France would go under unless the United States promptly entered the war. On the morning of the 15th, Roosevelt's answer arrived, expressing deep sympathy for France but unequivocally refusing the declaration of war which Reynaud besought. Meantime the French government moved again, since Tours was no longer secure, to take refuge in Bordeaux.

At Bordeaux, the drama was soon to reach its climax. A little before 4 o'clock on the afternoon of the 15th, as the members of the cabinet were assembling in the prefecture for their first meeting in the improvised new capital, Reynaud summoned General Weygand into a conference and made a new proposal. Reminding him of the circumstances of the Dutch capitulation some weeks before, when Queen Wilhelmina and her government had gone to London after authorizing the commanding general to order a general cease-fire, Reynaud suggested that General Weygand solve the problem by ordering the surrender of the army. The government would then seek haven abroad without opening political negotiations with the Germans. Thus, he argued, the vain sacrifice of lives would be avoided, and so would the breach of honor involved in an armistice.

To this, General Weygand responded with an unequivocal refusal. The scheme, he argued, was a trick of the civilian authorities, who would save themselves the price of their own follies by putting the whole humiliation upon the military. Once more, as so often before, Reynaud chose not to insist upon his stand.

At 4 o'clock, the meeting of the cabinet began. General Weygand presented a report on the military situation, then withdrew. Thereupon the debate resumed between those who advocated and those who opposed the armistice. By now the cabinet was separating into two hostile camps. But no one quite knew which was the larger, nor did either camp as yet wish to call for a vote. So again the argument went on to no clear conclusion, until at length Chautemps, who had emerged as one of the partisans of the armistice, proposed a kind of compromise. Without awaiting a decision of the cabinet as to whether or not to conclude an armistice, the Premier should seek the permission of London to enter into negotiations with the Germans, to learn what terms they would offer. If the Germans should impose dishonorable conditions, he argued, the cabinet would have no need to consider the matter any further. But if the terms should prove less than dishonorable, the cabinet could pursue the debate as to whether to accept them or continue the struggle abroad.

The suggestion seemed cleverly designed to win over those who were disposed toward an armistice but reluctant to take a stand. A consensus soon developed in favor of the proposal. Reynaud realized that this move would lead the government so far in the direction of an armistice that it would probably settle the matter by making peace. Accordingly, in order to thwart the scheme, he refused to accept the responsibility for broaching the question with the British. Instead, he proposed to resign as Premier. However, President Lebrun, who was anxious to avoid occasion for reorganizing the government at such a critical moment, simply refused to accept his resignation. Pointing out that the cabinet was not presently deciding upon a policy but merely seeking information, he instructed Reynaud to make the inquiry which the cabinet wished. Thereupon Reynaud backed down. The meeting of the cabinet adjourned about 7 o'clock, with the understanding that the Premier would sound out the British.

On his way out of the salon where the cabinet had been meeting, Reynaud encountered General Weygand, who had been waiting in an anteroom. There ensued a heated and confused interchange between the two, in the course of which Reynaud, returning to the notion he had advanced earlier that afternoon, demanded that General Weygand give the order for a military surrender, on the instruction of the government but without an armistice. Promptly Weygand answered:

"There is no power on earth that can make me sign the capitulation of an army that has fought as valiantly as the French army."

"You will, if I give the order," Reynaud retorted.

"Never! You will not find a French officer who will accept that disgrace!"

"You are here to take orders!"

"I am here to defend the honor of the army," answered Weygand. "You and the President of the Republic are trying to shift your responsibility. The government took the responsibility for the war, and it's up to the government to take responsibility for the armistice."

Thereupon Reynaud bowed to the bold defiance which General Weygand presented. Shortly the Premier got in touch with Sir Ronald Campbell, the British ambassador. Pursuant to the decision of the cabinet, Reynaud asked him to advise London that the French government wished to enter into negotiations with the Germans.

The morrow, Sunday June 16, proved to be the day of decision, crowded with a tumult of events and disordered with a welter of moves at cross-purposes. At 10 in the morning Reynaud held a conference with Édouard Herriot, the President of the Chamber of Deputies, and Jules Jeanneney, the President of the Senate, and asked them to approve the transfer of the government to North Africa. Both readily agreed and indicated their desire to support the Premier in urging this policy.

At 11, the cabinet met again. Reynaud opened by apprising the cabinet of Roosevelt's negative answer to his appeal for an American declaration of war. Then he reported that he had approached the British ambassador, in accord with the wishes of the cabinet, to inquire whether the British government would permit the French to sue for terms. The ambassador had replied, according to Reynaud, that despite whatever Churchill had said in Tours on the 13th, the British government regarded the French as honor-bound not to seek a separate peace. Thereupon, Reynaud continued, he had asked to confer with Churchill again. Arrangements had been made for them to meet at Nantes the same afternoon, at about 1:30.

Marshal Pétain then rose and read a letter of resignation, explaining that he would not put up with such maneuvers, the sole purpose of which was to postpone a decision. Once more, President Lebrun intervened to prevent the breakup of the cabinet, and at length he persuaded Pétain to withhold his resignation. Finally, the cabinet agreed to recess until after the Premier had had a chance to meet with Churchill.

As soon as the cabinet meeting concluded, Sir Ronald Campbell delivered to Reynaud a telegram from the Foreign Office, stating that the British government would not veto the French negotiations with the Germans, provided the French government immediately ordered its fleet into British ports. About an hour later, the British ambassador delivered another telegram, reaffirming the previous message and adding some further stipulations of minor importance.

Though these two telegrams cleared the way for Reynaud to seek an armistice, he made no move to exploit this opportunity. The reason was that he did not wish an armistice, whether or not the British were willing to give their sanction. Moreover, Reynaud had knowledge that the British government was soon to announce a new position, proposing a political union between France and Britain.

This startling proposal for a merger of the two nations, envisaging a single government and a single citizenship, was one of the more obscure developments of the day. Apparently the idea originated with members of the French economic mission in London, who induced General de Gaulle to become its sponsor. General de Gaulle had come into prominence some weeks before as the favored military adviser of Reynaud, and in the reorganization of the cabinet on June 5, the Premier had named him Under-Secretary of State for War. An unshakable partisan of continued resistance, De Gaulle had labored with utmost zeal to strengthen the determination of the Premier in this purpose. Evidently he had conceived the scheme for waging a siege war in the "Breton Redoubt" and had persuaded Reynaud to press this plan upon the government. Once the tide of battle had rendered this proposal quite out of the question, De Gaulle had gone to London to arrange with the British for the removal of the French government to North Africa. In London, where he had arrived on June 13, De Gaulle had remained in close touch with Reynaud by telephone. As the issue of the armistice neared decision, he had become desperate in his desire to help Reynaud thwart the advocates of a separate peace.

In his search for some means of buttressing the position of the hard-pressed Premier, De Gaulle had seized upon the suggestion of a merger between the two allied governments. Such a proposal would afford Reynaud a dramatic occasion for prolonging the discussion in the French cabinet, and if approved, the scheme would render an armistice impossible. De Gaulle had won over Lord Halifax and Sir Robert Vansittart, among others. These, in turn, had broached the idea to Churchill, at lunch at the Carlton Club on the 15th. Churchill professes that he remained dubious as to the wisdom of the move, but he agreed to present the idea to the War Cabinet. This he did the same afternoon, and the War Cabinet made a favorable response.

The next morning, the fateful Sunday of June 16, De Gaulle telephoned the news to Reynaud. But meantime Reynaud had presented the request of the French cabinet for British permission to seek an armistice. As soon as the French appeal reached London, the War Cabinet gave its alternative answer in the two telegrams sent to Sir Ronald Campbell, which he delivered to Reynaud shortly after noon. At 3 o'clock, the War Cabinet met again, and Churchill once more raised the proposal for an Anglo-French political union. Thereupon the War Cabinet decided to approve this proposal, as a substitute for its earlier statement releasing the French government from its pledge not to make peace. Forthwith word was sent to Sir Ronald Campbell, who informed Reynaud of the new proposal.

At 4 o'clock, an hour before the cabinet was to meet again, Paul Baudouin and Yves Bouthillier, the Minister of Finance, both of whom were advocates of an armistice, called upon Reynaud. He advised them of the scheme for an Anglo-French union. Baudouin responded that this was much too sweeping a proposal to be considered at the moment, and the government must not longer defer the termination of hostilities. Bouthillier spoke in much the same sense, then withdrew, leaving Baudouin alone with the Premier. A silence ensued, Baudouin relates, then he put the question to Reynaud: "What will you do after the meeting of the cabinet, when a clear majority will pronounce in favor of an appeal for an armistice?"

Tired and worn, the Premier at length replied, "We are inevitably heading for a Pétain government. I have already discussed the matter with the President of the Republic. What's worse, the marshal will name Laval to Foreign Affairs, and that will mean a complete break with England."

Baudouin acknowledged that Laval was sending emissaries to Pétain to urge him in that direction, but the marshal, according to Baudouin, was determined to give the position to Baudouin instead of Laval. Reynaud expressed his satisfaction with this news.

At 5 o'clock, the cabinet assembled again at the prefecture. Reynaud reported that the meeting with Churchill, which had been anticipated at the close of the morning session of the cabinet, had not taken place. Making no mention of the two telegrams by which the British government had sanctioned an armistice before changing its stand, he proceeded to read the new British proposal for a union with France. The idea evoked no response. Returning to his earlier tactic, Reynaud next proposed that the government order General Weygand to bring about a military surrender without conditions. But Pétain spoke in bitter opposition to this, and the consensus supported him.

The debate rambled on, with much impassioned rhetoric on both sides but no new ideas, until at last Mandel, one of the stubborn advocates of resistance, intervened with a stinging taunt, declaring that there were two camps within the cabinet—the brave men and the cowards—and each must now choose his side. Tempers blazed, and the mood of compromise and hesitation vanished. As the cabinet thus at length divided, it became apparent, though no vote was taken, that the larger number was in favor of an armistice. Thereupon Reynaud acknowledged that, since only a minority shared his position and he was unwilling to accept the decision of the majority, he must resign. Once more President Lebrun sought to dissuade him, but he stood firm, and at 7 o'clock the cabinet recessed to permit the President of the Republic to arrange for the appointment of a new Premier and a new cabinet.

Reynaud was promptly closeted with President Lebrun, to whom he recommended Marshal Pétain as his successor. At 10 o'clock Pétain was received by President Lebrun, still in the company of Reynaud. Pétain handed over a typewritten list of the ministers whom he proposed to name, and thus the aged soldier assumed charge of the government.

Not without some trouble did Pétain succeed in organizing his new cabinet. In his original choice of ministers, he had named Laval as Vice-Premier and Minister of Justice, and Adrien Marquet, who was a henchman of Laval, as Minister of the Interior, while he entrusted Foreign Affairs to Paul Baudouin, who had taken charge of this department, though not as minister, in the previous cabinet. About 10:30, however, while Pétain was completing his arrangements, Laval broke in upon him to announce that he would not serve as Vice-Premier and Minister of Justice unless he were also appointed Minister of Foreign Affairs. Pétain gave in and agreed to this.

But no sooner had Laval left than General Weygand, accompanied by Charles-Roux, one of the senior officers of the Ministry of Foreign Affairs, rushed in to dissuade Pétain. They argued that Laval was utterly unworthy of the responsibility for foreign policy, because he was notoriously hostile to Britain and friendly to the Axis. Thereupon Pétain again changed his mind, once more deciding to name Baudouin to Foreign Affairs. Learning of this, Laval then refused to take any office in the government. Adrien Marquet likewise turned down the Ministry of the Interior. This time Pétain stood fast, and neither Laval nor Marquet appeared in the new government.

As the cabinet eventually took shape, its personnel comprised mainly those members of the Reynaud cabinet who had supported the decision in favor of an armistice, while the minority that had opposed it was replaced. Besides Pétain as Premier, the more notable members were: Camille Chautemps, Vice-Premier; General Weygand, who now became Minister of National Defense; Admiral Darlan, who entered the government as Minister of Marine; and Paul Baudouin, who ultimately gained the Ministry of Foreign Affairs. A minor delay developed while the Socialist members consulted with Léon Blum to secure his permission, as head of their party, for their participation in the cabinet. But he raised no objection, and at 11:30, President Lebrun signed the documents appointing the new ministers.

The new cabinet met promptly and formally decided to seek an armistice, the deliberation taking no more than ten minutes. Shortly after midnight, Baudouin received Lequerica, the Spanish ambassador, for whom he had sent, and asked him to use the good offices of his government to transmit the French appeal for terms to the Germans. Lequerica immediately telephoned to the Spanish attachés at Saint-Jean-de-Luz, who relayed the message to Madrid. At 1 o'clock in the morning, Baudouin advised Sir Ronald Campbell of the French decision, and afterward he gave the same information to Francis Biddle, who was acting as United States ambassador.

The French had to wait two days before receiving a reply from the Germans, and not until the 21st did the cabinet learn the conditions which the Germans chose to impose. The anxious interval between the 17th and the 21st was crowded with events, the principal of which involved efforts by the British and American governments to ensure against the surrender of the French navy to the Germans.

London and Washington attached the gravest importance to the fate of the French navy for the reason that, if it should come into the possession of the Axis, it would give the Axis a larger seapower than either the British naval forces available for service in the Atlantic, or the whole of the United States navy. The principal French naval units were: two battleships and four cruisers in the British ports of Plymouth and Portsmouth; one battleship and four cruisers at Alexandria; two new heavy cruisers and two light cruisers at Mers El-Kébir, the naval base at Oran; the new battleship "Jean Bart," still unfinished, at Casablanca; the battleship "Richelieu," likewise uncompleted, at Dakar; seven cruisers at Algiers; three cruisers at Toulon; and numerous destroyers and submarines dispersed among these and other stations.

Few of these units were liable to pass under Axis control. The British could prevent the escape of the vessels stationed at ports in Britain or at Alexandria, and the Germans could not seize those at Dakar, Mers El-Kébir, or Casablanca without the sanction of the French government. Only the units at Toulon were in immediate danger of capture by the Axis.

At no time did the French government contemplate giving over any portion of its navy to the Axis. Reynaud naturally had no such thought, and while he was still Premier, he had induced both Pétain and Weygand, who were the principal advocates of an armistice, to declare themselves against the surrender of the fleet. On June 18, the Pétain cabinet formally decided to reject any Axis demand involving the surrender of the fleet, even if such a refusal were to prevent the conclusion of an armistice.

Nevertheless, the British and American governments did their best to induce the French to give their naval forces to the British. On June 16, President Roosevelt urged the French ambassador in Washington to induce his government to take this action. On the 18th, Biddle, the American ambassador in Bordeaux, made a similar representation to Baudouin, the new Foreign Minister. On the 19th, a British delegation, comprising A. V. Alexander, First Lord of the Admiralty, Sir Dudley Pound, First Sea Lord, and Lord Lloyd, Secretary for Colonies, arrived in Bordeaux for the purpose of pressing this action upon the French. The trio spent the day in consultation with various leaders in the government, especially with Admiral Darlan, who had it within his power to order all French warships to sail for British ports.

Neither the British mission nor the American ambassador could persuade the government to consider any such action, which probably would have resulted in the refusal of the Germans to offer an armistice of any kind. Nor would Darlan take so bold a step on his own initiative. However, Darlan added his personal word to the assurance of his government that no portion of the fleet would pass into the hands of the Germans or the Italians.

Meantime developed the affair of the "Massilia," involving the proposed removal of the government to North Africa, which remains one of the more obscure episodes in this chaotic period. The series of events that culminated in this enterprise originated as soon as the government reached Bordeaux on June 15, after leaving its previous seat at Tours. Various members of the government were fearful that the Germans would reach Bordeaux before the cabinet could arrive at a decision on what course to adopt. Pressure therefore arose to transfer the seat of government to North Africa, in order to make sure that the cabinet could deliberate with some degree of calm. Upon his assumption of the premiership, Pétain indicated his willingness to have Chautemps, who remained Vice-Premier in the new cabinet, proceed to North Africa, together with President Lebrun, the presidents of the two chambers of Parliament, and any other members of Parliament who wished to go along, although Pétain himself remained determined never to leave France under any conditions.

Accordingly the steamship "Massilia" was made ready at Port-Vendres, the harbor nearest Perpignan, to take aboard those who wished to leave. However, Laval took it upon himself to block the move, fearing that it would lead to the establishment of a rump government in North Africa which would continue the war in the colonies. Though not a member of the government, Laval therefore sought out President Lebrun and bullied him into promising not to leave the country. Thereupon Pétain, uncertain as to his course, ordered a postponement of the departure.

Eventually, the "Massilia" sailed, on the afternoon of the 21st, just as the government received the German terms. Aboard were about twenty-five members of Parliament, including Daladier and Mandel. While crossing the Mediterranean, the ship's radio received the news that the Germans had communicated the conditions of the armistice. Thereupon several of the members of Parliament aboard strove to induce the captain of the ship to turn back to France, so that they might take part in the decision as to whether or not to accept the terms. However, the captain refused, so the ship proceeded to Casablanca, arriving on the 24th. Promptly upon landing, Mandel, with the approval of Daladier, undertook to proclaim himself the head of a new government, which would continue the war. But the venture proved a fiasco.

Mandel was immediately arrested, and the others of the party confined aboard the "Massilia." Not until more than six weeks later were they taken back to France.

The question remains whether the departure of the "Massilia" represented an ill-consummated plan to remove members of the government and of Parliament to a safer haven or a deliberate plot to get rid of those who were likely to oppose an acceptance of the German conditions. As yet, the answer cannot be definitely established. It seems probable, however, that the operation was not meant as a trap. It is clear that Pétain gave his approval to the plan as a safeguard in the event that the German terms should prove unacceptable. He contemplated Chautemps's taking charge of the government in North Africa if, having refused the conditions of the armistice, Pétain himself should be taken prisoner by the Germans. For while Pétain was desirous of an armistice and determined under no circumstances to leave France, he was not committed to making peace on whatever terms the Germans might offer. On the contrary, he was pledged to refuse the armistice if the Germans should require, for instance, the surrender of the fleet.

But it also seems probable that others—perhaps Laval, perhaps Darlan, perhaps Baudouin—saw in the venture an admirable opportunity to get rid of those who were most likely to raise objections to the German terms. Likewise, it was a happy opportunity to place under surveillance those who might be disposed to set up a rump government in North Africa: this, at any event, was the practical outcome of the affair.

Meantime the negotiations with the Germans proceeded at snail's pace. Not until 6:30 in the morning of June 19 did Lequerica give word that the Germans were willing to negotiate. Pétain promptly summoned the cabinet, which designated General Huntziger as head of the armistice mission, and thereupon Baudouin gave the roster to the Spanish ambassador. Two more days passed before the Germans made answer with a radio message, picked up about 5 o'clock in the morning, advising the French to stand by for further instructions. At 11:15, another message ordered the French plenipotentiaries to set off by automobile on the road leading to Tours. At the designated hour, 5 o'clock that afternoon, the mission departed.

As the French plenipotentiaries were proceeding along the highway from Bordeaux, a German escort met them and guided them on to Paris, where they spent the night. On the morrow, June 21, they were conducted to their ultimate destination. This proved to be Rethondes, the site of the armistice negotiations of November, 1918, whither the Germans had brought the same railroad car in which Foch had dictated the conditions of the armistice on the previous occasion. General Keitel was the sole member of the German delegation, but present as observers were Hitler, Marshal Goering, Grand Admiral Raeder, General Brauchitsch, Ribbentrop, and Hess.

General Keitel began by reading a prepared statement which recalled the injustices the French had done the Germans in 1918. At the conclusion of this reading, Hitler rose, handed the French the text of the terms the Germans proposed, gave a Nazi salute, and withdrew from the car, followed by all the others save General Keitel and Dr. Schmidt, the interpreter of the Foreign Office. General Keitel then sat down again while the German text was translated into French, whereupon the session was terminated. The French delegates withdrew into a tent, provided for them nearby, to study the terms, then gained permission to communicate with their government at Bordeaux by telephone. The connection was made about 8:20 in the morning.

At the other end of the wire, in Bordeaux, were assembled Marshal Pétain, General Weygand, Admiral Darlan, Baudouin, Bouthillier (the Minister of Finance), and Alibert (the Minister of Justice).

"You guess where I am—in the railroad car," General Huntziger began. "My poor friend," responded General Weygand. The conditions as a whole, General Huntziger then reported, were harsh but not dishonorable. He proceeded to dictate the text over the telephone, while a stenographer typed up triplicate copies.

The terms contained twenty-four articles. The principal of these provided for the demarcation of France into two zones. One zone was to remain under German military occupation, the cost of which was to be borne by the French; the other was to remain wholly under French administration. The zone of occupation was to consist of northern and western France, including the whole Atlantic coast. The unoccupied zone was therefore confined to the southeastern quarter of France, but it included the Mediterranean shore. The army was to be demobilized, and the navy interned in French ports, under Axis supervision. The French were required to accept or reject the conditions the next day, June 22. But if they accepted, the armistice was not to become operative until they also had signed an armistice with the Italians.

Just after midnight, the cabinet was summoned into session in the residence of the Prefect at Bordeaux. The reaction of a number of the members, when the terms were made known to them, was adverse. Chautemps and Admiral Darlan, among others, were inclined to reject the terms, as was President Lebrun. However, the objections were not pressed while the articles of the armistice were examined in more detail, one by one.

Then the decision was taken to propose a number of modifications. Four of these were of some moment—a revision of the line of demarcation, so as to reduce the area of the occupied zone and leave Paris in the unoccupied zone; a stipulation that the navy was to be interned in North African ports, so as to give more assurance that the Germans would not seize it; provision that the matériel of the air force be stockpiled rather than handed over to the Germans; and a proposal that the question of the fate of political refugees be worked out on "an honorable basis," in subsequent negotiations.

The next morning, the 22d, the cabinet reconvened at 8 o'clock. At 10 o'clock, General Weygand established telephonic communications with General Huntziger, who had been brought back from Paris to Rethondes, and advised him of the amendments which the cabinet desired. General Huntziger transmitted these proposals to General Keitel, who summarily refused all save the one relating to the matériel of the air force, to which he assented. General Huntziger reported this response to Bordeaux, adding his own advice to accept the terms. The cabinet approved, with no vote in opposition. At 6:50 that evening, General Huntziger placed his signature on the document.

Thereupon, as the two delegations stepped down from the railroad car, in view of the German newsreel cameras, General Keitel unbent for the first time. Taking General Huntziger aside and saying to him, "General, as a soldier, I know what you must have gone through," he offered him his sympathy and shook his hand. With tears in his eyes,

General Huntziger answered simply, "Thank you, General. Excuse me, but I can say no more." Dr. Schmidt, the German interpreter, adding some ill-chosen remarks, concluded with the observation, "This marks a beginning."

The armistice with the Italians soon followed. Baudouin began negotiations with Rome at the same time as with Berlin. Upon the conclusion of the negotiations at Rethondes, the French government instructed General Huntziger and his delegation to proceed to Rome, where they arrived on the 23d. Count Ciano and Marshal Badoglio received the French mission and delivered the Italian proposals. These followed, in the main, the terms of the German armistice, save that no Italian zone of occupation was provided for. On the 24th, the French cabinet authorized the signature. The two armistices became effective at 12:35, just after midnight of June 24–25.

Thus, at length, after a month of anguished hesitation and debate, did the French government terminate its active participation in the war. The decision was at once a deep humiliation, and the source of a division of opinion that was eventually to split the nation into two hostile camps. That division of opinion had begun to develop as soon as the discussion of the problem of the armistice commenced; it reached a climax in the meeting of the cabinet on the night of June 16, when Mandel called upon his colleagues to take their place with either the brave or the cowards; and it persisted down to the moment when the cabinet authorized the acceptance of the terms.

In these decisive weeks, the issue did not involve public debate. On the 17th Marshal Pétain announced over the radio that the government was asking for terms, and on the 25th the public learned that the struggle was over. Other than this bare outline of events, the censorship released no news, nor did it permit comment of any kind upon the problem in the press.

Nevertheless, the debate persisted and broadened with the passage of time. Even while the negotiations were in progress at Rethondes and then Rome, some of the irreconcilables were beginning to look toward London, where already General de Gaulle was striving to rally those who would never make peace with the Axis. Gradually, as the chaos of

May and June slowly gave way to a grim new order, and the nation began to recover from its traumatic shock, men and women in all walks commenced to ask themselves: Did the government choose the right course? The issue remained unresolved throughout the war, even after the choice was quite irrevocable. Never was the debate keener than on the eve of liberation.

Though we cannot hope to settle the argument, neither can we hope to avoid considering the issues involved in it. For upon our estimation of the armistice depends our view as to whether Vichy represented the government of men who betrayed their nation or of men who did only what was necessary.

We have already seen the outline of the problem as it took shape in the deliberations within the government. We have noted that no one saw a real possibility of maintaining an effective resistance within France after May 25. We have also noted that, once the French found it impossible to keep up the struggle in their homeland, they were without means of rendering large help to the British, save insofar as concerned the disposition of their navy. At no time did the government contemplate giving this over to the Axis.

To be sure, the French government might have done the British a more positive service by handing over to them those vessels which were not already under their surveillance. However, neither Reynaud nor anyone else in the cabinet spoke up in favor of such an order. Nor, indeed, was this a *sine qua non* of friendship for the British, since the latter had much less need for the use of the French navy than for a guarantee that it would not become available to the Axis.

In sum, we may say that the question of the armistice did not involve the further question of whether the French would aid the British or not. Whatever their wish, the French were in no position to render decisive aid to their allies. Rather, the question involved the kind of diplomatic relations that France would maintain with Britain and the kind of domestic administration she would have while under the inevitable German domination.

The course of refusing an armistice would have had the advantage, as we have remarked, of maintaining the French alliance with Britain and claim upon American good will. Moreover, it would have left no question in the minds of the French but that the Nazis were to be held responsible for the hardships and humiliation which France was bound to suffer under German rule. On the other hand, this course would have been sure to worsen those hardships. For then the entire French army was likely to become prisoners of war, and the nation would pass under the administration of either the German army or a puppet government recruited among Frenchmen wholly subservient to German interests. In any event, the nation would have had no effective representation of its interests vis-à-vis the occupying power.

Unquestionably, the probable disadvantages outweighed the advantages, unless the British and Americans were to win a decisive victory sometime in a reasonably near future. Hence the rejection of the armistice would have meant subordinating short-run interest to putative advantages in the longer range. Thus it would have amounted to a wager upon an Anglo-American victory.

In the summer of 1940, that seemed a poor gamble. After seeing their own "impregnable" defenses crumble under the pummeling blows of the German air force and the grinding treads of German tanks, the French could well imagine that the Nazis had some new diabolic miracle to disclose which would solve their problem of crossing the Channel. And not even Churchill could hope to hold back the German hordes if they made a landing. Nor did the French have reason to presume that the United States, having refused their appeals for aid in 1940, would soon choose to enter the lists. Taking all such items into account, the course of resistance seemed a dubious venture. The arguments for it, though based in part upon considerations of honor, seemed quixotic.

Yet the arguments in favor of the armistice were not much more attractive. Certainly this course also involved a gamble, since a separate peace was bound to put a severe strain upon French relations with London and Washington and to prove embarrassing in the event that the Anglo-American bloc emerged triumphant at the close of the war. Moreover, it meant that the legal French government would have to become the instrument of German rule, since it would have to enforce decisions taken by the Germans in their own interest. Thus the French government had to be ready to take the blame for hardships that would really be the work of the Nazis.

On the other hand, an armistice could be expected to give the French government some means of minimizing these hardships. It would unquestionably mean a real boon to the millions of men still in service if they were discharged from the army under the provisions of an armistice, rather than be taken captive and shipped off to German prison camps. Moreover, it seemed that an armistice would leave the French government in a position where it might be able to change sides later on and reenter the war whenever the British and Americans proved capable of undertaking an offensive in Western Europe.

Considerations such as these, we must remember, came readily to the minds of men accustomed to the ways of parliamentary politics, who made their careers out of negotiation, compromise, and sudden shifts of alignment, and who habitually dealt with men whom they neither liked, respected, nor trusted.

In balancing these calculations, we must acknowledge that we cannot charge the men who concluded the armistice with treason, dishonor, or even a conscious preference for "collaboration" with the Axis. Furthermore, we must note that the French themselves, on the whole, shared this view. Naturally, those who advocated the armistice saw their choice as in no wise reprehensible. But even their adversaries, in the main, accepted the decision as a reasonable difference of opinion. Thus Reynaud himself proposed Pétain as his successor. Nor did he or anyone else in the government raise a protest at the constitution of the new cabinet for the express purpose of seeking peace. Even in 1945, when the Provisional Government, having taken over the administration of France in the wake of the Anglo-American liberation, brought the men of Vichy to trial, it chose not to rest its case against them on the ground that they had signed the armistice. Rather, the burden laid on them was that their actions subsequent to the armistice gave aid and comfort to the Axis.

We may also take as a matter of fact—so far as the evidence will permit us to establish facts—that the armistice was not the outcome of a plot to deliver France over to the Axis. Despite a rash of wild allega-

tions and rumors current at the time, there is no evidence that the
French government in May and June of 1940 was in the hands of men
who wished to see France pass under German rule, whether for personal or partisan interest.

To be sure, there were men in French political life who were pro-
Nazi. Some of these had an ideological preference for the principles
of the Nazi regime. Others hated Blum worse than Hitler, and still
others hoped to better their own fortunes by serving what seemed to
be the rising power in Europe. Some of these men—Déat and Doriot are
the conspicuous examples—were later to rise to positions of prominence.
But men such as these were not members of the government at the time
of the decision for the armistice, nor were they influential in shaping
its decision.

There were men within the cabinet who were pro-Nazi in the sense
that they had no deep opposition to Nazism on ideological grounds.
But that does not mean that they wished to see their nation under
foreign rule. Moreover, a number of these were Catholic conservatives.
Among them were Baudouin and Bouthillier. Probably Marshal Pétain
and General Weygand were also of this sort. Catholic conservatives
such as these were disposed to advocate an authoritarian or corporative
regime, but only within the bounds of a Catholic political orientation.
They were therefore sympathetic to the Franco regime in Spain, and
generally friendly toward Italian Fascism. But they were by no means
partisans of the neopagan and anticlerical Nazi dictatorship. All considered, it seems quite clear that the French government which signed
the armistice had no special fondness for Hitler and his associates.

We may also take as established that the men in the government
who urged the armistice did not choose this course in order thereby
to give France over to the rule of Marshal Pétain and thus to accomplish
a conservative counterrevolution in answer to the Popular Front. Without doubt, there were those in France who nursed an insane hatred of
Léon Blum and took immense satisfaction in the promise of Marshal
Pétain to undo the work of the Popular Front. But again, these were
not the men who decided the issue of the armistice.

Probably General Weygand was the most consistent and influential
advocate of the armistice, and he was unquestionably a conservative

in matters of social politics. However, he was a partisan of the armistice primarily because he conceived it as necessary to preserve what he regarded as the honor of the army. We need not inquire into the merits of his special conception of honor, but we have no occasion to question its sincerity.

Marshal Pétain certainly lent his support to the demand for an armistice, and unquestionably he developed an ambition for political prominence in this hour of crisis. But the evidence does not suggest that he was involved in intrigue to exploit the military defeat as a means of accomplishing his political advancement. Indeed, Pétain himself showed only a mild interest in whether or not the government should make peace—on more than one occasion, he expressed his readiness to approve the alternative course. His one obsession was to take upon himself the role of a martyr, by remaining in France and sharing the misfortunes of his compatriots. As best we can judge, he would have been nearly as well satisfied to achieve his martyrdom by becoming a prisoner of war, provided that could be done with *éclat,* as by becoming the captive head of the government.

To be sure, a plot to make Pétain dictator, utilizing the armistice as a pretext, would not have required the knowing help of either Weygand, though he was the principal partisan of the armistice, or Pétain. But the evidence does not suggest who, in that event, was the mastermind at work behind the scenes. Laval would have liked the role, it is obvious, and he did his best to win it. But he had no access to the Reynaud cabinet, where the issue of the armistice was being decided. So little was he in command of the situation that, as it turned out, he did not enter the new cabinet which Pétain organized upon his accession. Chautemps was the man within the Reynaud cabinet who began to talk in terms of Pétain as the next premier, but he reaped rather less advantage from the accession of Pétain than would have been due a principal conspirator. Though he retained his post as Vice-Premier, he never exercised a large influence in the Pétain regime. In the last analysis, it was Reynaud who played the decisive role in the rise of Pétain, since it was he who stepped aside and suggested Pétain as his successor in the premiership. Yet Reynaud certainly was not a member of a conspiracy in Pétain's behalf.

At any event, we must remember that Pétain took charge of the government in June of 1940 as Premier, in just the same constitutional position as Reynaud before him. He did not become the master of a personal government until July, some three weeks after the armistice was signed. And this came about only by virtue of quite another political operation.

Finally, looking back over the whole course of events leading up to the armistice, we cannot avoid the impression that much of the responsibility for the decision, whether this means praise or blame, lies with Reynaud. First, it was he who called Pétain into the cabinet as Vice-Premier and named Weygand to the supreme military command. Indeed, it was Reynaud who brought into the government every one of those who ultimately voted for the armistice. Then, as the debate developed in the cabinet, Reynaud proved weak and indecisive. Thus he ordered Weygand to prepare a retreat into the "Breton Redoubt," then backed down when Weygand objected; subsequently, he ordered Weygand to bring about a military surrender, then again yielded to Weygand's defiance; finally, he handed over the premiership to a man whom he knew to be an advocate of a separate peace.

Nevertheless, we must acknowledge that Reynaud was in a difficult position. Time and again Churchill cut the ground beneath him by indicating that the British would not hold it against the French if they were to make a separate peace. From the beginning of the debate, moreover, a considerable portion of the cabinet was against the Premier, and never did he have a clear majority in favor of continuing the war. Yet Reynaud had little or no chance of accomplishing his main purpose unless the cabinet supported him. For his aim, as we have seen, was to have the French government honor its pledge to make no separate peace, even though it could offer little more than a token resistance from a refuge in one of the French colonies, in order thus to maintain a moral hold upon the British.

A refugee government could not serve this purpose unless it was a legal government. But if Reynaud had left for Algiers, while a large portion of his cabinet remained behind and denounced him, he would no longer have been the head of the lawful government of France. He would have been only a pretender, such as De Gaulle became. Instead of pressing a claim upon the British, he would have had to depend upon their favor to maintain his position. Acting on his own initiative, by leaving France without resigning as Premier, Reynaud could have succeeded in preventing the armistice, but only at the price of depriving France of any legal government, either at home or abroad. And thus France would have lost the advantage of either making peace with the Axis or preserving her alliance with Britain.

VI

VICHY-ÉTAT

THE CONCLUSION of the armistice with the Axis opened the way for the revision of the French constitution, establishing the dictatorship of Marshal Pétain. The two occurrences were related to the degree that the armistice made some kind of change in the pattern of the French government seem advisable. Yet the connection between the events was not a simple and necessary link between cause and effect, for the exigencies of the armistice were not such as to dictate the particular kind of political reform that came about.

The explicit terms of the armistice made no stipulation requiring a change in the structure of the French government. Indeed, the armistice implied that there would be no such change. It was with the legal government of France that the German and Italian governments signed the armistice, and it was on the basis of the constitution of the Third Republic that this government professed to speak in the name of France. Moreover, the armistice envisaged that the French government which signed the armistice would remain in power to administer its provisions.

Nor did the armistice mean that the French government renounced the whole of its sovereign rights. In the zone that passed under German occupation, comprising about three-fifths of France, the armistice accorded the Germans the right to station their troops. Further, under the principles of international law providing for the case of a military occupation, it gave them the right to issue and administer such decrees as they might deem necessary to provide for the security and supply of their troops.

Other than this, the Germans had no right to tamper with the personal liberty or the property rights of the population of the occupied zone. The French government retained its basic responsibility for the rule of this area no less than of the unoccupied zone. In the latter region, the Germans could neither station troops nor issue decrees of any kind. They could affect the rule of this portion of France only insofar as they might make demands upon the French government on the basis of the agreements establishing the armistice.

In practice, however, the French government would have to accede to whatever demands the Germans might impose, provided these did not surpass the bounds of endurance. In the first place, if they considered it advantageous, the Germans could always violate the armistice and subject the entire country to an outright military rule. Having no power whatever with which to resist such a move, the French government could avoid this eventuality only by conciliating the Germans.

Even if the Germans should respect the terms of the armistice, the French had to be ready to make concessions in order to bargain with the Germans. For example, the French government would have to negotiate with the Nazis to induce them to liberate the 1,500,000 French soldiers who had been taken prisoners of war. Likewise, the government must deal with the Germans in order to solve the problem of the hundreds of thousands of civilians who had fled from northern France and taken refuge in what was now the unoccupied zone. Most of these wished to return to their homes, now that the fighting was over. At any event, the resources of the unoccupied zone were too meager to support them. In neither zone, indeed, could a normal pattern of life be restored until trade and travel were resumed between them. Yet the Germans were under no obligation to permit intercourse between the two regions of France, or between France and other countries of Europe, or between Metropolitan France and the French colonies. Finally, the French government faced the negotiation of a definitive peace settlement, since the armistice was only an agreement to suspend hostilities *ad interim*. If she was to avoid a Draconian peace in the event that the Axis proved victorious over the British, she had to demonstrate at least a reasonable amount of good will toward Berlin.

For the difficult task of pursuing continuous negotiations with the Axis, the French parliamentary system was ill-suited. The new situation made it imperative, as never before, that the government be able to develop a plan of action and hold to it, strike a bargain and keep it, balance immediate needs against possible advantages in the inscrutable longer range, and take a decision on the basis of secret information, without having to explain its calculations in public. No government could discharge such a responsibility if it constantly had to submit to interpellations in Parliament, hang upon the outcome of votes registering the ceaseless ebb and tide of alliances among political parties, and remain defenseless against six hundred deputies ambitious to gain places of personal political influence. The government must take on a more autocratic character than in time of peace.

But this did not mean a complete and permanent break with the traditions of the parliamentary system. Indeed, the executive had established its substantial independence of Parliament well before the armistice was signed. Parliament had had no voice in the decision to embark upon war in September, 1939, save to give its endorsement, *ex post facto,* to the decision of the cabinet. Throughout the next nine months, it had exercised virtually no control over the prosecution of the war. In the ultimate crisis, the cabinet had made the decision to seek terms of the Germans, then had signed the armistice, without even asking the endorsement of Parliament.

Yet the cabinet had assumed its dominating role only on a temporary basis, without a revision of the constitution. It had gained its freedom of action by virtue of an enactment of Parliament, which gave the Premier the right to issue decree-laws, subject to later review by Parliament.

Moreover, the cabinet had taken on a new character in assuming this new role. It had ceased to represent merely an alliance among a number of parties in Parliament, to the exclusion of others. Instead, it had become a council of the leading politicians of all shades of opinion, save only the Communists, whose party had been dissolved. Thus it had become the place where differences of opinion were reconciled, in much the same way as formerly had been done on the floor and in the lobbies of the Chamber and the Senate. In the situation that prevailed after the conclusion of the armistice, it was impossible to revert to the normal practices of open debate in Parliament. But it was not manifestly necessary to proceed further in the direction of an autocratic executive than the government had already gone.

But the atmosphere that prevailed in France on the morrow of the armistice made probable a broader political reform than the armistice itself required. For the shock and humiliation of the defeat produced a widespread, almost universal sense that something was gravely wrong with the institutions of France, and that the work of reform and regeneration must commence without delay. A chastened and sober new mood had descended upon France, and in its anguished determination to cleanse and redeem itself the nation showed a more nearly single mind than one could have imagined in a land so unhappily renowned for its internecine strife.

Then, too, the debacle provided a favorable occasion for those who had been urging changes in the structure of French institutions since long before the war. Among these proponents of reform, for whom the armistice was an unforeseen opportunity but not an original stimulus, there were three main schools. First, there were those who wished political reform within the traditions of the Third Republic, but tending to bolster the position of the executive. In earlier chapters, we have noted that in the 1920s and 1930s, though most of the republican parties favored the weak executive characteristic of the Third Republic, there were conservative republicans sharing the views of Poincaré, Millerand, and Tardieu, who wished to give larger powers to the President of the Republic or to the Premier. In the summer of 1940, men such as these thought in terms of strengthening the hand of Pétain as head of the government, intending thus to correct a vice of the Third Republic but not to suppress the republican regime.

Second, there were those conservatives who had never accepted the republican tradition but subscribed to the monarchist creed, more or less as expounded by the *Action Française*. In the crisis of 1940, men such as these saw the harvest of those vices of individualism and materialism which the Third Republic had misrepresented as virtues, giving free rein to each man's search for his own worldly aims and making no provision for the safeguard of larger interests than those of the individual. These conservatives thought of the task of national regeneration in terms of reestablishing the allegiance of men to the com-

munities of which they form part—the family first, then vocational
associations, and ultimately the nation—and thus overcoming the preoccupation of the individual with only his own welfare and happiness.
As part of the same scheme, they wished to see Marshal Pétain become
the personal embodiment of the nation, who would inspire loyalty to
the community as a whole, by commanding loyalty to his own person,
much as the King had done in times gone by. The reformers of this
school were not clear as to the details of their program, but plainly they
envisioned Marshal Pétain as something more than a stronger President or Premier of the Third Republic.

Third, there were the avowed fascists, such as Déat and Doriot.
These men advocated a regime which would place a dictator with
absolute power at the head of the state, which would recognize no
interest but that of the nation, and which would see the need of drawing the masses into a dynamic and enthusiastic support of the dictator,
and thus of the nation as a whole. They saw in the events of 1940 the
proof that German and Italian totalitarianism represented the wave
of the future, and evidence that France must make her institutions
conform to the new necessities of the twentieth century.

Thus it appears that most of the French drew no new lesson from
the monstrous happenings of 1940 but only saw confirmation of what
they had believed all along. This is hardly surprising. Seldom do men
suddenly discard old habits of thought, no matter how dramatic the
occasion. And the persistence of the familiar divisions of opinion foretold that in the new regime the same parties would soon be pitted in
struggle as under the Third Republic. Nevertheless, we cannot mistake
the sincere wish to break loose from the trammels of the past, nor fail
to mark the unshaken faith that France would eventually recover
from her sorry plight.

The choice which France made, as among the alternative paths to
her redemption, was almost fortuitous, so little was it the expression
of a clear trend of social and political forces. In the decision, public opinion played practically no part. The moves which led to the revision of
the constitution were planned within a narrow circle, comprising perhaps two dozen men, who did not make their proposals public until

a week before Parliament was summoned to approve the scheme. Even then, little chance was given for public discussion, since the censorship remained in force.

But the government had no need to circumvent or overpower an opposition to its plans, for the circumstances of the moment were not such as would encourage a public debate. Most of the nation was too preoccupied with personal problems to take a keen interest in public questions. A large proportion of the male population was still in military service—in the process of demobilization, unless taken prisoner by the Germans—while civilians were absorbed in the problems of reestablishing some kind of order in their private affairs, now that the tumult of the invasion was subsiding.

Nor was the situation such as to permit the normal maneuver of political parties and pressure groups. The parties had been in disorder ever since the middle of May, when Parliament, which was the hub of their organization, ceased to meet; after that, the deputies merely tagged along behind the cabinet as it migrated from Paris to Tours, then Bordeaux, and subsequently to Clermont-Ferrand and Vichy. The magnates of big business were no less preoccupied than the rest of the population with the problems arising in their personal affairs. Though ordinarily they kept in close touch with members of the government and of Parliament who were responsive to their pressure, presently they were in a poor position to exercise an influence upon politics. By the same token, the Confédération Générale du Travail, the principal trade union organization, was so disordered that its leaders could not maintain their normal liaison with the political parties of the Left. And the Church was so little accustomed to political influence under the Third Republic that, even though many in the entourage of Marshal Pétain were practicing Catholics, the leaders of the Church had not yet established close contact with the government.

The Nazis made no attempt to intervene. The German government had no communication with the French save through the Armistice Commission. This comprised representatives of the two governments who met at Wiesbaden to deal with problems arising out of the provisions of the armistice. The Germans had political agents in Paris, including both their own people and French sympathizers and sycophants who volunteered to do their bidding. But this network did not yet reach into the unoccupied zone, where the issue was to be decided, nor did the Germans ever establish an agency of large size in Vichy. Indeed, the Germans at this time had little interest in France. In the summer of 1940 they were preoccupied with the problem of how to press on against the British and inclined to dismiss the beaten French as no longer of concern to them. Moreover, as we shall note, they had no clear notion of what use they wished to make of their victory over the French, and when eventually they turned their attention to the problem, they were so divided in their counsels that they never did decide upon a clear-cut policy.

The preparations for the move to make Pétain dictator involved, in the first instance, the members of the cabinet, the President of the Republic, the presidents of the two houses of Parliament, and Pierre Laval, who at the beginning had no position in the government. Among these, the prime mover, according to the unanimous testimony of everyone who took part in the discussions, was Laval. It was he who planned the move, got the acquiescence of the members of the government, presented the proposal to Parliament, and conducted the intrigue which brought about a favorable vote. No one challenged his leadership or even sought a partnership in the venture. Pétain himself, who presumably was to be the principal beneficiary of the plan, was only mildly interested. By no means was he loth to accept the role of a dictator—he already had what amounted to absolute rule, for so large was his prestige that no one in the governing circle could oppose him or envisage a move to unseat him.

Most of the other members of the cabinet looked with favor upon the plan to give Pétain unlimited power, although they varied considerably in the degree of their enthusiasm. Some, such as Baudouin, would have preferred to see General Weygand in charge of the government, but Weygand lacked the immense public esteem which Pétain commanded. Moreover, he labored under the handicap of having had supreme command at the moment of defeat. Certainly the Germans would have taken it ill to see at the head of the French government the man who had led the French resistance to their armies. President Lebrun, Herriot, and Jeanneney remained unabashed partisans of the parliamentary system. They took the position, however, that they would not oppose the plan to give Pétain a personal rule, provided that the move should be freely approved by Parliament, as the institution representing the will of the people.

In engineering this coup d'état, Laval was moved primarily by his own ambition rather than any grand political design, either to preserve or subvert the republican regime. He judged that Pétain was a man without political ideas or even intuition, capable of no other role than that of a figurehead. By taking the initiative in a move to give him absolute rule, Laval apparently believed he would win the good graces of Pétain, become the grand vizier, and take over the actual management of the government. Perhaps he also reckoned that he would shortly succeed to Pétain's position on the aged Marshal's death. For a politician such as Laval, this was a natural line of calculation. Getting into power was his first thought, and developing a program was something to be attended to subsequently.

Yet Laval was not moved by mere personal ambition. Apparently he was sincerely convinced that he was the one man who could rescue France. As best we can discern the pattern of his thought, he had made up his mind that Germany was the paramount power of the moment and of the future. Henceforth France must seek her interest on the basis of a frank recognition of German hegemony, relying solely upon clever bargaining to wrest the utmost advantage for herself from a collaboration with the Nazis which she could not possibly avoid. He was sure, too, that he alone clearly perceived this basic reality. Other politicians still nursed a hope that somehow, some day, France would again be in a position to stand up to the Germans on the basis of equal power. Or else they abased themselves so humbly before the superior German might that they dared not think of outdoing their conquerors by resort to those devices of guile that are the weapon of the man of intelligence in outwitting a stronger foe.

Despite this sense of mission, Laval well knew that he could not command the trust of either the French people as a whole or of the governing circle. In a land where men in public life are universally viewed with suspicion, Laval stood out as a man whom everyone regarded as singularly shifty. Hence he had no chance of gaining power in his own name. He could do so only by gaining the confidence of Pétain, who commanded wide public respect, and by inducing Pétain to lend the weight of his name to the policy which Laval regarded as indispensable to the salvation of France.

Having decided on this course, Laval proceeded to his purpose by playing upon the weakness, vanity, and illusions of the men whose help he needed. He had little trouble in winning over the old marshal, even though Pétain disliked and distrusted him. Laval quickly learned how to gain Pétain's good graces by pandering to his senile vision of himself as the patriarch of his people. Nor did Laval find it hard to secure the compliance of the conservatives in the cabinet, such as Baudouin and Bouthillier, who hoped to see the dictatorship of Pétain as a transition to a new and more conservative regime.

Laval had no less success in persuading politicians who had spent their whole lives in the service of the Third Republic, to whom the parliamentary system represented both a religion and a livelihood. In his appeal to this element, he presented himself as a man who also owed his career to Parliament and who therefore would be a guarantor of the traditions of Parliament within the new regime. Besides, he pointed out, Pétain, becoming dictator by virtue of the vote of Parliament, would have no choice but to acknowledge the ultimate authority of Parliament. So well did Laval succeed in his campaign that, though the principal responsibility for the death of the Third Republic lies upon him, nearly everyone in a position of political influence in the summer of 1940 was to some degree his accomplice.

The sequence of events that was to culminate in the rise of Pétain to absolute rule began with the discussions in the cabinet concerning the armistice. Up to that time, Pétain remained simply a man who commanded wide public esteem as one of the victorious generals of the War of 1914, but he had no political aspirations. He had been called into the cabinet by Reynaud merely to lend the government the prestige of his name and reputation and thus to help bolster public morale, and he had been content with this decorative role. As the issue of the armistice arose, however, he took on new importance. For as it became apparent that the majority of the cabinet favored a separate peace, Marshal Pétain emerged as the logical successor to Reynaud. As early as May 26, Chautemps was beginning to talk of Pétain as the next Premier.

But the debate over the armistice did not approach a decisive stage, nor therefore did the resignation of Reynaud become imminent, until after the government moved to Tours, then to Bordeaux. It was at Bordeaux that Laval launched his campaign to ride to power in tow to Pétain, and apparently it was Laval who advised Pétain as to whom he should include in his cabinet. However, Pétain did not owe his rise to the premiership to intrigue on the part of Laval, who was not a member of the Reynaud cabinet and therefore in no position to wield a decisive influence. Nor was he indebted to Chautemps or anyone else. For everyone in the government agreed, whatever their differences as to whether France should make peace, that if the cabinet decided upon that course, Pétain was the only conceivable choice as the new head of the government. Accordingly, as we have seen, Reynaud himself proposed Pétain as his successor. The nomination was approved by President Lebrun, Herriot, and Jeanneney, even though these three were personally opposed to the decision to sue for terms.

Once the armistice was signed, discussion began at once among the members of the inner circle surrounding Pétain as to how to reorganize the government. As a minimum, apparently everyone agreed that Pétain must have the absolute right to govern in his own name, without consulting Parliament or even permitting it to meet, as long as the armistice was in force—in other words, until a definitive peace settlement was reached and the German occupation terminated. But as to what more should be attempted, opinion divided.

From the first, Laval insisted upon a bold venture. Regretting his earlier refusal to serve in the government unless he were named Minister of Foreign Affairs, he accepted appointment as minister without portfolio on June 23. Promptly upon his entrance into the cabinet, he declared that Parliament must be swept away, not merely rendered inoperative for the time being. He therefore proposed a revision of the constitution which would give Pétain not only the right to govern in his own name for the duration of the armistice but also the right to promulgate a new constitution. This would require that parliament be summoned into session once more, since the constitution could legally be amended only by the vote of the members of the two houses of Parliament meeting together as a National Assembly. Obviously, therefore, Parliament would have to be persuaded to vote its own death sentence. But Laval had complete confidence that he could browbeat Parliament even to this extreme.

In urging this course, Laval probably had no principled animus against Parliament as an institution. He simply believed that the Axis would retain its hegemony over Europe far into the future, and that France could not possibly preserve her parliamentary system of government while part of a Europe under the dominance of totalitarian powers. Since France had no choice but to abandon the Third Republic, he deemed it better to make a clean break, in such a way as to leave no doubt of the legality of the new authoritarian regime which Pétain must inaugurate. And he judged it wisest to do this at once, while the prestige of Pétain was so enormous that Parliament would not dare balk at whatever he might ask, and while the shock of the armistice would help overcome the inertia characteristic of French political life under the Third Republic.

By no means was Laval alone in his wish to have done with the Third Republic. On June 28 General Weygand submitted to Pétain a memorandum outlining the moral bases of a new regime, corresponding to the views of Catholic conservatives. In this sketch he advocated a corporative social order, stressed the need of nurturing the family as an institution, and proposed the slogan, *Dieu, Patrie, Famille, Travail*. A number of other men in the cabinet, including Baudouin, Bouthillier, and Alibert, shared much the same outlook.

However, Laval's scheme did not at once meet with unanimous approval. Baudouin opposed it, even though he was a partisan of some such broad reform as General Weygand outlined. In the first place, he thought it unlikely that Parliament would vote Pétain the right to promulgate a new constitution. In the second place, he considered it inopportune to undertake to revise the whole structure of national life at a time when France was still under German occupation. Accordingly, Baudouin urged that Marshal Pétain merely utilize the same *pleins pouvoirs* by which Daladier and Reynaud had previously been authorized to issue decree-laws without consulting Parliament, and that Parliament be prorogued. This would solve the immediate problem, but it would not require debate in Parliament on a measure having much less practical importance at the moment than for the future.

Moreover, not all the members of the government were eager to repudiate the republican regime, nor were they so sure as Laval that France must now accommodate her institutions to the German and Italian models. Pétain himself had no clear views on broad political issues, nor personal attachments that would determine his outlook. He was no more a foe than a friend of republicanism. Before his sudden rise to a position of political leadership, he had had associations with conservative Catholics who were known to be hostile to the principles of liberalism. But he had also had relations with conservative republicans, and he had made a successful professional career under republican auspices. Others in the cabinet had much the same ambivalence toward the Third Republic. In short, the members of the Pétain government were far from single-minded in a determination to institute an authoritarian regime on a permanent basis.

Nevertheless, Laval won Pétain's approval of his plan. The decision came at a conference on Sunday afternoon, June 30, at which were present Pétain, Laval, Baudouin, Bouthillier, and Alibert, the Minister of Justice. At the outset of the discussion, as Baudouin presented his objections to the venture, Pétain remained hesitant. He seemed disposed to favor the more cautious procedure which Baudouin espoused. At any event, he would not go ahead on the basis Laval proposed without the assent of President Lebrun. Promptly Laval made off to see Lebrun. Returning an hour later, he reported that Lebrun agreed to raise no objection to a revision of the constitution, provided that Parliament should approve. Thereupon Pétain ceased his vacillation and said to Laval, "Well, then, go ahead and try."

Forthwith Laval set to work. With Alibert, he began drawing up the text of the proposal which would be presented to the National Assembly and making arrangements to convene the two houses of Parliament, which had not met since May 17. Meantime Baudouin, who remained skeptical as to whether the members of Parliament would vote themselves into limbo, undertook to protect the marshal against a rebuff. In the event the National Assembly approved the resolution giving him complete power, Baudouin urged, Pétain was to make it clear that he owed this power to the National Assembly and not to Laval. On the other hand, if the National Assembly voted down the proposal, Pétain was to declare that the scheme was not his idea. Thus the vote would not redound to the discredit of Pétain but of Laval as its sponsor. Evidently Pétain heeded this advice. He carefully remained in the background, leaving Laval with the sole public responsibility for the venture, until just before the vote was to be taken in the National Assembly.

In the interval while the matter was under discussion in the cabinet, the government had moved from Bordeaux, since this city was included in the zone of German occupation. At the urging of Laval, it had chosen the town of Clermont-Ferrand as its new seat. But the facilities there were inadequate for the needs of the government, so another move had to be made. Lyons would have been an obvious choice, but Pétain did not wish to go there. Lyons was the political stronghold of Herriot, who was its mayor, and Pétain had a distaste for Herriot. So, at the suggestion of Baudouin, the government settled in Vichy, a fashionable watering resort, where there was an abundance of hotels suitable for use as offices for the various ministries and as housing for the horde that would inevitably cluster around the headquarters of the government.

On such practical grounds, the choice was good. In another respect, however, it was unfortunate, for the town was well known as a health resort for the aged and infirm of the upper classes. This provided perhaps too appropriate a setting for a government headed by an octogenarian and dedicated to the task of national rejuvenation.[1]

The government reached Vichy on July 2, and shortly members of Parliament began to arrive. The two chambers were not convened for a formal session until the 9th. In the meantime, meeting places were made available to the members of each house, the deputies in the Petit Casino, the Senators in the Salle des Sociétés Médicales. Throughout the

---

[1] The decision of the government to make Vichy its headquarters and to use the term État Français in its legal documents, rather than République Française, led to ironic references to Vichy-État. Frenchmen suffering from the national liver ailment, known simply as *le foie*, traditionally drink medicinal doses of mineral water, taken from the springs at Vichy and distributed throughout France by a governmental monopoly. Upon the label of this bottled water appear the words *Vichy-État*.

week, a ceaseless discussion developed, in shapeless conversations among groups of senators and deputies gathering in these quarters, or in restaurants and hotels, or in the streets, while Laval and his political lieutenants circulated among them, seeking to make sure of a favorable majority before the debate and vote in the National Assembly.

Laval waged his campaign with consummate skill. He had an immense advantage, to be sure, since other members of Parliament were in a poor position to challenge his arguments. A considerable number had been caught in the maelstrom of the invasion, and only with difficulty had they succeeded in making their way to the impromptu new capital. These had little or no knowledge of what had transpired since the exodus from Paris, a month before. Others had kept pace with the government in its migrations to Tours, Bordeaux, and Clermont-Ferrand and had therefore gleaned somewhat more news than the censorship released to the general public. But no one outside the immediate circle of the government had reliable knowledge of the precise state of relations with either Britain or the Axis, or of what progress the Germans were making in their attack upon Britain, or of what secret threats they were presenting to France.

In such a situation, Laval had little trouble in finding hopes and fears to play upon. Evidently he made use of nearly every kind of argument, according to his estimate of the man to whom he was speaking. To some, he promised positions of importance in the new regime if they proved cooperative in their vote. With others, who seemed more interested in the fate of the nation than their own advancement, he dwelt upon the horrors in store for France if she proved slow to take her place in the new Europe of the Axis, and the rewards open to her if she ventured upon a new orientation. And to those who remained intractable, he implied that General Weygand stood ready to order troops to Vichy to settle the issue by force if Parliament refused to vote its own disappearance.

On July 9 the two chambers met in formal sessions to take the necessary action providing for their deliberations as a single body, the National Assembly, in which alone was vested the right to amend the Constitution of 1875. The Chamber of Deputies met first, at 9 o'clock in the morning, in the theater of the Grand Casino, which provided an auditorium large enough for the occasion as well as an appropriate setting for a desperate gamble. Herriot, who presided, began with some words of tribute to the members of the Chamber who had died while in military service, then put the motion providing for a session of the National Assembly. The motion passed by 395 to 3. In the afternoon, the Senate met in the same auditorium, with Jeanneney in the chair, and promptly adopted the same motion, by a vote of 229, with only a single voice in opposition.

The next morning, the 10th, the members reassembled as a constitutional convention, to pass on the motion introduced in behalf of the government. This comprised a single article: "The National Assembly gives complete power to the Government of the Republic, under the signature and on the authority of Marshal Pétain, President of the Council of Ministers, for the purpose of promulgating, by one or more acts, the new constitution of the French State. This constitution shall guarantee the rights of Labor, the Family, and the Fatherland. It shall be ratified by the assemblies which it shall create."

Thereupon a confused debate began. But before the discussion reached a critical stage, Laval got up from his seat in the front row of the auditorium, mounted the stage, and read aloud a note addressed to him by Marshal Pétain. Its burden was unequivocal: "The constitutional proposals presented by the government over which I preside will come up for discussion before the Assembly on Tuesday the 9th, or Wednesday the 10th of July. Since it will be difficult for me to participate in the session, I ask you to represent me. The adoption of the proposal which the government submits to the Assembly seems to me necessary to assure the welfare of the country." Thus, disregarding the advice of Baudouin to avoid risking his own position on the outcome of the vote, Pétain threw his prestige into the balance.

Once Laval delivered this blow, the opposition crumbled. Though the debate rambled on several hours more, the outcome was not in doubt. The vote showed 569 in favor of the motion of the government, 80 against it. Thereupon the Assembly adjourned amidst cries of "Vive la France!" Some heard also a single voice that shouted, "Vive la République, quand même!"

Words to the number of millions have been spoken and written to

explain, or explain away, this vote of the National Assembly. Yet there
is little that is obscure in its action. First, it is clear that the vote con-
formed to the procedures prescribed by the Constitution of 1875. Neither
President Lebrun nor Herriot nor Jeanneney, who were the acknowledged guardians of republican legality, raised any objection at the time
to either the substance or the procedure of the enactment.

Second, it is evident that the vote represented the free expression of
the opinion of those who participated in the debate, insofar as free
opinion was possible in the helpless situation of France. Despite whatever threats Laval might have invoked in private conversations, there
is no evidence that the French army was prepared to use force against
the members of Parliament, nor that the Germans were disposed to take
such action.[2]

Third, it is manifest that the vote represented the views of a majority of the elected representatives of the nation. To be sure, not all the
members of Parliament were present to take part in the vote. Among
those absent were some seventy Communists, who had been expelled
from parliament in the course of the previous winter, and about thirty
deputies and one senator who had embarked on the "Massilia." But
even if the votes of all those absent were counted as against the proposal
of the government, the motion still would have gained a clear majority.
Finally, it is incontestable that the majority represented a broad cross
section of political opinion. It included the larger proportion of Socialist
and Radical-Socialist deputies as well as representatives of the parties
of the Right. Only the Communist Party, which no longer had seats
in Parliament, cast no vote in favor of the motion.

Nevertheless, while the circumstances of the vote were clear enough,
there were ambiguities in the text of the resolution, which doubtless
were far from inadvertent. Though the bill vested *pleins pouvoirs* in
Marshal Pétain as head of the government of the *Republic,* it envisaged
the promulgation of a new constitution for the French *State,* which
need not mean the French Republic. Moreover, although it indicated

---

[2] This excuse was made at the time, to explain the readiness of Parliament to do Laval's
bidding, and the charge was repeated during the trials of both Pétain and Laval. It is quite
possible that Laval led some members of Parliament to believe that the Germans or the French
army would intervene if Parliament proved stubborn. But there is no evidence to establish that this
was a real likelihood. At any event, no action was taken against the eighty men who cast their
votes in the negative when the test came in the National Assembly.

that the new constitution would come into force when approved by the nation and by the assemblies which the constitution would institute, it made no provision for universal suffrage. Doubtless Laval, who drew up the text of the bill, intended to gain the votes of those who remained loyal to the republican regime while also providing a hopeful prospect for those who envisioned an authoritarian or a corporative regime.

Promptly upon the decision of the National Assembly, Marshal Pétain made the first use of his prerogative to issue organic decrees. On July 11 he signed three such decrees repealing portions of the constitution of the Third Republic and instituting a new framework of government. Constitutional Act Number One abolished the office of President of the Republic and designated Pétain as "Chief of the French State." Constitutional Act Number Two established the general procedures of government that was to prevail until such time as a complete new constitution should be promulgated. Under its provisions, Marshal Pétain assumed the right to appoint to all public offices, the ultimate command of the armed forces, and the power to issue laws and conclude treaties on his own signature. He denied himself only the right to declare war without the consent of the "legislative assemblies." Constitutional Act Number Three declared that the Chamber of Deputies and the Senate should "subsist" until the promulgation of the definitive new constitution. But both houses were to remain adjourned until and unless the Chief of State summoned them into session again.

Though intended only as interim measures, these three Constitutional Acts of July 11, 1940, were to remain the legal basis of the government of France all through the period of the Vichy regime. Their provisions were to be amended in some details by later decrees. Eventually the text of a complete new constitution was to be drawn up. But this constitution was never put into force, nor were its terms revealed to the public.

So, as it happened, little practical consequence came of Laval's scheme to give Pétain constitutional prerogatives rather than merely temporary *pleins pouvoirs* to issue decree-laws. Its principal import, indeed, was only to mark the legal demise of the Third Republic.

A reorganization of the cabinet completed the measures which launched the new regime. This was required, in part, because the aged marshal lacked the stamina to preside over the meetings of a cabinet comprising two dozen or more ministers or to devote attention to the administrative problems of each of the ministries. Quite apart from Pétain's need to husband his strength, however, some such reform of the cabinet was needed in order to permit it to discharge its task. For the cabinet had grown to inordinate size under the Third Republic, numbering about thirty men. This was too large a group to permit the informal discussion of broad issues. Its growth had been due, in part, to the establishment of new administrative departments, each of which traditionally required a cabinet member at its head. But it had come about also because representation in the cabinet was needed, on grounds of practical politics, for each of the parties whose support was required to secure the cabinet a favorable majority in Parliament.

In the new situation such considerations no longer obtained, since the government did not depend upon Parliament. And because it now had a much heavier burden of decision on matters of public policy, in the absence of Parliament, it had much more urgent need to deliberate expeditiously and effectively. At the instance of Baudouin, the decision was taken to limit membership in the cabinet to about eight men, each with the rank of Minister. The heads of administrative departments of less than prime importance were reduced to the rank of secretaries or under-secretaries of State. These would continue to be responsible for the management of their respective departments, subject to the review of the cabinet, but would no longer take part in the cabinet meetings.

On the basis of this decision, Marshal Pétain on July 12 asked for the resignation of the members of his original cabinet. The next day, he appointed a new one. In this renovation, Pétain retained the position of Premier, of course. Laval became Vice-Premier; Baudouin kept his post as Minister of Foreign Affairs, Bouthillier as Minister of Finance, Marquet as Minister of the Interior, and Alibert as Minister of Justice. The other members brought the total number of ministers to twelve, not counting Pétain and Laval. This represented more than the optimum size, but it was an improvement over the previous number.

Of much larger significance was the decision of Pétain to name Laval as his heir. This was accomplished by a new organic law, Constitutional Act Number Four, promulgated on July 12. By its terms, Pétain decreed that if he became unable to fulfill his functions as Chief of State, Laval was to succeed him; in the event that Laval was unable to do so, the cabinet was to designate the next in succession. Thus was Laval rewarded for his services as king maker.

Perhaps the prize was more than he had earned. As we have seen, the action which the National Assembly took in response to the threats and promises of Laval added but little of practical importance to the *pleins pouvoirs* which the National Assembly was quite willing to give Pétain, even without the urging of Laval. But then, the designation of Laval as heir to Pétain also proved of little practical value. For though Laval doubtless thought his chances excellent of succeeding the octogenarian Chief of State, thereby winning for himself the unlimited powers he had labored to bestow upon Pétain, the old soldier proved so durable that he not only outlived his own reign, but ultimately survived the Dauphin.

VII

PROBLEMS, ISSUES
AND FACTIONS

IN THE COURSE of June and July of 1940, France had taken two momentous decisions—first, to withdraw from the war by way of an armistice, and second, to entrust to Marshal Pétain the sole charge of her government and the task of reforming her institutions. Thus she had apparently made a firm commitment of her future.

Actually, however, she had settled little by these decisions. She had only opened up a new complex of problems whose involutions and ramifications no one at the time clearly perceived. Not until well into the fall of 1940 did the French begin to recognize the problems they now faced, the alternatives among which their government must still make its choice, and the ultimate implications of each of the possible courses of action.

One series of problems arose out of the dislocation of the basic routine of national life, due to the cessation of hostilities. Conspicuous among these, and hardest to solve, was the problem of the 1,500,000 prisoners of war held by the Germans, who were under no legal or moral obligation to liberate them. France could hardly achieve a semblance of normality while so many of her men were absent from their families and their usual pursuits. Similar was the problem of the hundreds of thousands of refugees who had crowded into what was now the unoccupied zone of France. These included French citizens whose homes were in the regions under German occupation or who had escaped to the south of France to avoid the horrors of the *Blitzkrieg;* political exiles who had gained haven in Paris before the war and had fled before the Nazi advance; and a considerable number of Belgian civilians who had been swept into France during the German invasion of their homeland.

At the same time, Vichy had to cope with a host of economic tasks. The government was obliged to find means of meeting the heavy payments which the Germans levied to cover the costs of their occupation; to secure supplies of food and other essential commodities while virtually all channels of trade with either Axis Europe or the overseas world were shut off; to find work for the urban proletariat in towns where war industries were now grinding to a stop; to find ways of maintaining agricultural production, now more critical than ever before; and to find means of dealing with inflation, which could be expected as an inevitable consequence of the new economic crisis.

Another series of problems developed out of the anomalous position in the international scene in which France now found herself. By signing the armistice with the Axis, France had dropped out of the war. Nevertheless, the struggle went on. Gradually it became evident that France was in the curious position of being neither at war nor at peace but rather a nonbelligerent caught between two adversaries locked in a gigantic struggle. This meant that France would have to reexamine her position in relation to both Britain and the Axis. It also meant that the British and the Germans would have to reconsider their attitude toward France, as would also the United States, Russia, and other neutrals.

A third series of problems had their source in the accession of Marshal Pétain to absolute rule. As soon became apparent, nothing had really been decided by the action of the National Assembly on July 10. By their vote on that occasion, the representatives of the nation had given their trust to Pétain, and public opinion generally had approved this testimony of blind faith in the aged Marshal. But no one, including Pétain, knew what use he was to make of this new dominion. And in the multitude that acclaimed the "Victor of Verdun" as the new Joan of Arc, there were nearly as many shades of opinion as ever appeared in the Parliament of the Third Republic. Among the Pétainists, as we have noted, there were three main factions—a conservative clique, drawing inspiration from the tradition which the *Action Française* popularized; a small but vociferous band of avowed fascists, reveling in the bright prospect which the German triumph seemed to promise them; and an old guard of parliamentary politicians who, while acclaiming Pétain as the man of the hour, still hoped to preserve the familiar world of the Third Republic. It remained an open question as to which of these three factions would prevail over the others.

Each of these sets of problems interlocked with another. For example, Vichy could not make much progress toward the restoration of normal economic life unless France gained the good graces of the Axis. Conversely, Vichy could take a stiff-necked attitude toward Germany on diplomatic issues only if the government was prepared to see France suffer severe economic distress in the short run. Likewise, the debate that developed as to what kind of domestic political reform France should adopt was involved with differing views as to how long Europe would remain under the domination of totalitarian governments.

The task of choice was rendered more vexed because of the devious procedures for reaching a decision on public issues. Compared with the chaos that now prevailed in Vichy, the systematic vacillations of the previous regime seemed to represent resolute and single-minded purpose. In principle, Marshal Pétain had complete authority and complete responsibility, as had the King in the age of Bourbon absolutism. But the Vichy regime not only lacked organic laws other than the interim decrees which Pétain issued on July 11, but it had no history and therefore no traditional procedures to serve in lieu of a written constitution.

Nor did the dictator have such a firm mind as to give his regime a stable direction. On practically no issue did Pétain have a strong conviction. This is not surprising, since he had virtually no prior political experience. It is more remarkable that he showed little of the habit of decision which one might expect of a man whose profession as a soldier put him in a position of command. At any event, he was now an old man. He lacked the stamina required for the ceaseless round of conferences which is the routine of the head of a government. Being hard of hearing, he could not take part in a discussion involving more than a small number of persons. Because of his want of strength, moreover, he was in full possession of his faculties for only a few hours each morning. By afternoon, he betrayed his fatigue by forgetfulness and confusion of mind.

In practice, therefore, Pétain was wholly dependent on his advisers. Yet the men in his entourage were far from a homogeneous party. Apparently Pétain had no intimate associates before his sudden rise to political prominence in 1940. The men who gained positions close to him, upon his accession to the dictatorship, were not henchmen whom he had chosen long before but rather a chance aggregation recruited in the rush of events in June and July of 1940. Some had made their names in the army or the navy, like General Weygand and Admiral Darlan; others in Parliament, like Laval, or in the civil service, like Bouthillier, or in business, like Baudouin. Scarcely any had quite the same views as another, and some had none at all. Several had personal political ambitions which ill accorded with those of others in the group.

Consequently the cabinet of the marshal resembled the court of an oriental potentate, where all efforts are bent to getting next to the sultan, or the grand vizier, or the man likely to become the next grand vizier. And the outcome was also suggestive of such a despotism. For it is a fair rule of history that the closer a government approaches the absolute rule of one man, the more its policies become indecisive and erratic.

The situation which France now occupied was not simple to define in terms of international law and a good deal harder to define in terms of international politics. By virtue of the armistice, she was no longer engaged in hostilities, but neither was she at peace. Though not quite without precedent, this situation was irregular. In the past, for a hundred years and more, wars among the principal powers of Europe had ordinarily ended when the state or states on one side acknowledged defeat. In 1940, however, the armistice between France and the Axis powers had terminated hostilities only between these belligerents, while Britain and several of her Dominions remained at war. So all powers had to consider just what were the implications of an armistice.

From the start, it was clear that France remained a sovereign state. As we have seen, the armistice imposed a number of specific obligations upon the French government, but otherwise did not curtail its liberty of action. Since France remained sovereign, neutral powers had the right to maintain diplomatic relations with her government. Most neutrals chose to use this right. Foremost among them were the United States and Soviet Russia. Likewise, belligerent states not at war with France had the right to maintain normal diplomatic relations. Thus Canada allowed her minister to remain in France even after the British ambassador returned to London. Whatever the legal niceties, the Germans made clear that they would not allow Vichy to maintain relations with the governments-in-exile of those states whose territory was actually under German occupation. Hence the diplomatic corps at Vichy included no representatives of Belgium, the Netherlands, Norway, Poland, or Czechoslovakia. Nevertheless, the larger number of those governments which had ambassadors or ministers accredited to the French Republic before the war chose to maintain their representation, at least for a while, at the seat of the new French government.

In 1940, however, considerations of international law had little necessary bearing on the realm of world politics. In practice, both France and the two principal remaining belligerents had to reexamine their relations in terms of their own interests and their guess as to the probable course of events ahead. Examined in such a perspective, the armistice unmistakably marked a step on the part of France toward a rapprochement with Germany, but it did not represent a definitive commitment.

In the given circumstances, the course of events might take one of three directions. France might proceed further toward the Axis, seeking a partnership with the Germans and Italians; or she might seek to remain in the middle ground between the warring antagonists, hoping to avoid a wrong guess as to the ultimate victor, and thus gain advantage as the arbiter between them; or, despite the armistice, she might ultimately resume her struggle against the Axis. In determining which of these courses she should follow, legalistic considerations would weigh only lightly, while practical advantages bulked large.

The Germans did not escape this need to reconsider their attitude toward France, merely because they had overpowered the French army. In making their decision to grant an armistice, the Nazis had by no means thought out and adopted a long-range policy. They had had to make their answer to the French appeal for terms while in the midst of a chaotic battle. In reaching their decision on what response to make the Germans had had no need to grant an armistice in order to save themselves the exertion of overcoming French resistance. They had only to consider how their answer would affect their further struggle against the British. And this involved primarily the question of what would become of the French navy.

This was a matter of large importance, though not decisive. If the Germans had chosen not to grant an armistice, the French navy would doubtless have gone over to the British, either by order of the French government or by the spontaneous decision of the naval command. This would have rendered much more difficult either a German invasion across the Channel or a submarine blockade, and would have assured the British of a clear preponderance of seapower in the Mediterranean. On the other hand, if the Germans could have gained the French navy for themselves, they would have been in a much better position to wage economic warfare against the British, since the Axis would have been able to close the Mediterranean.

However, it would have been virtually impossible for the Germans to induce the French to hand over their fleet as a prize of war. Such a concession would have meant the utter humiliation of the French, whose one slim boast was that their navy had escaped the fate of their army. Moreover, it would have required them to surrender their sole item of bargaining power. Thus the Germans could hope to gain the use of the French navy only by ruse or by a diplomatic bargain between the French and German governments subsequent to the armistice. Thus they could accomplish the most by offering terms that would prove acceptable to the French while leaving Berlin room to maneuver later on. Such, in substance, were the terms the Germans offered.

But as the summer wore into the fall, Berlin had to develop its policy toward Vichy in view of broader calculations. As it became apparent that the war was not going to terminate soon, the Germans had need to weigh the relative advantage of exploiting their military superiority over the French by reducing them to a quasi-colonial status, as against the advantage of developing amicable relations with France as a kind of partner in the "New Order" which the Axis envisioned for Europe.

Viewing the problem in this perspective, the Germans revealed a cleavage of opinion the origin of which lay back in the prewar period. Much as the French in the 1920s and 1930s had been divided between advocates of a "hard" and of a "soft" policy toward Germany, the Germans had also been divided in their view of France. Some regarded France simply as the hereditary enemy, while others harbored a grudging respect for her as the epitome of European culture. Hitler himself had espoused the former view and had given it scriptural basis for the Nazis in *Mein Kampf*.

On the other hand, the Weimar Republic had made obeisance to those ideals of liberal humanism which France had long represented. In the era of Locarno, while the German government was seeking a diplomatic reconciliation with Paris, German intellectuals were rendering homage to *la ville lumière* as the home of that wit, warmth, grace, and taste that seemed the birthright of the Latins and so wanting in the German heritage.

This view had not died out in the Nazi era. It had gained classic expression, indeed, in a book published in 1929 under the title, *Gott in Frankreich*—whose author, Friedrich Sieburg, was to have a minor role in Franco-German collaboration in the period of Vichy. Even Hitler, having become master of the Reich, had chosen not to emphasize his hatred for the French in public statements. Instead, he had preferred to depict the Germans as a people who wished only to live in peace with their neighbors across the Rhine but who had met with one rebuff after another. At the same time, however, neither the Nazi Party nor the Reichswehr had ceased to think of the French as foes.

As the German government faced the problem of its relations with Vichy after the armistice, it reflected this division of opinion. In general, Hitler, Goering, and Goebbels adhered to the "hard" view of France as the *Erbfeind*. To be sure, this did not preclude giving France lenient treatment, as a matter of tactics. On occasion, Goering urged amicable relations with Vichy, in order to win French cooperation in

Axis campaigns in Africa. Nor was Hitler unequivocal in his attitude. But in the view of the Nazi doctrinaires, including Hitler, the defeat of the French in the war gave proof of their decadence as a people. This ruled out their making a contribution of importance to the Europe of the "New Order." In much the same spirit, the army was inclined to take a contemptuous view of French military prowess and to see no advantage in winning the friendship of the vanquished nation.

On the other side, Ribbentrop emerged as the advocate of a policy of generosity toward Vichy, looking forward to a partnership between Germany and France and banking on those French who were sympathetic to Nazi ideology to help bring about this cooperation. Ribbentrop himself had long-standing personal associations in France, where he had often visited and had mingled in French society. Moreover, the permanent staff of the Foreign Office, which he headed, was an inheritance from the Weimar Republic. Its personnel, lukewarm in their attachment to Nazi principles, had been habituated to both the idea of Franco-German rapprochement as envisioned at Locarno and the idea of a general European conciliation symbolized by Geneva.

Neither Ribbentrop nor his subordinates in the Foreign Office went so far in their benevolence toward the French as to merit the name of Francophiles. But the man whom Ribbentrop chose as his representative in France, Otto Abetz, did deserve such a reputation. A native of Baden, where the cultural influence of France is pronounced, Abetz was one of the generation of German intellectuals of the 1920s who became enamored of France. A student of architecture, he became a passionate admirer of the French Gothic, on which he had lectured both in France and in Germany. When he married, he chose a Frenchwoman as his wife.

In broad outline, then, we can say that the division of opinion corresponded to a difference between the Foreign Office and the military, with the leadership of the Party generally favoring the latter. But the question remained as to where, between the military and the Foreign Office, lay the responsibility for the policy regarding France. In one sense, the armistice implied that this was an affair of the military. Since the termination of hostilities between the armies clearly did not conclude the state of war between the two governments, the armistice did not involve the restoration of normal diplomatic relations, such as would naturally fall within the province of the Foreign Office.

On the other hand, the armistice was an agreement between the German and French governments, not between their armies. Inasmuch as relations between the two states were essentially political, the Foreign Office had grounds to concern itself with the questions involved in these relations.

In actuality, of course, the ultimate decision rested with Hitler, who took counsel—to the extent that he ever heeded advice—from both military and diplomatic advisers. In the main, as we have remarked, he leaned toward the policy of firmness which the military favored. Nevertheless, he did not foreclose the possibility of a more generous attitude, such as Ribbentrop and the Foreign Office bespoke. Perhaps he harbored some of that deference toward French culture which we have mentioned as common among Germans of his generation. Perhaps he imagined himself as a new Bonaparte, the magnanimous builder of a new and better Europe, in which the French would hold a rank below the master race but well above the Slavic barbarians.

On occasion, at any event, he made gestures toward reconciliation with the French, for reasons of military strategy. The principal such occasion came in the fall of 1940, when he contemplated a campaign for the conquest of North Africa. For this purpose, he hoped to gain French cooperation. Again in 1942, when he envisioned a new venture in the Near East, he was to come back to the same tack. Because he never quite made up his mind that the good will of France was valueless, he held back from endorsing a "hard" policy toward Vichy. Yet neither did he make a firm decision in favor of a "soft" policy. Thus the Germans developed their relations with France on the basis of an unresolved debate within their own councils. In the outcome, they missed much of whatever advantage they might have gained from either firmness or friendship.

The British were likewise of two minds in their attitude toward Vichy. Basically, Churchill seems to have maintained the relatively friendly position which he had expressed during the hectic weeks of May and June, when the French government was debating whether or not to seek peace. As he declared, the British would regard France as a comrade who had been struck down in battle, after an heroic combat, and not as a faithless ally who was selling them out. No more than a week after the French signed the armistice, however, the British government began to show deep concern over the possibility that Vichy might yet give over its navy to the Axis or even openly join the Axis in the war. One reason for this growing alarm in London was the entrance of Laval into the French cabinet on June 24, for Laval was known as a partisan of wholehearted collaboration with the Axis. As another factor in the British attitude of suspicion we can recognize the influence of General de Gaulle, who had every reason, and much opportunity, to worsen relations between London and Vichy.

De Gaulle had gone to London in June, we have seen, as a representative of Reynaud. While the Reynaud cabinet debated the problem of the armistice, he had done his utmost to strengthen the hand of Reynaud and the others who wished to continue the struggle. But De Gaulle had seen this hope disappear when Reynaud voluntarily handed over the premiership to Marshal Pétain. Immediately he had determined to organize a new French government in London, which he hoped to induce the British to recognize. Apparently he believed that a government-in-exile, such as he proposed to head, could do much to encourage the French at home to oppose the new Vichy regime. Evidently he also believed that such a government could rally a number of the French colonies to its support. In these expectations, he was certainly overoptimistic.

Yet we may reasonably presume that he did not base his movement solely upon these miscalculations. Doubtless he was shrewd enough to realize that a government-in-exile, which would have scarcely any strength save what the British might lend it, could not materially affect the outcome of the war. As best we can surmise, he was moved primarily by his sincere conviction that only if a government purporting to represent France waged war in partnership with the British would France have the right to share in the settlement of the war. And only thus could the French make sure that the British would not strike a bargain with the Germans at their expense.

Consequently, De Gaulle had reason to wish to see a breach between London and Vichy, since such a rupture was prerequisite to British recognition of the new French government he planned to organize. Accordingly, we may reasonably imagine that he played a large role in persuading members of the British government that the Vichy regime was being run by men whose sympathies were wholly with the Axis.

In response to these various impulses, the British adopted a much sterner attitude toward the French in the summer and fall of 1940. Since we shall need to examine the matter in more detail in the next chapter, we shall do no more here than note the main events in the worsening relations between the two former allies. First, the British announced that they would subject France to the same blockade as the Axis. Next, they undertook to use force to capture or destroy whatever units of the French navy they could reach. Finally, they transported a Gaullist expeditionary force to Dakar, in the hope of helping him to seize the capital of French West Africa.

This situation, which reached the stage of open hostilities between the two governments, did not at all displease those elements in France that hoped to see Vichy conclude an alliance with the Axis and reenter the war. But it produced grave consternation among those in Vichy who wished to steer a cautious middle course between the two belligerents or who hoped to see the British ultimately emerge victorious. Eventually it became clear to the British that their new attitude was helping to drive Vichy into complete partnership with the Axis.

So in September and October of 1940, London began to approach Vichy with a view toward working out a *modus vivendi,* and the French responded favorably. Gradually the British thus came around to much the same cautious and reserved attitude toward Vichy as did the Germans—distrusting Vichy but not dismissing the possibility of dealing with the new regime.

No less than the Germans and the British, the French also had to reconsider their diplomatic orientation. As the issue appeared at the time to a large segment of public opinion in Britain and America, the French people had to decide whether to follow Marshal Pétain in a course of collaboration with the Axis or to give its allegiance to General de Gaulle. As the issue appeared to the French, however, the choice did not lie between "resistance" to Vichy and "collaboration" with the Axis. Rather, the choice was between a freely accepted partnership with the Axis and a reluctant cooperation.

Scarcely anyone in France in the summer of 1940 thought in terms of open opposition to Vichy and the Axis. Apparently very few persons in France heard the dramatic address, launching his appeal for resistance, which De Gaulle delivered on the London radio on June 18, or the others which he broadcast in the following week or two. Subsequently, the number who heard De Gaulle's broadcasts increased, and some rare individuals began to contemplate opposition to Vichy. Thus the earliest organizations of the "Underground" began to germinate. However, scarcely anyone in France thought the time ripe to begin an open struggle in the homeland against the government of Marshal Pétain. No one knows how many persons were already looking forward to such a resistance some time in the future. But we can be sure that the number comprised only an extremely small minority of the nation. In short, we may dismiss the "resistance" as quite without practical importance in the summer and fall of 1940, however significant it might be as testimony to the integrity and heroism of those who pioneered in the movement or as a harbinger of the broad movement that was to develop later on.

Indeed, the French had little reason to consider resistance as practicable. In the wake of their own capitulation, they believed that Britain would soon be conquered or compelled to negotiate with the Axis. As the summer passed it became apparent that, contrary to this expectation, the British would hold out. But it still seemed probable that a prolonged deadlock would ensue and that the war would ultimately end in a compromise.

In 1940, the course of resistance to the Axis, such as De Gaulle advocated, had more chance of gaining acceptance in the French colonies, where the might of the Axis did not prevail, than in the homeland. Yet scarcely any of the French colonies rallied to De Gaulle in 1940. The local authorities in the French stations in India, the French island possessions in the South Pacific, and some of the colonies of Equatorial Africa recognized the Gaullist organization in London within six months after the armistice. From the outset, however, the North African colonies of Morocco, Algeria, and Tunisia, which comprised the principal portion of the French empire, remained loyal to Vichy, as did Indo-China, Madagascar, and the French West Indies. In sum, the French gave no serious thought in 1940 to an open struggle against the new regime.

As the French viewed their situation in 1940, collaboration with the Axis seemed inescapable, on one basis or another, because there was no possible means of their challenging the power of the Axis. Some thousands might slip off to Britain or elsewhere abroad, thus avoiding a personal submission to Nazi rule. But the entire nation could not emigrate. The mass of the people would have to remain in their homes, earning their livelihood by their usual pursuits and preserving as best they could their normal routine of life.

Since it was unavoidable that the nation must live under conditions which the Nazis would dictate, there was little room for doubt but that the French would get better terms if a government of their own were to negotiate in their behalf. Otherwise, each individual would be obliged to negotiate for himself with those German authorities with whom he must have contact.

The question still remained as to the basis on which the French government should conduct its dealings with the Nazis. At this point, two main alternatives appeared. One course was for Vichy to accept the hegemony of the Nazis as decisive and definitive and accordingly to seek a partnership in the Axis, going as far as to take up arms against the British as a token of the readiness of France to assume a binding obligation. This course we may call, for the sake of a convenient name, "broad" collaboration. The other alternative, based upon the premise that German hegemony was not necessarily permanent, was for Vichy to accommodate to German might as far as was unavoidable while retaining its freedom of action as far as possible. Whenever German dominion should begin to weaken, the French could either resume a struggle against the Axis or interpose as a neutral, swinging the balance of power between the Axis and its adversaries. This course we may label "narrow" collaboration.

In general, the two alternatives involved a difference in emphasis as between economic and political cooperation with the Axis. "Narrow" collaboration implied cooperation limited, as far as possible, to economic matters, since the restoration of some kind of normality to French economic life represented the *sine qua non* of national survival. "Broad" collaboration implied both economic and political partnership.

The course of "broad" collaboration naturally appealed to those elements in France that had long admired the principles of fascism. In the view of men such as Déat and Doriot, the events of 1939–40 had only given final proof that France must recognize the superiority of fascism, accommodating both her institutions and her foreign policy to this fact. But others, too, who before the war had remained unconvinced of this argument, now came to the same conclusion. Men such as these began to think that France had made a grave mistake in the 1920s and 1930s in thinking that she could survive only by a policy of antagonism toward Germany and friendship with Britain.

Those who favored "narrow" collaboration looked upon limited economic cooperation with the Axis as an expedient to keep France alive. To this extent they accepted the idea of a partnership. But they viewed the armistice as a kind of weapon which France could and should use in a continuing struggle against German power. Therefore they proposed to yield nothing to the Axis beyond the explicit terms of the armistice, save in return for an equal or greater concession on the part of the Germans. Unlike the advocates of "broad" collaboration, they had no desire to demonstrate the good will of the French toward their masters and thus win the good graces of the Nazis. Above all else, they wished to ensure that French collaboration with the Axis should not go so far as to make an irreparable breach with the British.

Some took this position because they regarded the eventual victory of Britain, backed by the United States, as probable. Their concern was that France should not be allied to the losing side. Still others favored "narrow" collaboration without believing an Anglo-American victory probable, for the reason that they expected the war to end in a stalemate and a negotiated settlement. Against that day, they believed, France should remain free of firm commitment to either side, so as to be in a position where she could interpose as an arbiter. Thus, even though she would lack military power, she might emerge at the end of the war with some advantage for herself, won in the bargaining at the peace conference.

The choice between these alternatives also involved preferences in the issues of domestic politics. In the minds of some, these weighed more heavily than calculations of foreign policy. Thus some advocated "broad" collaboration, whether or not it seemed the cleverest move in foreign relations, simply because it would imply that France must conform to the pattern of fascist totalitarianism. On the other hand, those who kept their allegiance to the liberal traditions of the Third Republic, and also some conservatives who drew their inspiration from the monarchist tradition expounded by the *Action Française,* resisted "broad" collaboration, regardless of its merits in terms of diplomatic advantage, simply because they were opposed to the kind of reform it would necessitate in French domestic institutions.

As between the two paths, France made no clear decision in the summer and fall of 1940. Like Britain and Germany, she developed a tentative and hesitant policy. In the next chapter, we shall examine in some detail the diplomatic involvements in this period among the three governments. At this point, we need anticipate the narrative only so far as to note that, at its inception, the Vichy regime passed under the direction of men who favored the reform of French domestic institutions according to conservative principles, but not on the basis of fascism, and who likewise favored "narrow" collaboration.

Within the cabinet, however, Pierre Laval soon emerged as a partisan of "broad" collaboration, and throughout the summer and fall of 1940 he labored to commit the new regime to this course. So well did Laval pursue his maneuvers that only by a slim margin were his adversaries able to prevent the commitment of France to complete partnership with the Axis.

However portentous the issues, public opinion in France in the summer and fall of 1940 did not take a keen interest in the diplomatic crisis. As for domestic problems of immediate concern, rather than proposals for long-range reform, there also was little public discussion. This unwonted quiescence was due in part to the immense veneration which

Marshal Pétain commanded. It is hard indeed for an outsider, even with due recognition of the traumatic condition of the French nation in that desperate summer of 1940, to understand the aura which surrounded the aged marshal. Though Pétain seems to have displayed in public a kind of simple dignity, he apparently had little or no warmth or personal magnetism. At times his public addresses attained a somber eloquence of pathos, but seldom did he give evidence of keenness of mind or of the power to dramatize an issue.

Yet the French saw in him the figure of the venerable patriarch, representing the timeless persistence of the race, the stern but loving parent who would protect his children from the shapeless terrors that threatened them, the embodiment of the military glory of a happier time, whose simple presence among them awakened memories that helped expunge the humiliation of the moment, and the image of what an American might call an "elder statesman" but the French would call "the aged king."

To be sure, the magic air surrounding Pétain became less and less potent as time passed. Eventually, public opinion viewed him as a well-meaning but senile old gentleman, who was being used by evil advisers to further their nefarious purposes. But never, down to the eve of the liberation, did the nation as a whole quite lose its awe of him, and at the inception of the new regime in 1940 his prestige was so enormous as to put the government he headed out of the reach of public criticism.

Other circumstances also helped bring about this political peace. One was the relative obscurity of the men who became members of the government in the summer of 1940. With the notable exception of Laval, whom no one trusted save to the degree that Pétain lent him credit, the men who assumed positions of prominence in the new regime had not taken a conspicuous role in the politics of the Third Republic. Hence they were relatively free of the embarrassments of a known past and from the suspicions that invariably surround the professional politician in France. Then, too, the enormity of the disaster that had befallen the land produced a mood of solidarity, much as men of all parties and classes put aside their differences when forced to cope with the ravages of a flood or an earthquake.

Vichy had need of such indulgence, for it proved unable to accomplish much toward the solution of the immediate problems arising out of the armistice. It made no progress whatever, in the summer and fall of 1940, toward inducing the Germans to liberate the 1,500,000 prisoners of war, whose absence from their homes disrupted the normal life of hundreds of thousands of families in France. By the terms of the armistice, the Germans were pledged to facilitate the return to their homes of the civilian population that had fled from what became the occupied zone. Other than to permit this repatriation, however, the Germans refused to reduce the barrier which the line of demarcation established between the two halves of France.

This demarcation rent the nation into two separate communities. No one could pass from one zone to the other without a German permit. Such permits were obtainable only by persons who were obliged to travel on business of urgent public importance, or who were known to the Nazis as politically reliable, or who were able to distribute generous bribes. Nor could goods be shipped between the two zones without German permission, nor newspapers published in one zone be distributed in the other. Not for some time did the Germans allow even personal mail to be sent between the two zones. Indeed, so separate were the two communities that many Frenchmen who passed the period of the war in one zone had only a vague notion, at the end of the war, as to what had happened in the other.

The division between the two zones was made sharper because it corresponded to other differences besides the distinction in political control. The occupied zone included the metropolis of Paris as well as most of the other urban and industrial regions of France, while the unoccupied zone, though including Lyons and Marseilles, was generally rural. Since the economic distress due to the occupation bore more heavily upon the urban population than the rural, which could better provide its own food, hardship was more widespread in the occupied zone than the unoccupied. Indeed, the people of the south, having no personal relations with the Germans under the armistice and not having been overrun in the course of the invasion, at first took the problems of the armistice less seriously than their compatriots of the north, who had memories of the German invasions of 1914–18 and 1870–71 as well as their present close association with their conquerors. Occasionally the southerners spoke of the north as the "conquered zone," in contrast to the "free zone." The illusion was nurtured by Vichy, whose censors permitted no criticism of the government of Marshal Pétain but allowed considerable latitude, in the press of the southern zone, to veiled attacks upon the Germans.

Of all the immediate problems pressing upon the new regime, the one of most general and urgent importance was the reestablishment of something approaching normal economic life. The work of agriculture proceeded throughout the summer of 1940 into the harvest time, save where the fighting in the spring had laid waste the land or where the shortage of manpower made a serious hindrance. The urban economy, however, was wholly disrupted. During the previous winter and spring most industries had been converted to war production, but with the signing of the armistice production on military orders naturally came to a halt. As factories shut down, industrial workers were laid off. Because of the barrier between the two zones, as well as because of the inevitable shortages of goods due to the war, commerce was thrown into disorder. Moreover, until Vichy worked out a *modus vivendi* with Britain as well as the Axis, France was shut off from normal sources of supply abroad.

On the whole, France made a reasonably quick economic recovery. In the unoccupied zone, the peasants, who made up the bulk of the population, were reasonably sure of providing their own minimum wants and of finding a good market for whatever produce they might have to spare. The north, including the principal industrial regions, was harder hit than the south. Economic collaboration with the Axis, which ultimately provided the only possible relief for the economic problems of the north, did not become considerable until after 1940. However, the mining regions along the Belgian border were separated from the rest of the occupied zone immediately after the armistice and were placed by the Germans under the same administration as Belgium. Accordingly, the mines in this region were promptly put back into operation in the service of the Axis.

Moreover, Paris soon regained a semblance of its normal life as a pleasure resort, no longer catering to British and American tourists but, instead, to German officers and soldiers on leave. Just like their predecessors, the new *feldgrau* sightseers thronged the cafés of the Champs-Élysées and the downtown shops and restaurants, took the same innumerable snapshots of the Arc de Triomphe and the Eiffel Tower, visited theaters and historic monuments, and everywhere spent lavishly, paying outrageous prices in good francs. To be sure, these francs were ultimately provided by the French treasury, in the form of payments to the German government for the costs of the occupation. But this was not immediately apparent to the shopkeepers and waiters who collected the same kind of money from Germans as anyone else.

So the economic situation, even in the occupied zone, was less than critical in 1940. Though harder times were ahead, shortages were not yet severe, and peace, after all, was worth some price. It was some compensation for their humiliation and distress that the French could sit in their cafés and sip wine, or spend their evenings in the theater, secure in the knowledge that whatever planes might pass overhead were bound for Britain or Germany, and not to bomb their cities.

The principal divergences of opinion developed over plans for the long-range regeneration of France, which engendered a good deal more interest than affairs of more immediate importance. Indeed, France in 1940 seemed to experience a fervor for reform, more intense and widespread than even during the tumultuous period of the Popular Front in the mid-1930s. In the renewed clamor for reform, two tendencies predominated, both of which had appeared, but failed to gain satisfaction, under the Third Republic. One represented the views of the avowed partisans of fascism, the other corresponded to the conservative tradition associated with the *Action Française*. In addition, however, we can also discern under Vichy virtually every other shade of opinion apparent in the political spectrum of the previous republican regime.

The open proponents of fascism comprised the most clearly defined political faction on the scene, though by no means the most unified. The leaders among them were men who had been identified with this position before the war. Very few persons of prominence under the Third Republic who had not espoused fascist ideas before 1940 became converts to fascism after the armistice. But among the men who had been associated with the "leagues" of the Extreme Right before the war, only two attained roles of importance in the period of Vichy. These were Marcel Déat, who had broken away from the Socialist Party in the mid-1930s to found the neosocialist movement on the basis of principles of nationalist socialism and had become one of the best-known champions of "appeasement," and Jacques Doriot, the renegade Communist who had organized the Parti Populaire Français.

Colonel de la Rocque, whose Croix de Feu and its later incarnation, the Parti Social Français, had been the largest and most formidable of the prewar protofascist movements, passed into eclipse in the new era. Evidently he sought no active role in the new regime and withdrew into virtual retirement. Perhaps a dozen others who had been minor luminaries in one or another of the various "leagues," or had attracted attention as apologists for the Axis, sought now to capitalize on their record. But none of these won a role comparable to that of Déat and Doriot.

The fascists made their headquarters in Paris rather than Vichy. Both Déat and Doriot, being members of Parliament, were present in Vichy for the meeting of the National Assembly on July 10, but neither gained position or influence in the new government. Finding the atmosphere uncongenial, they soon returned to Paris, where they could draw upon the good will of the German occupation authorities. With this help, each obtained the editorship of a daily newspaper. Déat took over *L'Œuvre*, which had been one of the dailies of large circulation before the war. Doriot assumed direction of *Le Cri du Peuple*, which blossomed for the first time. These two papers became the principal organs of fascist opinion.

As the first step toward the reconstruction of France, the advocates of fascism urged an authoritarian government, and therefore they professed to welcome the personal rule of Marshal Pétain. To be sure, they had misgivings. Certainly none of the fascists regarded the aged marshal as the optimum choice for the role of a French *Fuehrer*. But in view of his immense popularity, they were in no position to voice objection. Nor were they agreed upon any other candidate of their own.

While welcoming a dictatorship, the fascists were far from hostile to representative institutions. Indeed, they were insistent that the dictatorship must be accountable to the people. As the means of reconciling an autocratic government with the will of the people, they proposed a *parti unique,* or single official political party. In their view, this was the indispensable corollary to the personal rule of the dictator. For a dictatorship could avoid passing under the manipulation of a palace guard, and could remain in close touch with the nation, only by making use of elective institutions, including a parliament. And it could do so, without succumbing to the vices characteristic of the Third Republic, only by putting an end to the ceaseless warfare among rival political parties, which inevitably engendered division within the nation. Instead, all persons desirous of an active role into politics must be organized into a single, disciplined cadre of political leadership.

Further than this, the fascists were quite unclear as to what other institutional innovations the new regime should adopt. They were generally agreed that the government must purge the nation of the alleged influence of the Jews. Doriot was as rabid as the Nazis in his anti-Semitic utterances. Déat, however, was rather more enthusiastic in his assaults upon clerical influence. On occasion, he was assailed by his adversaries as a spokesman for the Free Masons. Both Déat and Doriot professed large concern for the welfare of the urban masses. Again and again, Déat argued the need of basing the new regime upon trade unions, and Doriot likewise championed various measures to relieve the distress of the working classes. Both launched increasingly bitter criticism of Vichy as the refuge of reactionaries, devoted to the interests of the rich rather than the poor, who had no thought but to wage a rearguard action against democratic ideas the logical conclusion of which, as Déat and Doriot argued, could only be fascism.

The other of the two political movements that dominated the scene after the armistice we shall designate as "conservative." The name is inadequate, and we use it in a special sense, since surely there were other kinds of conservative opinion in France besides that to which we refer, but none better is available. Most of these "conservatives" took their inspiration from the tradition of which the *Action Française* was the best-known voice. Its spokesmen denounced the liberal and democratic heritage of the French Revolution, urged the restoration of an hereditary monarchy, proposed the reorganization of national life on the basis of corporatism, and urged a return to the public recognition of the

Church as the guardian of the mind and conscience of the nation. To be sure, the argument in favor of hereditary monarchy was more symbolic than practical. Probably very few who upheld this position had a serious wish to see a king reestablished on the throne. Certainly even those who harbored such a hope recognized that the moment was inopportune, since a king who regained the throne in that time of national humiliation would begin his reign under the poorest imaginable auspices.

The common denominator among the "conservatives" was their repugnance for the parliamentary system as this had developed under the Third Republic. Their distaste for Parliament was due in part to their fear of the proletarian parties of the Left, which turned the institution of Parliament to their own uses. Without question, as Déat and Doriot charged, the "conservatives" were more concerned for the interests of the rich than of the poor. But their antagonism toward Parliament was perhaps due more to their hatred of the professional politician, who made Parliament the source of his livelihood, than to their distrust of the masses. In the view of the "conservatives," the man who made a career of politics was not much different from a man who made his living by blackmail. At bottom, his business came down to gaining the suffrages of the common people through systematic demagogy, then selling the power thus gained solely for his own corrupt advantage.

Like the fascists, the "conservatives" believed that the government should have a strong man at the helm. But they envisioned him as a kind of chairman of the board, using the prestige of his position to bring about agreement among the diverse corporate interests of the nation. They did not imagine him as the sole source of national inspiration. Nor did they see need for a *parti unique* which would serve to draw along the mass of the nation in his path. Indeed, the "conservatives" distrusted the *parti unique* as a haven for the professional politicians, whom they hoped to eliminate from the life of the nation.

The "conservatives" shared two other guiding ideas. One was devotion to the Church, which had proved itself the foe of those principles of liberal individualism which were the ideological basis of the Third Republic. The other was anti-Semitism. Like the fascists, the "conservatives" harbored a principled opposition to the Jews. Indeed, "conservatives" of this sort had proclaimed the ideas of anti-Semitism since before the time of the Dreyfus affair, long before fascism was thought of.

However, the "conservatives" expounded a more moderate kind of anti-Semitism than the fascists. They did not rest their argument, as did the Nazis, upon pseudo-scientific doctrines of race. They defined the Jews as a cultural community rather than a people whose characteristics represented an ethnic inheritance. They looked upon the Jews as a peculiar people, whose position within the nation was such as to make them especially quick to espouse the philosophy of individualism. The principal reason for this, in the view of the "conservatives," was that under a liberal regime, which recognizes no distinction among citizens, the Jews would be secure against discrimination. Accordingly, the "conservatives" were desirous of excluding Jews from positions of political and intellectual leadership. Otherwise, the "conservatives" believed, the Jews would make use of their influence in support of liberalism. But the "conservatives" did not go so far as to urge the complete extirpation of the Jews.

In contrast to the fascists, the "conservatives" had little eagerness for collaboration with the Axis. For more than a generation, men of this sort had viewed the Germans as the hereditary enemy, and in the aftermath of the First World War they had urged the "hard" policy toward Germany. To be sure, many "conservatives" had toned down their hatred of the Germans during the 1930s and, like the proponents of fascism, had endorsed the policy of "appeasement." But they had done so, not primarily because of ideological sympathy with Nazism, but because of their hostility toward the Popular Front, which represented the triumph of the liberal and Marxian parties in France. Now that France was subject to German might, the "conservatives" proved reluctant to remodel France in the German image.

The "conservatives" and the fascists remained separate factions and, under Vichy, became bitterly hostile to one another. The divergence between their views had not been apparent in the 1930s, when the disciples of the *Action Française* had worked hand in hand with such men as Déat and Doriot to break up the Popular Front. Nor was the distinction between them immediately obvious at the inception of the Vichy regime. Both the "conservatives" and the fascists bespoke an autocratic government under the leadership of Marshal Pétain, and a rupture with the parliamentary system of the Third Republic. Both factions shared the same detestation of Jews, liberals, and Marxians, whom they lumped together as the beneficiaries of the republican regime.

Yet the alliance between the two factions in the 1930s represented a cooperation in tactics, based upon their common desire to subvert the Third Republic, rather than an identity of views to a constructive purpose. Once the Third Republic disappeared, they no longer shared the same antagonism that previously had held them together. As they approached the new task of reconstruction, they soon discovered that their vague agreement as to the broad outline of the new regime was less important than the sharp cleavages between them as to the sources of their inspiration.

Within a matter of weeks after the inception of the Vichy regime, Déat and Doriot perceived that the "conservatives" were gaining the upper hand in the new government and were pursuing quite another purpose than the establishment of fascist totalitarianism. Thereupon, as we have noted, Déat and Doriot withdrew to Paris. Under the aegis of the German occupation, they began a press campaign directed against their "conservative" adversaries, who remained entrenched in Vichy. Soon the antagonism became so sharp that no one who assumed an active role in politics could avoid choosing between the two camps, thereby incurring the enmity of the other. Eventually the struggle became as bitter and envenomed as any that had occurred among rival parties under the execrated Third Republic.

Indeed, this struggle gave the appearance, which was not wholly illusory, of perpetuating under Vichy the same battle between Right and Left that had gone on under the previous regime. Thus, in problems involving social and economic issues, the "conservatives" emerged as champions of the élite, while the fascists proclaimed themselves the defenders of the masses. Likewise, the "conservatives" made a political principle of their devotion to the Church, whereas the fascists became heirs to republican anticlericalism. And in foreign affairs, the "conservatives" showed, in their preference for "narrow" collaboration, the predilection of the Right for what we have designated, in another context, as the "hard" policy toward Germany. On the other hand, the fascists, in their espousal of "broad" collaboration, revealed the same orientation of the Left which we have earlier identified with the "soft" policy.

Though the "conservatives" and the fascists held the foreground, the republicans of the previous regime did not wholly drop out of view. To be sure, men of the Extreme Left had little hope of influence in the new era. The Communists, whose organizations had been dissolved in the fall of 1939, remained an underground movement. For a time, they may have entertained some hope of rehabilitation, but they never played any significant role within the new regime. Likewise, the left wing of the Socialist Party, which had accepted the leadership of Léon Blum and had opposed "appeasement" in the late 1930s, found no accommodation with Vichy. However, some of those identified with the right wing of the Socialist Party, who had never disavowed "appeasement," made their peace with the new order, either in Vichy or in Paris.

So did many of those who had held positions in the republican parties of the Center and the Right. Very few men of prominence in the political life of the Third Republic chose to leave France and attach themselves to the Gaullist movement in London. Some dropped into retirement, whether from considerations of discretion or of high principle. But others did not dissemble their good will toward the new regime.

This is scarcely remarkable, since the new regime had been created by the vote of the republican members of Parliament, sitting as a National Assembly, and not by the "conservatives" or the fascists. Nor had the Parliament of the Third Republic quite disappeared. It had been adjourned indefinitely, but its members continued to hold their positions and to draw their salaries. And though the government gave little sign of summoning Parliament into session again, the presence of Pierre Laval within the cabinet seemed to give some assurance that the old order was not quite gone.

Those republican politicians who gave their allegiance to Vichy looked upon the dictatorship of Marshal Pétain as a temporary expedient. Ultimately, they hoped, the dictatorship would give way to a restoration of parliamentary government, modified in some details. In future, presumably, the executive would have more power than in the past, so that the former omnipotence of Parliament would be curbed. But such a reform would mean no more than what some republican politicians, such as Poincaré, had long urged as a necessary improvement of the liberal regime. It would only bring the practice of representative government in France a little closer to the pattern prevailing in Britain and the United States, where the head of the government has sufficient power to exercise an effective leadership, though far less than the power of a dictator.

Save the wan hope that Parliament would have some place in the new regime, the republicans had little or no program to propose. Naturally they did not look with favor upon the fascist scheme for a *parti unique*. On the other hand, they were not wholly averse to the principles of corporatism which the "conservatives" propounded. Indeed, the Third Republic had in practice moved a considerable distance in the direction of corporatism, even though the theorists of the republican regime had been reluctant to abandon the doctrines of individualism. However, those who remained loyal to republican liberalism had no common ground with the "conservatives" in the campaign of the latter to establish closer relations between Church and state, nor with either the "conservatives" or their fascist adversaries in the crusade against the Jews, which ran counter to the principles of 1789. Yet, whether or not the republican politicians of the previous regime wished to gain place in the new order, they always remained outsiders, scorned and distrusted in both Vichy and Paris. As time passed, their desire as well as their hope of assuming a role of importance in the new regime diminished.

In principle, the decision as to which of these various tendencies would prevail in the redesigning of French institutions should have been simple, since the choice rested with Marshal Pétain alone. Not only did he exercise the whole governing power, by virtue of the constitutional laws of July 10–11, but no other person commanded sufficient public esteem to challenge his leadership.

However, Pétain was far from decisive in his attitude toward the problem of national reconstruction, whether because he had a temperamental reluctance to command, which seems quite possible, or be-

cause the erosion of advanced age had worn away his firmness of character. By prior experience, moreover, he was not well fitted for the task
of constitution making. Though known as a scholar in his profession,
he had no broader intellectual horizon than the army. In a land where
it is by no means extraordinary for a man to be at once a professor and
a politician, or a policeman and a dramatist, or an engineer and a
sociologist, Pétain was remarkable for showing no sign of interest in
the arts, literature, history, or any of the other provinces of culture.

Nor had he gained a close pragmatic knowledge of the problems of
government, since his sole excursion into practical politics before 1940
was his short tenure as Minister of War in 1934. He was, to be sure, not
without acquaintance with ideas in the realm of politics. As an army
officer, he had spent his life in an environment where criticism of
republican liberalism was widespread. It is apparent that he nursed a
distrust of men who made their living in Parliament. But it is not evident that he had a principled opposition to republicanism, derived
from a body of ideas which we may dignify as a political theory. In
short, Pétain had neither deep principles nor deep prejudices to guide
him in his task of redesigning the institutions of French life.

Not only was he ill-qualified, but at bottom he was little interested
in his task. Assuming that we could reduce to a single impulse the
complex motives that moved Pétain in that vexed period of his career,
we would probably have to say that he was impelled primarily by a
kind of vanity. He did not assume his role as dictator because he was
determined to institute a particular program of reform but because he
was convinced that he had been singled out by Providence to become a
martyr for the fatherland.

If we interpret his thought in a generous sense, we may say that he
recognized that the government of France must now pursue a course
which would inevitably prove painful and humiliating, and he believed
that he was the only man with sufficient prestige to head the government and thus persuade the nation to give it its trust. As he put it, risking his own reputation and sacrificing the repose of his old age to the
call of duty, he "made to France the gift of his person."

If we interpret the motive less generously, we may believe that he
coveted a role of prominence above all else. Therefore he proved will-

ing to compound the national humiliation by offering to the Germans, as their agent in the subjugation of France, the person of the one living man whom the French revered as the embodiment of their military glory. Thus he snatched from his people their sole vestige of pride, merely to indulge his own ego. Under either interpretation, we must acknowledge that he did not assume his role of leadership primarily because he wished to determine the new bases of French institutions.

In practice, the decision as to what course the new regime was to adopt, in domestic politics as well as foreign relations, depended upon the pressures that bore upon Pétain. In part, these pressures arose out of the relations of France with Britain, and ultimately the United States, on one side, and the Axis on the other. Insofar as circumstances constrained France toward "broad" collaboration with the Axis, this strengthened the hand of the fascists. Insofar as the course of the war made "broad" collaboration seem a poor gamble, this strengthened the hand of the "conservatives," who consistently favored "narrow" collaboration, and improved the stock of those few republicans who had not broken with Vichy. In part, the pressure upon Pétain represented the influence of a small coterie of intimates and advisers surrounding the marshal.

In this inner circle, no republican politician save Laval ever gained admittance. Nor did Pétain ever admit the avowed partisans of fascism into his confidence. Apparently he had no acquaintance with either Déat or Doriot before the war, nor did he establish a personal association with them after he took power. He may have had some relations with the *Cagoulards* before the war, though the evidence of this is more obscure than the allegations. Even so, the *Cagoulards* remained closer in spirit to the *Action Française* than the new-model movements extolling German and Italian totalitarianism. What influence the fascists won in Vichy they owed either to the force of circumstances, when the course of the war made "narrow" collaboration difficult, or to the intercession of Laval, who frequently made use of the fascists to further his own purposes.

From the outset, it was the "conservatives" who had the ear of Pétain. Possibly this was due to his predilection for their ideas. More likely, it was due to the circumstances that placed men of "conservative" convictions close to him. Several of these "conservatives" Pétain appointed to positions in his original cabinet for the simple reason that they had been members of the previous Reynaud government and had favored the armistice, and not necessarily for the reason that he subscribed to their views on other issues. Thus he appointed General Weygand, who, as we have seen, promptly submitted to him a memorandum outlining a program of domestic reform in accordance with "conservative" notions, summed up in the slogan, *Famille, Travail, Patrie, Dieu.* From the Reynaud cabinet, likewise, Pétain inherited Paul Baudouin, who became Minister of Foreign Affairs, and Yves Bouthillier, who remained Minister of Finance, and both of these were men of "conservative" and Catholic views. Another in the clique was Dr. Ménétrel, Pétain's personal physician and a friend of long standing. Dr. Ménétrel made use of his daily visits to Pétain to discuss politics as well as health and thus exerted an influence in the direction of a "conservative" orientation.

Doubtless at the suggestion of these associates, Pétain also drew into his service, as a personal brain trust, several other men of the same opinions. Notable among them were Lucien Romier, who had made his name as an editor of *Le Figaro,* the newspaper favored by the fashionable upper classes of Paris; Henri Massis and Thierry Maulnier, both of whom were contributors to the *Action Française;* and Henri du Moulin de la Barthète, who had been on Pétain's staff when the marshal was serving as ambassador to Franco's government in Spain. These, and perhaps a dozen others sharing much the same views, became a palace guard, to which Pétain became a willing captive. Seldom appearing in public, they wielded their influence wholly behind the scenes, insinuating their ideas into the speeches they wrote for Pétain or the decrees they drafted for his signature, screening the visitors who came to see him, and maneuvering the appointment of their henchmen to key positions in the administration. Thus gaining an unobtrusive ascendancy over the aged marshal at the inception of his rule, they clung tenaciously to their position, down nearly to the end of the regime.

From the start, Laval emerged as the principal adversary of this "conservative" clique. The open proponents of fascism, such as Déat and Doriot, could inveigh in the Paris press against the machinations of the "reactionaries" surrounding Pétain and misleading him, but they had no means of breaking through the palace guard to win Pétain over to their views. As Vice-Premier, however, Laval had free access to Pétain, and because of his services in inducing Parliament to abdicate, he had a claim upon the marshal which he did not neglect to exploit.

Why Laval became a foe of the "conservatives," we cannot say simply, or with assurance. Certainly they never regarded him as one of them, and doubtless Laval reciprocated their dislike for the reason that the "conservative" côterie represented an obstacle to his personal ambition for power. Probably he fell out with them also because he did not share their views on long-range domestic reform. So far as we can perceive, in what remains an obscure problem, Laval was not a firm partisan of fascist totalitarianism, although he probably leaned in that direction. But assuredly he was not, and never dreamed of becoming, a disciple of the *Action Française*.

At bottom, Laval apparently had little interest in plans for redesigning France, whether on the basis of "conservatism," or fascism, or some improved version of the Third Republic, because the issue was of no immediate importance. Laval was not the man to take sides in a debate over ideas without practical significance at the moment. Hence he opposed the "conservatives," it seems most likely, primarily because they favored only "narrow" collaboration, whereas he regarded the Nazi hegemony as definitive, and therefore close partnership with the Axis as the only realistic course open to France.

In any event, within a matter of weeks after the inception of the new regime, Laval was locked in struggle with the "conservative" clique that surrounded Pétain. This struggle went on throughout the summer and fall of 1940, reaching a climax in December.

In the history of Vichy, the six months between July and December of 1940 thus constitute a crucial period. It was in this interval that the diverse problems which we have enumerated became apparent and that the decisions were made which were to define the orientation of the new regime. It was likewise in this interval that the strange new atmosphere of resolute leadership and willing obedience, which had marked the beginning of the new regime, gave way to the more familiar world of factions working at cross-purposes, while the government sought in vain to steer a steady course.

The interval includes two separate though interrelated series of occurrences. One was the struggle for power between Laval and the "conservative" côterie in Vichy. This struggle involved the question as to what approach the new regime would take to its domestic and diplomatic problems. The second was the inauguration of a program of institutional innovations, soon given the name of the National Revolution, which was the substance of the "conservative" attempt to redesign the bases of French national life. Not all the measures which made up this program were instituted before the end of 1941, nor was the program as a whole ever brought to completion. Nevertheless, the broad outline of the plan became evident within this period. In the next two chapters, we shall first consider in more detail the course of the struggle for power in this initial phase of the new regime; then we shall examine the measures of reform which constituted the National Revolution.

VIII

SIX MONTHS OF CRISIS

THE FIRST SIX MONTHS of the Vichy regime comprised its most critical period, for the reason that this was the time when the new government had to make the decisions which determined its character. As we have noted in the previous chapter, the circumstances of its origin were not such as to give the new regime a precise orientation. Gradually, in the course of the summer and fall of 1940, this ambivalence lessened, and the new regime began to take on a distinctive pattern. In its initial period, Vichy came to signify, so far as concerns the reform of institutions, an authoritarian government resting on a basis of corporatism and a moral regeneration emphasizing a larger public recognition of the importance of the family and religion. So far as concerns diplomacy, the new regime undertook to limit the inevitable collaboration with the Axis to those measures of economic cooperation which were required in order to sustain national life, while striving at the same time to avoid a complete break with Britain and the United States.

The Vichy regime was to retain this character. Eventually, from the spring of 1942 onwards, and especially after January, 1944, the government was to move a considerable distance in the direction of "broad" collaboration, and the partisans of fascism were to gain increasing influence. However, the fascists were to find it impossible to revise either domestic or diplomatic policy wholly according to their designs.

Moreover, we can readily recognize this ultimate movement toward fascism and "broad" collaboration as due to the mounting Axis pressure, whereas the initial commitment of Vichy to a "conservative" program of reform and "narrow" collaboration represented a more spontaneous choice. Hence we may reasonably regard the policies which Vichy adopted in the summer and fall of 1940 as representing the inner impulse of the men who guided the new regime, and the modifications of these policies after 1942 as the consequence of external pressure.

The initial problem confronting the government upon its arrival in Vichy was to improvise the facilities of a capital in the little resort town it had chosen as its provisional headquarters. Even if the French administration had been less prone to the proliferation of personnel and paper work, it could not expect to perform its functions without a staff of considerable size, an abundance of office space, and voluminous files of documents. For this reason, among others, the government had selected Vichy for its seat, since the numerous hotels there afforded some surplus of accommodations.

To be sure, no one anticipated that the government would long remain in Vichy. Under the terms of the armistice, the Germans had agreed to permit the return of the government to Paris as soon as feasible. Once it became evident, however, that the war was not to come to a speedy termination, the Germans became reluctant to let the French government return to Paris, because their hold upon the capital gave them valuable political leverage. Presently Vichy also became dubious of the advantage of moving back to Paris, for the reason that Pétain and the "conservatives" who surrounded him were unwilling to place themselves under the obvious tutelage of the Nazis. As it turned out, therefore, Vichy remained the "provisional" headquarters of the government for four years.

The impromptu capital afforded a marked contrast to the spacious magnificence and centuries-old grandeur of Paris. Situated on the banks of the Allier, a little stream flowing through the plains of central France to join the Loire, the town of Vichy normally had a population in winter of about 25,000, which rose each summer, with the influx of visitors in June, to about 75,000. The center of the town is a shaded park, provided in summer with benches, kiosks selling periodicals and refreshments, and glass-enclosed pavilions where the warm mineral waters bubble up from the springs which are the town's renown. There the summer visitors repair to obtain carefully measured rations of the water, according to prescription, for the cure of disorders of the liver and of other maladies. At one end of the park is a large casino, where gaming tables and a theater provide entertainment. On the streets bordering the park are large hotels and fashionable shops, and elsewhere in the town, hotels of lesser name, restaurants, cafés, theaters, stores vending curios and summer wear, clinics, and bathing establishments for those whose physicians recommend immersion in the therapeutic waters.

In July, 1940, when the government arrived in Vichy, a complement of summer visitors was already there. Many of these stayed on, and some even returned the next summer. However, the government took over the larger hotels for office space, and the horde of administrative personnel, hangers-on, and place seekers, which eventually swelled the population of the town to about 150,000, gradually squeezed out those who sought only their own physical recovery and mild diversion.

Marshal Pétain established his own headquarters in the Hôtel du Parc, the principal hotel of the town, and this became the hub of the government. Pétain had his office and a modest apartment on the fourth floor and commonly took his meals in the public dining room. Laval ensconced himself on the third floor. Unlike Pétain, however, he did not live in Vichy. Each night, he returned by automobile to nearby Chateldon, where he had his home. The Hôtel des Ambassadeurs, appropriately enough, was given over to the diplomatic corps. Other hotels were ascribed to the various ministries, save the Ministry of the Interior, which took over the Casino. Soon enough, the town had all the familiar attributes of a wartime capital, including a housing shortage, a shameless black market, a ceaseless buzz of rumor, and a sea of personal intrigue.

In the unoccupied zone, something approaching a normal pattern of life soon reappeared. The German armies had not overrun this region in the course of their invasion, nor had the armistice given them the right to station troops there. Not until the close of 1942 did the populace in the unoccupied zone have occasion to see a German soldier. Vichy readily reestablished contact with the prefects, *maires,* and other local authorities, and public institutions, such as schools, universities, and courts soon resumed operation. Lyons, which was always a thriving center of business and finance, became the economic hub of the unoccupied zone, and it also became the publishing headquarters of those newspapers, such as *Le Figaro* and the *Action Française,* which circulated throughout the zone.

In the summer and fall of 1940, however, Vichy had very little contact with the occupied zone. Not only did the Germans refuse permits to private persons who wished to visit the occupied zone on personal business, but they also proved extremely reluctant to allow even high officials of the Vichy regime to go to Paris to supervise the work of their subordinates in the occupied zone. Some ministries which were concerned with technical services, such as the administration of the railroads, were permitted access to their Paris headquarters. But the ministries of Justice and of the Interior, which were responsible for the enforcement of the decrees and laws of the central government, had scarcely any opportunity to deal with local authorities in the occupied zone, who were obliged to develop an unprecedented degree of initiative and independence.

Yet the Germans made little attempt to interfere with the routine of administration in the occupied zone. The German general in charge of the occupation established his headquarters in Paris, where his staff exercised a close censorship over the press and the radio. Decrees of the Vichy government were submitted to his office for approval before their promulgation in the occupied zone, but ordinarily this approval was given. From time to time, German regulations affecting the civilian population were published in a bilingual gazette. These decrees had the force of law, overriding the ordinances of Vichy or prior French legislation. In the main, however, the Germans permitted the local French authorities to handle the routine of administration at their own discretion, according to established French practices.

Moreover, the German commanders in the occupied zone saw to it that their troops behaved with scrupulous rectitude in their relations with the civilian population. Until nearly the eve of the liberation, indeed, the German occupation in France was surprisingly free of instances of illegal arrests and seizures by the military authorities, unauthorized pillage and rape by the soldiery, and street brawls between the troops and the populace, such as are common occurrences in a situation of military occupation.

On the whole, then, the new regime began its work under favorable auspices. Its moral hold upon the nation seemed secure. For their part, the Germans had granted an armistice on terms that, though onerous, were far from unbearable and well short of dishonorable. Even the British had made clear their acquiescence in the armistice, provided that the French keep their navy out of the hands of the Axis.

But the halcyon did not last long. Both the Germans and the British soon began to show an increasing degree of firmness. Within two months after the signature of the armistice, France found herself shut off from the worlds on either side, threatened with economic strangulation, and devoid of friends to whom she might appeal for support. The British revised their attitude because of their fear that the French would soon reenter the war in alliance with the Axis. The Germans, on the other hand, became more severe because of a feeling on their part that they were not reaping sufficient advantage from their military victory. As the summer wore on and their hopes of a prompt settlement with the British began to dim, the Germans began to apply pressure to induce Vichy to grant them advantages not stipulated in the provisions of the armistice.

As it happened, the pressure of both the British and the Germans worked in the same sense. For the British, by adopting a sterner attitude toward France, unwittingly played into the hands of those elements in France that were urging closer ties with the Axis, while the Nazis were striving to bring about such a partnership with deliberate purpose.

This diplomatic pressure produced a sharp division within the French cabinet, with Paul Baudouin and Pierre Laval emerging as the principal adversaries. Though Baudouin had been one of the advocates of the armistice, he was not a partisan of "broad" collaboration. He hoped to preserve a position of neutrality for France. Consequently he labored to avoid a complete rupture with the British and, at the same time, to avoid a complete partnership with the Germans and the Italians. In this endeavor, he gained support within the cabinet from Bouthillier, the Minister of Finance, and from General Weygand. Laval, on the other hand, did not disguise his wish to see France assume the role of a satellite to the Axis. He therefore was anxious to worsen the antagonism between Vichy and London. Within the cabinet, he won support from Admiral Darlan, who, though not at this time a partisan of the Axis, became violently enraged at the British, as we shall see, when they made an attack upon the French navy.

The issue between Baudouin and Laval was not settled by a decision of the cabinet, measuring the relative strength of the factions which each rallied to his support. Nor was it settled by the fiat of Pétain. Rather, Baudouin, and Laval each undertook maneuvers and intrigues outside the cabinet, with the hope of forcing a decision. Thus Baudouin sought to negotiate with the British in order to induce them to ease their pressure, which was driving Vichy into the arms of the Axis. Meantime Laval sought to incite the Germans to increase their pressure, in order thereby to crush his adversaries in the cabinet.

It was the British who first began to show a new firmness toward the French. Several circumstances contributed to their change of attitude. One was the rupture of top-level diplomatic communications between the two governments, as a consequence of which London lost touch with those elements in Vichy that sought to maintain a link with Britain and avert "broad" collaboration with the Axis. The breakdown of communications was in part fortuitous. Sir Ronald Campbell, the British ambassador to France, had left Bordeaux, where the Pétain government was then sitting, on June 23, though London did not give him specific orders to do so, on the basis of his general directive not to let himself be taken prisoner by the Germans. On the same day, the French ambassador in London resigned his position, because of his opposition to the decision of his government to seek an armistice. Thus the two governments ceased to have the normal facilities for an exchange of views, although neither had decided, up to that time, to sever relations with the other.

Another factor in the rift between the former allies was doubtless the influence of General de Gaulle, who, as we have observed, had every reason, and ample opportunity, to persuade British political leaders that the new Pétain regime was committed to a partnership with the Axis. Even without such prompting, the British had good reason to fear that the French navy might yet pass under the control of their enemies. For it was quite possible that the Germans would offer Vichy a prompt peace treaty, on favorable terms, in return for the use of the French fleet. Or the Germans might seize the fleet by force. Finally, the British had reason for alarm upon the entrance of Pierre Laval into the cabinet on June 24, since Laval's readiness to cooperate with the Axis was well known.

In view of this situation, the British government determined to take action to forestall the seizure or surrender of the French navy. At the time of the armistice, we have noted, the larger French warships had been dispersed, some of them at anchor in English ports, some stationed with the British squadron at Alexandria, and others in various ports of the French colonies in Africa. Before concluding the armistice, the French had ordered the ships then at their naval bases on the Atlantic coast, among which were the uncompleted battleships "Jean Bart" and "Richelieu," to make for colonial ports in order to avoid capture by the German armies sweeping down the western seaboard of France. Hence only a small force, comprising three cruisers and some lesser vessels, which were stationed at Toulon, remained in the French homeland.

On July 3, the British launched their attack, designated as "Operation Catapult," in three separate theaters at the same time. In England, an overwhelming force seized the French vessels, including two battleships and four cruisers, which had been held since the armistice in the ports of Plymouth and Portsmouth. Simultaneously the British naval commander at Alexandria delivered a message to the admiral in command of the French units which lay at anchor there, offering him the choice of ordering his men and ships into the service of the British navy or proceeding under British escort to ports in England or the western hemisphere, to be interned for the remainder of the war. The French admiral refused either alternative. But, realizing that the British would attack and sink his ships if he attempted to leave Alexandria, he made no move, and the British chose not to press the issue. An agreement was worked out which provided, for all practical purposes, that the French vessels be interned at Alexandria.

Meantime, under the same plan of concerted action, a British task force arrived at Mers El-Kébir, the naval base near Oran, in French Morocco, which harbored the two new battle cruisers "Dunkerque" and "Strasbourg" as well as a number of other warships. The British commander delivered the same proposal that was made to the admiral commanding the French units at Alexandria. As at Alexandria, the French response was negative. Dreading the necessity of firing on their erstwhile comrades, the British continued to negotiate throughout the day, July 3, but the French proved adamant. As night approached, the British opened fire, and the French replied. A vigorous action ensued, in the course of which two French cruisers were sunk, the "Dunkerque" disabled, and about 1,200 French sailors killed. Thereupon the British withdrew. Under cover of darkness, the "Strasbourg" escaped and raced to Toulon. Meantime a number of cruisers that had been stationed at Algiers, hearing the news of this attack, likewise took refuge in Toulon.

Shortly the British struck again. On July 5, they launched an air attack upon the disabled "Dunkerque," which had run aground during the action at Mers El-Kébir on the 3d, and caused additional French casualties to the number of about two hundred. Then, on July 7, a task force appeared at Dakar, the port in French West Africa where the uncompleted battleship "Richelieu" had taken refuge after escaping from its base in France. A message was delivered to the French, requiring them to order their vessels to a British port, to be interned, or to the French West Indies, to be disarmed, or else to scuttle them at Dakar. Once more, the French refused. Thereupon, early in the morning of the 8th, a British torpedo boat dashed into the harbor and launched a torpedo which struck the "Richelieu" in her stern, damaging the propellers and rendering her incapable of moving. Then, as the French opened fire in answer, the British withdrew.

In the outcome of their operation, the British thus gained a measure of success. Yet a considerable portion of the French navy remained out of their grasp, and either actually or potentially serviceable. This included the unfinished battleship "Jean Bart," which had taken refuge at Casablanca; the "Richelieu," which, though immobile, remained a serious concern; the "Dunkerque," which it proved possible to repair; the "Strasbourg," which had escaped from Mers El-Kébir to Toulon; and some other cruisers, which also put in to Toulon.

Offsetting the advantage which the British had won was the widespread resentment which their attack produced among the French. This reaction was due in part to indignation at the loss of lives which the French suffered at Mers El-Kébir—the more outrageous, in the French view, because the bloodshed was the work of erstwhile allies. In part, the French reaction was doubtless due to a sense of humiliation. For the British attack exposed the impotence of the French navy, which so far had escaped defeat, and thus struck another blow at French pride in their armed services.

Within the French government, the news of "Operation Catapult" produced a sharp crisis. Admiral Darlan, then the Minister of Marine, who up to that point had been generally friendly to the British and had personally given a promise to Churchill that he would not permit his fleet to pass under Axis control, was beside himself with anger. This one incident transformed him from a valuable friend into a dangerous foe. Laval, who scarcely concealed his wish to see France assume a partnership with the Axis, naturally welcomed news of this crisis and did his best to exacerbate the ill will it aroused. On the other hand, Baudouin and Bouthillier, though no less indignant than the others, labored to prevent the crisis from leading to open warfare between the two countries.

Darlan gave a report of the British attack at a meeting of the cabinet on the afternoon of July 3. Thereupon he asked approval of an order which he had drafted, instructing the "Strasbourg" and a flotilla of cruisers to search out and retaliate upon the British squadron in the western Mediterranean. Baudouin, realizing that this would mean war, succeeded in persuading Pétain to withhold his approval. But, as a compromise, he agreed to sever formal diplomatic relations with London. Two days later, on the 6th, Admiral Darlan reported to the cabinet that he had approached the Italian Ministry of Marine with a proposal for a raid by combined units of the French and Italian navies upon the British base at Alexandria, for the purpose of freeing the French warships held captive there by the British. With the support of Weygand, Baudouin killed this project, too. But on the 8th, Darlan came up with still another scheme, this time involving a French naval bombardment of Gibraltar. Pétain gave his approval in principle, and July 14 was chosen as the tentative date for the operation. But subsequently the date was deferred to the 16th, then postponed indefinitely. As it turned out, then, the French made no immediate response, save the gesture of severing relations with London.

Meantime the Germans sought to take advantage of the Anglo-French strife by drawing the French into their orbit. Immediately after the naval action at Mers El-Kébir, in which the French showed their readiness to fire upon their former allies if provoked, the Germans began to give signs of a more favorable attitude toward Vichy. On July 8, they granted the French permission to resume trade with their North African colonies. Next, they accorded Vichy permission to maintain its colonial army in North Africa at the level of 120,000 men. Then, on July 15, they proposed that the French allow them the right to maintain eight air bases in North Africa, with the use of the Tunis-Rabat railroad, and the right to take over some twenty weather-stations in the French African colonies.

This proposal produced consternation among those in the cabinet who favored only "narrow" collaboration. If Vichy were to agree, they feared, this would probably lead to the reentrance of France into the war on the side of Germany and Italy. But if Vichy were to refuse, no one could predict what the Germans might do in retaliation. Despite the risk, the cabinet decided on July 17 to make a negative response, pointing out that the German proposal had no basis in the provisions of the armistice. An answer in this sense was delivered on the 18th to the German representatives at Wiesbaden.

Thereupon Laval, who evidently now came to the conclusion that he could not presently induce the cabinet to approve his position, determined to take action on his own. On July 19 he left Vichy for Paris, where he remained three days. In the course of this visit, he undertook to establish personal relations with the Germans, in order to advance his scheme for "broad" collaboration.

It was by no means easy for him to do so. In the first place, there was no regular means of communication with the German government, since diplomatic relations had not been restored by the armistice. In the second place, Laval had little or no acquaintance with men of prominence in the Nazi regime. For their part, the Nazis generally had an unfavorable opinion of him. To be sure, he had gained some name before the war as one of the partisans of "appeasement," inasmuch as he had shown his willingness to allow Mussolini virtually a free hand in Ethiopia. However, Laval had been much better known for his endeavors to preserve friendship with Italy than for pro-German utterances. On occasion, he had made talk of a "Latin bloc," in which France and Italy were to join together to offset the growing power of Germany. Moreover, he had made gestures toward a Franco-Soviet rapprochement and had given evidence of his desire to maintain the diplomatic alignment of France with Britain and the United States. In view of the ambivalence in his record, as well as his notorious reputation as one of the slipperiest politicians in the French Parliament, the Germans were inclined to regard him as untrustworthy. Indeed, Hitler was unequivocal in his attitude, dismissing Laval as merely "a dirty democratic politician."

As the go-between in his campaign to gain the good graces of the Nazis, Laval sought to make use of Otto Abetz, who was more than willing to serve in this role. As we have seen, Abetz was one of the numerous German intellectuals who, in the period of the Weimar Republic, had become enamored of France as the heart of European culture, and he had remained a Francophile even after becoming a Nazi. He had gained the attention of Ribbentrop, whose protégé he soon became. In the aftermath of the Munich settlement, he had been appointed German ambassador to Paris, where he developed a wide circle of acquaintance among pro-Nazi French intellectuals. Because of his propagandistic activities, which exceeded the usual role of an ambassador, the French government had requested his recall in June, 1939. Upon the outbreak of the war three months later, Abetz had seen the prospects of his career in the Foreign Office suffer a sharp reverse, since there now seemed to be little need for a German Francophile.

No sooner had the Germans overrun France, however, than Ribbentrop ordered Abetz to return to Paris as his personal representative. The choice was reasonable enough, in view of Abetz's connections with pro-Nazi elements in the French capital. But Ribbentrop had a personal interest in sending Abetz back to Paris, for he was anxious not to permit the military to monopolize relations with conquered France, to the exclusion of the Foreign Office. Naturally, Abetz had no less desire to accomplish this, since only by so doing could he reestablish his career on a secure footing.

Laval had no acquaintance with Abetz before making his visit to Paris on July 19. The two were brought together through the efforts of Fernand de Brinon and Jean Luchaire. Both of these, destined for roles of some importance under the Nazi occupation, were old friends of Abetz. Brinon had risen to some prominence in the 1920s as editor of the *Journal des Débats,* then of *L'Information.* As a newspaperman, he had made numerous visits to Germany in the period of the Weimar Republic, where he had established connections with influential persons in business and politics, including Stinnes, Thyssen, Rathenau, Stresemann, and Brüning. He had remained sympathetic to Germany after the rise of the Nazis. In February, 1933, he had scored a coup by gaining an interview with Hitler, which was the first the Fuehrer gave to a French journalist. Promptly Brinon reported that Hitler meant the French no harm. Subsequently he became active in the Comité France-Allemagne, an association of various pro-German elements in French business and politics, the counterpart in Paris of a similar committee in Berlin in which Abetz was a leading personage.

Luchaire, also a journalist but much younger than Brinon—being, like Abetz, still in his thirties—had served on the staff of various Paris newspapers. In 1927 he had founded a magazine, *Notre Temps,* in which he espoused the cause of Franco-German reconciliation. Briand, who, as Foreign Minister at that time, was developing such a policy, gave him a subsidy from the secret funds of the Foreign Office. In this period, Luchaire came to know Abetz, who was then making his living in Paris as a teacher of art, and the two worked together in organizing a Congrès de Jeunesse Franco-Allemand in 1930–32. In 1933, Luchaire made over his magazine into a daily newspaper, which lasted, without prospering, until 1939. Undisturbed by the rise of Hitler, he remained an advocate of Franco-German reconciliation even in the Nazi era. He renewed his association with Abetz, whose wife was formerly Luchaire's secretary, when Abetz rose to new prominence as an agent of the Nazis in Paris. Such, then, were the two men who put Laval in touch with Abetz. Each was to have a generous reward.

No one knows just what passed between Laval and Abetz during their conversations in Paris at this time, but evidently each recognized their common interest. Subsequently, the two worked together closely, with every sign of trust in one another. Indeed, circumstances were to make them confederates rather than representatives of opposing governments. For both Laval and Abetz had made a personal wager on "broad" collaboration between their countries; each had yet to persuade his government to adopt such a policy; and each had need of the other's help to bring this about. Laval required Abetz's endorsement in order to gain the confidence of Berlin. Abetz, recognizing him as the one man in Pétain's entourage who was an advocate of unreserved partnership with the Axis, had every reason to wish to see Laval's political fortunes prosper.

On his return to Vichy, Laval gave the cabinet an optimistic report on his conversations with Abetz. Meantime Abetz returned to Berlin to report on his talks with Laval and to gain the approval of his superiors. On August 5 he arrived back in Paris, now vested with the personal rank of ambassador, as the delegate of the Foreign Office, attached to the headquarters of the commanding general of the German military occupation in France.

Despite the combined efforts of Laval and Abetz, however, relations between France and Germany became more tense. No matter what glowing report Abetz might make of his talks with Laval, or what promise he might hold out of winning Vichy over to "broad" collaboration, the fact remained that Vichy had turned down the request of Berlin for the establishment of German military bases in North Africa. And even though Ribbentrop might back up Abetz, the fact also remained that the German Foreign Office did not determine German policy toward Vichy, while both the army and the party leadership, which had the larger voice in the decision, distrusted the personnel of the Foreign Office as Francophile.

Berlin soon gave unmistakable evidence of its new firmness. On July 20, while Abetz and Laval were conferring, the German military authorities in Paris ordered the closing of the offices which the various technical ministries had established in the capital, and they tightened their control over the border between the two zones so firmly that they even refused to allow mail to be sent across the line of demarcation. Meantime they began to ship French prisoners of war to camps in Germany, dashing the hope that they would soon release them. On July 24 they set up German customs houses in Alsace and Lorraine, treating these regions as part of the German Reich. On August 9 they set the cost of the occupation, which the armistice made a charge on the French budget, at the sum of twenty million marks a day, to be paid in francs at the rate of twenty francs to the mark. When the French government, protesting the huge sum, asked for evidence that the costs of the occupation actually ran so high, Berlin curtly refused to discuss the matter. Presently the Germans announced that Vichy must institute a system of food rationing under which the French would be allowed no more food than the Germans had had in the winter of 1918.

This increasing German pressure might have driven the French into closer relations with the British had not the latter chosen, at the same time, to reaffirm their hostility toward Vichy by tightening their blockade. Though the French had ample reason to expect that the British would shut off French trade with neutral countries, they counted on continuing their trade with their colonies. Even in time of peace, France depended heavily upon her colonial empire, obtaining supplies of phosphate for use in fertilizer, wine, wheat, fruit, and other food-stuffs from North Africa; peanut oil, palm oil, bananas, and chocolate from West Africa; rice and rubber from Madagascar and Indo-China.

Under the circumstances of the time, no longer having access to other sources of these necessities, the homeland became still more dependent upon this trade. Accordingly, Vichy had sought to induce the Axis to allow resumption of trade with the colonies. On July 8, as we have seen, permission had been given for trade between France and North Africa. Subsequently, on August 23, similar permission was granted for trade with the more remote possessions. But in the meantime, on July 31, the British had announced that their warships would halt and seize French merchant vessels, even though these were plying only between French ports.

Forthwith a new crisis developed in the French cabinet. Admiral Darlan hotly demanded that he be permitted to order French warships

to escort merchant vessels and to fire upon the British if they attempted
to halt the convoys. Once more, Baudouin and Bouthillier succeeded in
postponing so rash a move, while Baudouin, through the mediation of
the U.S. State Department, sought to persuade the British to back
down. Roundabout negotiations were thus begun between Vichy and
London. But on August 20 Churchill, in a public statement on the
question of relations with France, gave voice to such a pronounced
antagonism toward Vichy that French hopes of compromise were
dashed. Thus by the end of August, the French found themselves on
the verge of warfare with their former allies and no nearer to peace
with the Axis.

As Laval and Baudouin were pursuing their contrary purposes, with
neither as yet making substantial progress toward his goal, on September 6 Marshal Pétain reorganized his cabinet. Apparently Laval
took the initiative in bringing about this renovation. In order for his
plans to mature, he judged it necessary to eliminate from the government some of the persons least favorably known to the Germans. Especially, he wished to be rid of General Weygand, who never concealed
his distaste for Laval. To gain the approval of Marshal Pétain, who had
a high regard for General Weygand, although they were not personal
friends, Laval intimated that the Germans would never relax their pressure upon France so long as the government included the general who
had commanded the French armies in their struggle against the
Wehrmacht in the spring of 1940. With his criticism of General Weygand, Laval coupled an attack upon the members of the government
who had been members of Parliament under the previous regime, playing in this way upon Pétain's dislike of the republican politicians.

Baudouin and Bouthillier, the leaders of the opposition to Laval
within the cabinet, did not attempt to block the move. Instead, they induced Pétain to name General Weygand as his representative in charge
of the North African colonies. Thus, although Laval accomplished his
desire to remove General Weygand from the cabinet, his adversaries
had the satisfaction of knowing that Weygand was in a position to block
any move on the part of Laval to give the Axis the use of French North
Africa as a base of military operations.

In the course of September, relations between Vichy and London took a turn for the better. First, the British began to retreat from their decision to enforce their blockade against trade between France and her colonies. The French gained an inkling of this when Vichy, after prolonged discussion within the cabinet, determined to defy the British by sending a ship through Gibraltar to Casablanca. This ship passed through the straits on September 7 with the British making no move to halt it.

Meantime, conversations proceeded between Vichy and London. Because normal diplomatic relations were suspended, the interchange took place by various circuitous routes. On occasion, the U.S. State Department served as a go-between, as did the Spanish Foreign Office, and the Portuguese. Eventually, a cautious contact was established between the British and French embassies in Madrid. By this avenue, an agreement was reached on September 18 under which the British engaged not to interfere with French merchant vessels passing Gibraltar, provided the French kept them informed of the movements of their warships in the western Mediterranean.

However, the improvement in Franco-British relations did not continue without interruption. Early in September, the Spanish ambassador in Vichy advised the French that the British were planning to help General de Gaulle make an attack on one of the French colonies in Africa. Forthwith Vichy ordered naval reinforcements to Casablanca and Dakar, the two principal French bases on the Atlantic coast of Africa. On September 19 British warships intercepted this force, comprising three cruisers and three destroyers, and made it put in to Casablanca. The French then drew the obvious conclusion that Dakar, rather than Casablanca, must be the place where the British were planning to make their raid.

Hence the local authorities at Dakar were not taken by surprise when a British squadron, bearing a detachment of Free French troops under the command of General de Gaulle, arrived offshore on September 23. Hoping to persuade their compatriots at Dakar to rally to their cause, the Gaullists spent two days in a vain attempt to parley, while the French warships in the harbor, including the disabled "Richelieu," opened fire whenever the British squadron drew near. At length, on the 25th,

London ordered the admiral in charge of the operation to give up the venture and withdraw.

The immediate reaction in Vichy, as the news arrived of this episode at Dakar, was a new surge of hostility toward the British. Laval, always working toward an alliance with the Axis, naturally made the most of what seemed to be evidence that the British were *de facto* waging war upon France. Once more Admiral Darlan demanded authorization to retaliate upon the British base at Gibraltar, and a bombing attack was carried out on September 23. Baudouin and Bouthillier were no less enraged, since the British attack on Dakar seemed to presage a larger campaign against the other French colonies still loyal to Vichy. Such an attack, directed against North Africa, would certainly make it impossible for Vichy to pursue a course of neutrality. The Germans and Italians would surely take over the whole of the French homeland and the North African colonies if Vichy should prove unwilling or unable to strike back against the British.

In the outcome, however, the episode proved decisive in bringing about better relations between London and Vichy. For at Dakar the British discovered that General de Gaulle was unable to make good his assurances that the French colonies would break away from Vichy and rally to his standard if only the British would provide a favorable opportunity by lending him support. And since they had no desire presently to undertake a large-scale military campaign in North Africa, the British did not again underwrite De Gaulle's schemes for the liberation of the French empire.

Other circumstances also worked to relieve the tension. One of these was the failure of the German air war upon Britain. The Germans had begun their intensive bombing attacks in the first week of August, as soon as it became evident that the British would not make a favorable answer to Hitler's proposals of a negotiated peace. Throughout August and September, it had remained an open question whether the British could hold out. But by early October it became clear that the *Luftwaffe* was unable to secure a decision. As this crisis passed, London could make a calmer appraisal of the international situation and could perceive that Vichy was as yet far from committed to a partnership with the Axis. Accordingly the British at last, in October, gave evidence of their readiness to establish a *modus vivendi* with the French.

Negotiations to this purpose had been in course since September. As we have seen, an interchange of views between London and Vichy had developed through their respective embassies in Madrid, and an agreement had been reached providing for a relaxation of the British blockade. Meantime another move to resolve the differences between the two governments had been started on the private initiative of Professor Louis Rougier, of the University of Besançon.[1] During a visit to Switzerland early in September, Professor Rougier had called at the British consulate in Geneva and asked to have a message transmitted to Professor Lionel Robbins, of the London School of Economics, with whom Professor Rougier had a close personal acquaintance. The message asked that Professor Robbins secure permission for him to make a trip to London, in order to negotiate with the Foreign Office as a representative of Marshal Pétain. Shortly Professor Robbins sent back word that the Foreign Office would cooperate.

Thereupon, on September 17, Professor Rougier called on Baudouin in Vichy and outlined his plan, which Baudouin approved. He also secured the approval of Marshal Pétain. On October 22, after much delay, Professor Rougier at last reached London, where he conferred first with Lord Halifax, then with the Prime Minister. On the basis of his conversations, he drew up a memorandum on the 28th, incorporating the provisions of a *modus vivendi,* which Churchill approved. This memorandum stipulated that the British would refrain from further public denunciation of the government of Marshal Pétain, make no new attempt to seize French colonies recognizing his authority, and continue to permit trade between France and her African colonies. In return, Vichy pledged to make no attempt to reconquer those colonies that had already gone over to General de Gaulle and reaffirmed its de-

---

[1] The Rougier mission has brought forth an abundance of testimony and minor controversy. The fact that there had been negotiations between London and Vichy, culminating in a gentleman's agreement, did not become public knowledge until after the liberation of France. The revelation, which came during the trial of Pétain, was not welcome either to those in France who were demanding vengeance upon Pétain as a willing agent of the Axis or to Churchill, who was not happy to appear as having collaborated with a "collaborationist." Professor Rougier has published his account of the affair in *Mission secrète à Londres: les accords Pétain-Churchill* (Geneva: Les Éditions du Cheval Ailé, 1948).

termination not to give over the French navy to the Axis or permit the Axis to make use of bases in the colonies under its rule.

On his return to Vichy, Professor Rougier delivered this memorandum to Marshal Pétain on October 11. Shortly thereafter, Vichy sent word to London of its willingness to abide by this arrangement. For the following two years, until the American landing in North Africa in November, 1942, this agreement remained the basis of relations between the two governments. Though it fell far short of a rapprochement, it proved adequate to avert new tension between the former allies. Thus it made much easier the task of those in Vichy who favored a course of *attentisme,* or a watchful and provisional neutrality, as against a close alignment with the Axis.

No sooner did the French reach a working agreement with the British than their relations with the Axis approached a new crisis. By October, it became apparent to Berlin that the British and French were not going to declare war upon one another. At about the same time, it also became apparent that the *Luftwaffe* was unable to liquidate the R.A.F. Hence the Germans were compelled to give up their dream of either invading Britain or bombing their enemies into a readiness to negotiate a peace. Consequently, by the fall of 1940, Hitler and his henchmen were impelled to seek some new target for their attack, which would give better promise of success.

As the new focus of their operations, the Germans decided upon the Mediterranean. The choice was made at the urging of Marshal Goering, who persuaded Hitler that it was more feasible to force the British to terms by striking a blow at their position in the Near East than by hammering at their homeland. The first step was to be for the Axis to secure command of the western Mediterranean and thus make possible an Axis drive along the shore of Africa into the Near East. Accordingly, Hitler arranged to meet with Mussolini and Franco, whose assistance would be needed. Likewise, he determined to demand the cooperation of Pétain.

On October 4, therefore, the Fuehrer and the Duce met together for a conference, which was held in a railroad car on the Brenner Pass. As Hitler outlined his plan, Mussolini proved less than enthusiastic. He regarded the Mediterranean as the proper scene of Italian grandeur and did not relish the prospect of sharing the glory with his partners in the Axis. However, he was in no position to veto the scheme. Somewhat irked at the tenor of the conversation, Hitler then set out for Hendaye, on the French-Spanish border, where he was to meet with Generalissimo Franco. En route, he arranged also to meet with Pierre Laval, to announce to him the role in the Axis plan which the French must assume.

It was Abetz who apprised Laval of Hitler's intentions. The news that he was to meet the Fuehrer was a pleasurable surprise to Laval— "No kidding?" was his response, when Abetz told him. But, unabashed at what he seemed to regard as the high honor of meeting the man of the hour, Laval determined to make bold use of the chance to win a place for France within the "New Order."

The interview occurred on October 22 in the village of Montoire, near Tours. At the start, Laval adopted an audacious tone. The Germans, he admitted, had France wholly at their mercy, and they could wreak whatever vengeance upon her they might desire. But, he pointed out, some day France would surely revolt. In the course of history, more than once the Germans had beaten the French, but likewise more than once the French had whipped the Germans. "Must this go on forever?" he asked.

As he hoped, this approach drove Hitler into a pose of statesmanship. "I shall not make a peace of vengeance," the Fuehrer replied. "I shall not fall into the errors of Versailles." Pressing his advantage, Laval then assured Hitler of his warm desire to see a speedy Axis victory. However, Hitler well knew that, whatever Laval's intentions, he was not the master of the situation in Vichy.

Accordingly the Fuehrer indicated that he wished to discuss the whole problem of Franco-German relations with Marshal Pétain himself. Laval made quick to promise that Pétain would welcome such an interview. It was decided that the two chiefs of state were to meet two days later, as soon as Hitler returned from his conference at Hendaye with Generalissimo Franco.

Laval returned to Vichy on October 23 to report to Pétain and the cabinet. The news was a smashing blow to Baudouin, Bouthillier, and the others who opposed "broad" collaboration. Obviously they could not prevent the meeting between Pétain and Hitler. But they had every reason to fear that Hitler would raise demands, amounting to French participation in the war on the side of the Axis, which Pétain would not or could not refuse. In a desperate attempt to save the situation, Baudouin spent two hours in a private conversation with Pétain, arguing that the involvement of France in open hostilities with Britain would prove ruinous to France without even giving the Axis help. Pétain declared that he had no intention of agreeing to the reentrance of France into the war. But he refused to take Baudouin with him to the meeting with Hitler.

The next morning, October 24, Pétain set out by automobile for Moulins, on the edge of the occupied zone. Besides Laval, he took with him only two members of his personal staff—Dr. Ménétrel, his physician, and Du Moulin, his aide. Upon their arrival at Moulins, a German escort took them in charge, guiding them to an unannounced destination, which proved to be the same little village of Montoire where, two days before, Hitler had received Laval. As on the previous occasion, the armored train which Hitler used as his traveling headquarters was drawn up at the station, and the Fuehrer himself was waiting on the platform. Seeing Pétain approach, he stepped forward to receive him, with stiff but polite formality, returning the handshake which Pétain offered. Apparently the one-time German corporal was not without a trace of awe for the "Victor of Verdun." For his part, Pétain did not dissemble his curiosity at meeting the man whose armies had silenced French boasts of military glory. The exchange of introductions accomplished, Hitler ushered Pétain and Laval into the car which he used as his office, leaving Du Moulin and Dr. Ménétrel to wait in the dining car.

As it turned out, contrary to the fears of the "conservative" clique in Vichy, the conference between Hitler and Pétain proved void of immediate practical importance. The main reason for this was that Hitler had had poor success in his meeting with Generalissimo Franco at Hendaye the day before. The Fuehrer had tried to induce Franco to declare war upon Britain, in alliance with Germany and Italy, and to approve a combined Spanish and German operation for the capture of Gibraltar, which would prevent the British from making use of this entrance into the western Mediterranean. But Franco had refused to enter the war unless Hitler provided large supplies of food and munitions, assured the defense of the Azores and the Canary Islands against any British retaliation upon these Spanish possessions, and permitted the Spanish to take over French Morocco. It remains unclear whether Franco wished to exact the maximum compensation for his support or meant to keep out of the war, choosing to disguise his intention by setting impossible conditions.

At any event, Hitler had seen that Franco would not cooperate with him. And at his earlier meeting with Mussolini, as we have noted, he had already learned that the Italians were unenthusiastic about their share in the venture. Indeed, Hitler himself had never had a keen interest in the enterprise, which he had taken up only for want of a better alternative, after it became apparent that the *Luftwaffe* could not bomb the British into submission. In view of all this reluctance, the plan for an Axis campaign in the western Mediterranean gave such poor promise that, by the time Hitler encountered Pétain, he was about ready to give up the whole idea.

Consequently the Fuehrer had little or no immediate need of French cooperation, and therefore no specific demands to put upon Pétain. So he simply delivered a long monologue on the general topic of Franco-German relations, scarcely allowing Pétain a chance to open his mouth. Striving to strike a pose of magnanimity but achieving only a ludicrous air of injured innocence, Hitler declared that Germany had never wanted war with France and had taken up arms merely in self-defense. Despite the pain she had suffered as a consequence of French provocation, he averred that Germany would give the French another chance to establish amicable relations, provided they showed a genuine desire to collaborate with the Axis in the "New Order."

In response, Pétain affirmed the readiness of his government, as a matter of general principle, to achieve this collaboration. But he refrained from making any specific pledge, indicating that the details of cooperation between the two countries could best be worked out in further negotiations. The conversation thus terminated with no agree-

ment sought or reached, save on the professed desire of the two governments to develop better relations with one another.

At the time, this interview at Montoire seemed to mark a new departure. It appeared to initiate a willing agreement of France and the
Axis to work together for common purposes far beyond the terms of
the armistice. The French partisans of "broad" collaboration lost no
time in celebrating their apparent triumph. Thus Doriot, for example,
declared in the columns of his paper, *Le Cri du Peuple,* that the accord
reached at Montoire represented "a decisive break with the policy of
the past fifty years," a break which "liberates France from the democratic system of Britain and America and provides her a place in the
continental European bloc." France had no choice, he pronounced,
save "either to perish with England or survive with Europe." By the
same token, the news produced grave consternation among those who
advocated the opposite course of "narrow" collaboration. Likewise,
alarm developed in London and Washington, where Secretary of State
Hull took occasion to deliver a stern warning to Gaston Henry-Haye,
the ambassador whom Vichy had newly appointed as its representative
in the United States.

In actuality, however, the conversation between Pétain and Hitler
did not afford a new occasion for either celebration or concern, because their agreement was so vague as to be nearly meaningless. The
time was already past when France could choose, simply as a general
principle, whether or not she would cooperate with the Axis. The only
question that still remained open was as to the specific terms of Franco-
German cooperation. This was a matter of *quid pro quo,* involving the
questions of how much concession the Germans would make and
what price the French would have to pay. It was a matter, therefore,
requiring continuous deliberation on the part of Vichy as well as Berlin, since both governments would have to decide whether a particular
concession was worth its price. But as to such calculations, the interview
at Montoire advanced matters not a whit.

Nevertheless, Montoire represented progress in the direction of
"broad" collaboration insofar as it gave new strength within the French
government to Pierre Laval, who was unequivocally committed to this

policy. Evidence was soon forthcoming of his new advantage. On October 28 Baudouin insisted that Pétain accept his resignation as Minister of Foreign Affairs, since he, Baudouin, was unwilling to accept the task of developing the "broad" collaboration which Montoire seemed to presage. Upon his resignation, Laval took over the position.

Laval proceeded with plans to enlarge the vague agreement reached at Montoire into a practical accord. This was by no means an easy task, even though Laval now had the upper hand in Vichy. For the Germans were growing lukewarm toward the idea of "broad" collaboration. As we have noted, Hitler had begun to lose interest in the plan for an Axis campaign in North Africa after his disappointing conference with Franco. He therefore had ceased to have an urgent need of French military cooperation. This was a hard blow to Laval. Instead of being in the position of inducing Pétain to agree to German demands, he was put in the need of developing, on his own initiative, some scheme for Franco-German partnership that would prove attractive to the Nazis. Perceiving this setback to his hopes, Laval had not returned from Montoire directly to Vichy but had gone to Paris to talk with Abetz.

The plan which these two worked out, probably with the help of Ribbentrop, envisaged an attempt by Vichy, with German backing, to reconquer French Equatorial Africa, which had gone over to De Gaulle. This was expected to serve the cause of the Axis by cutting the line of supply between Brazzaville and the Sudan, which was a base of British operations against the Italians in East Africa. Moreover, it would break the gentlemen's agreement between London and Vichy whereby Vichy had undertaken not to reconquer colonies recognizing De Gaulle. Thus it would give proof of Vichy's good faith toward the Axis by leading to an embroilment with both the British and the Free French.

In the fortnight following Montoire, Laval broached this plan to Pétain and the other members of the cabinet. Then, on November 9, he betook himself to Berlin, where he had an audience with Marshal Goering, who proved quite receptive to the plan. So Laval returned to Vichy, confident that no obstacle remained in the way of his determination to initiate a close military and political partnership with the Axis.

But Laval was overconfident, for his position in Vichy was not so secure as he supposed. His adversaries in the cabinet had been momentarily stunned by his apparent triumph at Montoire. But by the middle of November, as Laval proceeded with his plans, those who opposed "broad" collaboration realized that the time had come for them to make a bold effort to force him out of the cabinet, or else he would draw France back into the war on the side of the Axis. The leaders in this move were Bouthillier, the Minister of Finance; Peyrouton, the Minister of the Interior; Baudouin, who remained in the cabinet as Minister without portfolio after relinquishing Foreign Affairs; and Du Moulin, who held no position in the cabinet but was a member of Pétain's personal staff.

As the first step, the conspirators had to settle on a candidate of their own to succeed Laval as Vice-Premier, since Pétain lacked the vigor to assume the whole burden of managing the government. Obvious practical considerations dictated that their choice must go to someone who had considerable political stature and was not known as hostile to the Axis. The man who met these prerequisites was Pierre-Étienne Flandin. A former premier, Flandin had been identified before the war with those who favored "appeasement." Since the armistice, however, he had withdrawn from public affairs to his family property in the *département* of the Yonne. Thus he had neither attracted the unfavorable attention of the Nazis nor given sign of a desire to gain their good graces.

On November 21 Bouthillier paid a visit to Flandin to sound him out. Finding him receptive to the proposal, Bouthillier broached the question with Pétain on the 23d. While making no commitment, the marshal indicated a wish to be rid of Laval, whom he did not trust, listened with interest to Bouthillier's recommendation of Flandin, and expressed a desire to meet and talk with him.

The next step was to gain the agreement of the other members of the cabinet. This presented no insuperable problem, since the adversaries of Laval had succeeded, in the reorganization of the government two months before, in keeping out of the cabinet men known to be close friends of Laval or inclined to give him backing. Yet the conspirators were not sure of the attitude of Admiral Darlan, the Minister of Marine. Much depended upon the position he would take in the event of the ouster of Laval, since the Germans, in retaliation for the dismissal of their best friend in the French government, might decide to march into the unoccupied zone of France and attempt to seize the French colonies in North Africa. Darlan would then have to decide whether to permit the Axis to seize the navy or order it to go over to the British and the Gaullists.

As it turned out, Darlan proved amenable. He was quite averse, he told Bouthillier, to the scheme which Laval was urging for an attempt to reconquer Equatorial Africa. This would provoke a British counter-attack, he was sure, and in the outcome the Germans would move into North Africa. Under the pretext of helping to ward off the British, they would probably take over the French fleet. Darlan was not unwilling to use his fleet in cooperation with the Axis, provided it remained under his control, but he was not at all willing to see it taken out from under his command. So, once Darlan gave assurance of his cooperation, no obstacle remained within the cabinet.

However, the coup could not be launched without some occasion to provide an excuse. For a time, it seemed that Laval would forestall his enemies by setting in motion his own plan for military cooperation with the Axis. On November 29 he made a visit to Paris, taking with him Admiral Darlan and General Huntziger, the Minister of War, to confer with Abetz. At this meeting, his German partner announced that Berlin expected Vichy to begin its operation for the reconquest of Equatorial Africa without further delay. Upon his return to Vichy, Laval urged the cabinet to make immediate preparations for the expedition. His adversaries realized that the time was at hand for them to strike or it would be too late. Their hopes of saving the situation rose on December 6, when Flandin at last arrived in Vichy to confer with Pétain. But, though the marshal expressed satisfaction with the conversation, he still held back from the decisive step of dismissing Laval.

His reluctance is not easy to understand. There is more than adequate evidence that Pétain really did not approve of the policy of "broad" collaboration which Laval was pushing, and that he resented Laval's connivance with the Nazis to force him into a path he did not wish to follow. Doubtless his hesitation was due in large measure to his fear of the reprisals the Germans might inflict upon France for what they would regard as an affront. But his reluctance also reflected an ambivalence in his attitude toward the Vice-Premier. For Pétain evidently felt himself less than equal to the difficult task of dealing with the Germans. Even though he regarded Laval as too quick to give ground, he could not be sure that anyone else whom he might name as his deputy would not provoke a complete rupture with Berlin, with dire results for France, whether through an ill-contained animosity toward the Germans or by sheer clumsiness in handling them.

At the eleventh hour, an unexpected new development brought the crisis to a head. On December 12 Vichy was notified that the Germans wished Marshal Pétain to come to Paris to be present at a ceremony, which Hitler himself would also attend, to symbolize the new Franco-German amity. As the feature of the occasion, scheduled for the 14th, the Germans were bringing to Paris the remains of *L'Aiglon*—the son of Napoleon and his second empress, the Austrian Archduchess Marie Louise—to be placed alongside those of his father in the Invalides. The idea for this gesture had apparently originated with Abetz, who, like so many German Francophiles, was an admirer of Bonaparte. He had evidently urged the notion on Ribbentrop, who had gained Hitler's approval. Actually, the idea was ill-conceived. The French had a good deal less than a single-minded devotion to the memory of Napoleon himself. Certainly, few of them had the slightest sentimental regard for his son, who had been exiled from France at the age of three and had spent the rest of his short life in Vienna, where he had died at the age of twenty-one.

But, whatever the French might think of *L'Aiglon,* the German plan for the return of his remains presented a vexing dilemma. Obviously it would be difficult for Marshal Pétain to refuse the invitation to such a ceremony as was planned, the more so since Hitler would be present. Yet it would be personally humiliating to the marshal, and politically tactless, for him to make what would be his first visit to Paris since before the armistice under such conditions, surrounded by German uniforms. Pétain himself was incensed at the news of the invitation, which he regarded as another trick of Laval to make him willy-nilly do the

Germans' bidding. Accordingly, the little group that was plotting to unseat Laval seized their opportunity to exploit Pétain's displeasure.

In the afternoon of Friday the 13th, a cold, damp, dark, winter's day which well suited the ominous date and perilous occasion, the conspirators made their final plans. Just after lunch, Bouthillier encountered Peyrouton in the park outside the hotel where Pétain had his headquarters in Vichy. In a mood of desperation, the two agreed that they could delay no longer. "It must be tonight," declared Bouthillier. Forthwith they summoned their confederates. About three o'clock, an impromptu council assembled in Du Moulin's office. Those present were Du Moulin, Bouthillier, Peyrouton, Baudouin, Admiral Darlan, General Huntziger, and Alibert, the Minister of Justice. Quickly they decided to go as a group to see Pétain and press him for his sanction.

The marshal received them in his office and listened in silence as Admiral Darlan, the spokesman for the group, presented the plan. His answer was at last decisive: "The time has come. Let's have it over with."

The procedure was then decided upon. A meeting of the cabinet, over which Laval would preside, was already scheduled for five o'clock. This meeting would be held as planned. But another meeting would be called for eight that evening, at which Pétain would ask for the resignation of all members of the cabinet. He would then accept the resignation of Laval, but not the others. Thereupon Peyrouton, as Minister of the Interior, would have Laval arrested, to prevent his sending an appeal to the Germans to intervene in his behalf.

In essentials, the operation was accomplished according to this plan. The meeting of the cabinet at five o'clock took place without incident. At the second meeting, Pétain made his request for the resignation of the cabinet, without explaining his purpose. Laval, believing that the marshal wished to drop Belin, the Minister of Labor, raised no question as he put his signature to the collective letter of resignation. He was therefore thunderstruck when Pétain announced that he was accepting the resignation of only two ministers, one of whom was Laval.[2]

---

[2] The other was Ripert, Minister of Public Education. His dismissal had nothing to do with Laval's. Pétain wished to give a position in the government to Professor Jacques Chevalier, who was then engaged in negotiations with Lord Halifax, and the marshal chose to accept the resignation of Ripert simply to make an opening for Chevalier.

"What does this mean, *monsieur le maréchal?*" he protested. "You received me this very afternoon without saying anything of this to me!"

Pétain made a weak response, placing blame on Laval for the attacks on the government which were appearing in the Paris press. But when Laval sought to expostulate, the marshal cut him off with a curt answer: "Every time you go to Paris, I ask myself what new ruin you will bring down on us. The French people don't trust you, and neither do I."

Seeing that Pétain was resolute, Laval gave up the struggle. After shaking hands with Pétain, he returned to his office, then went to dinner in a restaurant. Two hours later, as he left the restaurant, he was arrested and taken under guard to his home at Châteldon, where he was kept incommunicado.

Though the conspirators thus gained their purpose, none of them was sure they could hold their ground in the face of what would certainly be an extremely unfavorable reaction on the part of the Nazis. Accordingly, they took steps to buttress their position. Peyrouton promptly established a state of siege in Vichy, prohibiting telephone or telegraph communications with Paris save by members of the cabinet, and likewise banning travel to the metropolis. Alibert took similar measures, posting detachments of a special new police, known as Groupes de Protection, at strategic points throughout the town. At the same time, he took it upon himself to telephone General de La Laurencie, the delegate of the French government in Paris, and ordered him to arrest Marcel Déat, who was both a partisan of Laval and a personal enemy of Alibert. Meantime notice was given Berlin, by way of the Armistice Commission at Wiesbaden, that Marshal Pétain would not attend the ceremony at the Invalides which was scheduled for the next day. Word was also given of the ouster of Laval, for reasons professedly of domestic politics.

For the next two days, Vichy waited with bated breath for the German reaction. No one would have been surprised to see German troops cross the line of demarcation into the unoccupied zone, establishing military rule throughout France. Nevertheless, the clique that brought about the dismissal of Laval had rightly guessed that the Germans would not take such a bold and decisive step.

Berlin received the news of the coup at Vichy with seeming calm. A ceremony, much curtailed, was held as planned at the Invalides on Saturday the 14th, when the remains of *L'Aiglon* reached Paris. Naturally, Hitler did not attend, since Pétain had turned down the invitation to be present. Yet the Fuehrer failed to become enraged. He realized, of course, that the men who had encompassed the downfall of Laval were enemies of "broad" collaboration. But, as we have seen, Hitler himself was far from a firm advocate of close cooperation between the two countries. He was now disposed to take a more favorable view of Laval than before, but he still regarded the deposed Vice-Premier with considerable suspicion, and he was by no means ready to assume the risks involved in a breach of the armistice, merely in order to see Laval restored to his previous position in the French cabinet.

Abetz, however, took quite another view of the situation. Berlin might wash its hands of the French Vice-Premier, since Hitler had no firm preference for "broad" collaboration. But Abetz would see his own role dwindle in importance in the measure that ill will developed between the two countries. He therefore had every reason to take a keen personal interest in the matter. Accordingly, he determined to make a visit to Vichy, in order to browbeat Pétain into reappointing Laval.

Meantime Laval's enemies strove to bolster Pétain's determination. Bouthillier would have liked to have Pétain name Flandin Vice-Premier at once, since this would make it so much the harder to reinstate Laval. However, others in the clique that had ousted Laval were not as enthusiastic as Bouthillier at the prospect of Flandin's taking over a position of such prominence. Besides, Flandin was suffering from heart trouble. He was therefore in poor condition to bear the nerve-wracking strain which this would involve. So it was decided that Flandin would become Minister of Foreign Affairs but that Pétain would make no new appointment, at the moment, to the position of Vice-Premier.

In the evening of December 16 Abetz arrived in Vichy, accompanied by a swashbuckling motorcycle escort of armed guards. The next morning, he was closeted with Pétain and Darlan. At the demand of Abetz, Laval was brought from Châteldon to take part in the discussion. A heated debate ensued, in the course of which Abetz depicted the evil consequences which would descend upon France unless Laval were taken back into the cabinet. To these dire prophecies, Laval added his own angered protests.

Nevertheless, Pétain held his ground, making clear his determination to resign as Chief of State rather than give in. Thereupon Abetz, who dared not provoke such a serious crisis as this would mean, began to back down. As a compromise, he proposed that Pétain agree to name a quadrumvirate, comprising Laval, Flandin, Admiral Darlan, and General Huntziger, to share with the marshal in the direction of the government. Even under this condition, Pétain still refused to take back Laval.

Finally Abetz made another proposal. This envisioned, first, the appointment of a three-man directorate, comprising Flandin, Darlan, and Huntziger; second, the dismissal of four ministers—Peyrouton, Alibert, Caziot, and Belin—who had taken part in the opposition to Laval within the cabinet; and third, the dismissal of General de La Laurencie, the delegate-general representing the French government in Paris, and the nomination of Fernand de Brinon to replace him.

On this basis, which did not involve the recall of Laval, Pétain deemed it wise to reach an accord with Abetz. Accordingly he agreed to dismiss La Laurencie and give his post to Brinon and likewise agreed to make Flandin, Darlan, and Huntziger his principal advisers. So far as concerned the dismissal of the four ministers whom Abetz had named, he indicated his readiness to consider the German ambassador's views and to give thought to the problem of reorganizing the cabinet as a whole. Abetz chose not to press the matter further at the moment. Putting the best face he could on what was an unmistakable defeat, he returned to Paris.

This interview between Pétain and Abetz proved decisive, but it did not quite terminate the crisis. Having defied Abetz and seen him back down, Pétain did not thereafter weaken. However, Abetz was still determined to keep up his pressure in behalf of Laval. He therefore gave the word to the Paris newspapers, all of which operated under German censorship and as willing agents of the German authorities, to open an attack upon the "reactionaries" in Vichy who were pushing Pétain along a road that could lead only to the ruin of France.[3]

In answer, Vichy ventured to by-pass Abetz and open negotiations directly with Hitler. Pétain entrusted this mission to Admiral Darlan, who made known to Berlin his desire to meet the Fuehrer, as the personal representative of the marshal. The Fuehrer received Darlan in a little town near Beauvais, in the occupied zone, on December 25. Darlan did his best to begin the interview on a note of peace and good will, with Christmas greetings and words of appreciation for the kindness of the Germans in giving back to France the remains of *L'Aiglon*.

But Hitler was not in a genial mood. He promptly launched upon one of his monologues, expressing his displeased surprise at the dismissal of Laval. Darlan gave profuse assurances that the ouster of Laval was merely a matter of domestic politics, which did not at all indicate a reluctance on the part of Pétain to continue in the course of "collaboration." Nevertheless, he made clear that Pétain would not take Laval back into the government. Though he would replace Alibert as Minister of Justice, he would not dismiss Peyrouton, Caziot, or Belin, the other three of the four ministers whose discharge Abetz had demanded. Hitler chose not to insist. But Darlan was obliged to acknowledge, on his return to Vichy, that his mission had evidently accomplished nothing toward settling the prolonged crisis.

So matters remained at an impasse until January 10, when Bénoist-Méchin appeared in Vichy. Bénoist-Méchin was one of those French intellectuals, such as Brinon and Luchaire, who had been apostles of Franco-German reconciliation since before the advent of the Nazis, and he had risen to new prominence after the armistice as one of the protégés of Abetz. It was evidently as Abetz's emissary that he now sought an interview with Pétain, to renew the argument in favor of the reinstatement of Laval. He succeeded in inducing the marshal to meet and talk with Laval once more.

The interview thus arranged took place in the village of La Ferté-

---

[3] Déat in *L'Œuvre* and Jean Luchaire in *Les Nouveaux Temps* took the lead in this press campaign. Doriot's *Le Cri du Peuple* was slower to respond. It is indicative of the ill will between Doriot and Déat that Doriot's first public comment was to accuse Déat of championing Laval out of sympathy for the old guard of Free Masons and parliamentary politicians left over from the previous regime.

Hauterive on January 17. At the start, Laval made an effort to regain Pétain's good graces, apologizing for the immoderate language he had used during their previous meeting. With the same design of conciliation, Laval chose not to raise the question of his own return to the cabinet. Instead, he besought Pétain only to dismiss Flandin and the others in his councils who were intent on opposing the Germans and thus on bringing down upon Pétain the menace of German ill will.

This approach seemed to work, for Pétain gave sign of a favorable response. Thereupon Laval proposed that at the termination of their interview, he and Pétain issue a public announcement that they had reached an accord. Pétain agreed.

Arriving back in Vichy, Du Moulin promptly made a report to Flandin on the interview and gave warning of Laval's plan to issue a press release which would make it appear that he and Pétain were now of one mind. Forthwith Flandin moved to thwart Laval by issuing an announcement of his own, which acknowledged that the marshal had met with Laval but made clear that Pétain had no intention of reinstating him. This move served its immediate purpose, for it forestalled Laval from making use of the news to his own ends. But it proved a Pyrrhic victory for Flandin, because it put him in a position of unequivocal opposition to Laval. As a result, the Germans, who hitherto had been willing to see Flandin remain in the cabinet, provided that Laval returned, now came to the conclusion that they must ultimately insist upon Flandin's departure.

This new setback spurred Abetz to redouble his exertions. He had made no appreciable progress in the month that had passed since the coup of December 13, and he could not help knowing that the longer Pétain made good his defiance, the poorer became the chances of forcing him to retreat. Accordingly, Abetz inspired the Paris press and radio to step up its attack upon the "reactionaries" and "hidden Gaullists" in Vichy.

Indicative of the tone of this campaign, which reached a climax in the last two weeks of January and seemed to presage some kind of German *coup de main* against the entire Pétain regime, was a lengthy article in *Les Nouveaux Temps* of January 30, by Jean Luchaire. "Unless nearly all the members of the Vichy government give way to a fresh crew, in which new men will take their places alongside those whom a detestable conspiracy has temporarily removed from office," Luchaire declared, "there will be no further Franco-German collaboration. And without that collaboration, France will lose, no matter what else may transpire, her best chance for recovery and progress. That is the truth of the matter. Frankly, we say this in both anger and despair. But we do so in order to point to where the responsibility lies, and in order to provoke a wholesome reaction throughout the breadth of France. . . ."

But time ran out on Abetz. By the end of January, Berlin gave up its interest in Franco-German collaboration. Hitler had again approached Franco with the plan for a German-Spanish attack on Gibraltar, and once more Franco had rebuffed him. Thereupon the Fuehrer had written off the scheme for a large-scale Axis offensive in the western Mediterranean, which had given point to his earlier interest in gaining the cooperation of Vichy. Besides, Hitler was now becoming absorbed in plans for a much bolder venture in another quarter, which were to eventuate five months later in the invasion of Russia. For this enterprise he had no need of French help. Such being the mood in Berlin, Abetz could not hope to secure the backing of his government for his schemes to reinstate Laval in Vichy. Without such support, he lacked the power to force Pétain to do his bidding.

As time thus worked against Abetz and his henchman Laval, it likewise brought nearer the hour of Darlan's triumph. By the end of January, it was clear that Laval could not return to Vichy, and it was equally clear that Flandin could not long remain. Meantime Darlan had become Pétain's right-hand man, upon whom alone the marshal could depend to negotiate with the Germans. Yet Darlan had given the Germans the impression that he himself had no wish but to ease the tension between the two governments. Thus Darlan emerged as the only person, acceptable to both Pétain and the Germans, who had sufficient stature to fill the office of Vice-Premier. Doubtless he was not unaware of this logic. Quite probably, he had perceived the shape of things to come at the time when he decided to throw his lot in with those who were planning the overthrow of Laval, and as he watched Flandin become embroiled with the Germans.

At any event, Pétain had little choice but to turn to Darlan for help.

Early in January, the marshal had made a gesture toward conciliating the Germans, when he accepted the resignation of Paul Baudouin, whom Abetz knew as one of his adversaries. And on January 28 Pétain had dismissed Alibert, the Minister of Justice, whose replacement Abetz had long been demanding. These gestures proved insufficient to ease the tension between Vichy and Paris. So Pétain had asked Darlan to reopen negotiations with Abetz. After considerable delay, word was sent to Vichy that the German ambassador would receive him, whereupon Darlan betook himself to Paris, on February 3, for a new conference. At this meeting, Darlan apparently succeeded at last in convincing Abetz that the return of Laval was quite out of the question, while at the same time presenting himself as an acceptable second choice.

On his return to Vichy, Darlan quickly reaped his harvest. On February 5 Flandin, his one possible rival, resigned as Minister of Foreign Affairs, and Darlan took over the portfolio. Then, on February 10, Pétain named him Vice-Premier, thus filling the position for the first time since the dismissal of Laval on December 13. On February 15 Peyrouton handed in his resignation as Minister of the Interior, whereupon Darlan added this position to his several others. Finally, on February 25, Pétain renovated the entire cabinet at Darlan's behest, giving the rank of minister to only four others besides Darlan, none of whom could become a rival to him. Thus Darlan emerged as the ultimate beneficiary of the crisis that had begun on December 13. Not only did he replace Laval, but he gained a more secure command of the government than his predecessor had ever had.

It is by no means easy to appraise the outcome of the coup of December 13 and the crisis it unloosed. Certainly it did not mean even a temporary repudiation of Franco-German collaboration, or the choice of "narrow" as against "broad" collaboration. As Vice-Premier, Darlan was soon to give his sanction to a political and military cooperation with the Axis that went well beyond the requirements of the armistice.

From one point of view, therefore, the crisis led to nothing more than a personal advantage for Darlan without materially changing the policy his predecessor had inaugurated. Laval was not the only one who had grounds to complain of the injustice of this turn of events. Within two months of his ouster, Baudouin, Peyrouton, Alibert, and Flandin, all of whom had been instrumental in bringing about his dismissal and blocking his return, had likewise been squeezed out of the government. Thus they had jeopardized their own positions only to open the way for Darlan.

From another point of view, however, the consequences were of more considerable moment. For the downfall of Laval made it apparent to the entire nation that Marshal Pétain did not regard "broad" collaboration as in the best interest of France. At the moment, his reluctance to sanction close cooperation with the Axis made little difference in the course of affairs, since he found it necessary to replace Laval by a man who would carry on much the same policy. Nevertheless, the attitude of the marshal had immense influence upon public opinion. For in 1940, as we have noted, the mass of the nation looked upon Pétain as a God-given savior, to whom was owed absolute trust and obedience. Stunned by the immensity of their misfortune and humiliation, confronted with the task of finding their place in a world that no longer had familiar contours, having no means of gaining reliable knowledge of the true state of relations between their government and those of the belligerents, the French could not help but hang upon what sign Pétain might give them. They knew that he had access to the information they lacked. With what seemed good reason, they believed that a man who had already attained the full span of a normal life, and the full measure of high honor open to him, would judge their interest without the bias of personal or partisan ambition.

Had Pétain given ungrudging support to the policy of "broad" collaboration which Laval was urging, surely a considerable portion of the nation would have drawn the conclusion that the outcome of the war was now determined and that France had no choice but to accommodate herself to the "New Order." By the same token, we cannot doubt but that the visible reluctance of Pétain made it easier for public opinion to recognize that such a course did not represent the free choice of the man who occupied the best position to judge their interest, but only a constraint which he and they must endure so long as France remained helpless to resist.

Further, the banishment of Laval helped avert a complete rupture with London and Washington. In the weeks between Pétain's interview with Hitler at Montoire on October 24 and the coup of December 13, the British had watched with alarm the signs of a new Franco-German rapprochement, since this seemed to undo the gentlemen's agreement which Professor Rougier had worked out in the course of his visit to London. But in December Lord Halifax established communication with Professor Jacques Chevalier, of the University of Grenoble, whom he had known personally since the days when both were students at Oxford. Promptly Professor Chevalier approached Pétain, who indicated his readiness to reopen conversations with the British.

The ouster of Laval on December 13, coming just at this moment, gave sign that Pétain was acting in good faith. Moreover, in the reorganization of the cabinet which ensued upon Laval's dismissal, he appointed Professor Chevalier Minister of Public Education, thus giving him direct access to the cabinet. Shortly thereafter, negotiations between Halifax and Chevalier reaffirmed the *modus vivendi* between their governments, in much the same terms that Professor Rougier had earlier worked out.

Meantime President Roosevelt named one of his personal advisers, Admiral William D. Leahy, as ambassador to Vichy, filling a post which had been vacant since the armistice. Arriving in Vichy early in January, Admiral Leahy soon assured himself of Pétain's genuine desire to avoid a definitive involvement with the Axis.

Moreover, the coup of December 13 marked a decisive setback to the hopes of those elements, making their base in Paris, that wished to see a thoroughgoing reform of French institutions on the basis of fascist totalitarianism. As we have noted, the avowed partisans of fascism had not won representation in the cabinet at the inception of the new regime. In the course of the fall, however, Laval had begun to establish a political alliance with Déat and some of the others in Paris who were now proclaiming the need of France to remake herself in the German and Italian pattern. Laval apparently had no large interest in their schemes for domestic reform. He sought, rather, to make use of their support in his own struggle to bind the new regime to the diplomatic policy of "broad" collaboration, which he regarded as the one pivotal issue of the moment.

Had he emerged victorious over his adversaries in Vichy in the crisis that opened on December 13, Laval probably would have soon thereafter drawn men such as Déat into positions of importance in the government. Once Laval was dislodged, the zealots of fascism were without a *point d'appui* in the unoccupied zone. For Darlan, though by no means an irreconcilable enemy of fascism, had no personal links with Déat or Doriot or any of the other prophets of the "New Order." Nor was he in urgent need of their support in order to maintain his own position in Vichy. Though he was to admit into the government some of the minor prophets of fascism, such as Bénoist-Méchin, he was never to give place to either Déat or Doriot, the two principal figures in this faction. By the time he, in his turn, had to give up the vice-premiership, the moment was past when the fascists could hope to realize their program for the "regeneration" of France.

Therein lay what was probably the crucial importance of the struggle between Laval and his enemies. We have already noted that the coup of December 13 did not mean a complete reversal of diplomatic policy. Perhaps we may further acknowledge, contrary to the conviction of both Laval and those who sought to displace him, that it probably made little difference whether Vichy chose the course of "broad" or "narrow" collaboration. For France was in no position to withhold her collaboration altogether, and yet she could not largely affect the outcome of the war simply by the greater or lesser degree of her willingness to cooperate with the Axis.

Nevertheless, while it might not have had much effect upon the course of the war, it might well have involved grave consequences for the national life of the French themselves, had avowed proponents of fascism gained admittance to the government in the winter of 1940–41. Given power at that time, when the liberation of France from German occupation was more than three years distant, these zealots could have wreaked such vengeance upon their political opponents, and produced such an utter moral and intellectual chaos, that the traces of their rule would have endured, no one can say how long after their ultimate downfall.

To be sure, the preservation of the *status quo* was not the intention of the "conservatives" in the clique that unseated Laval and thus postponed the triumph of the fascists. But these revolutionaries of reaction were men of much more scruple, or inhibition, than were the champions of democratic dictatorship. And though the reform of French institutions which the "conservatives" strove to inaugurate was not without enduring consequences, the "National Revolution" which they initiated involved no measures that the French could not reconsider and undo, if they wished, once the Vichy regime had disappeared.

Thus we begin to see a familiar pattern emerge again. For the outcome of this, the first sharp inner crisis of the new regime, was the same sterile conclusion that had so often terminated the political battles of the Third Republic—one faction thwarted another, without winning a decisive victory. So the net result was that no decision was reached, save to forestall what might have been a new departure.

IX

FAMILLE, TRAVAIL...

FROM ITS START, the Vichy regime had a dual mission. As its immediate task, it sought an answer to the strange new diplomatic problem confronting France in the aftermath of her military defeat. As a longer-range purpose, the new regime also undertook a complete reform of the social and political institutions of the nation. At bottom, the two tasks were aspects of the same problem. One attempted to cope with the consequences of the disaster of 1940; the other, to remedy the weaknesses and vices in French national life that had helped bring about the debacle.

At the outset, the manner in which Vichy was to pursue either mission was uncertain. Among the multitudes in high and humble rank who acclaimed Pétain as the savior of the nation, there were wide divergences of opinion as to how his new regime should proceed. To be sure, only two factions—the avowed fascists and those whom we have called the "conservatives"—had a real chance of gaining influence in the government. Yet the "conservatives" and the fascists differed sharply in their outlook and aspirations.

As the fascists saw the problem of national reform, the basic need was for "national integration." That meant a new framework of institutions that would compel the entire nation to move with a single purpose in pursuit of its collective interest. In their view, the fault of the Third Republic was that it recognized no other political entities than the citizen and the nation. In practice, therefore, it proved incapable of suppressing a class struggle between the bourgeoisie and the proletariat, which reduced political life to a condition of unremitting civil war.

The remedy must involve, first, authoritarian leadership embodied in a dictator. In pressing this demand, the fascists found themselves in an embarrassing position. An old soldier near his dotage, with little clear notion of the broad problems of politics, was a poor figure of a *Fuehrer*. Yet there was no chance of displacing Marshal Pétain, so great was his prestige. Nor were the various factions among the fascists agreed upon another candidate for the office. So there was nothing for it but to wait for his overdue demise and hope that in the meantime someone who better understood the requirements of the office would emerge as his logical successor.

Next after the dictator, the essential was a single official political party—the *parti unique*. This was indispensable, both as a means of linking the dictator with the mass of the nation and as a means of recruiting personnel for subordinate positions of political leadership.

Provided these two principles—the dictatorship, and the *parti unique* —were established, the fascists had no repugnance for the institution of Parliament. Of course, they thought in terms of a Parliament without debate or division of opinion. But for such a Parliament, they envisioned a role of much importance, as a means of drawing the nation in the path which the dictator and the *parti unique* would mark out. The fascists also flirted with the idea of corporatism, seeing in the public recognition of the separate interests of ownership and labor the first step toward the conciliation of the differences between them. But corporatism, in their scheme, was in no sense a substitute for political organization. For the fascists were thoroughgoing *étatistes*. They had an unbounded trust in the competence of the state to solve problems, and they conceived of the nation as essentially a political community, with the citizens at the base of its structure, the dictator at the apex, and the *parti unique* and Parliament as the bonds between top and bottom.

The "conservatives," on the other hand, placed much less reliance upon the state, and attached much less importance to the role of the authoritarian national leader.[1] In their view, the vice of liberalism was

---

[1] The *Action Française* was the pontifical voice of the "conservative" point of view. However, it did not speak as an authoritative voice of the government nor even of those within the councils of the government who subscribed to "conservative" doctrines. Neither Charles Maurras, who had founded the paper and remained its master, nor Maurice Pujo, who had succeeded

its presumption that men are primarily citizens and, as such, essentially identical one with another. Such a conception, according to their argument, strips a man of all those attachments to his fellows which alone give him individuality. Instead of real persons, whose distinctive attributes are defined by their position within a family and their role in a business, profession, or trade, the liberal state recognizes only shapeless abstractions who, as citizens, are neither fathers nor sons, peasants nor landlords, workmen nor *patrons*. A state based upon this uniformitarian premise inevitably becomes a machine which the professional politician manipulates for his own advantage, while the real men who make up the nation become his pawns. Men do not live as atomistic individuals, each by and for himself, but only as members of social communities, of which the more important are the family and the fellowship of men who earn their livelihood in the same vocation. These social communities are the only proper basis of the state.

In the "conservative" view, therefore, the family and the "corporation," in the sense of a vocational association, were first premises. The family, being an institution of private rather than public character, lay outside the province of the state. The "corporation," on the other hand, must become the cornerstone of the entire structure of public life. The state could do no better than recognize the separate communities of interest among businessmen, workingmen, and peasants, help give a legal organization to these associations, and delegate to them, so far as possible, the right to manage their own affairs.

Under such a corporative regime, leadership in the nation would be vested not in a corps of professional politicians but in an élite chosen from among those who have earned the good regard of the men working alongside them. The voter would not be called upon, as under the liberal regime, to give his suffrage to one or another among a dozen rival professional office seekers, none of whom he knew personally. Instead, he would be expected to choose a representative from among men with whom he has had some degree of personal association, on the basis of their opinion on issues that have arisen in his own experience in his trade or business.

---

him as its editor, was in close touch with the government. Few of the men in Pétain's entourage who adhered to the ideas Maurras had popularized were willing to take orders from him. Nor did Maurras, who was in his late seventies, wish to take an active role in practical politics.

The state, in this scheme, would have only a limited role in national life. It would not disappear, but it would confine itself to action upon problems of general public concern—such as those arising out of the diplomatic relations among governments—which bear equally upon all members of the nation, without regard for distinctions of vocation among them.

From this starting point, the "conservatives" developed a position quite distinct from that of the fascists. Like their rivals, the "conservatives" wished to see the head of the state provide the nation with a more decisive leadership. In their conception, however, he would not be a kind of heroic superman, discerning the path of destiny by some mystic inner light and dragging along the mass of the nation like so much dead weight. He would serve, rather, as a kind of chairman of a board of directors, presiding over the deliberations of a network of corporative councils and striving to bring about a reconciliation of differences among them. The ultimate wisdom of the nation would arise out of these councils, not from the personal inspiration of the dictator.

Because of the lesser role they envisioned for the head of the state, the "conservatives" were much less interested in the *parti unique* than were the fascists, who regarded this as the indispensable link between the dictator and the people. Some of them did not disguise their distrust of an official party. They suspected that it would soon become a refuge for the professional politician, whose disappearance from public life must be, in the view of the "conservatives," one of the inevitable consequences of any wholesome political reform.

It is apparent, then, that the distinction between the "conservatives" and the fascists did not arise because one faction favored certain political innovations while the other endorsed quite a separate program. On the contrary, the two factions were agreed on the need for a more decisive and more personal leadership in government, on the need for an armistice in the struggle between rich and poor, and on the need for an end to the legalized warfare among rival political parties. The disagreement between them involved the ultimate intention behind these practical proposals. It was no whit less sharp for being subtle.

In determining the domestic character of the new regime, as well as its diplomatic orientation, the interval between July and December of 1940 proved crucial. The new government proceeded to its task of revising French institutions with astonishing alacrity. One reason for this promptness was that the struggle over domestic issues was more heavily weighted to one side than was that over the proper degree of collaboration with the Axis. From the outset, the Vichy regime was identified with the "conservative" point of view as far as internal policy was concerned. Despite some concessions that were made in response to the pressure of the fascists, it retained a "conservative" character down to its end.

There were numerous reasons for the advantage of the "conservatives" in this sphere of action. One was that the Axis had much less interest in what the French might do at home than in their attitude toward the course of the war. Though the Germans used their influence on several occasions to support those in France who urged "broad" collaboration as against "narrow," they made scarcely any attempt to influence debate in France concerning the reform of institutions.

Another factor was the success of the "conservative" faction in gaining positions of influence in the government at the moment of its inception. This was, in some degree, fortuitous. In June of 1940, Marshal Pétain had a free hand to choose his counsellors as he wished, and he had no clear commitment to any political faction. He had links with some persons in the milieu of the *Action Française,* but he was by no means at home in aristocratic and monarchist circles. After all, he had sprung from humble peasant stock, and he had accomplished his rise to the apex of his profession under the auspices of the Third Republic. Doubtless he called upon some men of "conservative" views, such as Baudouin, simply because they had been members of the previous Reynaud government and had spoken up in favor of the armistice, as had Pétain himself. Others, like Peyrouton, he chose because they had made a career in public administration without becoming involved in the politics of Parliament. Once established in office, these "conservatives" used their influence to draw others of like mind into the service of the new regime.

On the other hand, Pétain had little occasion to call upon the men who now became the chief advocates of fascism. Apparently he had no prior personal acquaintance with either Déat, whose background was

Socialist, or Doriot, whose origins were Communist. Whatever his relations with moderate republicans or the disciples of the *Action Française,* Pétain had no ties whatever with Marxian or proletarian political movements. Nor had either Déat or Doriot risen to such positions of importance in the politics of the Third Republic as to have a claim, by virtue of experience in the work of government, to a share in the leadership of the new regime. Perhaps Pétain would have made use of Colonel de la Rocque, who before the war had had links with both "conservatives" and fascists. But Colonel de la Rocque apparently chose not to seek an active role in the new regime and went into virtual retirement.[2]

The proponents of fascism could not look to Pierre Laval to represent their point of view in the cabinet on domestic problems, as he did on diplomatic questions. Laval showed scarcely any interest in their notions on internal reform. Perhaps this was because he regarded the discussion of long-range plans as premature while the war was still in course; perhaps, because he had no personal convictions on this topic; perhaps, because he remained loyal to the basic traditions of the Third Republic, under which he had first risen to prominence. At any event, he made his alliance with the fascists because he shared their wish for "broad" collaboration with the Axis rather than their views on the need of reform within France. So, while having to wage a relentless struggle against Laval and his allies on issues concerning relations with the Axis, the "conservatives" found themselves virtually unopposed on issues of reform at home. Their adversaries had no *point d'appui* within the cabinet.

Even though the domestic reforms of Vichy were drawn up by men who shared the same general outlook, these measures did not constitute a complete and self-consistent program. The decrees that embodied them were not all drafted by the same persons, working as a group, nor published at the same time, nor ever consolidated into a code or constitution. Some were prepared by members of Pétain's personal staff, others were worked out in meetings of the cabinet, and still others

[2] Remarkably little has come to light on Colonel de la Rocque's activities in this period. Evidently he chose not to reactivate his Parti Social Français, and he made no conspicuous public appearances. More than once, Doriot denounced him in *Le Cri du Peuple* as pro-British, and for a time the Germans had him under arrest. Nevertheless, he was put to death by members of the Resistance in 1944.

developed by the Conseil National, a consultative commission which Pétain appointed in January, 1941. Some measures necessary for a comprehensive reform were never promulgated—notably, the constitution providing for a national legislature—and some measures that were proclaimed as law were never put into operation. Other reforms were initiated that did not correspond to the intentions of the "conservatives." These were either grudging concessions to the demands of the fascists in Paris or responses to practical needs of the moment. Hence the work of reform reveals gaps, inconsistencies, and inner contradictions.

Moreover, the movement for reform soon began to lose momentum. In the summer of 1940 nearly everyone agreed on the need of a new departure of some kind, and the "conservative" clique in Vichy, making haste to exploit this sentiment, proceeded to the task of reform with vigor and enthusiasm. Within six months, the "conservatives" committed the new regime to their principles. With the organization of a "Corporation of Agriculture" in December, 1940, and the establishment of a scheme for corporative institutions in commerce and industry in October, 1941, they wrote their basic prescription into law. But thereafter they made little or no further progress. By that time, the war had blazed up again, after Hitler launched his invasion of Russia. Hence, diplomatic problems became so acute that proposals for the future regeneration of France became a matter of academic debate.

From the fall of 1941 onward, the "conservatives" were no longer thinking of completing their domestic program but were striving simply to wage a rearguard defense against their adversaries. Ultimately the fascists gained representation in the government, and at last began to remodel the Vichy regime according to their predilections. But they did not gain influence in Vichy soon enough, nor did they ever win a sufficiently clear mastery, either to accomplish a broad reform of their own or to efface the earlier work of the "conservatives."

Hence we may reasonably regard the measures which the "conservatives" introduced in 1940–41, as representing the intentions of the Vichy regime in the matter of reform. Likewise, we may treat these measures as the sketch of a comprehensive and logical program. For we have sufficient indication of the ideas which the "conservatives" espoused to enable us to distinguish their intentions and to make interpolations bridging the gaps in their work. Of course, we must recognize that the scheme of reform we thus construct is more ideal than actual. Nevertheless, it is not a wholly imaginary creation. Both its "conservative" sponsors and its fascist critics recognized that the work of reform initiated in 1940–41 constituted a single, rational structure, to which was soon given the name of the National Revolution.[3]

In the view of the "conservatives" who guided the National Revolution, as we have remarked, the foundation of social life was the family, which must be the corner stone of national reconstruction. This was not a new idea. It had figured in French conservative social thought throughout the nineteenth century, from the time of Bonald and De Maistre onwards. Its principal proponent had been the Catholic sociologist Frédéric Le Play, the founder of a movement for conservative social reform which had gained considerable following in the latter half of the nineteenth century.

In the doctrine of Le Play and his disciples, the *famille souche,* or "root-and-branch family," was presented as the natural and efficacious instrument of social well-being. It is in contrast to the "unstable family," which comprises only parents and their children and dissolves as soon as the children reach marriageable age and leave the parental home. The *famille souche,* on the other hand, comprises, besides the parents and their children, the grandparents, unmarried aunts and uncles, and those married children who choose not to set up homes of their own. Its members pool their economic resources, each drawing his sustenance from it. Under ideal conditions, the patrimony remains undivided from generation to generation.

Such an institution, Le Play taught, not only provides for the needs of the young, as does any family, but also furnishes security and affection to the aged, who can no longer fend for themselves but have a claim to repose and respect; to the spinster or widowed daughter, who can satisfy her hunger for close companionship only within the family

---

[3] It is not clear who originated the term National Revolution. Déat used it as the heading of an article in *L'Œuvre* as early as July 10, 1940. Pétain gave it official sanction in a speech on October 11, 1940, in which he first described the general program of reform which his government would institute. The *Action Française* never relished the name, because it seemed to reawaken memories of the Revolution of 1789.

of her parents; and to those who are physically or mentally handicapped, or temperamentally ill-equipped to make their way in the
world by themselves. In a land where such families flourish, there is
happiness for all, and it is a matter of little importance what kind of
political institutions prevail. On the other hand, in a land where the
"unstable family" is normal, no reform of the constitution or of the
economic system can assure the well-being of the people. Hence the
state can do nothing better—and little else of value—than encourage
and support the institution of the *famille souche*.

This approach to the problem of social welfare never attracted wide
public interest. It did not correspond to the preoccupation with political issues which was common among conservatives as well as liberals.
Nor did these doctrines lend themselves to the publication of manifestos
and the organization of parties or leagues. Nevertheless, this conception
found favor among those persons, outside the arena of public affairs,
who shared the conservative distrust of liberalism and Marxism. It also
gained support from the Catholic Church, since it accorded with the
Christian emphasis on the family as a sacramental institution as well
as with the growing desire among French Catholics for some program
of social reform that would acknowledge Christian religious principles.

But others, who had little or no sympathy with either Catholic or
conservative views, also favored a policy of nurture of the family. They
deemed such action necessary to check the decline in the birth rate,
which, in turn, seemed a factor in the decline of French military power.

From one point of view, to be sure, family life in France was always
closely knit. In rural regions where small-scale agriculture survived
with some degree of prosperity, the family still had roots in the soil and
drew sustenance from it. The peasant handed down his small holding
to his son, with the family remaining intact over a span of many generations. In towns and cities, the family business firm remained more
characteristic than the impersonal business corporation. Many an urban
family passed on its shop from father to son, just as though it were a
parcel of land. In village and town alike, the family gave evidence of
its vitality in the gatherings of the clan on the occasion of a wedding
or a funeral, and in the sacrifices which humble families often made

to provide an education for a gifted son or to give a daughter the dowry that would gain her a good marriage.

Nevertheless, the fact remained that the family was ordinarily small, marriages were often late, and irregular unions not uncommon. An obvious reason for this situation, as everyone realized, was that child rearing is expensive. Some were too poor to afford the luxury, while others, though better able to bear the cost, were unwilling to make the sacrifice of their personal comfort which numerous offspring would impose. The peasant family frequently forebore to raise more children after the birth of the first son, because its plot of land was usually too small to provide an adequate patrimony for more than one heir. The bourgeois postponed marriage so long—a man of thirty-five would regard himself as just becoming eligible—that he and his wife were past the best age for parenthood. The workingman, earning a meager pittance, was staggered at the cost of setting up a home.

An attempt to deal with the problem by means of subsidies to large families was begun two decades before the inception of the Vichy regime. Even before the First World War the state took steps in this direction by providing a differential wage, in certain categories of the civil service and for noncommissioned officers in the army and the navy, in favor of married men with children. Likewise, trade union agreements with the railroads and with coal-mine operators in the 1920s specified premium rates of wages and pensions for heads of large families.

More notable was a movement that developed in the 1920s, when certain philanthropic businessmen began to grant subsidies to their workers, in addition to their wages, according to the number of their children. Businessmen who made a practice of paying such subsidies began to band together with others, in the same branch of industry, who followed this custom. They would establish a common fund, known as a *caisse de compensation,* to which each employer would contribute a sum proportional to the size of his payroll. The *caisse* would then pay the bonuses to those workmen who qualified for them. The system gradually spread, wholly on a voluntary basis, until by 1930 the number of *caisses de compensation* reached about 230 and the number of workers covered by the plan totaled about 1,800,000.

The depression of the 1930s at first threatened to undo the progress made in the previous decade, since the burden upon the employers became more onerous. But rather than permit the *caisses* to disappear, the patrons of the movement demanded that the state require all employers to bear their fair share of the expense and allow all workers to share in the benefits. And because the scheme responded to the interest of the state in increasing the birth rate so as to provide for the future needs of the army, the demand was heeded. In 1932, a decree-law established the principle of requiring employers to contribute to a *caisse de compensation*. Simultaneously, the system was extended to include most workers in commerce and industry.

The system still showed serious deficiencies. The most obvious was that it provided benefits only for wage earners, not for employers or for the self-employed. Hence, it did not take in a considerable number of urban artisans. Nor, what was more important in terms of practical politics, did it include peasants who owned or rented their land, since these were working for their own account and not for wages.

Largely because of the complaint of the peasants, the government appointed a commission to review the entire problem and make recommendations for the improvement of the plan. Following the report of this commission, the previous legislation was brought together in 1939 into a single, comprehensive *Code de la famille*. At the same time, the earlier decrees were amplified so as to remove shortcomings in the policy.

The *Code de la famille* of 1939 made the system of subsidies to the family so inclusive as to cover the entire population and relieve nearly all the kinds of economic pressure that arise as a consequence of family life. Because it was impractical to require contributions to the *caisses de compensation* at a rate which would support the plan with its enlarged coverage, the state undertook henceforth to meet a portion of the costs out of public funds.

The subsidies which the legislation authorized were to be paid under one or more of a number of articles. First, in the order in which a family might present its claims, a bonus was paid upon the birth of the first child, provided this occurred within two years after the parents' marriage. The sum was determined according to the average monthly wage of a semiskilled workman in each locality. The bonus for the birth of the first child was fixed at 100 percent of the average local monthly wage.

After the birth of the second child, the family became eligible to draw a regular monthly allotment, known as the *allocation familiale,* at the rate of 10 percent of the average local wage. At the birth of the third child, the rate was raised to 30 percent, and it was increased by another 20 percent for the fourth and each succeeding child.

Still another allotment was paid to encourage mothers to remain at home and devote their whole time to the care of their children, instead of seeking work outside the home. Unlike the other premiums, this allotment to the mother-at-home (*la mère au foyer*) was payable only to families of wage earners in urban communities, not to employers or the self-employed, nor to peasants. The sum, paid each month, might run as high as 10 percent of the average local wage.

Yet another subsidy, this one available only to families in rural communities, involved the loan of a small sum to be used toward the purchase of farm land or the furnishing of a home. Such a loan was granted to newly married couples, on condition that the couple earn its livelihood in agriculture or a rural artisan trade. A portion of the loan was canceled upon the birth of each child. But the unpaid balance became due at once if the couple were to separate from one another or move into town.

Hence, Vichy had no need to make a large-scale legislative innovation in order to attain its purpose of nurturing the family. Vichy had only to take over the *Code de la famille* and put its provisions into operation. These measures, representing the product of a long prior development, did not constitute a narrow, partisan program, identifiable with the Third Republic. Indeed, they remained in force, after the Vichy regime disappeared, under the Fourth Republic. Yet the policy embodied in the *Code de la famille,* which clearly bespoke a concern for the family, not merely the birth rate, corresponded fully to the principles of the National Revolution. Its acceptance by Vichy did not in any sense involve an opportunistic compromise of the intentions of the new regime.

Besides undertaking the administration of the *Code de la famille,* which represented a task of some considerable magnitude under the chaotic conditions of wartime, Vichy introduced a number of modifications in the plan. For example, the rate of payments was increased; the *allocation familiale* was made payable to the mother, rather than the father, in order to avoid the misuse of the funds by an unworthy father; women who were beneficiaries under any of the provisions for the subsidy of the family were required, in the event of subsequent pregnancies, to submit to prenatal medical examinations; and social workers were authorized to check up on the care of children in homes which were receiving *allocations familiales*. To supervise all matters of public policy relating to the family, a new Secretariat General for Youth and the Family was established under one of the ministries.[4]

Further evidence of public favor was also accorded to *familles nombreuses*. For instance, landlords were forbidden to refuse to rent their premises to families with children—though this proved impossible to enforce. Mothers of large families were given priority when waiting in queues, which was a privilege of no mean importance in a period of rationing and general shortages.

Other measures modified procedures for marriage and divorce. Couples about to be married were required to take a medical examination. Each was notified if he or she was suffering from a disease prejudicial to family life—although such a person would not be prevented by law from proceeding with the marriage, nor obliged to inform the opposite partner. Once married, neither partner could enter suit for divorce until after the lapse of three years. In order to avoid reminding the public of this alternative to marital stress, the press was forbidden to publish testimony given in divorce suits. Nor were persons other than the interested parties admitted into the court room during such trials.

Associated with this concern for the family was a campaign for the protection of public morals, which afforded a contrast to the laisser-

---

[4] In general, the Paris press endorsed the policy of subsidies for the family. However, Déat and Doriot were not of one mind as to the motives behind it. Déat denounced as reactionary the conception that the wife should devote herself to "the stove, the scrubbing board, and the cradle." But Doriot argued that the French labor movement had traditionally and quite properly held that the proper place for the wife was at home, and that one of the evils of capitalism was the drawing of women out of the home into shops and factories.

faire attitude of the Third Republic toward such matters. In the main, this involved pronouncements on the part of public officials in favor of virtue, denunciations of those who made a business of selling pornographic books, magazines, and photographs, and reproving remarks upon women who wore shorts or immodest bathing suits.[5]

In the same spirit, Vichy launched a crusade against alcoholism. To Americans, remembering their own experience with "prohibition" and knowing France as the home of choice potables, this French campaign against strong drink seemed somewhat ludicrous. Yet, in truth, the abuse of alcohol was a serious problem of France. Statistics were available in lush abundance to bear sober witness to this charge.

In an attempt to reduce the level of consumption, Vichy promulgated a series of complicated decrees for the regulation of the traffic in wine and spirits. In themselves, these measures achieved less than mediocre success. They were not well enforced, and they left many loopholes. Indeed, the new regulations perhaps worsened the situation. The toper who was unable to order his usual red wine was free to obtain strong distillates, to which an herbal concoction was added, on the ground that the infusion was a "digestive" and therefore medicinal. Eventually, however, the consumption of alcohol was considerably reduced by virtue of a shortage of the cheaper grades of wine.

Vichy also showed an interest in organizations for youth. In part, this was an endeavor to develop agencies for the control of public opinion in behalf of the new regime. It resembled the practice of the German, Italian, and Russian dictatorships, which made use of youth movements as an auxiliary to the official political party. But it arose also, in part, out of the interest of the "conservatives" who were directing the National Revolution in the welfare of the youth of the country, on much the same grounds as their concern for the family. Responsibility for both aspects of public policy was vested in the same new Secretariat General for Youth and the Family.

Foremost among the youth organizations which the new regime sponsored were the Équipes Sociales and the Compagnons de France.

---

[5] *Le Figaro* reported an official pronouncement that it was not improper for women to wear ski pants while skiing.

The members of these organizations undertook such tasks as helping with the harvest in regions where there was a shortage of agricultural labor.

Also notable were the *chantiers de jeunesse,* or youth camps. These were set up to provide a substitute for the military service that young men were formerly required to undergo, since the armistice did not permit the induction into the army of the annual classes of conscripts. The members of these camps, therefore, unlike the other youth organizations, were not volunteers. At the outset, they were required to provide labor for public works, such as the reforestation of wastelands. Eventually, however, after the Nazis began to require the French to furnish manpower for their war industries, Vichy became so preoccupied with the conscription of labor to serve in Germany that the system of compulsory service in the *chantiers de jeunesse* became a dead letter.

The success of the various Vichyite youth movements in the unoccupied zone was meager. On the other side of the line of demarcation, the Germans proved scarcely more favorable to the youth organizations which Vichy sponsored than to those surviving from the Third Republic, which soon disappeared from the scene in the occupied zone. Some of the proponents of fascist totalitarianism in Paris undertook to set up youth movements of their own, in competition with those originating in the south. But these fared no better. In the outcome, therefore, no organization won wide influence among the youth until late in 1942, when the various underground "resistance" movements began to win their allegiance.

In the plan of the National Revolution, corporatism was of only a little less importance than the nurture of the family and concern for the young. In this sphere, Vichy made a more distinctive, though evanescent, innovation. To be sure, despite the premise of individualism upon which the previous regime rested, there had been an appreciable drift toward corporatist practices under the Third Republic. There had even been a movement in the interbellum period to establish a national commission the members of which would represent the corporative interests of capital and labor rather than those of citizens irrespective of class, and to give this commission the right to deliberate upon problems of national concern and to make recommendations to the cabinet. Such an organism, the Conseil National Économique, had been created in 1925. It had persisted, without gaining large influence, down to the demise of the Third Republic. However, Vichy made a much more comprehensive attempt to develop corporative associations than had ever been undertaken by the Third Republic, and the new regime avowed the purpose of giving over to these "corporations" a larger voice in public affairs than had previously been contemplated.

We have already indicated the place which corporatism occupied in the "conservative" critique of the earlier regime. We have also noted that the fascists, as well as the "conservatives," paid lip service to this idea. But the corporatism of Vichy owed its inspiration much more largely to "conservative" and Catholic sources than to the example of Nazi Germany or Fascist Italy. The ventures which the new regime made in this kind of reform drew warmer criticism than applause from the zealots of fascism who directed the Paris press.

For all their serious intention, the "conservatives" accomplished least in this portion of their work. Little more came out of their eloquent theories on this subject than a series of decrees establishing, on paper, a corporative organization of agriculture and outlining the prospectus of a similar scheme for the urban business world. In practice, the government relied upon the old, established methods of bureaucratic regulation which they had so long denounced under the Third Republic.

The corporative organization of agriculture proved easier to draft than the parallel system for the urban economy. The basic decree, setting up a "Corporation of Agriculture," was dated December 6, 1940. The new association was to include as members all persons who gained their livelihood from agriculture. It was to have three levels. At the top, there was to be a national council, appointed by the government. Beneath this, there was to be a number of regional councils, the members of which were to be designated by the national council. At the bottom, there were to be local branches, each headed by an officer known as the syndic, who was to be named by the regional council. These branches were to include in their membership the entire agricultural population of each rural community. It would therefore comprise peasants, wage laborers, and large-scale landholders, without distinction among them. Though the organization was thus built upon the principle of appointment from above, a measure of democratic influence would ultimately be provided, by giving the local branches the right to propose candidates for appointment as syndic. Likewise, the regional council would eventually be given the right to make nominations for appointment to the national council.

No decree ever made clear the powers or functions of the Corporation as a whole, nor the role of its local and regional organs. Presumably these questions were to be answered on the basis of practical experience. But as it turned out, the Corporation never attained a role of sufficient practical importance to provide such an empirical answer, nor even for the problem of the definition of functions to be sharply posed. The national council hardly met, the regional councils only slowly took shape, and the local branches lagged still farther behind.

As a gesture, however, the Corporation of Agriculture had some importance. It helped offset the impression, which held over from the period of the Popular Front, that the government was more sensitive to the needs and aspirations of the laboring people of the cities and towns than to those of the villages. So it seemed to give some shadow of substance to the verbal tributes to the peasantry which the leaders of the new regime, from Marshal Pétain on down, never tired of delivering. Such declarations of intent, together with the real material prosperity which the war brought to the farmers of France, as of every other country, gave Vichy probably a better name among the peasants than with any other section of the population save big business.

Vichy also took other measures to protect the corporate interests of the agricultural population. For example, it made an attempt to reclaim wastelands. Likewise, it encouraged resettlement in regions where the migration of the peasants into the towns had led to depopulation. It also ventured a timid modification of the inheritance laws, so as to check the partition of small peasant holdings upon the death of the owner.

As soon as the problem of a shortage of food began to develop, moreover, Vichy quickly decided not to enforce price control as against the farmers. It chose to encourage them to raise as much as possible and sell their produce at whatever price they could get. Consequently a good many peasants and large-scale farm operators made substantial profits on the black market, with the tolerance of the government. By no means did all the peasants grow rich in this illicit trade, and those who did had difficulty either in spending their gains or finding a way to protect their savings against the eventual depreciation of the franc. But, naturally, the entire rural population was less affected by the shortage of food than were the town dwellers. Certainly most of the peasants suffered much less hardship throughout the occupation than the urban working class.

It proved harder to establish even a plan for corporative institutions in commerce and industry than for agriculture. It required more than a year to bring forth the basic legislation. After another three years, the scheme still remained largely paperwork. This was due, in large measure, to a struggle within the leadership of the new regime between the proponents of two different conceptions of corporatism.

One faction, which we may generally identify with the "conservatives," insisted that the new "corporations" must emphasize an autonomous cooperation between capital and labor. The other faction leaned toward the organization of capital and labor in separate institutions. This latter conception corresponded to the views of the proponents of totalitarianism, since it gave promise of "integrating" the two antagonistic classes under the guidance of the state. It also made an appeal to some elements of the trade-union movement. Such a scheme gave promise of strengthening the position of organized labor by creating a single trade-union structure and making membership in it compulsory. The chief spokesman of this point of view was René Belin, whom Pétain appointed, at the instance of Laval, as Minister of Industrial Production and Labor.

A first proposal for the solution of the problem, drawn up by Belin, was presented to the cabinet in September, 1940. It was turned down, at the insistence of the "conservatives," because it seemed to express the spirit of trade unionism, rather than corporatism. A second proposal, representing the ideas of the "conservatives," was blocked by Belin. A third draft, brought before the cabinet in December, 1940, fared no better. Thereupon, in February, 1941, the problem was referred to a special commission, comprising representatives of the various trade unions and of business interests. After six months of debate, this commission finally agreed on the terms of a statute, which the government promulgated under the date of October 4, 1941.

As a preliminary to the new economic organization, the government had ordered the dissolution of the principal existing national organizations of capital and labor. In particular, it had suppressed the Confédération Générale du Patronat, the Comité des Forges, the Comité des Houillères, the Confédération Générale du Travail, and the Confédération Française des Travailleurs Chrétiens. This action, taken under a decree of November 9, 1940, did not require the disappearance of trade unions or trade associations within particular industries, although in point of fact, most trade unions ceased to operate. It aimed, rather, at those organizations that cut across the boundaries of a single business or trade to bind men together primarily on the basis of their class.

The Charter of Labor, as the decree of October 4, 1941, came to be known, did not itself establish "corporations"; it only prescribed the procedure by which they were subsequently to be created. According to its terms, the government was to designate appropriate divisions of the national economy, to which the term "families" was applied. Each of these "families," or subdivisions of a "family," was to become the province of a separate corporative union. Only one such corporative union was envisaged for each "family," and membership in it was to be compulsory. Separate categories of membership within the corporative union were provided for workmen, foremen and supervisors, technicians and sales staff, managers and proprietors.

Each of these categories of members within a single corporative union might organize and take action separately, on a local, regional, or national scale, in matters concerning them as a group and not of interest to the other categories of members. For instance, master printers could meet together to consider problems relating to the allocation of paper supplies. But on issues concerning all categories of members within a single corporative union, action could be taken only by *comités sociaux,* or "social committees," comprising representatives of each of the various categories. Such problems would include the determination of wages and other matters normally subject to collective bargaining, the conditions of apprenticeship, or practices bearing on the recruitment and training of the labor force, and, in some instances, welfare activities such as recreation programs, or measures to protect the health of the workers and reduce industrial accidents.

The Charter of Labor also specified principles for the determination of wage rates, which had so often been the occasion of strife between capital and labor. Wages should involve three components—a "living wage," or *minimum vital,* representing the least sum sufficient to support a person at a decent standard, which the government would prescribe; a supplement according to the size of the worker's family, which would be provided, under the *Code de la famille,* by the *allocation familiale;* and a differential which would take into account, either in the form of piece rates or a kind of bonus, such factors as superior skill, hazardous conditions of work, night shifts, and the like. Each corporative union would establish its own schedule of rates, in the light of these principles, either for a particular enterprise or for all workers in the same trade in a particular region. Neither strikes nor lock-outs would be permitted.

Such was the prospectus; the realization of the scheme was much less impressive. The government proceeded only slowly with the task of dividing up the urban economy into "families," each of which was to define the boundaries of a particular corporative union. Indeed, this work was not completed before the demise of the entire regime in the summer of 1944. In order to make a start at the construction of the corporative edifice without waiting for the blueprint to be finished, it was decided to begin at once at the base of the structure by setting up *comités sociaux* in particular shops and factories. It was thought that these *comités sociaux d'entreprise* could immediately commence their work of conciliating the interests of business and labor at a local level, which was the crux of the entire scheme. Subsequently they could be linked together according to whatever system of filiations the government might eventually announce.

Perhaps two thousand such *comités sociaux d'entreprise*—the number is vague because many existed only on paper—were thus organized. Most of these were in Paris and other cities of the occupied zone. Some of them made a serious attempt to develop a program of action. Even with the best of intentions, however, these *comités sociaux* were unable to accomplish much. It was beyond their competence to set aside the proliferating economic decrees of the government, which was striving to cope with the immense economic dislocations resulting from the occupation and the state of war abroad, or to relieve the shortages of power, materials, and transport, which soon became the principal source of economic distress, affecting management and labor alike. So the *comités sociaux* could do little but talk, or busy themselves with minor matters such as sports programs. In many instances, the *comité social* amounted to no more than a committee of foremen, appointed by the owner and under his orders.

Vichy did its best to make up for its want of achievement in the practice of corporatism by a profuse exposition of its theory. Pétain himself made repeated declarations, in his public speeches, of the crucial importance of corporatism in his plans for the new France. The various propaganda agencies of the regime pursued a sustained campaign to develop this theme. In the same vein, private persons, on their own initiative, published books and pamphlets to the number of some hundreds, extolling the merits of the corporatist approach to social and economic problems. In the main, the exposition gave expression to the views of the "conservatives," drawing upon the ideas of Catholic social theorists such as La Tour du Pin, presenting corporatism as rooted in French experience under the Old Regime, and seldom making reference to the corporatist theories of the Axis countries.

Yet the public response was far from enthusiastic. The Corporation of Agriculture drew rather little comment, favorable or otherwise. But the Charter of Labor received considerable open criticism, while much of the praise of it came from intellectuals, who approved its principles but lacked personal acquaintance with the actual problems of business or labor.

To be sure, some businessmen shared the Catholic and "conservative" point of view which had inspired the experiment. Others took satisfaction from what seemed to them a device for curbing the independence of the trade-union movement and permitting monopolistic combinations for the suppression of business competition.

By a contrary calculation, some elements identified with the labor movement also hoped to turn the Charter of Labor to their own uses.

In their interpretation, the new plan gave promise of strengthening labor as against capital, since it would compel all workers to belong to a single, strong trade-union movement, thus putting an end to the warfare among rival unions that had so long plagued the French labor movement. It would also put the stamp of public approval upon the process of collective bargaining. Moreover, the government, by prescribing what it regarded as a basic living wage and continuing its subsidies to the worker in consideration of the size of his family, would guarantee that the process of negotiation could only raise wages above an ample minimum.

Only relatively few businessmen, however, paid serious heed to the Charter of Labor, one way or the other, and most of the spokesmen for the labor movement remained suspicious of it. The leaders of the Catholic trade-union movement—the Confédération Française des Travailleurs Chrétiens—were not pleased with the prospect of seeing their members merged with the irreligious hordes which had hitherto adhered to the Confédération Générale du Travail. For their part, the larger number of militants who had hitherto belonged to the C.G.T. were committed to either the Socialist or the Communist version of Marxism. Most of them soon wrote off the entire National Revolution as the work of clerical reactionaries. Those who subscribed to the idea of "pure" unionism were no better disposed toward what seemed to them a device for curbing the independence of the labor movement. Especially, they distrusted the prohibition of strikes.

Moreover, Vichy itself helped undermine confidence in its intentions by creating a parallel structure of new economic institutions which seemed destined for a more decisive role. This was done under a decree of August 16, 1940, which was promulgated and put into force while the cabinet was still debating the issues involved in what later became the Charter of Labor. By the terms of this decree, provision was made for the appointment by the government of a *comité d'organisation* for each branch of industry, comprising members of the principal business enterprises in the industry, and a *commissaire* representing the government.

The relationship between these *comités d'organisation* and the corporative unions envisioned by the Charter of Labor was never clear.

In the mind of Belin, who sponsored both plans while serving as Minister of Industrial Production and Labor, the two were to be correlative. The *comités d'organisation* were to be the instruments of national economic planning, by means of which the government would bring about what it deemed a proper balance among the various branches of industry. The corporative unions were to be the agencies for the conciliation of the diverse interests of capital and labor within each branch and for its self-regulation, within the bounds of the directives of the government.

But, as we have noted, the plan for the corporative unions never came into operation on a large scale, whereas a prompt start was made on the scheme for *comités d'organisation,* and these soon gained practical importance. Subject to the Office Central de Répartition des Produits Industriels, which became the key agency of the government in matters of wartime economic policy, the *comités d'organisation* were given the right to help determine the allocation of raw materials, control prices, determine methods of production, and regulate other business practices. They soon became the instrument of a more thoroughgoing economic *dirigisme* than France had ever known under the Third Republic.

Hence no one could avoid a considerable skepticism toward the corporatist theories according to which Vichy promised to curb the power of the bureaucracy and give over the regulation of social and economic life to autonomous associations of those who gained their livelihood from the same vocation. Nor, since the government gave representation in the *comités d'organisation* principally to the larger business enterprises, could anyone take very seriously the promise of an equal voice for labor and ownership. In sum, the corporatist experiment in the urban economy not only proved ineffectual: it failed even to demonstrate an honest intention of settling social and economic problems on the basis of equity, instead of accepting the basis of the systematic opposition of class interests.

X

... PATRIE

IN THEIR SCHEME for national regeneration, the "conservatives" who designed the National Revolution put their hope mainly in strengthening the family and developing corporative associations. They had but little expectation of accomplishing positive improvements through changes in the structure of the government. As a common denominator in their thought, and in contrast to the point of view of their fascist adversaries, they shared a distrust of the state and a desire to reduce its role in national life to the minimum. They conceived of personal and public well-being as depending much more upon private and semipublic associations than upon statutes and decrees.

Yet they acknowledged that certain functions were within the proper province of the state, and they insisted upon the need of correcting certain notorious deficiencies of the Third Republic. Despite their wish to lessen the pressure of politics upon the nation, they soon found themselves compelled by practical imperatives, arising out of the armistice and the occupation, to saddle France with a more pervasive *étatisme* than the prior regime had ever sponsored.

As they approached the problem of political reform, the "conservatives" saw two main tasks. One was to revise the institutions of the national government in such a way as would provide a more resolute national leadership, capable of defining a policy and putting it into practice. The other was to afford a larger degree of influence to the local and regional agencies of government. But it was not sufficient simply to define the need for reform. It was equally important to propose specific measures which would attain the desired purpose. In this latter respect, the "conservatives" who presided over the National Revolution proved no more capable than the liberal politicians who had managed the prior regime.

No one opposed the aim of making the national government more decisive. The Third Republic had given ample evidence of its failure to fulfill the function of policy making, which was seemingly vested in the cabinet but actually usurped by the upper echelons of the civil service—unless, as too often happened, the solution of problems was simply postponed until they became utterly insoluble. The "conservatives" were not alone in recognizing this. The proponents of fascism had made much the same point, in their criticism of the liberal regime. Even the partisans of the Third Republic had acknowledged this weakness in French political life.

But this consensus did not make it easier to reach agreement on how to accomplish a reform. In the view of those republicans who supported the National Revolution, the head of the state was to have much the same role as the Prime Minister in Britain, or the President of the United States. In the view of the fascists, however, he was to be a *Fuehrer,* accountable to the nation in some mystic or symbolic fashion but acting on his own impulse and drawing the nation along behind him.[1] For their part, the "conservatives" never made up their mind as to what they meant by a personal leader.

In the opinion of some of the "conservatives," the necessary key reform meant the restoration of an hereditary monarchy. In the summer and fall of 1940 there was some speculation in France, and a good deal more abroad, as to the likelihood of such a restoration.

So far as can be ascertained, however, the chance was never large. In the first place, not more than a small minority, even among the "conservatives," seriously contemplated such a possibility. For the institution of monarchy had been so long supplanted in France, and the previous attempts at a restoration so ludicrous, that the whole idea seemed Graustarkian. In the second place, Pétain, whose cooperation would be indispensable, gave no sign of eagerness for such a venture. Whatever his sympathies as between royalism and republicanism, he was in no haste to relinquish his role as the martyr-savior of France in

---

[1] It is perhaps not without significance that there is no word in French quite equivalent to *Fuehrer.* The French sometimes gallicize the English word "leader," for lack of a word of their own.

order to become merely the senior henchman of an obscure pretender. For their part, even the few zealous devotees of royalism had reason to hesitate at the thought of restoring a king at once, since the monarchy would have to begin its precarious career under the taint of collaboration with the Axis.[2]

There being no realistic likelihood of the reestablishment of hereditary monarchy, there was little alternative to a reaffirmation of the principle of an elective chief of state. To be sure, Pétain assumed the right to designate his political heir, and conceivably he might have made this the regular constitutional practice of the new regime. But such a solution would not have suited the French conception of a constitution, and none of the various factions espoused it.

There remained the question of how to choose the members of the councils, comparable to Parliament or substituting for it, to which the head of the state must turn for advice and assistance. For this problem, the fascists had a pat answer—establish a *parti unique,* then permit popular election of both the head of the state and a legislature.[3] Since the head of the state would also be head of the *parti unique,* and all the members of Parliament would be members of the *parti unique,* the government would then have a single mind. With only a single party presenting candidates, popular elections would be a mere pretense, of course, while the official party, which would dictate policy, would recruit its members by cooptation.

This did not appeal to the "conservatives." Such a solution of the problem would make the *parti unique* a secure haven for the professional politician, whose disappearance from the scene was one of the promised blessings of the National Revolution. However, the "conservatives" never worked out an answer of their own to the problem of how to reconcile election with leadership. For this reason, if no other,

[2] Since the extinction of the senior French Bourbon line, upon the death of the Comte de Chambord in 1883, the Orléans family had been generally recognized as having the best claim to the French dynastic succession. At the inception of the Vichy regime, the pretender was the Duc de Guise, who was the son of a son of Louis Philippe. An exile, since French law did not permit any member of a dynasty that had ever reigned in France to reside on French soil, he died in Spanish Morocco in August, 1940. Thereupon his son, the Comte de Paris, succeeded to the dynastic claim. Subsequently the Comte de Paris made a visit to Vichy, but nothing came of it. Ultimately he declared himself for the Gaullists.

[3] Déat was the principal advocate of the *parti unique.* Doriot's *Le Cri du Peuple* gave less prominence to the idea, and *Les Nouveaux Temps* was unenthusiastic.

their schemes for a new constitution never amounted to more than vague talk.

In the endeavor to reinvigorate local and regional government, likewise, the National Revolution set forth a commendable purpose but never solved the practical problem. In their criticism of the liberal regime, the "conservatives" had long complained of the centralization of political decisions in the capital. The simpler minds among them put the blame for this upon the Revolution of 1789. The more astute perceived the same vice under the Bourbon absolutism in the Old Regime. Because of the preponderance of Paris over the rest of the nation, so the argument ran, a man of ambition, with an interest in politics, could never hope to find an outlet for his talents in his native town or village, while those who chose to seek a career in Paris were obliged thereby to cut themselves off from the nation as a whole. This contention was not without an element of truth, as many French and foreign observers had recognized long before the crisis of 1940.

However, the interest of the "conservatives" in lessening the disproportionate role of Paris was entangled with romantic schemes for restoring the historic provinces of France as these had been under the Old Regime. Thus linked with extraneous notions, the proposal unnecessarily aroused the opposition of all who cherished the traditions of 1789. No less unfortunately, it was also linked with still more chimeric dreams for reviving the distinctive language, literature, and culture which some regions, such as Provence, had developed in the Middle Ages.

Not only did the "conservatives" becloud the issue with these other considerations, but they made no serious attempt to solve the stubborn practical problem involved in political decentralization. For France is not well suited to federalism; she is so compact and homogeneous that local governments have little basis for autonomy as against the national government. Yet any solution that did not involve a clear distinction of power and responsibility between the national and the regional or local governments would mean only a minor readjustment in the structure of the bureaucracy. This would not necessarily mean an increase of efficiency, and it certainly would not achieve the broader purpose which the "conservatives" sought.

Since the sponsors of the National Revolution made so little advance from the realm of general aims to that of specific plans, it is not surprising that Vichy accomplished little or nothing. The few measures of a quasi-constitutional order which the new regime introduced did not reveal any clear pattern, and none outlasted its short tenure of power.

At the base of the political structure, the new regime proceeded no further than to disrupt the existing institutions, without devising new ones. Thus the elective municipal councils were abolished in towns with a population of more than two thousand, and their administration was put under appointive rule. In part, this move was inspired by the notion that in a village or town of small size the voter could choose his municipal councillors from among men of whom he had some personal knowledge. In a larger town, he could only vote for one as against another of a number of professional politicians, none of whom he knew. But another inspiration for this move was doubtless opportunistic. For the municipal councils in the larger urban centers, which were thus swept away, were the breeding ground of those politicians who had been the stalwarts of the previous regime. However, a measure which gave over the government of these towns and cities to the appointive administration certainly did nothing to decentralize political power. It therefore ill accorded with the criticism which the "conservatives" directed against rule by the bureaucracy.

At the intermediate level, between the town or village and the national government, Vichy made only slightly more progress. The elective councils of the *départements,* like those of the larger cities, were dissolved. Though a return to elective regional government was envisioned as soon as circumstances permitted, the prefect thus gained, for the time being, complete charge of the *département.* Because of the disruption of the normal means of communication, the prefects now exercised a larger independence of action than ever before. In order to establish a closer control over them, therefore, Vichy created a new echelon in the administrative apparatus, comprising twelve regional prefects, or super-prefects, each of whom had authority over the prefects of a number of *départements.* This move was not merely a response to the immediate need of supervising the prefects. It was also part of the scheme for reestablishing provinces as an area of government comprising several *départements*. Nevertheless, its effect was not to implement the plan for decentralization but quite the opposite, to strengthen the apparatus of bureaucratic administration from the capital.

As to reform at the apex of the political structure, Vichy was still less decisive. Even the obvious question of the relationship between the new regime and its predecessor was never cleared up.[4] From one point of view, it could be argued that the Third Republic did not terminate with the accession of Marshal Pétain to absolute rule. Manifestly Pétain held this rule by virtue of a delegation of power according to the constitutional procedures of the Third Republic. Moreover, the two houses of Parliament remained in existence, even though they no longer held meetings. Pétain himself acknowledged their ultimate authority, when he proposed, in October of 1943, to summon them into session again as a National Assembly, in order to enact a constitutional law determining the succession to his office.

On the other hand, the legislation that created the new regime in July of 1940 explicitly empowered Pétain to issue organic laws by his own decree, to draft a whole new constitution, and to secure the ratification of such a constitution, if he wished, without again consulting the National Assembly of the Third Republic. It would be unreasonable to presume that the members of Parliament gave him this right without expecting him to make use of it. And Pétain made clear that he regarded his government as the inception of a new regime, not merely an extension of the Third Republic. For within a few weeks after his accession, public documents began to appear under the name of *État Français* rather than *République Française*.

Pétain made an attempt to change more than the name. In January, 1941, he appointed a Conseil National, to which he gave over the task of drafting a complete new constitution, as well as considering other reforms. A commission of the Conseil National promptly set to work on this assignment. From time to time, rumors spread that the text was soon to be revealed, and speculation developed as to its provisions.

---

[4] A bon mot of the time: "To the monarchy without a king which MacMahon established, Pétain has added only the absence of the republic."

But the commission did not complete its work until late in 1943. Thereupon it was announced that the new constitution would not become operative until the return of peace, and its terms would not be made public in the meantime.

In the absence of a new constitution, Pétain continued to exercise an unlimited personal rule. From the start, he took the title of Chief of State, but he also assumed charge of the deliberations of the cabinet. Thus he combined the roles that had been filled, under the previous regime, by the President of the Republic and the President of the Council of Ministers, or Premier. In 1942, after Laval returned to the government, Pétain gave him the title of Chief of the Government, with the former functions of the Premier. The Marshal, remaining Chief of State, kept only a role comparable to that of the President of the Republic. Subsequently Pétain empowered Laval to issue decrees on his own signature alone. However, this delegation did not represent a deliberate change in the structure of the regime but only a feeble gesture on the part of Pétain to indicate that he did not wish to assume personal responsibility for some of the measures of "broad" collaboration which Laval urged.

In practice, of course, Pétain never pretended to exercise his rule unaided. Not only did he delegate the management of the routine of government to his principal subordinate, Laval or Darlan, and to the cabinet. He also took counsel in other quarters. He made much use of his personal staff, which soon rivaled the cabinet in importance. He planned to turn over questions involving basic reforms of long-range significance to the Conseil National. For a time, this new consultative commission, comprising luminaries from various vocations of leadership, seemed destined to take over the role of the previous Parliament. Actually, however, the Conseil National never amounted to much. Its main accomplishment was to draw up the text of the new constitution, which never became operative. It was never consulted on issues of immediate importance. Nor was it ever summoned into a plenary session after its first such meeting.

As it turned out, the Conseil d'État took over much of the role that had been envisioned for the new Conseil National. Under the previous regime, the Conseil d'État, comprising the top level of the civil service,

had long exercised a strong influence upon the government, albeit behind the scenes. Some observers had considered it more decisive than
the cabinet itself. In the Vichy period, with Parliament in limbo and
the Conseil National stillborn, the Conseil d'État gained a crucial importance in shaping day-to-day policy on all questions save those involving foreign relations.

In its attempt to redefine the role of the cabinet, the new regime had
a bit more success than in establishing a regular procedure of legislation.
From the outset, Pétain made it a point to keep the cabinet small in
size, including no more than about ten men with the rank of minister.
Secretaries of state, responsible to one or another minister but excluded
from the top-level deliberations of the cabinet, handled the technical
routine of the administrative departments. In principle, this promised
a considerable improvement over the practice that had developed under
the Third Republic, where the cabinet, comprising twenty or thirty
men, had become so large as to be cumbersome. But in practice, the
smaller cabinet of Vichy proved no more effective. Even though it
no longer represented a committee of delegates from a coalition of
political parties, it was never well-knit. It still included antagonistic
factions, working at cross purposes. Indeed, in the two intervals when
Laval participated in the government, he seldom kept his colleagues
informed of his actions. Much less did he heed their opinions.

Nor did the autocratic regime make the cabinet more stable than
before. In the fifty months of the Vichy era, there were two major
reorganizations of the cabinet, besides a number of replacements of
particular ministers. So the three successive ministries had an average
span of only about eighteen months, which was scarcely an improvement over the record of the Third Republic.

Vichy proved no clearer in its attitude toward political parties. Both
the "conservatives" and the fascists were agreed in their repugnance
to the system of a multiplicity of parties that had been characteristic
of the Third Republic. But the two factions did not make the same
diagnosis of this malady. As we have remarked, the "conservatives"
generally were hostile toward political parties of any kind, which they
regarded as the nest of the noxious professional politician, whereas the
fascists proposed to substitute a single party for the swarm of rival or-

ganizations that previously had shared the role of political leadership in the nation. Yet, by the irony of events, it was the "conservatives" who took the first step toward the creation of a *parti unique,* while the fascists sponsored a number of antagonistic political movements.

At the start of the new era, the political parties of the Third Republic disappeared. Almost immediately, Vichy set up a new political organization in the unoccupied zone. This was the Légion des Combattants Français, which began in August of 1940 as a league of veterans of the two wars. At its start, the movement was under the leadership of "conservatives"—General Weygand was one of those instrumental in creating it. Its tone was less political than moralistic. Its members pledged loyalty to the marshal and the National Revolution, but in terms of dedication to the task of national regeneration rather than a partisan outlook. Because of the tension that developed between Vichy and Berlin in the fall of 1940, the Germans did not permit the Légion to operate in the occupied zone.

There, instead, the fascists gained a free hand, and two political parties rose to prominence. One of these was the Parti Populaire Français (P.P.F.), which Doriot had founded before the war. The other was the Rassemblement National Populaire (R.N.P.), which Déat resuscitated. Since Doriot and Déat both controlled Paris newspapers and had the confidence of the Germans, they were in a position to give wide publicity to their parties and hold meetings of some size. In addition, a number of lesser organizations, such as the Mouvement Social Revolutionnaire, under the leadership of Eugène Deloncle, and *Francisme,* identified with Marcel Bucard, made a bid for attention, though with little success. Repeated attempts were made to fuse these separate organizations in a single fascist front. But none of the ventures at a union of their parties proved successful. The reason was quite simple—neither Déat nor Doriot was willing to take second place to the other. So the advocates of totalitarianism, while denouncing Vichy for its failure to make a complete break with the past, themselves proved unable to overcome the vice of political schism which was so characteristic of the liberal regime.

After the summer of 1941, there was some progress in the direction of establishing a single, nationwide political organization. As soon as the

Nazis became involved in their war with the Russians, the spokesmen of fascism in Paris took the initiative in organizing a military formation. Known as the Légion des Volontaires contre le Bolchévisme, this was destined to serve with the *Wehrmacht* on the Eastern Front. About the same time, the Légion des Combattants Français, in the unoccupied zone, began to take in others besides veterans. Thus it assumed the character of a general political movement. Shortly its name was changed to Légion des Combattants et des Volontaires Français. Subsequently, as Vichy bowed under the German insistence upon "broad" collaboration, this Légion des Combattants et des Volontaires Français was permitted to operate in the occupied zone as well as the unoccupied. The military formation which the fascists had organized in the occupied zone, now renamed the Légion Tricolore, was made part of it.

Then a special branch, known as the Service d'Ordre Légionnaire (S.O.L.), was organized. Ostensibly, this was meant to maintain order at public meetings of the Légion. Actually, its task was to help combat the underground Resistance movement, which was becoming a serious problem. From the S.O.L., in turn, another organization was eventually detached. The Milice, as this was christened, became a special police for the suppression of "terrorism," as the government termed the Resistance. Ultimately the Milice was put under the command of the Minister of the Interior.

In the outcome of this evolution, the movement that had begun as the Légion des Combattants Français thus became an official political organization, operating in both zones, with the Légion Tricolore as its fighting arm on the Eastern Front, and the S.O.L. and the Milice as its paramilitary formations at home. But by the time this evolution was complete, Vichy was nearing the end of its days.

In respect to the control of public opinion, the new regime likewise fell far short of a police state. Vichy took over from the republican regime the censorship that had been introduced at the outbreak of the war, but this censorship was not so strict as to prevent the appearance in print of a wide range of opinion on public affairs.

Indeed, the press revealed much the same spectrum of opinion under Vichy as before the war, save that the Communists had no legal organ of propaganda. Those whose allegiance to liberalism remained unshaken could find their views developed in *Le Figaro,* which removed from Paris to Lyons and continued to appear until the fall of 1942. Socialists could take comfort from *L'Effort,* a new paper published in Lyons under the editorship of Charles Spinasse, who had been Minister of National Economy in the Blum government of the Popular Front and a member of the staff of the Socialist organ *Le Populaire.* The "conservative" *Action Française* carried on sharp polemics with the two principal organs of the fascists in Paris, *L'Œuvre* and *Le Cri du Peuple.*

The publication of books was even freer. A veritable torrent of titles appeared all through the era of Vichy, dealing with public issues of all kinds. As in the newspaper press, no expression of Communist doctrines was permitted, nor, of course, open attacks upon the Germans. But books in defense of such Marxian heroes as Jean Jaurès, or in defense of the interests of labor as against capital, were not suppressed. Works whose tone was unmistakably hostile to the Germans, such as Maurras's *La France seule,* were freely offered for sale.

On the positive side, in the direction of shaping rather than suppressing public opinion, Vichy accomplished little more. The Agence Havas, the principal commercial news service of France before the war, was nationalized. It became an instrument of propaganda for the government, under the name of Agence Française de la Presse. Newspapers were required to subscribe to its services and to print particular items of news which the government wished to have reach the public. But even with this help, Vichy never had much chance of forcing an official opinion upon the nation.

One reason for this was that the men in charge of the government were not themselves of one mind on basic issues. The regime was therefore unable to define its official position. Another reason was that Vichy could not exercise its censorship in the unoccupied zone, where the Germans kept control over the media of mass communication. Though Vichy could prevent the circulation in the occupied zone of newspapers published in the other zone, it was powerless against the radio transmitters of Paris, subject to German control, which could be heard in the unoccupied zone. As a consequence of these various circumstances, the atmosphere in the unoccupied zone was much more favorable to free discussion than might be supposed. Indeed, while northern France was under about as tight control as Germany, the southern zone was probably in closer touch with the outside world, and more open to public debate, than any other part of continental Europe save Switzerland and Sweden.

On the whole, Vichy was at first surprisingly lenient toward persons out of sympathy with the regime. To be sure, a number of the men who had held positions of leadership in the Third Republic in the 1930s, including Blum and Daladier, were arrested on political charges and kept in prison. This was an exceptional procedure, however. The number of persons thus imprisoned was small, and the victims were not ill-treated.[5] As a general rule, the government did not molest those who were lukewarm in their enthusiasm for the National Revolution, or even hostile to it, provided such persons did not undertake an open opposition. Most of the leading figures of the republican regime were permitted to retire to private life.

Later, as an underground Resistance movement developed to some size and began to wage a campaign of sabotage and violence, Vichy became more severe. Ultimately, the government resorted to all the devices of a ruthless political police, even utilizing the assistance of the Gestapo and the S.S. Thus it put itself in the shameful position of hunting down French patriots and handing them over to German executioners.

The measures taken to put down the Resistance give rise to one of the unanswerable reproaches directed against the Vichy regime. There is no excuse for these measures sufficient to redeem its honor, for no honorable man would have accepted responsibility for this policy, no matter what arguments of expediency might be urged. Recognizing, however, that there is no adequate defense of these measures, we must not proceed to the conclusion that the men who endorsed them were quite without a sense of shame. Once the men who supported the new regime accepted the premise that France was better off for having a government of her own, even though this government was obliged to do the Germans' bidding, they were compelled by their own logic to

---

[5] Georges Mandel, who was among those held in prison, was put to death in 1944. But his death was not, apparently, by order of the government.

proceed to measures many of them did not relish. Among these measures were those combatting the Resistance.

We must also acknowledge that the measures which Vichy took to put down the Resistance did not necessarily represent a campaign of terrorism directed against persons who were merely out of sympathy with the regime. For the activities of the Resistance involved a kind of lawlessness which no government could countenance. As always in guerrilla warfare, the Resistance waged its struggle by means which, under the law, amount to murder and banditry. Certainly we do not give Vichy an endorsement when we recognize that the measures taken against the Resistance do not necessarily bear witness to an intention of the government to hunt out and persecute law-abiding citizens who disapproved its policies.

Another avowed aim of the new regime, besides the revision of social and political institutions, was to purge the nation of "alien" and "cosmopolitan" influences. Accordingly, Vichy introduced a series of measures directed against the Jews, naturalized aliens, and Free Masons. In the broad conceptions underlying this campaign, the "conservatives" seemed to be in agreement with the fascists. But in the implementation of their common purpose, the two factions soon found themselves working against one another.

The principal enactment in this campaign was the "Statute of the Jews." This measure, promulgated in August of 1940, established a legal discrimination against persons defined as Jews, with the avowed aim of eliminating them from positions of influence in national life. A considerable number among those whom we have designated as "conservatives" had long demanded some such action. Ever since the time of the Dreyfus affair, anti-Semitism had been one of the slogans of the critics of liberalism, and the *Action Française* had espoused this campaign a generation before the Nazis. In the decade of the 1930s, the French apostles of fascism had also taken up the attack upon the Jews, since this was a cardinal point in the doctrine of their German exemplars.

Yet the initiative in the enactment of anti-Semitic legislation did not come solely from the spontaneous impulse of either of these factions. Neither the fascists nor the "conservatives" attached such overshadowing importance to the crusade against the Jews that action had to be taken within a matter of two months after the armistice, before the reform of social and political institutions was well begun.

Some of the more zealous champions of close collaboration with the Nazis urged prompt action on the ground that the Germans would regard this as evidence of the readiness of France to take her place in the "New Order." Others, less enthusiastic about a partnership with the Axis, also favored the quick enactment of anti-Semitic laws—in order to forestall the Germans rather than to conciliate them. For their part, the Germans put no pressure upon Vichy to take action against the Jews before Vichy adopted its anti-Semitic statute. Nevertheless, the impression prevailed in Vichy that, unless the French government immediately introduced such legislation in its own name, the Germans on their own initiative would begin a persecution of the Jews in the occupied zone, in which lived most of the Jewish population of France. Even some of those Frenchmen who did not dissemble their repugnance for the Jews were loath to see the Germans perpetrate on French soil the unspeakable atrocities which they had inflicted on the Jews of Germany.

In its definition of a Jew, the French statute provided two alternative criteria. According to one of these tests, a person was to be considered Jewish if three of his grandparents were Jewish. According to the other, he was to be regarded as Jewish if two of his grandparents were Jewish—and he himself either practiced the Jewish religion or married a woman who was descended from two Jewish grandparents. Thus the law was based, primarily, upon considerations of a presumed "ethnic" or "racial" inheritance. However, it made some provision for the possible "assimilation" of persons of Jewish background. Thus it defined Jewish grandparents as persons born into the Jewish religion; it did not envision an investigation into the "ethnic" origin of families that had practiced the Christian religion for three generations. In dealing with persons whose Jewish inheritance stemmed from only two grandparents, it placed decisive importance on the choice which the individual made of his religion and his spouse, as indicative of the degree of "assimilation."

Once a man or woman was legally classified as a Jew, he or she was narrowly restricted as to vocation. For example, no Jew could own or be employed by a newspaper or magazine, or engage in radio broadcasting or the production of motion pictures, or deal in securities and foreign exchange, or hold mortgages, or operate as a real estate broker, or own or manage any business enterprise employing Gentiles. In the liberal professions, a *numerus clausus* was established for Jews according to their proportion of the population. No Jew could hold political office.

A grave blame lies upon the men who drew up the Statute of the Jews if this is to be regarded as a measure of long-range reform adopted on its presumed merits. The legal discrimination which it imposed upon the Jews was about as severe as that which the Nazis incorporated in the Nuremberg code. Some of the French anti-Semites even boasted that the French legislation was more severe than the German. However, a plea in extenuation of the blame upon its sponsors may reasonably be made if the legislation is to be regarded only as a temporary expedient, conceived as the only alternative to the introduction into France of the Nazi kind of persecution. For the Nazis did not content themselves with the persecution of the Jews which their own Nuremberg decrees defined; they proceeded, beyond the scope of these decrees, to a persecution which aimed at wiping out the Jews as a subhuman species. In its enforcement of the Statute of the Jews, Vichy, on the other hand, was relatively lenient.

The administration of the anti-Semitic statute was given over to a special Secretariat General for Jewish Affairs, and Xavier Vallat was named to head the office. Vallat was a "conservative" known before the war as having ties with the Croix de Feu. He was remembered especially for having made an anti-Semitic attack upon Léon Blum on the floor of the Chamber of Deputies. Vallat set to his new work with no repugnance for the task nor any desire to temporize. But he moved so slowly that the Germans soon became impatient, eventually insisting on his replacement. Darquier de Pellepoix, who thus succeeded Vallat in the spring of 1942, evidently proved more satisfactory to them. Yet down to the end, the unoccupied zone remained a haven to which those Jews who could escaped from the German-dominated north.

One reason for the relative moderation of Vichy was that the anti-Semitic campaign did not prove popular, and the Catholic Church did not disguise its opposition to extreme measures against the Jews. Repeatedly, churchmen insisted upon the recognition of the right of Jews to adopt the Christian religion, and many churchmen, privately and publicly, testified to the duty of Christians to show charity and kindliness toward the Jews no less than to other fellow men.

With much the same xenophobic impulse as inspired the anti-Semitic campaign, Vichy also took action against naturalized aliens. A comprehensive review was ordered to inquire into the circumstances under which citizenship had been granted to all persons naturalized since 1927, and citizenship was revoked wherever evidence was found of fraud, corruption, or other irregularities in the proceedings. This worked hardship upon thousands of persons who had fled to Paris or other parts of France, in the troubled decades before the war, to escape persecution in Central and Eastern Europe, or upon the collapse of the Spanish republican regime. Undoubtedly, French citizenship had at times been given to adventurers, swindlers, and other undesirables who had left their native lands for other reasons than to escape despotism; but the measures of the Vichy government could easily be made to apply to naturalized aliens who did not fall into this category.

So far as concerned the measures against the Jews and naturalized aliens, the spokesmen of fascism qualified their approval of the work of Vichy only by complaining that Vichy was too lenient. But the further extension of the purge once more produced an opposition between the two capitals. For the "conservatives" who were guiding the National Revolution were no less hostile to the Free Masons than to the Jews, and on much the same grounds, denouncing the Masons as disciples of a cosmopolitanism that negated pride in the special heritage of France. However, some of the champions of fascism, Déat in particular, had close links with the Masons. Hence, in the continuous polemics between *L'Œuvre* and the *Action Française,* Déat denounced the "reactionaries" in Vichy for sheltering the Jews, while Maurras and his henchmen accused Déat and his friends in Paris of protecting the Masons.[6]

[6] Doriot, always happy to embarrass Déat, gave his backing to the charge of the *Action Française* that Déat was an agent of the Free Masons. Déat denied the charge on numerous occasions.

Some of the "conservatives" went further. They attacked their adversaries in Paris as men who would sacrifice the interests of France as a nation to the interests of a new "international" of fascism, no whit less cosmopolitan than the international movements of Marxism or Zionism. For example, the *Action Française,* in an article entitled "Le Briandisme des vaincus," dismissed the talk in Paris of a new organization of Europe under German leadership as only a new version of the old and discredited idea of the League of Nations. "M. Déat and his friends," declared the editor, "are the heirs of those Radicals and Socialists who were the backers of Briand."

In answer to such attacks, Déat and some of the other prophets of fascism charged Vichy with subservience to the Church, which bespoke a kind of cosmopolitanism in the service of reaction. The argument struck home. In truth, the "conservatives" were seeking to reverse the anticlericalism of the previous regime. The more utopian among them were dreaming of some kind of partnership between the Church and the state.

But more was involved than pious pronouncements by men in high political position. On a number of issues of public policy, the government of Marshal Pétain showed its desire to assist the Church. For example, a number of religious orders that had been expelled from France in the sequel to the Dreyfus affair, including the Carthusians, were permitted to return, and their property was given back to them. Provision was made for religious instruction in public schools, and subsidies were paid from public funds for the support of "free" schools, that is, private schools, most of which were maintained by the Catholic Church. These measures aroused so much grumbling on the part of anticlerical elements, however, that the government never pressed further in this direction. There was no serious thought of requiring religious ceremonies of marriage, nor of prohibiting divorces, nor of revising the legal separation of Church and state that had been effected in 1905.[7]

For its part, the Church gave ample evidence of its favorable attitude toward the government of Marshal Pétain. It could hardly do other-

---

[7] There was some discussion in the *Action Française* and *Le Figaro* of the wisdom of a law that would preclude the divorce of couples who chose, at the time of their marriage, to have a religious ceremony. But apparently such a law was never considered by the government.

wise than welcome a government that paid such unwonted tribute to religion and that included so many practicing Catholics in its high councils. Moreover, the basic principles of the National Revolution, including both the concern for the family and the ideas of corporatism, corresponded to Catholic doctrines of social reform. However, the Church never officially endorsed the policy of collaboration with the Axis, for the Vatican was by no means on friendly terms with the Nazi Reich nor desirous of an Axis victory in the war. Moreover, as the Resistance movement developed in France after 1942, the illegal opposition recruited much of its support among practicing Catholics. The Church had little reason to alienate these adherents by insisting upon obedience to Vichy. Apparently it succeeded in holding aloof from the new regime, while endorsing some of its intentions, since no serious attempt was made, after the downfall of Vichy, to accuse the Church of sponsoring "collaboration." Indeed, the Church not only escaped discredit but found itself in a more favorable position in the Fourth Republic than before the war.

On the whole, the National Revolution was a disappointment to its authors. For two generations or more, the "conservative" critics of liberalism had denounced the vices of the Third Republic without being able to gain political power. Under the aegis of Marshal Pétain, men of these convictions at last found themselves masters of the government. But in the outcome of their tenure, they accomplished virtually nothing. In a sense, the historian must share their disappointment. Since he must take note of the argument which the French "conservatives" had for so long developed in their appraisal of the ills of their nation, he would find it illuminating to learn what these critics of the Third Republic had to offer in its place. Yet it must be acknowledged that the experience of Vichy was hardly a fair test.

Manifestly, the National Revolution was undertaken in a situation that was ill suited to social and political experiment. Only a national disaster made possible the inception of the new regime, by wiping away the Third Republic. But the same catastrophe implied that the men who assumed power as heirs to the republican regime would not be free to govern France in accordance with their views of the needs and interests of the nation, but only under the relentless pressure of the armistice and the worldwide war that still raged unabated. And because the new French government had no choice but to collaborate with the Axis, it was virtually certain that its works would disappear with the downfall of the Axis, no matter what the merits of the innovations it introduced.

Taking the plans of the "conservatives" as the substance of the National Revolution, we must acknowledge that the venture at reform was based upon a reasonable analysis of the problems of social and political life that had become evident under the Third Republic. We need not agree with the "conservative" critique to recognize that there was much evidence to support a criticism of the republican regime for its excessive reliance upon individualism, the unremitting tension between social classes, the want of resolute leadership in the solution of problems of public affairs, the preemption of political life by a few hundred men who made a career of service in Parliament, and the growing weight of a bureaucracy that was more the master than the servant of the people. We must also acknowledge that this criticism of the Third Republic, which served as the intellectual basis of the National Revolution, had its roots in French experience rather than in the example of Germany and Italy.

But if this was one of the merits of the National Revolution—that it rested upon a telling criticism of the republican regime—the same virtue implied its weakness. For the reforms of the new regime were, from start to finish, the work of intellectuals. Vichy made its strongest appeal to the kind of man who read the *Action Française* or *Le Figaro* —men of means who were not men of affairs, men who had an interest in public issues but little practical experience, men who had ambitions for a role in politics but lacked the aptitude or temperament for a career in the arena of Parliament.

To be sure, the new regime could count upon the benevolence of businessmen, who had reason to see in the National Revolution a safeguard against the proletarian parties and the trade-union movement. For a time, the industrialist could take comfort in his revenge upon the Popular Front and tell himself that he was once more "master in his own home." Yet "big business," such as it was in France, never quite responded to the National Revolution. Nor, indeed, was there much reason for men of affairs to trust a regime headed by an aged soldier, who had little acquaintance with politics and none at all with economic problems, and who took his counsel from a weird assortment of discredited republican politicians, such as Laval, utopian theorists of reaction, and zealous visionaries of an ultramodern totalitarianism.

The urban working class had much less reason to hail the new gospel. Under the Third Republic, the proletarians had looked upon the two Marxian parties as their bulwark against the rich in the realm of politics, and upon the trade unions as their one dependable weapon in economic relations. In the decade or so before the war, they had given little or no sign of a readiness to accept the leadership of men such as Doriot and Déat, who preached the new doctrine of national socialism as opposed to Marxism. Certainly they had never shown the slightest interest in the message of the *Action Française*. There is no reason to presume that the events of 1940 could have changed their convictions or inspired confidence in a government that thrust aside their political parties and supplanted their trade unions with a complicated diagram of new "unions" representing foremen, engineers, managers, and owners, along with plain workingmen.

There was, it is true, a "proletarian" wing to the new regime. René Belin, who took a leading role in drawing up the Charter of Labor while he was Minister of Industrial Production and Labor, made a serious attempt to interest the working class in the scheme of corporative unions. Moreover, a considerable number of trade union leaders, as well as some men who had occupied the lower echelons of leadership in the Socialist and Communist parties before the war, gave their allegiance to the new regime. However, these were neither men of the rank and file nor men whose names were well known. Most of them looked to Paris rather than Vichy. Déat, in particular, became their principal spokesman. The government itself included no one whom the working class at large regarded as a proven champion of its interests. Nor, so far as the evidence permits us to determine, did the working class ever place its hopes in the promises of the new era.

The rural populace, it seems probable, was somewhat more positive in its attitude. The peasant could not help relishing the lavish praise which Vichy heaped upon the man of the soil. Nor could he be heedless of the contrast between this message and the concern which the Popular Front had shown for the urban proletariat. Besides kind words in abundance, he had another reason for feeling that his position had improved. For in France, as in all other countries, the shortage of food, arising out of the conditions of the war, gave the peasant an economic advantage. At worst, he could be sure of food enough for his own needs, and if he could produce a surplus, he could sell it on the black market at whatever price he chose to set. This does not mean that the French peasant was well off in the period of the Vichy regime. Even if he increased his income, he could find little to buy with his money. Nor, in a time of inflation, could he readily save it. Nor was he content to see his homeland under German occupation, provided he could profit on the black market. Yet it would have been surprising if the peasant had harbored ill will toward the government, which manifestly was not the cause of the occupation, so long as he was faring somewhat better than most of his compatriots.

On the other hand, the rural regions of France never gave clear sign of having repudiated the republican regime. The Third Republic had proved more durable than the First and the Second for the reason that, unlike its predecessors, it had won the confidence of the provinces. Moreover, the peasants had gained a larger measure of influence in politics under the Third Republic than ever before. However much he and his champions might complain of the preference of Parliament for the urban voter, the moderate parties, such as the Radical-Socialists in the interbellum period, had never dared neglect the rural constituencies.

Even had the peasants been more dissatisfied with their situation under the Third Republic, they were not apt suddenly to change their allegiance. By temperament, the French peasant is normally a partisan of the *status quo* no less than he is disposed to grumble. Despite the dramatic events of the summer of 1940, the Third Republic, rather than the tentative and provisional regime of Marshal Pétain, still seemed to represent the *status quo*. As best we can conclude, then, the peasantry seems to have viewed the National Revolution as a venture that held good promise, but this cautious approbation never amounted to a firm commitment to its support.

At the start, Marshal Pétain unquestionably commanded wide support among all classes. But this trust in him did not represent a general acceptance of the principles of the National Revolution. Rather, it represented a traumatic response on the part of the nation to the image of the aged and venerable old soldier, rising up as a figure from the heroic past to lead France out of the abyss. As distinct from Pétain, the regime over which he presided retained the unreserved trust of the nation as a whole for no more than a few months. By the summer of 1942, it commanded the partisan loyalty of only a diminishing band of zealots.

This gradual loss of public confidence is not hard to understand. Quite apart from the disaffection which arose because of its commitment to collaboration with the Axis, the new regime never gave evidence that it was capable of solving the long-standing problems of France. Of all the items in the program of the National Revolution, the only one that proved viable and popular was its family policy, and this was in no sense a distinctive achievement of Vichy. Corporatism amounted to no more than it had been before—an interesting but ambiguous proposal, wholly in the realm of theory.

The most striking failure of the new regime was its want of success in establishing a strong and stable personal leadership at the apex of the government. No other aim of the National Revolution was more distinctive than this determination to overcome the vacillations of the Third Republic by giving the ultimate authority and responsibility to the Chief of State. And no one could doubt that Marshal Pétain held such a position, for he commanded no less absolute power than Louis XIV at the zenith of his reign.

Yet at no time, not even in the summer of 1940, did Pétain actually control the government he headed. From beginning to end, he was the puppet of the men who surrounded him, being pushed or pulled or wheedled or duped into each of his decisions. On scarcely any issue did he show a mind of his own. Often he apparently did not even have knowledge of what his subordinates were doing in his name. Save on one occasion—the crisis of December 13, 1940—he never exercised a decisive personal influence—not even to the extent of tipping the balance in favor of one or the other of the rival factions that were waging a bloodless civil war within the inner circle of his government. By 1944 the old man who seemed to be dictator had become merely a figure-head, no whit more important in the determination of policy than had been the President of the Republic before him.

Doubtless the weakness of Pétain was due, in part, to the personal character and the advanced age of the vain old soldier whom chance had placed in power. Remarkable as was his stamina, considering that he was an octogenarian, Pétain was not in full possession of his facul-ties. Moreover, his judgment was sapped by his obsessive eagerness to play the role of a martyr, to "make France the gift of his person."

But it does not suffice to explain away, as due to the deficiencies of the man who held the office, the failure of the dictatorship to provide a single-minded guidance. Though his strength was flagging, Pétain was by no means physically incapable of following a discussion in the cab-inet. And his weaknesses of character, which were mainly those of an egotism untempered by either a sense of personal loyalty or firm convictions of principle, were of a kind that is not uncommon among men who aspire to positions of prominence in politics. While we can scarcely deny that another man would have made different use of un-limited personal power, we may doubt that such a person would have been wholly invulnerable to the temptations and pressures that bore upon Pétain.

At any event, no other man could have had the advantage which Pétain drew from the blind public confidence he commanded at the outset of his rule. Probably not more than three or four Frenchmen in a hundred years—perhaps Clemenceau, more likely Boulanger, perhaps Napoleon III—ever captured the loyalty of so much of the nation as did Pétain in the summer of 1940. In a land so little given to hero worship, no aspirant to dictatorship could have hoped to gain a wider popularity. And after the experience of Vichy, no one can again put forward a plausible argument that a dictatorship in France is apt to produce firmer rule than Parliament.

Despite its intentions to the contrary, Vichy soon developed into a distorted replica of the Third Republic. The cabinet, instead of serving as a committee of advisers to the autocratic Chief of State, once more became a committee of representatives of diverse political factions, each working against the others, while the nominal head of the government labored to maintain his position in the midst of a welter of intrigue which he could only partially control. Before the close of the Vichy era, the Chief of State was no longer even pretending to determine policy. Instead, he was devoting his energies to the time-honored duties of the President of the Republic—signing decrees which the premier delivered to him, delivering public addresses in favor of civic virtue, and handing out medals. And while one minister succeeded another in the ceaseless parade passing through the cabinet, the civil service remained the real government of France, inexorably extending its control into new segments of national life.

No other lesson that emerges out of the experience of the Vichy era is clearer, or more portentous, than this stubborn persistence of the traditions of the Third Republic under a regime dedicated to its utter extirpation.

XI

DARLAN AT THE HELM

THE DARLAN INTERLUDE began with a deadlock between the "conservatives" in Vichy and their adversaries in Paris. In the first six months of the new regime, as we have seen, the "conservatives" had won the upper hand. But their ascendancy was far from complete or definitive, and the tide soon began to run against them. In the sequel to the coup of December 13, 1940, under pressure from Paris and Berlin, Pétain had named Admiral Darlan as Vice-Premier, as the only alternative to recalling Laval.

This represented only a partial victory for the fascists, but clearly it marked a setback for the "conservatives." For, though Darlan was not in league with Abetz and his henchmen in Paris, neither was he a disciple of the school of Charles Maurras. He had but one clear purpose—to remain in power, and only one guiding strategy—to remain the second-best choice of all the rival parties.

By temperament, Darlan was not ill-suited to this role. According to all who knew him, he was an affable and easygoing person, without the imperiousness of General Weygand or the reserve of Marshal Pétain. In the broad divisions of political opinion, his position was not ambiguous. No one doubted but that he was a man of the Third Republic. Other than a vague allegiance to republicanism, however, Darlan showed no sign of firm political convictions. He had spent his whole life in the navy, rising to a position where he had no rival in the high command. He had not accomplished this without astute operations in the intramural politics of the navy and probably some connections in Parliament. But he had never taken a conspicuous stand on public issues outside the province of the navy or become known to the public otherwise than as a naval commander.

As a naval officer, Darlan had had little occasion to concern himself with diplomatic questions. The crucial problem of Franco-German relations was always of prime concern to the French army but of much less relevance to the navy. On the other hand, Britain loomed large in the thought of French naval men, in view of the long-established preeminence of British seapower. For more than a generation before 1940, the French navy had made its plans upon the assumption that, in the event of a general European war, the French and British navies would operate together. Nevertheless, the French naval command could not avoid a certain resentment of what must be a junior status in this joint enterprise.

In 1940, Darlan gave sign of this ambivalence. In the harrowing months of May and June, he had earned the good esteem of the British by his readiness to lend help in the evacuation at Dunkirk. Then, during the period of the French negotiations for an armistice, he had given the British his personal pledge that under no circumstances would he permit the French navy to pass under the control of the Axis. In July, however, when the British launched their attack upon the French warships at Mers El-Kébir and other ports, Darlan had given vent to an unbridled Anglophobia and had proposed one after another plan for French reprisals. Others in the cabinet—Baudouin, in particular—had prevented any rash move of this kind, and Darlan had later regained his outward composure. Nevertheless, he remained bitter and suspicious in his attitude toward the British.

This ambivalence was responsible for both the elevation of Darlan to political leadership and the ineptitude of his administration. Because he was known as an Anglophobe, after Mers El-Kébir, he was acceptable to the Germans as the successor to Laval. And because he had no prior record of a pro-German orientation, he was likewise acceptable, as a compromise candidate, to those who opposed "broad" collaboration. But because, in truth, Darlan had no views of his own on the basic problems confronting France at the time, nor even an understanding of them, it was obvious that his government would not hold a steady course.

Darlan seems to have regarded this as a merit. Like Laval, he thought of himself as a shrewd bargainer and a master of intrigue. He was confident that he would emerge the winner, and so therefore would France, in the inglorious but beguiling game of pitting one side against another. Even by his own uninspiring standard, Darlan flattered himself. Whatever his skill in the politics of personal advancement, he lacked the wit needed for the larger duplicities of international relations. As a diplomat, he tricked no one but himself.

Under his aegis, Vichy was steadily to drift away from a position of neutrality into what amounted to a partnership with the Axis. Yet, because Darlan never took a clear-cut decision in favor of such a course, his government was hesitant and grudging in its gestures of cooperation with the Axis. So France did not win the good graces of Berlin, while she accomplished no improvement of her relations with London and Washington. Consequently France suffered much of the disadvantage involved in both "broad" and "narrow" collaboration, without the profit of either.

Though Darlan took over charge of the government without having the firm support of either of the two principal political factions, the "conservative" or the fascist, he soon secured a tight grip on the reins. On February 25, 1941, two weeks after his designation as Vice-Premier to succeed Laval, he announced the appointment of a new cabinet. He chose the members without consulting Pétain in advance, and he gave the rank of minister to only three men besides himself. None of these was apt to become his rival. The other ten members of the government were reduced to the rank of secretaries of state or delegates general. Pétain continued to attend meetings of the cabinet but no longer took an active role in the discussions.

The membership of the new government did not give a clear indication of its political orientation. It included some men known to favor the point of view of the "conservatives" and others who had links with the avowed proponents of fascism. But gossip had it that the real masters of the government were members of a clique to which the name of the "Synarchy" was attached.

The more lurid versions of this rumor depicted the Synarchy as a secret society, with international ramifications. According to these stories, it was the political instrument of a combine of French banking and industrial interests, in league with large chemical and metallurgical firms in Germany, Britain, and the United States. From behind the scenes, it had controlled such prewar "leagues" as the *Cagoulards* and had been instrumental in establishing the dictatorship of Pétain. Such legends, which are the common coin of political rumor in Europe, cannot be wholly dismissed as patently absurd, but they are quite unsupported by evidence.

There was conceivably some particle of truth behind this talk of the Synarchy. It is clear that certain members of the Darlan cabinet had a close association with one another. Some of these had ties with leading French banking and business interests. The anchor man on the team, it appears, was Jacques Barnaud, one of the directors of the Banque Worms, who became Delegate General for Franco-German Economic Relations. Identified with Barnaud, who seems to have been responsible for their inclusion in the government, were François Lehideux, a leading figure in the French automobile industry, connected by marriage with the Renault family, who now became Delegate-General for National Equipment; Pierre Pucheu, an agent of the French steel cartel, who became Secretary of State for Industrial Production, later Minister of the Interior; Paul Marion, a renegade Communist, disciple of Doriot, and Jacques Bénoist-Méchin, known since before the war as an apostle of Franco-German rapprochement. These last two became secretaries general without portfolio.

We may credit the report that these five men formed a faction in the government, even though we need not heed the more imaginative allegations concerning the Synarchy. There is ample indication that they used their influence in favor of collaboration with the Axis on terms favorable to French business and financial interests. But there is no sign that they proposed a new solution, other than those advocated by the "conservatives" or the fascists, for either the domestic or the diplomatic problems of the regime. They may have been clearer than Darlan in their conception of what interests, besides their own, they hoped to serve, but they were no clearer than he as to how to gain their purposes.

At any event, the emergence of this new clique in the cabinet did not obscure the cleavage between the "conservatives" and the fascists. The same warfare between them went on throughout the new administration as in the previous months of Laval's ascendancy. To be sure, the "conservatives" suffered a setback, after their success in dislodging Laval, when Darlan gained the office of Vice-Premier. Baudouin and Peyrouton, who had been leaders in the struggle against Laval, had been obliged to retire. But others, such as Bouthillier and Caziot, continued to represent the "conservative" point of view within the government, while henchmen, including Du Moulin de la Barthète, remained entrenched in Pétain's personal staff.

The work of developing the National Revolution went on throughout the new administration, though with diminishing vigor. Meantime the *Action Française,* which had become the principal public advocate of "narrow" collaboration, continued to give warning, in terms as clear as the censorship would permit, against the pressure for partnership with the Axis. There are "d'autres Sedans que le militaire," Maurras pointed out. "On peut en subir d'économiques, de moraux."

On the other hand, the Paris press endorsed the new administration as giving promise of a sounder counsel in Vichy. *Le Cri du Peuple* was unequivocal in its support of Darlan, and *Les Nouveaux Temps* demanded that he take the title of Premier, instead of Vice-Premier, as an open sign of Pétain's relegation to the role of figurehead. Déat, who had become Laval's man, was never quite reconciled to Darlan, and *L'Œuvre* was therefore more reserved in its approbation. The new government was under the dominance of the "trusts," its columns warned, whereas the true path of the National Revolution must lie along the road to socialism. But this emphasis in *L'Œuvre* was more of the nature of partisan support than of opposition to the new government.

In respect to foreign affairs, the omens seemed favorable. Relations between Vichy and other governments were never better than in the first months of the Darlan interlude. Though Berlin regarded the ouster of Laval as an affront, Darlan had convinced the Nazis of his good disposition toward them. Besides, the Axis now became preoccupied in other quarters, so Berlin no longer attached large importance to France. In the wake of the Italian invasion of Greece, the Germans became involved in Southeastern Europe, whereupon the schemes for an Axis campaign in the western Mediterranean, which had earlier made the cooperation of Vichy a matter of concern to Berlin, now languished again.

For their part, the British had no immediate occasion to reconsider the *modus vivendi* which had been worked out in the course of the Rougier mission to London and the negotiations between Halifax and Chevalier. Relations also improved between France and the two principal neutral powers. In January, 1941, Admiral Leahy arrived in Vichy to fill the post of U.S. ambassador to France, which had been vacant since the summer of 1940. In March, 1941, the Soviet government raised its chargé d'affaires in Vichy to the rank of ambassador. Vichy likewise took action to reestablish its full diplomatic representation in Moscow.

But this diplomatic equilibrium did not last long. Darlan himself disturbed it by a singularly feckless attempt to win favor with Berlin. The occasion arose out of developments in the Near East in the spring of 1941. A revolt which broke out against the pro-British government of Irak gave the Germans a chance to plan an intervention in that region. In connection with this operation, the Germans desired to make use of the French base in Syria, which remained under the control of an administration loyal to Vichy.

Hence Darlan was summoned to Paris on May 3 to talk with Abetz. In this conversation, Darlan readily agreed to cooperate. Accordingly, he was invited to make a visit to Berchtesgaden, to discuss the matter with Hitler himself. In the course of this conference, which took place on May 11–12, Hitler held out glittering promises of the advantages which might be accorded France in the settlement of the war if Vichy should now prove cooperative. However, the Fuehrer conspicuously omitted to propose any specific commitment at the moment. Nevertheless, Darlan signified his willingness to accede to the desires of the Axis, apparently without attempting to secure a definite promise of a *quid pro quo.*

On his return to Paris, he and Abetz drew up a protocol, which both signed on May 27–28. According to its provisions, the French promised, *inter alia,* to permit the *Luftwaffe* to make use of French airbases in Syria in connection with the German operations in Irak, to permit German submarines patroling the North Atlantic to make use of the

French naval base at Dakar, and to permit the use of French transport facilities in North Africa for the supply of Axis ground forces engaged against the British in Egypt. In return, the German government made only trifling commitments, bearing principally upon the reinforcement of the French military establishment in the African colonies.

This agreement provoked a sharp reaction on the part of those who opposed "broad" collaboration. In the first place, because it represented an engagement over and above the terms of the armistice, it would mark a clear departure from the position of neutrality which Vichy had so far preserved. In the second place, it was a poor bargain. Under its provisions, France would be exposed to the risk of a rupture with the British and the Americans (who were by now virtually allied with the British) without being sure of any advantage in return.

On both grounds, General Weygand voiced an adamant opposition. In a conference with Darlan in Vichy on June 2, he induced the latter to revoke the portion of the protocol bearing on North Africa and to reaffirm the earlier decision to defend the African colonies against any foreign power.

The portion of the agreement bearing upon Syria was not revised. However, this proved of little practical importance. Early in June, a Gaullist force, backed by the British, launched an attack upon Syria, and by the middle of July it gained control of the region. Meantime the Germans lost interest in the Near East, since they were soon absorbed in their attack upon Russia. So Darlan was saved from what might have been a serious crisis with Berlin had the Germans continued to have a large interest in the plans which gave rise to the agreement. But the episode scarcely gave substance to his reputation as a master of intrigue.

The German attack on Russia, beginning on June 21, 1941, was an event of prime importance in the history of Vichy. In the short run, it was to give a new stimulus to a partnership between France and the Axis. This was not, as we shall see, to be its ultimate importance for France. But at the outset, the campaign in Eastern Europe served to take up the attention of the Nazis, so that, for the present, they no longer had time to devote to the riddle of how to exploit their military victory over the French.

Upon receiving the news of the German attack, to be sure, Vichy took a cautious stand. On July 1 the French ambassador in Moscow was recalled and diplomatic relations with the Soviet government were severed. But as the ostensible reason for this action, the French government did not mention the rupture between Berlin and Moscow. Instead, its announcement alleged that the Soviet diplomatic mission in France had been engaged in espionage. Nor did Vichy proceed to declare war on Russia. For some months, the censorship even permitted the *Action Française* to publish both the Nazi and the Soviet war communiqués, with no indication of partisanship as between the two camps.

An obvious consideration inducing Vichy to maintain an official position of neutrality was doubtless that the Germans had no need of French help in this new venture. Consequently, Berlin was not disposed either to permit the French to take a share in the crusade or to reward them for a meaningless expression of their preference for an Axis victory. Another consideration was that Vichy could not take a stand against the Russians without also taking a stand against the Anglo-American bloc. For the British did not hesitate to conclude an alliance with the Russians as soon as the Nazi-Soviet war began, and Washington made evident its approval of this *entente*. Though the "conservatives" were in complete agreement with the fascists in their opposition to Bolshevism, not many of them were willing to sanction a break with London and Washington.

From the start, however, the proponents of fascism sought to use the Nazi-Soviet war as the occasion for binding France to a role in the Axis. One expression of this campaign was a barrage of propaganda expounding the "New Order" which the German theorists of National Socialism described. This was not a new idea in the summer of 1941. German propagandists had begun to develop it in the 1930s, and in France some of the advocates of "appeasement" had drawn upon their arguments. With the beginning of the German invasion of Russia, the French partisans of fascism took up the theme with new zeal. In the vanguard of the campaign was Marcel Déat, writing in *L'Œuvre*. But the mission was not his alone. The propaganda was presented, at various levels of discussion, in all the Paris press, in the magazines circulating in the occupied zone, and in books and pamphlets.

The argument involved more than a mere glorification of the Nazis. Its basic premise rested upon an analysis of the position of Europe in the modern world. The nation-state is no longer the ultimate unit in world affairs, so the argument began. The world now comprises a congeries of power blocs, each of which includes a number of nations. One such is Britain, together with her Dominions and dependencies around the world. Another includes the United States and the Latin American republics which lie within the orbit of their northern neighbor. A third takes in the Moslem lands stretching from Morocco to Afghanistan. Still another involves the Russian domain in Eastern Europe and Northern Asia.

Potentially, according to the argument, Europe exclusive of Britain and Russia constitutes another community of the same order. Actually, however, Europe is still partitioned among warring nation-states. Because she is divided, she is unable to maintain her position as against such adversaries as the British Empire or the Russian colossus. The only salvation for Europe lies in some kind of union. The only feasible means of establishing such a union is through the leadership of a strong nation, which will impose order upon the others. And the only nation which has shown the strength requisite to this task is Germany.

In the new, integrated Europe, so the reasoning proceeded, France would be sure to prosper. Her guarantee is that both the skill and the deficiencies of France complement those of Germany. Among the peoples of Europe, the Germans are the unrivaled masters of modern industrial technology, while the French have little talent in this realm. In the new Europe, France will secure her basic manufactures from across the Rhine. On the other hand, French agriculture is quite capable of feeding the French nation and producing choice comestibles for export. Moreover, the French artisan has no rival in the manufacture of luxury wares, and Paris has no possible peer as the home of wit and art.

No doubt, the Germans might attempt to use their political and economic predominance to reduce France, along with other countries, to a servile status. But there is also a guarantee against this. For any nation which understands the nature of the modern economy as well as do the Germans must realize that slave labor is much less profitable than free labor. The Germans can achieve their own goals only by tapping the potential strength and riches of Europe as a whole, and they can do this only by becoming the leaders, not the oppressors, of the other peoples of Europe.

The logic was not unpersuasive. No one could refute the proposition that the regime of nation-states is anachronistic and that Europe has need of integration. Indeed, this diagnosis was to take on new meaning at the close of the war, when America and Russia were to pit their worldwide might in a titanic new struggle and Europe was to pass into a nearly total eclipse.

Moreover, this picture of the "New Order" made a certain appeal to French national pride. What Frenchman could believe that, even if the Germans were to remain the masters of Europe, Berlin would supplant Paris as the citadel of elegance? that a woman of taste would ever choose a German dressmaker, or that her husband would turn aside from the treasured vintages of France? that the world would ever cease to make its centuries-old pilgrimage to the streets of *la ville lumière?* Were not the Germans themselves rendering homage to France even as their troops occupied her capital? Were not the *feldgrau* hordes in the streets of the metropolis but another wave in the ceaseless stream of tourists? Was it not rumored that Hitler himself had planned to put the whole of France under the rule of *Gauleiters,* until he paid a secret visit to Paris and viewed for the first time the awe-inspiring spectacle of the Champs Élysées? No one knows to what degree such dreams beguiled the French, or to what extent the more formal exposition of the "New Order" proved convincing. But it would be as rash to presume that all the French remained impervious to its appeal as that all were won over.

We can better appraise the other principal expression of the new campaign for "broad" collaboration. This was the Légion des Volontaires contre le Bolchévisme. In August, 1941, Déat and Doriot began recruiting volunteers for this brigade, destined to give France representation in the crusade against the Soviet regime. The initiative came from Doriot. Eventually he resigned from the management of *Le Cri du Peuple* in order to devote his whole attention to the Légion, in which he held the rank of colonel. However, Déat gave the scheme his unqualified support. Indeed, it became the one enterprise in which the rival prophets of totalitarianism proved capable of working together. Its sponsors announced that the Légion had the approval of both Pétain and Hitler. Its members were to wear a uniform of their own, save while in action on the Eastern Front, when they would wear the German *Feldgrau*. The Légion would have its own officers, but would operate as part of the *Wehrmacht*.

Though the Paris press gave unstinted space, the response to the appeal for recruits was minimal. In September, 1941, announcement was made that the first contingent was leaving for Germany, where the recruits would undergo training. From time to time, other announcements of the same kind were released. But these seldom mentioned the number of men involved or the total strength of the Légion. Probably the muster never reached more than about five thousand men. For more than a year, communiqués reported that the Légion was "in training" in German-occupied Poland. Ultimately the organization saw action against the Russians. But its record was so uninspiring that, even with the help of an imaginative press in Paris, little could be done to create the impression of heroic exploits. No one with a shred of skepticism could help but discern that the venture was an utter fiasco.

But the drive for Franco-German cooperation against the Reds was not the sole consequence of the Nazi march into Eastern Europe. The new phase of the war also helped undermine the basis for a partnership between France and the Axis. In the long run, this was the more important effect. For the stubborn resistance of the Red Army soon brought German military supremacy into question. By the time of the battle of Stalingrad, in December, 1941, the primacy of the Axis over continental Europe was far from sure.

Inevitably this gave hope to the mass of the French nation, which had accepted the Vichy policy of collaboration with the Axis only because there had seemed to be no other choice. Thus the Nazi-Soviet war marked the second milestone—the first being the failure of the German air attack upon Britain in the summer and fall of 1940—in the evolution of French opinion toward thoughts of resistance to the conquerors. Yet, while the mass of the nation grew more restive, Vichy became more firmly committed to the Axis. Thus the cleavage began to widen between the nation and its government.

The Resistance—let us use the term henceforth in the sense of illegal opposition to the government—did not become a serious concern to Vichy until after the outbreak of the Nazi-Soviet war. This was not, to be sure, the beginning of the opposition. As we have noted, the Free French movement had taken its start, under the leadership of General de Gaulle, in the immediate aftermath of the armistice in 1940. Within six months, the Gaullists had gained a kind of recognition from the British government and *de facto* rule of a number of the minor French colonies. Throughout the summer and fall of 1940, over the winter and during the following spring, a thin stream of *émigrés* had escaped from France and rallied to this movement of opposition. From London and other bases abroad, the spokesmen of "Free France" had addressed innumerable radio appeals to their compatriots at home, denouncing the government of Marshal Pétain and the regime of collaboration with the Axis which the armistice had inaugurated. These broadcasts were heard in France, and the government took sufficient heed of them to launch a counterpropaganda against what it termed the "dissidence."

Yet this "dissidence" did not produce grave alarm. None of the principal colonies went over to the Gaullists, and after the inglorious venture at Dakar in September of 1940, the British made clear that they would not again permit De Gaulle to make an armed attack upon colonies remaining loyal to Vichy. The number of persons escaping to England or the Gaullist colonies was negligible, and the disaffection within France was of no immediate importance. Only a small minority of the population ventured to make protest against the new regime, and these did no more than issue an occasional pamphlet.

The Communist Party, which had been declared illegal before Pétain assumed power, was another matter. Vichy continued the drive to break up this illegal organization. But during the period of the Nazi-Soviet alliance, the Communists were not attempting to arouse public opinion against Franco-German collaboration.

From the summer of 1941 onward, however, the Resistance took on new importance. A notable reason for this was that the Communists now threw their whole strength into the struggle and soon modified the character of the Resistance. For the outbreak of the Nazi-Soviet war put the French Communists in a new position. First, it clarified the aims of the Communists themselves, who were now relieved of the need to take an equivocal attitude toward the Nazis. Instead, they were called upon to lead an unrelenting struggle against the Axis, as though they were themselves members of the Red Army. Furthermore, it put them in a position where they could seek to rally wide support throughout the nation, since they were now appealing to the French hatred of their conquerors. Finally, the entrance of the Communists introduced into the Resistance a band of disciplined revolutionaries, who did not hesitate to make use of terrorism as a weapon of political warfare.

Hitherto the illegal opposition had involved mostly individuals inspired by motives of personal idealism, who were not schooled in the techniques of eluding the police or steeled to the grim exigencies of sabotage and assassination. But such desperate works of blood and darkness were part of the tradition of Bolshevism, which was the inspiration of the French Communists. Under their guidance, the Resistance ceased to be a movement of propaganda and protest. It became a guerrilla army.

The new temper of the Resistance soon became apparent. A dramatic indication appeared in the public press on August 28, 1941, when an assassin shot at and wounded both Pierre Laval and Marcel Déat, as these two notorious champions of "collaboration" were attending a review of the Légion des Volontaires contre le Bolchévisme. The assassin, later identified as a ship's stoker, named Paul Colette, was captured and condemned to death, but at the instance of Laval the sentence was commuted to imprisonment. Because of the prominence of the victims, the news attracted wide attention.

More ominous was the news, made public on October 22, 1941, that two German officers had been shot and killed near Bordeaux. Doubtless this was not the first such occurrence. But this time, the Germans chose to make a public announcement of the assassination. Moreover, they presented to the French government a demand that the persons responsible for the crime be discovered and delivered to justice, or else the Germans would require the French to hand over fifty persons as hostages, to be shot by the Germans in reprisal.

This posed a crucial issue, which epitomizes the kind of problem facing all parties in the situation. Viewed according to the principles of international law and the moral principles which hold in normal times, the rights and wrongs are obvious. First, it is plain that the men of the Resistance had no right to assassinate German soldiers, who were present in France on a legitimate military assignment as occupation troops, under the provisions of the armistice, which were in accord with the customs of international law. Up to this time, we must remember, the German officers and men in France had behaved with unimpeachable rectitude. This we know by the admission of the French as well as the affirmation of the Germans. For a Frenchman to assassinate a German soldier was to cause the death of a man who had done no wrong —unless the wearing of a German uniform was in itself a crime—to violate the laws of his own government, and to bring down upon the whole French population the threat of severe German reprisals.

It is no less plain that the Germans had no right to take hostages and put them to death. They would have been within their rights if they had required the Vichy government to take measures to discover and punish those who had committed acts of terrorism, if they had imposed a collective fine upon the population in the town where an act of terrorism was committed, or even if they had established an outright military rule throughout France in order to protect their troops. But they had no legal right, under the armistice or the customs governing a military occupation, to take hostages and put them to death. And they had no moral right to sacrifice innocent persons for the wrongs of others, even though the German soldiers who had been assassinated were themselves innocent victims.

It is likewise plain that Vichy had no right to accede to the German demand. The government was under a legal obligation to do all it could to prevent terrorism, but only by normal police procedure. If it was unable or unwilling to do so, it should have abdicated, leaving the Germans to assume the responsibility for whatever police measures they might take to protect their troops in France.

But the issues did not appear to the parties involved in terms as simple as these. This was not a time when men recognized as binding the usual rules of morality and law. As the men of the Resistance saw the issue, the assassination of German soldiers was not a crime but a proof of patriotism. For this reason, the French government was under a strong temptation to condone these crimes and take half-hearted measures to catch their authors. Hence the German authorities in France had some reason to believe that only under the threat of dire reprisals would Vichy bestir itself to put down terrorism. This does not excuse the German demand for hostages. However, we must not confuse this measure of German severity with the insane cruelties committed in Belsen or Dachau.

From the standpoint of Vichy, the issue presented a grave dilemma. One possible answer would have been for Vichy to refuse to give up the hostages, promising instead to redouble its efforts to prevent terrorism. It is open to question whether the Germans would have been satisfied with such a promise. It is also open to question whether Vichy would have saved its honor by assuming responsibility for hunting down the men of the Resistance who were risking their lives in a guerrilla for motives of patriotism. But at any event it is plain that the French police simply could not track down and punish the particular members of the Resistance who were responsible for each murder of a German soldier. In apprehending a common criminal, the police can rely upon the help of ordinary, law-abiding citizens. In searching for men who committed acts of terrorism in the name of patriotism, the police could not depend upon this help.

Another possible answer would have been for Vichy to refuse the German demand, even though this might mean that the Germans would sweep aside the government of Marshal Pétain, establish outright military rule throughout France, and call upon the Gestapo and the S.S. to help the *Wehrmacht* in its police operations in France. This plainly would have saved the honor of the French government. But with equal certainty it would have brought down worse hardships upon the French people. For it would make an enormous difference—often the difference between life and death—if any ordinary Frenchman, caught walking down a street without a pass after the hour of the curfew, had to explain himself to a patrol of German soldiers instead of a French policeman. And it would be a meager comfort to know that the policing of France was putting a drain upon German manpower and worsening the French hatred of their German conquerors.

Obliged to choose among these evil alternatives, Vichy chose to accede to the German demand and deliver hostages. The man who resolved the issue was Pierre Pucheu, who had become Minister of the Interior a short time before. Others in the government demurred, but none urged a different course. Even those who were aghast at Pucheu's decision raised protest when Marshal Pétain contemplated giving himself up to the Nazis, in lieu of other hostages.

To be sure, no one foresaw that the campaign of terrorism would continue and develop into the dimensions of a partisan war, and that the German demands for hostages would increase in proportion. But once taken, the decision proved irreversible. Thus the government that had taken office in order to protect the nation against the horrors of a Nazi rule became responsible for handing over Frenchmen to German executioners, in whatever number and at whatever time the Germans might choose.

Though the summer and fall of 1941 saw portentous developments within France, these months brought little change in the relations between France and the Axis. Berlin had become so preoccupied with the opening campaigns on the Eastern Front that the problem of France dropped into the background. As winter approached, however, the Germans again returned to the question of how to wrest advantage out of the conquered land across the Rhine.

This time, the Germans made General Weygand their target. From the outset of the Vichy regime, Berlin had looked with distrust upon the generalissimo who had held supreme command during the Battle of France. His reputation with the Germans had not improved after his nomination, in December, 1940, as delegate general in charge of the French empire in North Africa. For Weygand had consistently taken the stand that Vichy must defend its African possessions with no less vigor against the Axis than against the Gaullists and the British. He had thrown his whole weight against the provisions in the "Paris Protocols" that promised the Axis the use of French communications to supply the forces operating in Libya and Egypt against the British. And he had maintained close relations with American diplomatic agents —in particular, Robert Murphy. An agreement which he had concluded —the so-called Murphy-Weygand accord—providing for American economic aid to French North Africa, had become the pretext for the establishment of American espionage operations throughout the French colonies under his administration.

Watching these developments with increasing displeasure, the Germans eventually came to the conclusion that Weygand must be replaced. Word to this effect was given Darlan. The latter was not at all dismayed. On the contrary, he was eager for an opportunity to be rid of Weygand, whom he distrusted as a rival for political influence. Accordingly, Darlan made use of the German intimations as a means of inducing Pétain to approve the ouster of Weygand. Ultimately, in November, 1941, the marshal gave in. Weygand was recalled to France and put on the retired list. The position of Delegate General in North Africa was then abolished. So Darlan had no occasion to fear a new proconsul in the colonies. Washington made haste to express displeasure at this turn of events, but to no avail.

A few weeks later, Pétain and Darlan met with Goering for a further discussion of the general problem of Franco-German relations. In a pitiful confession of the failure of their efforts, the two representatives of France gave voice to a querulous complaint that Berlin had so far offered France no concession of value to her, despite the desire of Vichy to cooperate with the Axis and the German professions of a willingness to accept the friendship of the French. Dismissing this lament with a blunt answer, Goering made clear that Berlin would promise nothing until the French gave surer proof of their unequivocal readiness to "collaborate." After all, he concluded, "Who are the victors, we or you?" Ruefully, Pétain replied, "Never have I been more aware of our defeat."

In the upshot, the interview marked no new progress toward an understanding. And nothing more constructive came of a meeting between Darlan and Count Ciano, the Italian Foreign Minister, at Turin on December 10-11.

Nevertheless, Vichy persisted in the dogged attempt to win the good graces of the Nazis. Now, at last, the French government undertook to stage the trial of "war criminals" which the Germans had long awaited. The inception of this prosecution antedated Darlan's administration. It went back to the first weeks of the Vichy regime. In the summer of 1940, Pétain had announced that his government would call to account those persons responsible for the defeat of the nation in the war. In principle, this decision corresponded to the desires of a large segment of the populace, which was demanding punishment for those who had brought down disaster upon the nation. Probably any government taking office at such a time would have had to seek a scapegoat, and few persons would have taken the stand that none of the men in high position in the Third Republic was blameworthy.

But Vichy proceeded only slowly. One reason was that it was difficult to decide what persons to punish. Another was that it was not clear on what grounds to rest the charge. Obviously some person or persons had been at fault for leading France into a war for which she was ill prepared. But did the fault arise because France went to war, or because she was unable to win? And was the locus of the blame in the army, which had the professional responsibility for preparing for war, or in the cabinet, which always insisted upon the ultimate authority of the civilian government over the military?

Faced with such issues, Pétain had determined to give the entire problem over to a special tribunal, the High Court of Justice, which he appointed in July, 1940. This court had established its seat in the town of Riom, and had proceeded to deliberate, but without reporting progress. Meantime, in the fall of 1940, a number of persons had been placed under arrest, in view of their probable prosecution. These included Blum, Daladier, Reynaud, Gamelin, and Mandel, who had remained a prisoner since his participation in the affair of the "Massilia." At length, in September, 1941, Pétain had decided to take action in his own name, without waiting longer for the formalities of a trial in open court. In consultation with a new Council of Political Justice, which he appointed *ad hoc,* he declared the prisoners guilty of "treasonable dereliction in the discharge of their responsibilities" and sentenced them to continued imprisonment for an indefinite term. So the matter seemed to be settled.

But no sooner had this decision been announced than voices were raised within the government, urging that the High Court at Riom proceed with a public prosecution. The suggestion originated in a group including Pucheu, Barnaud, Bénoist-Méchin, Marion, Lucien Romier, and Henri Moysset, the two latter being members of Pétain's entourage. Darlan does not seem to have taken the initiative, but he made no opposition to the move.

Ostensibly, the logic of this maneuver was based on the presumption that public opinion would not accept the punishment, simply by decree, of men guilty of such faults. Moreover, the marshal would put himself in a bad light if he were to exercise judicial power as well as constituent, legislative, and executive.

Such considerations may have troubled some members of the group. But others were motivated by the thought that a public prosecution of the leading "war mongers" of the Third Republic would prove to Berlin that Vichy had completely broken with the tradition of Franco-German enmity. Thus it would help allay the suspicions in Germany that were preventing the development of "broad" collaboration.

But the plan miscarried. Prodded into action, the High Court cut short its legalistic labors concerning the grounds of the indictment. A public trial was begun at Riom on February 18, 1942. However, the defendants—Daladier and Blum in particular—succeeded in turning the tables on the prosecution. As the debate developed, the crucial issue became that of determining who was at fault for France's not having won the war, rather than who was culpable for having caused France to oppose German aggression. Furthermore, the defense brought out considerable evidence putting blame upon the leadership of the army, including Pétain himself. Even the utmost exertions of the censorship were insufficient to keep these implications out of the French press, much less the foreign.

After six weeks of the farce, the Germans themselves put a stop to it. On March 21 one of Abetz's men, Dr. Friedrich Grimm, called upon Pétain to report to him the displeasure of Berlin. The Fuehrer was incensed, he reported, at the unrepentant assumption of the French that they should have waged the war with better success. The *Wehrmacht* was no more pleased to see a parade of French generals testifying that the Germans would not have prevailed if the French government had not been so parsimonious in voting the military budget before the war.

Pétain had no choice but to accede. Forthwith he adjourned the trial *sine die*. And thus the scheme that was to have won Vichy the good graces of Berlin served only to increase German suspicion and ill will.

After the inglorious outcome of the Riom trial, the days of Darlan's primacy were numbered. The latest fiasco was only further evidence of the ineptitude he had shown from the time he assumed the office of Vice-Premier. In more than twelve months under his guidance, Vichy had seen no improvement in relations with Berlin despite repeated endeavors on his part to demonstrate his eagerness for "broad" collaboration. Meantime opposition within France to this pro-Axis orientation had become much more serious. The protests of the dwindling clique of "conservatives" in Vichy had become a minor matter, now that the terrorists of the Resistance were leading the struggle.

Having failed to demonstrate statesmanship, Darlan had been no more proficient in developing personal alliances within the governing circle. He had, to be sure, warded off his principal rival, Laval. He had also helped bring about the retirement of Weygand, whose reputation outshone his own. But he had never established a close personal relationship with Pétain, nor had he become identified with any of the various political factions in Vichy or Paris. Another man might have made this isolation into a source of strength, pitting one faction against another, to his own advantage. But Darlan was not that astute. He was simply without friends or allies.

By March of 1942, everyone on the "inside" in Vichy was wondering who would succeed Darlan, and how soon. With this speculation, there developed a welter of intrigue, as whenever, in a despotism, the grand vizier begins to lose his grip. It is quite impossible to unravel this tangled skein, so as to establish who pulled the strings that brought about Darlan's demotion and Laval's return. It is possible, however, to identify some of those who were working to this purpose.

Foremost of these was Laval himself. Even those who detested him could not help but admit that he was the obvious choice to take over leadership in the government. No other politician of comparable prominence was acceptable to Berlin. Moreover, even those who were hostile or lukewarm in their attitude toward "broad" collaboration had to acknowledge that Laval was more apt than Darlan to reap the meager rewards of such a policy.

For his part, Laval was eager to be back in office. Ever since his ouster, he had kept in touch with his partisans in Paris. In particular, he had

cultivated Déat, with whom he had developed a closer personal association after Colette's attempt on both their lives. Doriot was never as
enthusiastic as Déat in his endorsement of Laval, as might be expected,
in view of the bad blood between Doriot and Déat. But Luchaire did his
bit to keep Laval's name in view.

Laval also had the backing of Pucheu and the others in the government identified with the Synarchy. Evidently this clique was interested
in Laval because he gave promise of developing better economic relations with the Axis, which would work to the profit of French business
and banking interests. Pucheu also gave sign of a personal ambition
for a larger role in the government, which he imagined he would
achieve quicker as a henchman of Laval.

The attitude of the Germans was another factor. Darlan had proved
worse than a disappointment to them; he had become a vexation.
Though far from enamored of Laval, Berlin could not help but have
a better view of him after he had been squeezed out of the cabinet because he was too pro-German. Abetz was more positive in his preference for Laval. Most of the Nazis, as we have noted earlier, were never
so much interested in a Franco-German partnership as were their
French apologists. But Abetz, whose Francophile sentiments were of
long standing, was a sincere advocate of rapprochement between the
two nations. Besides, his personal position as ambassador, which opened
the perspective to higher position in the German Foreign Office, depended upon amicable relations between the two countries. So Abetz
did his best to induce Berlin to use pressure upon Vichy in behalf of
Laval.

On the other hand, the U.S. State Department was known to be
hostile to Laval. Admiral Leahy, who had remained in Vichy as American ambassador even after the outbreak of war between the United
States and the Axis, went so far as to call upon Pétain in an endeavor
to dissuade him from bringing Laval back into the government. As it
turned out, this *démarche* proved to have the opposite effect from that
intended. For the Germans took this as further evidence that Laval
must be their man.

The remnants of the "conservative" clique made a feeble gesture to
block the return of their *bête noire*. But this faction was now reduced

to a mere handful of men in Pétain's personal entourage, who were becoming less and less sure of their position. None of them showed much acumen in this crisis. Du Moulin de la Barthète, who remained Pétain's *chef du cabinet civil,* initiated a maneuver to reorganize the cabinet, in the outcome of which he hoped to elevate Lucien Romier to the top position. Pétain expressed interest in the scheme, but nothing came of it.

For his part, the marshal seemed resigned to Laval's return. Pétain was probably sincere in his many protestations of dislike for Laval. Yet the latter had a strange personal hold upon the old man, who could scarcely ever hold firm against him. At any event, Pétain took the initiative in opening negotiations with Laval looking toward his possible reinstatement in the cabinet.

The first such interview took place at Randan, near Vichy, on March 25. Sensing that he had the advantage, Laval indicated that he would return to Vichy only on condition that he have complete charge of the government. Pétain evidently took offense at this stand, which seemed to mean his own abdication, and no agreement was reached. But another meeting between the two, on April 2, seems to have issued in a closer accord.

The upshot was that on April 14 Vichy announced that Laval would reenter the government and would organize a new cabinet, in consultation with Pétain and Darlan. Forthwith the Darlan cabinet submitted its collective resignation. On the 18th, the names of the members of the new government were released.

At the head of the roster was Laval, who took the new title of *Chef du Gouvernement* as well as the ministries of Foreign Affairs, Interior, and Information. Among the holdovers from the preceding government were three of the five men regarded as agents of the Synarchy, as well as others likewise known to favor economic collaboration on a basis advantageous to French "big business" and high finance. Most of the remainder were men known as advocates of "broad" collaboration, but none was of preeminent rank.

Darlan himself passed into a twilight zone. On the 19th, Pétain announced that Darlan would remain in general charge of the ministries concerned with defense and the armed services and would be respon-

sible to the Chief of State rather than the Chief of the Government. So
he did not pass into retirement. But neither did he continue to have a
role in the direction of the government.

Thus the Darlan interlude came to its close, with little in its record
to reflect credit upon Darlan. For if there was any ground, other than
his personal ambition, upon which he could explain his acceptance of
the vice-premiership in February of 1941, it was upon the ground that
he was the candidate of the faction opposed to "broad" collaboration.
Yet Darlan proved as ineffectual in resisting the pressure for "broad"
collaboration as in gaining the good graces of the Nazis. To be sure,
he held back from the decisive step—a declaration of war upon Britain
and Russia, and ultimately upon the United States—which would have
meant a binding commitment to the "New Order." Hence he did not
permit the Axis to make use of the French navy.

But he showed himself quite willing to strike a bargain with the
Nazis transcending the terms of the armistice. That he stopped short
of open participation in the war on the side of the Axis was doubtless
due, in part, to the fact that the Germans did not have need of French
help and did not regard their assistance as worth a price. At any event,
Darlan did not shrink back from putting the French police at the service of the Germans, nor from punishing as traitors those leaders of the
Third Republic who had incurred the enmity of the Nazis simply because of their timorous and belated declaration of war in 1939. Having
gone so far, Darlan had little chance to cloak himself in high principle
when the Germans and their French spokesmen ultimately demanded
his dismissal for the reason that, whatever his intention, he was not
effective enough to suit them as their agent.

So it happened that Vichy became more deeply committed to the
Axis than ever before, precisely at the time when this ceased to be the
course of obvious advantage. In the summer of 1940 there had been
some logic in the argument for "broad" collaboration. At that time,
the British had seemed doomed to lose their single combat with the
Axis, while America and Russia remained neutral. Hence there had
been reason to believe that a rapprochement with Berlin was the only
course open to France and that a ready acceptance of this choice was

the part of wisdom. But Vichy had not yielded to this logic at that time.

Now, however, Britain was no longer alone—the United States and Russia were both in the war by her side. Strong as the *Wehrmacht* might be, it no longer seemed invincible, nor did the *Luftwaffe*. Hence the choice of partnership with the Axis no longer seemed a stern necessity. Rather, it represented a wager on one of the two warring camps. At best, this was a bold gamble. As it turned out, it was a losing gamble.

In retrospect, knowing what lay ahead, we cannot help but wonder why men with any degree of shrewdness accepted the risks to which Vichy was now exposed. We can perhaps explain the position of men such as Doriot and Déat on the ground that these were men of principle, albeit satanic principle. They were prepared to stake the fate of France upon that of the Axis because they believed that Europe could survive only on the basis of the "New Order." Or, more simply, we may note that these men were so deeply involved with the Nazis that they could not hope to save their own skins if the Axis should lose the war. Consequently they were willing to compass the ruin of France, if need be, to preserve their own lives and fortunes.

We cannot so readily explain Laval's motives. Certainly he was not wedded to the Nazis because he espoused their ideology. Nor was he, up to that time, so closely identified with the Nazis that he could not conceivably separate his future from theirs. However, we shall not pursue the question here; we shall have occasion to consider Laval's motives in the next chapter.

But we cannot defer, nor easily solve, the puzzle posed by those "conservatives" and others, apart from Laval, who without being committed to the principles of fascism remained loyal to Vichy after April, 1942. To be sure, only a few of the "conservative" coterie still remained in positions of influence in Vichy after the return of Laval. Most of these were attached to Pétain's personal staff rather than to the ministries responsible to the new Chief of the Government. Nevertheless, none of these stalwarts of the palace guard took the occasion to retire. Nor did many of those who had earlier been identified with the leadership of the new regime but had already been squeezed out of the governing circle now wash their hands of the whole venture.

A partial explanation is that some of these men remained loyal to Pétain, who continued to give the government the sanction of his name and prestige. So those who trusted Pétain as the one man whose patriotism was above question could presume that he regarded the recall of Laval as a further humiliating necessity for the preservation of France. They could hope that, when the time proved opportune, the marshal would take back the reins.

The question then arises, why did Pétain lend his endorsement to Laval? Why did he not take the occasion, instead, to terminate the fiction that France was under the rule of a French government? The charitable answer is that the old man was too senile to understand the situation. Though there is no doubt of his mental competence in 1940, there is some indication that his age was now telling on him, and that he was no longer in sufficient possession of his wits to be accountable for his actions. But the evidence is not conclusive, and this explanation is not convincing. The answer must lie, rather, in the considerations, compounded of personal vanity and political calculation, that led Pétain to deem a captive French government preferable, under any conditions, to the outright rule of the Germans, and that caused him to believe he was sacrificing his repose and reputation to shield France from her conquerors.

Yet among those who continued to support the Vichy regime, while disapproving of the government of Laval, there were many who were by no means committed to a blind devotion to Pétain. What of these men? We need not tarry here to consider in full the apology which many of them were to set forth after the liberation. But, in order to keep a perspective on the situation that obtained at the moment when Darlan gave way to Laval, we must take notice of a portion of their argument.

First, we must recognize the dilemma confronting the man who had served Vichy, thinking the new regime represented a humiliating but not dishonorable necessity, and had now begun to waver in this conviction. Where would he turn? He might, of course, go over to the Free French movement abroad. But what kind of reception would he have? Ever since the summer of 1940 the Gaullists had been denouncing the men of Vichy as traitors, and the latter had been castigating the *émigrés* as deserters and rebels. Even if he were prepared to confess his errors and beg a welcome in London, the disillusioned Vichyite might wonder what he would accomplish thereby to better the situation in France. The Gaullists were in no position, at the moment, to do more than hurl invective against Pétain and Laval in broadcasts on the London radio.

Nor was the Resistance within France a likelier avenue of protest. A man of the kind who had held office in the new regime was not the sort to begin now distributing leaflets in the dark of the night, helping derail trains, or knifing German soldiers in the back. Even if he were willing, he would wonder whether acts of terrorism and sabotage really weakened the Nazi rule or merely brought down ruthless reprisals and tighter repression.

Presuming he was not prepared to embark upon an illegal opposition to Vichy, he might retire to private life and give no positive support to the regime. This was the choice of those whose honor would stand no more compromise as well as of those whose sense of personal opportunism was keenest. Yet it was easy for a man of good intentions, with a gnawing hunger for a role in public affairs, to convince himself that such a course of withdrawal meant only an abdication of responsibility, a subtle form of cowardice.

Moreover, the same arguments could be adduced for the further support of Vichy as had earlier served to justify the inception of the new regime. For if it was worthwhile for France to avert an outright German rule in 1940, it was still important in 1942. Though the military superiority of Germany was no longer as impressive as before, the Axis was far from the verge of defeat. Even if the Nazis were eventually to lose the war, they still had more than ample time to wreak immense havoc upon France. And no one, in the spring of 1942, could be sure that ultimately they would prove the losers. At the moment when Laval supplanted Darlan, the Russians were barely holding back the German advance; the Japanese, having dealt a heavy blow to American seapower by their attack upon Pearl Harbor, were swarming over Southeast Asia and the East Indies, while the United States was still in the process of mobilization.

In view of the war map at the time, it would hardly have been unreasonable to predict the victory of the Axis. Certainly there was better reason to believe the war would end in a stalemate than in an unconditional surrender. In that event, France would surely have an opportunity to work loose from the domination of the Axis, provided she preserved a legal government of her own. She might even gain a voice in the negotiation of a compromise peace. In a land where the memories of both Talleyrand and Stresemann were alive, no one was unaware of what miracles might be accomplished, even by a powerless nation, if her diplomats were shrewd enough.

By some such reasoning, most of the "conservatives" persuaded themselves that the part of wisdom was to continue to support the Vichy regime. Whether their logic was sound, as judged by an Olympian omniscience, we may not presume to settle here. We may note, however, that this same kind of argument was to lead them still further. Just as the logic of the armistice in 1940 drove them to accept the return of Laval in 1942, so the logic of this decision was to induce them to continue their support of the regime in the succeeding months, even after Vichy, far from sheltering France from German might, served only to facilitate German rule in the conquered land.

Thus the last act of the tragedy began.

XII

THE BITTER END

VICHY seemed to have the destiny of thwarting the hopes of everyone
who had to do with it. In the earlier phases of the venture, from the
summer of 1940 to the spring of 1942, it was the "conservatives" who
were the victims of this frustration. At its inception the new regime
presented them with the opportunity of putting their ideas into practice for the first time, after more than a generation of vainly criticizing
the leadership of the Third Republic. But their hopes soon withered.
The National Revolution proved stillborn, and the dream of achieving
diplomatic independence died a slow and anguished death. So the "conservatives" had to step aside, while the champions of "broad" collaboration took over leadership.

Thereupon it became the turn of their adversaries to suffer the same
kind of disappointment. In the final phase, from April, 1942, to August, 1944, Laval and his henchmen held the reins in their own hands,
at last, without having longer to wage a struggle against the "conservatives." For his part, Laval imagined that, by virtue of what he believed
was his singular gift for bargaining, he would win for France a place
among the partners in the Axis, quite as though she had shared their
victory instead of having been their victim.

Perhaps he might have achieved this coup—we may admit the
hypothesis without necessarily believing it true—if he had not been
squeezed out of office in December, 1940. But by the time he worked
his way back into power, it was too late. By the spring of 1942, France
was no longer in a position to bargain with the Axis, because she had
nothing of large value to offer as a *quid pro quo*. So, instead of swin-
dling the Germans, Laval found himself forced to become the humble
agent of their will.

Those who were avowed disciples of fascism were no better off. Indeed, their cup was tinctured by an even more bitter irony. From the morrow of the armistice, or even before the outbreak of the war, these zealots had insisted that there was no conflict between the true interests of France and those of the Axis. Now that Vichy was finally committed to doing whatever the Germans might dictate, they could only declare that such a course was right and proper.

But for them, as for Laval, their triumph came too late. In 1940 or 1941, a case could be made for French acceptance of the "New Order." By 1942, however, the Nazis manifestly had no serious interest in the "New Order." Forced to pit their whole strength against the Russians and still unable to smash the resistance of the Red Army, the Nazis were now concerned only with winning every possible advantage at the moment, trusting to the future to take care of itself. Hence the Germans no longer had the slightest interest in France save insofar as they could draw upon her manpower and her resources for their own use. Consequently the French fascists gained a leading role in the government only in time to give the lie to their own specious promises of a prosperous fraternal union of the two neighbors across the Rhine.

On his return to the government in April of 1942, Laval became the undisputed master of the Vichy regime, as he remained down to its close. Pétain passed into a nearly complete eclipse. As a sign of his virtual abdication, the marshal established, by a decree of April 19, 1942, that the ministers were now responsible to Laval as Chief of the Government and not to himself as Chief of State. Subsequently, on November 26, 1942, Pétain delegated to the Chief of the Government the right to promulgate decrees of all kinds, save those having the character of organic laws, on his own signature alone.

Laval had had no such preponderance during the previous period of his participation in the government. He had never won the confidence of Pétain, even though the latter was unduly grateful to him for his role in handling the National Assembly. Pétain had been much more trustful of men such as Baudouin and Bouthillier, who did their best to discredit Laval. Nor, at that time, had the Germans singled out Laval as their man.

In 1942, however, Laval's position was much stronger. The Germans now looked upon him as their best bet among French politicians. To be sure, the Nazi leaders still had reservations about him. They recognized that Laval was an opportunist who advocated "broad" collaboration only because he deemed it a wise expedient at the moment. Men such as Doriot and Déat, on the other hand, were so deeply committed to the Axis that they must remain apologists of a Franco-German rapprochement no matter what might happen. But the Nazis also knew that neither Doriot nor Déat was the man to head a puppet French government. Neither had large public appeal or the experience and skill in political intrigue that Laval had acquired in his career in the politics of the Third Republic. So, despite their doubts of him, the Germans continued to place their reliance in Laval rather than in the more forthright advocates of fascism.

Pétain had also modified his attitude toward Laval. He now knew that Laval was the only man, save Doriot or Déat, whom the Nazis would accept as the head of the government. As among the three, Pétain preferred Laval. So did the remnants of the "conservative" clique in Vichy. While Laval was committed to such an abject subservience to Berlin that only a shade of difference distinguished him from the avowed fascists, there still remained a discernible distinction between them. For the French fascists could never break with the Nazis, no matter how certain the defeat of the Axis might become. But Laval might conceivably betray the Germans if circumstances should ever make this seem advantageous to him as well as France.

While we can perceive the circumstances that made Laval nearly indispensable to the continuance of the Vichy regime, we cannot so easily understand the considerations that led him to accept the responsibility of office at this time. In the spring of 1942 the likelihood was that the Axis would either suffer defeat or gain, at best, a stalemate. Looking ahead to either of these eventualities, Laval should have deemed it safer to remain in retirement. If the Germans should lose the war, he would have much less to explain away. If a stalemate should develop, he could emerge at a later time to try his hand at bargaining under more favorable conditions.

We can do little more than speculate as to Laval's calculations, for the documentation so far available is not sufficient to permit us to be sure of his motives. We might dismiss the problem quickly by assuming that Laval simply made a gross error of judgment—overestimating the strength of the Axis, he believed that the ultimate defeat of the Allies was certain. But we cannot be quite satisfied with this answer. Laval was generally regarded as a man of too shrewd judgment ever to join the losing side.

Or we might assume that Laval had become a convinced partisan of fascism who sincerely wished the victory of the Axis, whether or not he regarded this as highly probable. We have evidence for such a view in a number of public pronouncements in which Laval affirmed this desire to see the Axis win. Despite his words, however, we must discount this explanation. For there is little to bear out his professions of a sincere conversion to the cause of the Axis. In his earlier career, he had given little evidence of such an inclination. No doubt, he had been an advocate of Franco-German reconciliation in the 1920s and a champion of "appeasement" at the time of the Italo-Ethiopian war in 1935, but he had never been conspicuous as an apologist of the Nazis, nor had he established ties with those Frenchmen who earned this kind of fame.

Moreover, he was so well known as an opportunist that it seems unlikely he would ever risk his neck for a matter of principle. His enemies, who included representatives of virtually every shade of political opinion, all agreed that Laval was so much the man of intrigue, and so little the man of conviction, that he seemed to have a neurotic compulsion to seek his purposes invariably by devious means and to shun an open clash of issues as the Devil fears holy water. Apparently Laval himself took pride in his reputation as a wily trickster. He seemed to think he had a special gift for bargaining, a heritage of his peasant stock, which gave him a mystic bond with the common people.

It is not hard to imagine that precisely this self-delusion led him to his undoing. For Laval evidently became the victim of his own conceit, taking office in the spring of 1942, despite the malign omens, because he believed himself the one man in France capable of cheating the

Germans. As it happens, this is not far from the explanation which Laval himself offered, *ex post facto,* as to why he accepted the obvious risk involved in his return to office.

Whatever the mixture of his motives, Laval proceeded to his task with resolute decision. Without the slightest hesitation, he committed his government to the path of "broad" collaboration. Even French opinion, which was by now inured to nearly any kind of monstrosity of politics, was shocked to hear the Chief of the Government declare, in a radio address of June 22, 1942, "I wish to see the victory of the Axis." Nothing in his actions gave proof that he did not mean his words. Whatever the Germans demanded of him, he promised without protest; he asked only for time enough to do their bidding.

So far as concerns domestic affairs, he gave a free hand to the fascists. Thus Déat was permitted to establish branches, in the unoccupied zone, of the Rassemblement National Populaire, a federation of various small political associations of fascists, which Déat had earlier established in Paris as the nucleus of the *parti unique.* Likewise, Doriot was allowed to extend the recruitment of the Légion des Volontaires contre le Bolchévisme, his pet project, which hitherto had been active only in the occupied zone. As the fascists thus found new freedom and official approval, the "conservatives" saw their one remaining stronghold collapse when Laval dissolved the Conseil National, the commission charged with the task of deliberating on general problems of long-range reform, which had given evidence of a "conservative" bias.

But gestures such as these were of no importance, compared with the two principal endeavors of the new administration. One of these was the recruitment of workers for German war industries. This was the main problem confronting the government at the time Laval returned to office, as it remained for the next eighteen months. The other was the repression of the Resistance, which became an ever greater concern to Vichy, until by the winter of 1943–44 it was the sole preoccupation of the little band of desperate men who still called themselves the government of France.

The German interest in French labor did not begin with the return of Laval. It was a gradual outgrowth of their involvement in the war on the Eastern Front. During the twelve months of the armistice prior to the outbreak of the Russo-German war, the Nazis had had no problem of manpower. Their armies were not engaged in large-scale operations, and their factories were not short of labor. So the Germans were content to exploit France by other means than the conscription of her workmen. The charges which they levied upon France for the costs of the occupation, which they fixed at 400,000,000 francs per diem, afforded them a surplus. Part of this surplus they used to purchase French business enterprises and to subsidize their political agents in the occupied zone.

But as the deadlock developed in the fall of 1941 in their war with the Russians, the Germans became concerned about their reserves of manpower. By the winter of 1941–42 they were making plans for the extensive use of foreign labor in their factories, so as to release more of their own men for service with the *Wehrmacht*. Hence they began to recruit workers in France, as well as in other occupied countries, at first on a volunteer basis. They offered attractive terms—good wages, the privileges of German social insurance, and permission to send savings back to France or to return home on vacation.

At the same time, to make sure that volunteers would come forward in sufficient numbers, they began to take steps which would produce unemployment in France. Thus they began to cut down on the placement of war contracts with French firms, restrict the supply of raw materials used in French industry, and prohibit the repair of factories damaged by air raids. By these and similar devices, the Germans succeeded in obtaining about 150,000 volunteers. The enlistment of these workers was accomplished through offices which the Germans opened in various French cities and towns. The French government, at the start, had no official part in the recruitment.

But by the spring of 1942 this campaign for the volunteer recruitment of labor broke down. One reason was that not many more Frenchmen were willing to go to Germany. Even though the Germans offered all kinds of blandishments, the fact remained that work in their factories was hard and hazardous—war plants were the obvious target of air raids—and Germany was a strange and hostile country, where no

French workman could ever be quite at ease. The other reason was that, while voluntary enlistments were drying up, the Germans were making plans for a still larger use of foreign labor.

However, because the armistice made no provision for forced labor, the Germans themselves could not compel French workmen to take work in Germany, unless they were willing to sweep aside the armistice, establish a complete military rule in France, and then conscript whatever number of workers they wished. Such a step might involve as much disadvantage for the Axis as it would give benefit. Consequently the Germans were obliged to accomplish their purpose by putting pressure upon Vichy to see to it that the quota of volunteers was met.

Laval came face to face with this problem within a matter of weeks. Early in May he was summoned to a conference with *Gauleiter* Fritz Sauckel, to whom Berlin had given charge of the entire program of recruiting foreign labor. Sauckel announced that Germany would require a sufficient further number of French volunteers to raise the total of French workers in Germany to 250,000 by the end of July. He made clear that Vichy must bend every effort to encourage enlistments, under pain of stern consequences if the French failed to meet their quota. Laval made quick to indicate his willingness to cooperate. However, he urgently besought Sauckel to offer some kind of concession in return, which Vichy could use to make enlistments more attractive. Reluctantly, Sauckel agreed to this plan—for every three French workmen who volunteered for work in Germany, the Germans would release one French prisoner of war out of the 1,500,000 still held in German prison camps.

Thereupon Laval launched an intense press and radio campaign, presenting the voluntary enlistment of workers for service in Germany as a patriotic duty, to ransom their less fortunate countrymen from German captivity. The scheme was christened the *relève,* or "relief." The public was given the impression that each worker would replace a prisoner, rather than three for one.

Despite the utmost exertions of the government, scarcely any more volunteers signed up. By the end of July, which Sauckel had set as a deadline, the French were still far from their quota. So, too, were the other occupied countries under Axis domination, where the same kind of recruitment had been launched. Consequently, on August 20, 1942, Sauckel announced that a system of conscription would be introduced to supersede the reliance upon volunteers.

This ominous news bestirred Laval to a new effort to appease Sauckel. Knowing that the introduction of German conscription into France would leave no pretense of French independence, he begged Sauckel to make an exception of France and give Vichy another chance to meet the quota. Sauckel agreed, on condition that Vichy itself establish a French system of conscription, to make sure that the quota be met. Accordingly, by a decree of September 4, 1942, Laval instituted the Service du Travail Obligatoire (S.T.O.), or compulsory labor service. The decree provided that the government might call up and put to work, as it might see fit, all French men between the ages of eighteen and sixty-five, and unmarried women between twenty and thirty-five. However, it stipulated that only men between the ages of twenty and fifty, and no women, would be required to work elsewhere than in their usual place of residence.

Laval hoped that the threat of conscription would induce a sufficient number of "volunteers" to sign up, so that the government would not have to have recourse to this law. Hence the decree was not put into operation at once. Instead, the propaganda for volunteer enlistment was redoubled, with the new menace of conscription to back up the appeals to patriotism. Under the pressure of Laval's piteous pleas, which Abetz endorsed, Sauckel grudgingly agreed to give the French until November of 1942 to show results.

Still, no more than a trickle of "volunteers" came forward. By the beginning of November, Laval was in a tight spot. He had stalled off the Germans for more than six months, with promises that he would meet their quota, if only they gave him time—and he had conspicuously failed. Never quite trustful of him, the Nazis were again wondering whether Laval was really their man. Rumors were insisting that he would soon be swept aside in favor of a new government, headed by Doriot. No one knows how Laval would have made out had not the Americans launched their invasion of North Africa at this time, giving Vichy and Berlin a new preoccupation, just as the crisis over the problem of forced labor was reaching its climax.

In the series of crises that mark the hectic fifty months of Vichy, none was more chaotic than the upheaval which followed the American landing in North Africa in November of 1942. Even though everyone had long been aware that such a move was likely, and the Americans had been making their actual preparations for some months, Vichy apparently had little or no precise foreknowledge of the plans for the landing. And neither Vichy nor Berlin gave evidence, when the operation was launched, of having thought out in advance what would be their general policy.

The news of the invasion reached Vichy promptly on the morning of November 8. Immediately the government broke off diplomatic relations with the United States and reaffirmed its orders to the civilian and military authorities in the colonies to resist the attack. Nevertheless, the Germans took matters into their own hands. On November 11 their troops crossed the line of demarcation into what the armistice defined as the unoccupied zone. Apparently this decision was reached simply on the grounds of military considerations. No one could be sure that the Americans would not proceed at once to strike against the southern shores of France, and the Germans would hardly trust Vichy with the task of warding off such a blow.[1]

But the move also had political implications. Since the occupation of southern France represented a clear breach of the armistice, it raised the question of the legal position of the Vichy regime. Hitherto it had been possible to argue that the French government remained sovereign, with quite the same freedom of action as other governments, save insofar as it had assumed a certain number of legal obligations under the stipulations of the armistice. Though one might have challenged this argument, hitherto one could have dismissed it out of hand. Now it became quite impossible to allege that the German power over France was in any way effectively limited by the armistice. This presented Vichy with only two alternatives. The French government must either resign or admit that it was nothing more than an instrument of German rule.

[1] A consequence of the German move into southern France was that the French naval command at Toulon scuttled all the vessels stationed at this base, to keep them from falling into the hands of the Germans.

Apparently the Germans did not care which way the issue was re-solved. On the one hand, they showed no desire to force Vichy to abdi-cate. While they did not hesitate to send their troops across the line of demarcation, they made no move to set aside the French rule over the civilian population in either zone. On the other hand, they showed no concern whatever as to the possibility that the French government might resign in protest.

At Vichy, there was no serious question as to what course to take. Among those few in the government or in Pétain's entourage who still held out against a complete commitment to the Axis, there was some vague and aimless talk of protest. But neither Pétain nor anyone else made even a motion to resign, and no lesser kind of protest was worth the trouble.

We cannot help but wonder at the relative ease with which Vichy accepted this new stage in its degradation. At the time, Anglo-American opinion regarded the events of November, 1942, as marking the ultimate hour of decision. Up to that point, the more charitable observers would acknowledge that Vichy had some slight title of legitimacy. But after the occupation of southern France, virtually no one in Britain or America would admit that a man of honorable purpose could remain loyal to Vichy. Actually, however, the moment of decision seems to have come in the previous April, when Laval returned. Evidently anyone who was willing to support Vichy after Laval came back was willing to support the regime down to the bitter end.

The invasion of North Africa had another consequence, besides the extension of the German occupation. It produced a rival French govern-ment. This was not, of course, the first challenge to the authority of Vichy. Since the summer of 1940, General de Gaulle had been pre-tending to speak in the name of France, and in September, 1941, he had organized the National Committee of Free France as though it were a government. The United States and Soviet Russia, as well as Britain and a number of other governments and governments-in-exile, had accorded him a qualified diplomatic recognition. Yet the status of the Gaullist movement had remained ambiguous until the invasion of North Africa made it a practical necessity for the Allies to create a *de facto* French government which would cooperate with them. This necessity became De Gaulle's opportunity.

However, his definitive success did not come at once upon the landing. The Americans, who took the lead in the North African operation, had remained lukewarm toward General de Gaulle. At the time when plans for the invasion were being drawn up, moreover, the Americans had decided not to make use of the Gaullists. Instead, they intended to seek the cooperation of the Vichyite authorities who were in command of the French colonies in North Africa, in the hope of reducing or even obviating the French resistance.

To the surprise of all parties, Admiral Darlan happened to be in North Africa at the time of the American landings. Promptly the Americans established contact with him. Once they made clear to him that they commanded a superior force, he threw his lot in with them, ordering the French civil and military authorities to abandon their resistance. Because he had remained in supreme command of French ground, sea, and air forces, by the express delegation of Marshal Pétain, his word required obedience even from those who still remained loyal to Vichy. In consideration of the assistance he thus vouchsafed them, the Americans then recognized Darlan as *de facto* head of the government of French North Africa, with the title of High Commissioner.

No one knows what would have become of De Gaulle had Darlan lived to consolidate his new position. But on December 25 Darlan died at the hands of an assassin, who shot him down in the streets of Algiers. Thereupon the Americans, still anxious to avoid dealing with De Gaulle, named General Giraud as the successor to Darlan.

But this was a losing game. De Gaulle had too strong a following among the French, and too good a press in Britain and America, to be denied a place in the French government which the Allies were sponsoring. Nor could Washington longer urge against him the argument that he had no legal basis for his rule, since the Americans themselves were now supporting General Giraud as High Commissioner, and he had no warrant for his position save their endorsement.

So Washington could do no better than insist that De Gaulle come to some kind of agreement with Giraud, which would merge the *de facto* government he headed with the quasi government which De

Gaulle represented. Accordingly, negotiations between the two were begun. The discussions dragged on until June, when ultimately De Gaulle emerged as the head of a new Provisional Government, while Giraud retained only command of the French military forces obedient to this new government. We shall not pursue the career of this Provisional Government from its proclamation in June, 1943, to its eventual establishment in Paris in August, 1944. This belongs to the story of the liberation rather than of Vichy, and a substantial literature has been written on it. Yet we must take note that its emergence meant a new challenge to the authority of the government in Vichy to which Pétain still lent the sanction of his name.

Up to this point, the Frenchman in the homeland had little choice but to recognize Vichy as the legitimate government of France. He might bitterly disapprove the policies of this government, as earlier he might have opposed policies of the Third Republic. But he could not blink the fact that Marshal Pétain had gained office lawfully and that a large number of foreign governments, including others besides those favorable to the Axis, had recognized him as head of the French state.

Now, however, the ordinary Frenchman had much more reason to question the legitimacy of Vichy. By their action in occupying southern France, the Nazis themselves set aside the armistice. At the same time, the Americans, British, and Russians had given recognition to another French government.

Consequently, those in France who remained loyal to Vichy now became partisans of one side, in what amounted to a civil war, quite as much as did those who gave their support to the Resistance. As ordinary citizens were thus obliged to choose between the two camps, inevitably the larger number put their hopes in the Provisional Government, now established in Algiers. By the same logic, those who continued to give their active support to Vichy now became more firmly bound by their decision than ever before and more completely committed to the cause of the Axis.

Indeed, the Gaullists took the position that anyone who supported Vichy was an agent of the Axis and a traitor to France. The Provisional Government gave an ominous proof of its determination to uphold this position when it sponsored the trial of Pierre Pucheu. Though the

political meaning of this case was simple, its background was complicated. In April, 1941, as we have seen, Pucheu had become a member
of the Darlan government, in which eventually he took the post of
Minister of the Interior. Upon the recall of Laval, however, he had
been excluded from the cabinet. Subsequently he had come under suspicion of opposition to the government, and in November of 1942 he
had escaped from France, taking refuge in Spain. Then, after the
American landing in North Africa, he had passed to French Morocco,
intending to throw in his lot with the American-sponsored regime in
North Africa. Instead, he had been put in prison, and the Communists,
who by this time had gained a large representation in the Gaullist
movement, had raised a demand that he be brought to trial on the
charge of treasonable collaboration with the Axis while a member of the
Darlan government.

Unquestionably Pucheu had been one of the advocates of "broad"
collaboration, but this was hardly the reason for bringing him to trial.
His record was no worse than that of Darlan, whom the Americans
had invested as High Commissioner of North Africa. However, Pucheu
had incurred special disfavor because, as Minister of the Interior, he had
taken the immediate responsibility for handing over hostages to
the Germans, and he had selected Communists in preference to others.
At the insistence of the Communists, the Provisional Government of
Algiers drew up an indictment in August, 1943, and launched a prosecution. The case was tried in March, 1944, and Pucheu was condemned
and shot. Thus Algiers gave an unmistakable indication of the fate
promised those who had participated in the Vichy government, and
made it clear that a last-minute apostasy was of no avail.

So those who remained in Vichy found their retreat cut off. We may
not presume to determine whether it was the part of wisdom for Algiers
to set such a grim pattern for the future. But, wise or not, the decision
helped to embitter the civil war then brewing in the homeland. Had
not the Provisional Government taken such a hostile stand toward turn-
coats, probably a larger number of Vichyites would have gone over to
the Resistance in the latter part of 1943 and early in 1944. Unquestionably this would have opened an avenue of escape for many opportunists,
but it would also have meant that no one would remain loyal to Vichy to

the bitter end save those who were through-and-through fascists. These might ultimately have been brought to justice without involving in their fate the larger number of those whose faults signified weaknesses of character or judgment rather than deliberate treason.

Of the four years that comprise the span of Vichy, 1943 proved the least eventful. The twelve months that followed the crisis of November, 1942, brought no new moment of decision in domestic politics and no new climax in the international arena. Vichy persevered in the dismal endeavor to prove its subservience to Berlin, while the Germans launched still another great offensive against the Russians, once more without achieving a decisive success. As yet, however, the Russians were unable to undertake a counteroffensive with more than modest tactical perspective.

Meantime the Allied offensive in the Mediterranean theater bogged down. To be sure, once the Americans were established in Morocco, Algeria, and Tunisia, the Axis was obliged to liquidate its operations in North Africa. In July, the Americans crossed from North Africa to Sicily, then invaded the southern tip of Italy. Shortly afterwards came the coup that overthrew Mussolini, and in September the new Italian government concluded an armistice with the Allies and declared war upon Germany. But after the capture of Naples the Americans came to a standstill, spending the next six months in inconclusive fighting in Italy, while preparations proceeded for the grand assault upon "Fortress Europe" in the spring of 1944.

Yet the situation in France was far from static. Indeed, the polarization within France became sharper than ever before and revealed an ominous new pattern. Hitherto political problems had attracted more attention than economic, and the division of opinion had been as between Vichy and Paris. In the main, the nation had given its trust to the government of Marshal Pétain, while Paris, having become the bastion of the French apologists for the Axis, had developed into the center of criticism, protest, and disaffection. Now, instead of Vichy against Paris, it became an opposition of France against her rulers. For now Vichy spoke with the same voice as Paris, which was the voice of Berlin, and the nation as a whole could no longer regard its pretended government as other than an instrument of the Axis. And instead of politics, the interest of the nation was now absorbed in the bare economic problem of how to keep alive.

Until 1943 the economic problems of France had been much less critical than might have been supposed. The worst distress so far had been the unemployment which developed right after the armistice. This had risen to the point where some 1,500,000 persons were out of work, even though 1,500,000 prisoners of war were withdrawn from the labor supply. But this unemployment had been largely liquidated by the winter of 1940-41, partly because of the normal process of reconversion from a war economy to production for civilian needs, partly because of the minor boom resulting from German expenditures in France. In the long run, these German purchases of goods and services represented a kind of expropriation, since the Germans made payment with francs which they received from the French Treasury for the costs of the occupation. In the short run, however, the German expenditures had the effect of an economic stimulus, since they afforded a good market for French agricultural and industrial products and assured a prosperous clientele for the restaurants, theaters, and other such facilities of Paris.

To be sure, shortages had begun to develop before the end of 1940, and some of these had become vexatious. The shortage of fuel made it virtually impossible to heat private houses, apartments, or public buildings. Throughout the winters from 1940 to 1945, motion-picture theaters were crowded, not so much for the sake of the entertainment as for the animal warmth which the audience itself generated. Gasoline was unavailable, save for cars used by high officials of the government or at exorbitant prices on the black market. Nevertheless, trucks and buses continued to operate, making use of a wood-burning contraption, attached to the outside of the vehicle, which generated charcoal gas for fuel for the motor. Even in 1940 the supply of edible oils and fats fell far below the minimum needed for proper nutrition. Until late in 1942, however, these shortages were not so general as to make it impossible for the mass of the nation to meet its basic living needs, albeit with some hardship and inconvenience.

In this period, the problem of shortages was not so serious in itself as in relation to the problem of inflation. In part, of course, the rise in prices was the consequence of an insufficient supply of goods on the market. But it was also due to other factors, including the drain upon the reserves of gold in the Treasury, to meet the payments to the Germans for the costs of the occupation. As a general policy, the government undertook to stabilize all prices at the levels prevailing before the armistice. In practice, however, the government made no serious effort to control the prices which the peasants charged for their produce, deeming it better to allow them to sell their surplus on the black market, where it would pass into the hands of French consumers, than to require it to be sold through legal channels, where it could be bought up by the Germans.

The natural result was that food prices rose faster than the general level of prices. This worked to the advantage of the peasants and the disadvantage of the urban population. In particular, it meant a hardship for the working class, since wages were not permitted to rise in proportion to the costs of living. Likewise it would bring distress to other elements in the populations, such as pensioners, rentiers, and civil service personnel, whose income was fixed. The business classes, on the other hand, were in a position to increase their income in proportion to the rise in the costs of food, or at a higher rate. Thus the economic problem, at the outset, involved a disturbance in the relative position of the various economic classes rather than a severe burden upon the nation as a whole.

But in 1943, the economic distress worsened to the point of desperation. No longer did the factors of economic benefit in the short run, such as the German expenditures, offset the long-range pressures on the economy. Textile supplies virtually disappeared, since the black market could not furnish such exotic commodities as cotton, nor wool in large amounts. Without replacement, personal supplies of clothing became depleted. Leather became so scarce that the streets of Paris resounded with the clatter of wooden-soled shoes.

The shortage of food became much worse. For want of chemical fertilizers and insecticides, the peasant found his harvests shrinking. Nor could he keep up his herd of livestock when the harvest of grain was insufficient for human needs. Even on the black market it became hard to obtain eggs, butter, cheese, milk, and meat. Nor was it possible to purchase bread and table wine in ample quantities. For all save a favored few, potatoes, turnips, and other cheap vegetables became nearly the whole of the daily diet. To obtain this humble fare, the ordinary town-dwelling family often had to send one or more of its members, by bicycle or on foot, from one farm to another in the outlying countryside.

Meantime the Germans at last had their way in the matter of forced labor. Early in 1943 the decree for the conscription of labor was put into effect. Soon trainloads of French workers—sometimes the whole staff of a factory, engineers and foremen along with unskilled and semi-skilled workers—were moving eastward across the Rhine. We cannot determine with any degree of exactitude the total number of men who thus became *déportés*. Nor can we distinguish them from those others who signed up for work in Germany of their own volition because they saw no other way of keeping their family alive. Naturally, the wife of a man who enlisted under the pressure of economic stress would find it wiser to tell her neighbors that he had been conscripted than to admit he had voluntarily taken service with *les Fritz*. Suffice it to say that the number of French workers in Germany eventually reached a total in the order of magnitude of about 600,000, exclusive of those prisoners of war whom the Germans "liberated"—on condition that they remain in Germany as "free" workers.

The consequence of this growing economic pressure—together with the obvious degradation of the French government and the approach of the liberation—was an increase of the Resistance. From the beginning of 1943 onward, the various movements of the illegal opposition became a factor of formidable importance, no longer simply an heroic gesture or a nuisance. The Resistance now comprised three separate branches. One was the political Resistance, which included a number of disciplined organizations, waging a struggle against Vichy and the Axis by means of illegal propaganda, sabotage, and terrorism. This movement had taken its start in 1940, as we have noted, but it had not gained large importance until after the outbreak of the Russo-German war in June, 1941, which brought the Communists into the struggle, and the entrance of the United States into the war in December, 1941, which gave new courage to the non-Communist opposition. The partisans of this branch of the Resistance gained new boldness in 1942, as the Red Army once more withstood the German attack on the Eastern Front, and as the Anglo-American allies opened their offensive in the western Mediterranean. Gradually the Gaullist movement established contact with these elements in the Resistance, who, by 1943, began to think of themselves as agents of the rightful French government, in opposition to a band of traitors.

A separate branch of the Resistance developed in the army. Like the rest of the nation, the army had welcomed the accession of Marshal Pétain in the summer of 1940. But this was not because of an affection for the Axis. The career officers of the French army were generally "conservative" in politics but not advocates of Franco-German rapprochement, much less of French subservience to the Axis. As it became apparent that Vichy was hopelessly committed to the cause of the Axis, which now seemed even less likely to prevail against the Allies, the military leadership of France began to make plans for resuming the struggle. Against the day when the Anglo-American armies should land in France, the army began to husband stores of munitions and draw up plans of operations, all in secret and in violation of the armistice. This movement in the army had its center in the Deuxième Bureau, or Intelligence Section, of the General Staff. It had no ties with the political movements of the Resistance. Indeed, military men generally regarded the campaign of sabotage and terrorism as more harmful to France than to the Axis, since a war of pin pricks did little to weaken the Axis while the reprisals wrought havoc on the French people.

The other branch of the Resistance was the *maquis*. This did not begin to develop until the winter of 1942–43, and it arose wholly as a reaction against the conscription of labor for Germany. Without any kind of prearrangement, without the leadership of any illegal political organization, thousands of young men simply slipped away into "the brush" (*maquis*), in order to avoid deportation to work in German war plants. Some of them established contact with the political organizations of the Resistance, but the larger number drew together into desperate little bands which had to live like criminals. In contrast to the members of the political Resistance, who continued their habitual vocations and directed their terrorism against the Germans and those Frenchmen who were known as notorious apologists for the Nazis, the *maquisards* were obliged to hide out by day somewhere in the hills, and make raids by night upon nearby villages in order to obtain food, clothing, and other necessities. In some regions, the *maquisards* became a scourge of the villagers rather than the Nazis. Nevertheless, the movement, which eventually involved upwards of 100,000 men, bore witness to the spreading disaffection within France.

The repression of the illegal opposition became the only important task of Vichy in 1943, other than the provision of labor for Germany. And in its grim work of political repression, Vichy no longer showed any sign of hesitation or mercy. This attitude is not surprising on the part of men who made public profession of their desire to see the Axis prevail. But it is more remarkable that others, who had no preference for the Axis as against the Allies, also approved of the measures of repression directed against the "terrorists," as Vichy termed the Resistance.

In order to understand this point of view, we must bear in mind that, however laudable the motives of the Resistance, its activities were bringing down severe reprisals upon the French, while the effectiveness of its blows against the Axis was never obvious. Furthermore, we must recognize that, while an immense number of Frenchmen risked their lives in the Resistance in response to deep moral or patriotic impulses, not everyone who committed acts of violence in the name of the Resistance was a man of sincere high purpose. As in any movement embracing thousands of persons, the partisans of the Resistance included representatives of the whole range of human character, from the finest examples of selfless heroism down to instances of the insane urge to murder concealed behind the guise of political principle.

Finally, we must acknowledge that the French government had no choice but to strike down the illegal opposition, or its authority would collapse at once. In that event, the Germans would simply take over the task. In sum, it is clear that even a government of the most honorable kind, if it were to remain in office, would have had to combat the Resistance. It is no less clear that men of the nicest sense of honor would not have accepted positions in a government which had no other choice but to serve as a branch of the Nazi police.

At any event, Laval and his henchmen showed no scruple. Finding the regular police organizations inadequate for coping with the Resistance, Laval created a new instrument for the task. This was the Milice, or Militia, which had originated as an outgrowth of the Service d'Ordre Légionnaire, the strong-arm detachment of the moribund Légion des Combattants et des Volontaires. In January, 1943, Laval made the Milice into a special police, separate from the gendarmerie, and assigned it the sole task of tracking down "terrorists." Its director, Joseph Darnand, was notorious even among fascist fanatics for his long-standing ambition to become the head of a French counterpart of the Nazi S.S. He had sought such a role, before the war, in the Cagoule, the Croix de Feu, and Doriot's P.P.F., but without ever achieving his purpose. Now, as head of the Milice, he found scope for his talents.

Under his command, the Milice became a band of freebooters, recruited in the underworld and given license to proceed to their task without regard for law. It was never so much the scourge of the "terrorists" as of the simple, law-abiding citizen, who could make no protest at whatever crimes the Milice might commit in the name of "the maintenance of order."

In November of 1943 Pétain made one last, fumbling gesture to halt the drift toward ruin. He set in motion a plan to order a new meeting of the two houses of Parliament as a National Assembly. Apparently he intended to resign his *pleins pouvoirs* and ask the National Assembly to name his successor. But word of the scheme reached the Germans, and Berlin promptly intervened to put a stop to it.

As low as Vichy sank in 1943, this was but a portent of the depths of its degradation in 1944. For in its last, doomed months, Vichy could no longer offer even a pretense of serving France. In 1940, there had been honorable grounds on which to argue that France had need of a legal government of its own. Even in 1942, there had been some measure of substance in the argument that France still had need of Vichy. But by the beginning of 1944, there was no reasonable doubt that the liberation was close at hand.

A compromise settlement of the war was now out of the question. Nor was there any room to argue that Vichy was now shielding France from the horrors of a complete military occupation, when the pretended French government had no other task but to wage war upon the Resistance. Nor was there any question but that the Nazis were entrusting this task to Vichy only because a puppet French government could do so more expeditiously than could the Nazis themselves. Hence none remained of the varied multitude that once had hailed the government of Marshal Pétain as the herald of a French resurrection save some scores of wretches so irrevocably bound to the Nazis, whether by a fanatic devotion to what they conceived as principle or by a common complicity in the subjection of their country, that they had no alternative but to go down to ruin with their German masters.

The ultimate transformation of Vichy into a Nazi rearguard began in the winter of 1943–44. No one could mistake the signs of this evolution as Laval proceeded to purge the government of those few men within it who might still be capable of protest, replacing them with men of whose loyalty to the Nazis there could not be the slightest question. Thus Darnand was given rank as Secretary of State for the Maintenance of Order, and Philippe Henriot, one of the stalwarts of Doriot's P.P.F., was made head of Information and Propaganda. In March, 1944, Déat attained his ambition, when at last he became Minister of Labor. In April the government, abandoning all pretense of a distinction between the two zones, moved its seat to Paris, leaving only Marshal Pétain and a skeleton staff in Vichy.

Through the press and the radio, meantime, the government now developed a single theme, in the vain hope of keeping some slight hold upon the allegiance of the nation. This was the argument that, unless the Axis prevailed, the Red Army would surely sweep across the ruins of Germany into France and the whole of Europe would pass under the rule of the Bolsheviks.

But this appeal proved of no avail. The government was now plunged into open warfare against the mass of the nation, which now had no thought but of its approaching liberation. The Resistance, hitherto a conspiratorial élite comprising only those exceptional persons who were willing to accept the hazards of a political struggle outside the bounds of the law, now swelled to the dimensions of a mass movement. Acts of sabotage, such as the derailment of trains bound for Germany or Italy, became commonplace occurrences, as did the assassination of men whom the Resistance marked out as archapostles of treason. Among the latter were Philippe Henriot, the new Minister of Information, who was shot as he entered a studio to make a broadcast, and Colonel de la Rocque, who was apprehended by a band of *résistants* as he stepped out of a church, taken to a nearby thicket, and shot. On the other side, special courts martial were now set up to give a semblance of trial to those whom the Milice designated as "terrorists." And, to supplement the resources of the Milice, the Gestapo and the S.S. now began to take a conspicuous share in the work of repression.

No one knows how many men and women perished in this grim struggle, under the fire of either the Milice or the Resistance, or at the hands of the Germans themselves, nor how many were innocent of the crimes for which their lives were forfeit. Probably the number was not less than 25,000, and perhaps as high as 125,000. This represents a smaller proportion of the population than perished at the hands of the Nazis in some other countries. But the anguish of France was worsened by the knowledge that her people were suffering death at the hands, not only of their conquerors, but of their compatriots.

At last, on June 6, the nation heard the news for which it had so long been waiting, whether with tense impatience or the dread of retribution—the Allies made their landing in Normandy. As soon as the news reached Paris, the government proclaimed its position as one of neutrality, calling upon the people to "maintain order" and take no part in the struggle between the armies. Clearly, this stand was motivated by the hope that "Vichy" (we shall keep the familiar term, even though the seat of the government was now in Paris) would eventually reach a compromise with the Gaullists, if and when the Allies should prove victorious.

"Vichy" could hope to interest the Gaullists in such a compromise, for the reason that Pétain could offer the Provisional Government an aura of legality, which otherwise it would lack. For, from a legalistic point of view, Pétain still held *pleins pouvoirs* by the delegation of the National Assembly, whereas the Provisional Government had no sanction but the endorsement of the Allies. If such a merger could be effected, of course, it would be impossible for the Gaullists to bring the

Vichyites to trial on the charge of treasonable relations with the Axis.

At this eleventh hour a new schism appeared within "Vichy." Evidently it was Laval, with the approval of Pétain, who made the decision to proclaim the neutrality of the government. Deep as was his involvement with the Nazis, he clung to the hope that he could switch sides at the last moment and save his skin. Doriot and Déat knew better. Warning France of the reign of terror which the "Gaullo-Communists" would surely visit upon the land, they proclaimed their allegiance to the Nazis, down to the bitter end.

But by now, "Vichy" was powerless to affect the situation, no matter what stand it took. Its authority simply dissolved. In the regions where the *Wehrmacht* was now engaged in battle to hold back the invaders, the Germans established a military rule. All over the rest of France, the Resistance now came out into the open and established what amounted to a new, *de facto* government. For about two months, from mid-June to mid-August, France was thus reduced to virtual anarchy.

In this period, moreover, the Germans no longer maintained a strict discipline over their troops in France. Hitherto the *Wehrmacht* had been scrupulous in preventing German soldiers from molesting civilians. Even after the Germans had begun to take hostages, to be shot in retaliation for the attacks of the Resistance upon German soldiers, the *Wehrmacht* had made gestures of deference to legal procedure. But as France now became an active theater of war and the Resistance became bolder in its guerrilla, the German troops in some localities—especially the *Waffen SS*—began indiscriminate reprisals. This, in turn, incited the Resistance to fiercer attacks upon the Germans. We cannot determine how many persons perished in the course of this savage warfare, but the number doubtless runs to tens of thousands. Certainly more French civilians perished at the hands of the Germans in the last three months of the occupation than during the previous four years.

Fortunately the issue was not long in doubt. The Allies quickly consolidated their beach head in Normandy and began to spread out into northwestern France. The Germans then fell back, waging a rearguard action but not making a decisive stand until they reached Alsace and Lorraine.

However, the Germans decided not to permit the government of

"Vichy" to remain in France after their withdrawal. Accordingly a message was transmitted to Pétain, who had remained in Vichy, to make ready to leave for Germany. Holding fast to his one unshakeable political principle—that he would never leave France—Pétain refused. Thereupon, early in the morning of August 20, a convoy of German military trucks drove into Vichy. A German general demanded admittance to the Hôtel du Parc, where Pétain made his residence. Pétain was roused out of bed, ordered to prepare to leave at once, and taken off as a prisoner. He was brought first to Belfort, then removed to Germany. Meantime the Germans delivered a similar order to Laval, who was taken by force and transported, via Belfort, across the Rhine.[2]

As the Germans were abandoning the struggle on French soil, the leaders of the Resistance in Paris gave the signal for a general uprising in the capital. The German garrison, numbering about 17,000 men, was thus pinned in the city. To avoid the prolongation of street fighting, which would have worked needless damage and destruction, an arrangement was worked out to permit the peaceable surrender of the German troops. Thus by the 20th, when the Allied forces reached the city, it was already in the hands of the Resistance. Six days later General de Gaulle made a triumphal entry, and Paris once more became the capital of the French Republic. As the liberation of northern France thus neared completion, another Allied landing had been made on the Mediterranean coast, whereupon other Allied columns began to drive northward. The two bodies of Allied troops made a junction on September 13, and shortly thereafter the last German troops were driven out of France.

With the retreating Germans disappeared the government which had promised to shield France from their might and the National Revolution which had promised to inspire the regeneration of her people.

[2] The week before, Laval had proposed to reconvene the National Assembly, hoping to induce the members to vote approval of all that had been done by the government since the investiture of Pétain in July, 1940, and then reestablish the Third Republic. The desperate hope behind this plan was to make it harder for a Gaullist Provisional Government to arraign those who had taken part in the Vichy regime on a charge of treason. In a countermove, Déat tried to induce the Germans to name him, Déat, the head of a new French government, which would follow them in their retreat and take up a role comparable to that of DeGaulle's Free French movement in London. The Germans put a stop to Laval's plan, but not until later did they take up Déat's proposal.

XIII

DAYS OF WRATH

In the ecstatic popular enthusiasm which hailed the liberation in August of 1944, the French nation seemed single-minded, not only in its acceptance of the new Provisional Government of General de Gaulle, but in its utter repudiation of the previous regime. Even before the Liberation was completed, the authority of Vichy melted away. Though the new government had never received the mandate of a popular election, there was no doubt whatever that it commanded the allegiance of all but a minute proportion of the people of France.

Indeed, if one were forgetful of the dazed and pathetic trust with which France had acclaimed Marshal Pétain in the summer of 1940, one would have declared that no French government ever took office with a more nearly universal popular approbation than did the Provisional Government in the summer of 1944. Its partisans included representatives of the whole, broad spectrum of French political opinion, from monarchists to Communists. Its irreconcilable adversaries, numbering probably no more than one or two percent of the population, comprised only those who were so completely compromised by their willing service in behalf of the Germans that their lives were now in danger. Many of these fled across the Rhine with the retreating German armies. The rest, finding it impossible to escape abroad, did their best to drop out of public view.

With this all but unanimous popular endorsement, the Provisional Government reaffirmed its determination to wipe away all traces of the Vichy regime and punish all persons who bore responsibility for its works. No task seemed more obvious, less partisan in motive, or more pressing. It became one of the immediate preoccupations of the gov-

ernment, along with its endeavors to relieve economic distress and organize French participation in the continuing Allied campaign against
the Axis, which was still to reach its climax.

The simpler part of the task was to expunge the marks which Vichy
had left in the laws, decrees, and other public records. In principle, the
Provisional Government refused to admit that Vichy ever had the legal
or moral right to govern France. In logic, it should have followed that
the Third Republic, never having been lawfully terminated, would
once more become the rightful French government. It should also have
followed that no public act since July 10, 1940, remained valid, since acts
in the name of Vichy lacked legitimate authority.

In practice, it proved impossible to sustain this position. First, French
opinion was no more favorable to the resuscitation of the Third Republic in 1944 than it had been toward its continuance in 1940. Its leaders now bore blame, not only for the defeat of 1940, but also for their
abdication in favor of the dictatorship of Marshal Pétain.

Furthermore, it would have produced chaos, had the Provisional
Government simply swept away all public acts since the summer of
1940. Innumerable actions had been taken by authority of Vichy which
were in the normal routine of administration and were in no way
affected by German pressure or the predilections of the men in charge
of the government. For example, it would have been out of the question to declare that every expenditure of public funds under Vichy
was unlawful, that every license or university degree was invalid, that
every appointment or promotion in the civil service—which would
include professors of biology, engineers on the railroads, clerks in the
post office, and traffic policemen—must be revoked. Nor was it feasible
to invalidate administrative orders or decrees bearing on such non-
political problems as the repair or condemnation of bombed-out buildings, or to dismantle the apparatus for rationing and price control.

So the Provisional Government had to accept much of the work of
Vichy as valid, while revising or repealing other parts. Since this portion of the labors of the Provisional Government has its main significance for the founding of the Fourth Republic, which involves a number of factors outside our purview, we cannot examine this work in
detail. We need only note that, though the Provisional Government was

obliged to validate some of the acts of Vichy, it repudiated all that were distinctive of the National Revolution.

Thus the Provisional Government resolved the constitutional dilemma by simply continuing to rule *de facto* until such time as circumstances should permit the election of a new representative assembly, which would draw up a new constitution. This did some violence to legal niceties, but it answered the practical question of how to invalidate the grant of *pleins pouvoirs* to Marshal Pétain without thereby restoring the constitution of the Third Republic and reinstating the prewar Parliament. With no more hesitation the Provisional Government also brushed aside the Charte du Travail and the legislation creating the Corporation Agricole, and likewise the Statute of the Jews. All that remained of the pillars of the National Revolution was the Code de la famille. This, as we have seen, had its basis in legislation antedating Vichy and corresponded to the views of nearly every party.

The other aspect of the liquidation of Vichy—the "purge" (*épuration*), or punishment of persons deemed guilty of collaboration with the Axis—lies closer to our theme, since it involves the problem of the moral responsibility of those who shared in the leadership of the fallen regime. In retracing the course of the "purge," we shall not presume to sit as an ultimate court of review. And we shall put off to the next chapter our general reflections on the issues of political morality which are presented by the history of the Vichy regime. However, we shall find it helpful to take note of the attempt of the new French government to define and assess the guilt associated with Vichy for what light this throws on the problems arising in the endeavor to make an historical appraisal of the regime.

There were numerous factors behind the decision of the Provisional Government to undertake the "purge." First was the general commitment of the Allied governments—Russian, British, and American, as well as the Gaullist and other governments-in-exile—to the principle that the leaders of the Axis were not simply the heads of a hostile alliance but enemies of the human race, who had become outlaws by virtue of their own contempt for every moral commandment known to man. Hence, a damning guilt attached to any man in the degree to which he knowingly and willingly gave aid to the Axis.

This conviction wholly corresponded to the sentiments of the French people at the time of their liberation. Though France had suffered less than some other nations, such as Poland, ultimately the Nazi rule had become so ruthless that the French had more than ample reason to share the general hatred of the entire German people, and of all those who have ever served, praised, or condoned the Nazis.

Much more bitter in their hatred than the passive millions of the French were those scores of thousands who had taken an active role in the Resistance. These men and women, who had risked their lives in the struggle against the Nazis, harbored all the passion of vengeance that is engendered in the course of a civil war. They directed a worse reproach against those of their compatriots who had served the Germans than against the Germans themselves. Since the Resistance was the one dominating moral and political force in France on the morrow of the liberation, it was inevitable that the Provisional Government would pursue the struggle against the "collaborationists." Nor were those members of the Provisional Government who had not themselves taken part in the civil war within France, having instead escaped abroad and taken up with the Gaullist movement, inclined to oppose the cries for vengeance. For Vichy had denounced the Gaullists as traitors, while striking down the men of the Resistance as rebels.

We must remember, too, that the liberation of France did not mark the close of the war. The collapse of the Nazi regime did not come until eight months later. In the meantime, some thousands of French "collaborationists" who had escaped across the Rhine, continued to give allegiance to the Nazis. Neither the Provisional Government nor French popular opinion was apt to take a cool view of the "purge," in the face of such a demonstration of unrepentant guilt.

There were other factors, of a more partisan nature, involved in the pressure for the "purge." First, the Provisional Government itself had a special interest in the matter. Even had the guilt of "collaboration" been more obscure, the new government would have been desirous of establishing that Vichy had been captive to the Axis. For, unless Vichy was the instrument of a treasonable surrender to the Nazis, Marshal Pétain would have a better legal right to head the French government than General de Gaulle. Furthermore, the Socialist and the Communist

parties had other considerations in mind besides collaboration. However vacillating and ambiguous had been its attitude toward the Axis,
clearly Vichy had represented the victory of the Right over the Left,
a revenge upon the Popular Front. Just as, in 1940, men of the Right
had used the defeat to discredit their political opponents, so now men
of the Left were inclined to use the guilt of "collaboration" as a means
of ruining their adversaries.

The Communists, in particular, saw in the "purge" a priceless opportunity to exploit the moral indignation of the people for their own
purposes. Though the Communists were by no means *résistants de la
première heure*—their attitude toward the Axis had remained ambiguous until the outbreak of the Nazi-Soviet war—they had taken a leading role in the illegal opposition after the summer of 1941, and some of
their people had proved themselves brave, dauntless, and capable fighters in the "underground." Hence the Communists were in a good position to take the lead in demanding retribution upon the men of Vichy.
Thereby they were liable to gain not only a political advantage: because
the outstanding business and banking interests of France were especially tainted by "collaboration," the Communists could hope to use
the "purge" as the springboard for an attack upon the bastions of
French capitalism. It would be quite wrong to suggest that the Communists were the prime factor in raising and pressing the demand for
the "purge," or that the two Marxian parties were in league with the
government to make partisan use of the issue of "collaboration." But
we must bear in mind that such considerations of advantage, as well as
the widespread popular sense of moral outrage, were elements in the
situation.

It proved much easier to demand justice, however, than to define
and administer it. In the first place, it was impossible to treat "collaboration" as a crime without affronting the basic legal principle that
no man should be punished for an action which was not defined as a
crime at the time he performed the deed. Certainly the armistice, which
gave the occasion for "collaboration," was not unlawful, nor was the
government of Marshal Pétain, which after the Pétain-Hitler meeting
at Montoire, gave official sanction to it. *A fortiori,* it was not unlawful for a citizen to support a policy approved by the proper public

authority. This legal problem might have been resolved simply, by declaring that acts of "collaboration" involved so gross an outrage to patriotism, or to the moral sense, that no one would be permitted to invoke the protection of a mere legal principle, to shield himself from the retribution he had earned by his own willing acts.

But even this would not have solved the larger problem. For if it were a crime to collaborate with the Axis, the whole of France shared the guilt. Obviously the French nation had lived since 1940 in obedience to German dictates, and the Germans had had no thought save how to gain advantage for themselves from their power over France. Nor did the French as a nation "collaborate" only involuntarily. Nearly everyone had endorsed the accession of Marshal Pétain and had continued to trust him even after Montoire. Gradually French opinion had shifted, until by 1944 virtually the whole nation was hopeful of an Axis defeat, and much of the nation was engaged in active or passive struggle against the Nazis.

Consequently the crux of the matter was not whether a man had endorsed "collaboration" or opposed it. Rather, the question involved the degree of enthusiasm with which he had originally espoused it, and at what point in time he had changed his mind. Manifestly it was impossible to use such a subtle standard for a legal definition of guilt. Even if it had been feasible, it would have exempted from punishment men whose chief claim to virtue was their quick sense of when to shift their allegiance from one side to the other.

Taking into account the intense pressure for a merciless vengeance, as well as the complexities of the problem of blame, we need hardly be surprised if some punishments were too severe, or too light, or misplaced, or if some persons escaped who were culpable. We should marvel, rather, that the "purge" did not become a more serious political problem, and that it gave rise to as much complaint of excessive leniency as to protest at its undue severity.

The "purge" was not a single episode but a process. It involved more than one stage and extended over a period of several years. The first phase was a period of summary justice, beginning in the midst of the chaos of the liberation and continuing until the Provisional Government reestablished order throughout the land. An interval of about three months supervened between the Allied landing in Normandy in June, 1944, and the withdrawal of the German troops from France. In this interval the Resistance undertook a general uprising which affected all parts of France, though not every locality, and reached the proportions of a popular revolution.

In the course of this uprising, bands of guerrillas, or local committees representing the organizations of the Resistance, frequently undertook to punish persons known in the locality as notorious "collaborationists." Sometimes this vengeance was mild, verging on the frivolous, as when a crowd would fall upon a woman of the town who had become conspicuous for preferring to consort with the Germans, and would cut off her hair. Sometimes it was an incident of warfare, as when a band of the Resistance would ambush and massacre a detachment of the detested Milice. Sometimes it took the form of an impromptu court martial, which would accord the accused a chance to answer the charges made against him, then would order his execution. Sometimes it took on a form resembling assassination, when a partisan of the Resistance would simply shoot down a man who he believed had been an informer for the Germans or a member of the Milice.

No one knows how many persons died in this initial phase of the purge. Eventually the government released an estimate which put the number at about three thousand. Probably this estimate tends to err on the side of minimizing the number. Hostile critics of the "purge" put the figure several times higher. But presumably it indicates the proper order of magnitude. Certainly the number of persons killed in this manner was much greater than the number later put to death by order of regularly constituted courts, after the government took over responsibility for the "purge."

No one will ever know what proportion of justice and injustice was involved in these executions. We can only note, as a general observation, that such direct action affords the accused little or no protection against a personal enemy who brings false charges against him, or against the passions of the mob and the moment. On the other hand, it also makes possible the punishment of culpable persons who would escape their deserved doom if they could only have recourse to the legalistic maneuvers possible in a courtroom.

This stage of the "purge" came to a close as the Provisional Government took over its management. In order to terminate the unauthorized executions, as well as to prepare for an orderly prosecution, the government made haste to place under arrest all persons against whom a charge of "collaboration" was lodged, if the evidence was sufficient to make eventual prosecution a reasonable likelihood. Within six months, the number of persons thus detained reached about 50,000, which was the high-water mark.

Meantime procedures for prosecution were worked out. Though consideration had been given to this problem before the Provisional Government quitted London, and some plans had been embodied in decrees, the work of preparation was not completed until December, 1944.

Ultimately it was provided that the regular courts would handle the cases of those persons charged with acts of "collaboration" that could be punished under the existing codes. But this would provide only for exceptional cases, since "collaboration" as such was not an offense. Moreover, it was obvious that the regular courts could not dispose without unreasonable delay of such an immense number of cases as must be heard. And there was considerable suspicion that many of the magistrates in these courts, having continued to serve in their office throughout the Vichy era, were not themselves free of the taint of "collaboration." So a new apparatus of courts was established, and specifications were developed to define a new crime.

At the apex of this structure of new tribunals was the High Court of Justice, appointed in November, 1944. This court heard cases against men who had held leading positions in the government, including ministers, secretaries of state, commissioners general, and governors of colonies. Its personnel included three magistrates and twenty-four jurors, drawn by lot from a panel named by the Consultative Assembly, the appointive council which served the Provisional Government in lieu of a Parliament. For the purposes of the High Court, "collaboration" was defined as treasonable intelligence with the enemy, or acts damaging the external security of the state.

Below this in rank came twenty-seven special courts of justice. One of these courts sat in each of the principal cities, while the one in Paris was divided into ten sections, in order to handle the larger docket in the capital. Each of these courts, or sections of a court, comprised a magistrate and four jurors. For the purposes of these courts, "collaboration" was defined as actions revealing the intention of aiding the enterprises of the enemy.

Then came the *chambres civiques,* which handled cases involving offenses of a less serious nature. These civic chambers comprised a magistrate and four jurors. The latter were chosen, at the start, from a list drawn up by the local organizations of the Resistance. The offense within their purview was defined as *indignité nationale,* or "national unworthiness." It involved deeds that gave aid to Germany or her allies or did damage to the unity of the nation, the liberty of the French people, or the equality among them. Unlike the courts of justice, the civic chambers could not impose the sentence of death or imprisonment. But they might refer to the appropriate higher tribunal cases which seemed to warrant such punishment. The sanction within the power of the civic chamber was the deprivation of civic rights, such as the right to vote or hold public office.

Still lower in the structure were the "courts of honor," one of which was set up in each branch of the public administration. These had no power save to propose to a civic chamber that it take action against persons who seemed to have incurred the guilt of "national unworthiness."

All these new tribunals began their work while the war was still in progress. Some thousands of cases were heard, and verdicts rendered, before the surrender of the Germans in April, 1945. The larger number came before the civic chambers. But those of wider public interest were reserved to the special courts of justice or the High Court. Before the close of 1944, the special courts of justice disposed of 2,200 cases. Sentence of death was imposed in 300 of these, and imprisonment in 1,700 others. In the next six weeks, up to the middle of February, 1945, another 5,000 cases were completed. The High Court was much slower. It did not begin its first trial until March, 1945, when Admiral Esteva was sentenced to imprisonment for life on charges arising out of the assistance given to Axis forces in North Africa while he was Resident General in Tunis.

Among those condemned during this period was Charles Maurras, who was tried before the special court of justice sitting in Lyons, in January, 1945. He was prosecuted at the same time as Maurice Pujo, the managing editor of the *Action Française,* in consideration of the endorsement their paper had given the government of Marshal Pétain. Maurras made no attempt to defend himself, save to expound his doctrines before the court. He was sentenced to imprisonment for life, and Pujo, for five years. As the verdict was announced, Maurras delivered his last epigram: "C'est la revanche de Dreyfus!"

But the "purge" could not reach its climax, no matter what might be the fate of the subalterns of "collaboration," so long as their principals remained outside the reach of French courts. Of the three men— Pétain, Laval, and Darlan—who had accepted prime responsibility in the Vichy regime, one was out of reach forever, since an assassin had determined the fate of Darlan. The other two had been removed to Germany, on orders of Berlin, when the German armies were driven from France. With them had gone a number of the others who had the most to answer for. These included Déat, Doriot, and Luchaire, who had been the outstanding apologists of the Axis in the Paris press; Brinon, who, as French ambassador in Paris, had been Abetz's opposite number and *alter ego;* and Darnand, the head huntsman of the Milice. We must now turn aside to take note of the fate of these and the other French *émigrés* who had taken haven in Germany, in August, 1944.

There is an element of historical irony, though none of pathos, in the penultimate phase of the downfall of the French partisans of the Axis. We cannot help but note the parallel between their situation in 1944 and that of the little band of French refugees who had gathered in London in 1940, when the prospects of Britain had seemed as dark as now those of Germany. But in the plight of these *émigrés* of 1944 there is no sign of that personal dedication, Quixotic idealism, and dauntless courage that lent grandeur to the Gaullist movement, even when its hopes seemed dimmest. Instead, these new exiles lived only in the dread of an inexorable doom, hoping against hope that some unimaginable disaster might yet save them and their Nazi hosts from the grim fate in store for them.

As the residence of their French accomplices, the Nazis set aside the small town and the castle of Sigmaringen, situated on the headwaters of the Danube, not far from the borders of France, Switzerland, and Austria. Within a few weeks, some thousands of refugees swarmed into the town. Along with the luminaries of "collaboration" came an assortment of fugitives of lesser rank, together with their wives and children. Among them were the remnants of Darnand's Milice. About six thousand of these hated special "police" had escaped with the German armies—after robbing a branch of the Banque de France to obtain funds for their withdrawal. But the Germans permitted Darnand to keep only two thousand of his men with him at Sigmaringen, as an "honor guard." The others were either dispatched to the Eastern Front or required to take work in German factories.

Even in their exile, the prophets of authoritarian discipline continued their schisms and quarrels. From the outset, Pétain and Laval insisted that they were being held against their will and must be treated as prisoners. The Germans were not inclined to argue the point. But the others made no such pretense, and the Germans soon determined to make use of them as a kind of government-in-exile.

Thus a Commission Gouvernementale was established, with the approval of Hitler, and was authorized to "represent the interests" of the French workers and prisoners in Germany, who now numbered about 2,000,000. Brinon became president of this commission, while Déat served as Minister of Labor, Darnand as Secretary General for the Maintenance of Order, and Luchaire as Delegate in Charge of Information.

Doriot remained aloof. He pinned his hopes upon the chance that the Communists would undertake a revolution in France, thus setting off a civil war and giving him a chance to return to France as the head of the Anti-Bolshevik Legion. However, he did not live to see his hopes disappear. He met his death in February, 1945, when the automobile in which he was riding, near Sigmaringen, was strafed by an Allied airplane.[1]

In April, 1945, with the disintegration of the Nazi regime, time at last ran out. In the complete disorder of their defeat, the Germans simply abandoned the French at Sigmaringen to their own devices. Left free to meet or dodge their fate, none chose to return to France and face his accusers. Even Pétain did as much as an old man could to avoid his doom—he asked the Swiss to give him haven. But they agreed to let him cross their border only on the understanding that they would hand him over to the French authorities whenever Paris should so request. He accepted this condition. Accordingly he was taken to the French-Swiss border, and thence to Paris to await trial.[2]

Laval resisted longer, but to no more avail. Failing to induce the Swiss to give him refuge, he obtained the use of a German airplane, which took him to Barcelona. His arrival there, on May 2, was apparently an unwelcome surprise to the Spanish authorities, who dared not give him shelter but did not wish to hand him over to the Allies. Their solution of the dilemma was to intern him in Barcelona, on condition that he leave Spain within ninety days. Laval spent the three months of grace without finding another refuge. So, on July 31, he could do no better than take a plane from Barcelona to Linz. He was arrested by the Americans as soon as he landed and then was given over to the French.

Of the other notables, only Déat fared better. On April 15 he and his wife left Sigmaringen in an automobile, heading for the Tyrolean Alps. Apparently he made good his escape, since he was never taken prisoner, nor is there reliable evidence to indicate that he met his death. Darnand, with six hundred of his *miliciens,* made his way to Italy, where he was soon captured and taken back to France. Luchaire sought the same refuge. He hoped to pass himself off as an Italian, since he knew the language and the land as well as his own. But his stratagem proved vain. He, too, was taken prisoner and shipped back to France.

---

[1] This account of Doriot's death comes from persons who were his associates. It is possible that he made his escape, arranging with his friends to report that he had been killed.

[2] The newspapers at the time reported that Pétain asked the Swiss for asylum. However, testimony at his trial represented him as having sought only to pass through Switzerland in order to return to France.

Nor did Brinon escape, even though he and his wife had taken the precaution of keeping 4,000,000 francs at hand with which to purchase their freedom. Most of the others were also taken captive by one or another of the Allied armies swarming over Germany. Some proportion, however, disappeared among the millions of liberated prisoners, slave workers, and other displaced persons, and were never identified.

The return to France of Pétain and the others who had hitherto been out of reach gave rise to a redoubled clamor to hasten the "purge" to its completion. As the months wore on after the liberation without the condemnation of any person of first rank among those identified with Vichy, the suspicion developed that the government was intentionally temporizing and, in response to hidden pressures, was seeking to appease the public demand for retribution merely by sacrificing a few scapegoats of minor importance while shielding the principal wrongdoers. So the preparations for the trial of Marshal Pétain were speeded up, and the public hearings began on July 23, 1945.

The case of Pétain became, of course, the center of intense public interest. Even though the principle had long since been established that participation in the Vichy regime constituted a crime against the nation, the prosecution of the Chief of State could not be other than the climax of the "purge." Inevitably it would be the occasion for a full-length presentation of the arguments for and against the regime he had headed, to which reference would be made in every later public or private debate upon the issues.

Moreover, the witnesses would include most of the men still living who had had a leading role in the successive crises of 1939–44. Among them would be Blum, Daladier, Reynaud, Herriot, Jeanneney, Lebrun, Weygand, Laval, Peyrouton, Bouthillier, Brinon, and Darnand. Since each of these would be more intent upon defending his own record than either damning or defending Pétain, the hearings would develop into a general debate upon the great issues of French politics since the outbreak of the war, with most of the leading figures confronting and challenging one another.

In view of the scope and importance of the issues involved, the conduct of the trial left much to be regretted. Even the normal procedures of a French court are less rigid than those in Anglo-American lands, permitting the introduction of evidence that has little or no apparent bearing on the issues of the case and testimony based upon hearsay. In this case, which was far from normal, the High Court allowed both counsel and witnesses a still looser rein. For instance, Reynaud and Weygand were permitted to engage in a long, rambling interchange with one another over their respective roles in the decision for an armistice. This testimony threw no light whatever upon the guilt or innocence of Pétain. Virtually any witness was free to offer his guess as to Pétain's motives, or to repeat, in the guise of evidence, the speculations of still other persons on this topic.

The jurors did no better than the witnesses to help create an atmosphere of cool and rigorous investigation. All of them were known as adversaries of Vichy. Half were former deputies and senators of the Third Republic who had axes of their own to grind. Furthermore, both the Presiding Magistrate and the Public Prosecutor were under suspicion of having been partisans of Vichy. Both were therefore desirous of allaying these doubts by giving public sign of their antipathy for the defendant and those who spoke in his behalf.

Nor did the Court prove firm in maintaining order on the part of the audience. Frequently the proceedings were interrupted by outcries from the spectators, sometimes in support of the defense, sometimes on the other side. The least figure in the courtroom was the deaf old man whose fate and fame were at stake. From the outset, he refused to take part in the proceedings and declined even to answer questions put to him. He did his best to maintain an attitude of dignified indifference. But, from time to time, he fell asleep in his chair.

After a motion *pro forma* by counsel for the defense to challenge the competence of the High Court, the trial began with the reading of the act of accusation, which summarized the case the prosecution proposed to develop. This was an ambiguous exposition. It did not make clear whether the prosecution would hinge its case upon the thesis that, even before the armistice, Pétain had conspired to overthrow the Third Republic and become dictator, or would accept his accession as lawful and would levy charges on him only for his actions while in office. The two items of the indictment, which concluded the act of accusation, permitted either interpretation. These specified both "an attempt upon the internal security of the state," and "intelligence with the enemy, with the intention of furthering his purposes." Subsequently, however, in the course of the debates, the prosecution clarified the question by indicating that its case would rest upon only the evidence of events after the signature of the armistice.

As soon as the reading of the act of accusation was concluded, Pétain delivered a prepared statement. With the simple eloquence he sometimes achieved, he declared that he had received power from the French people, that he had done his best to shield them from their conquerors and reestablish their institutions on a sounder base, and that he would make no other answer for his actions, since "a marshal of France asks pardon of no one."

Then began the parade of witnesses. We need not take note here of their various depositions, since the evidence thus brought out has been incorporated into the narrative in the previous chapters. We must, however, summarize the main arguments that emerged on either side. For its part, the prosecution devoted more attention to the relations of Vichy with the Axis than to its actions in the sphere of domestic politics. As we have remarked, it soon gave up the effort to prove that Pétain had been party to a conspiracy to subvert the Republic. It made but little more endeavor to indict the National Revolution for its repudiation of the principles of liberalism. Though reference was made to the Statute of the Jews, this did not loom large among the reproaches directed at Pétain.

The prosecution made no serious attempt to reproach Pétain for having signed the armistice. It would have been difficult to do so without incriminating Reynaud, who seemingly had given his approval by handing over the premiership to Pétain. Nor did the prosecution develop evidence to show that Pétain himself ever evinced a desire to aid the Axis, or wished to see the Germans win the war. Hence the case came down to the charge that, no matter what the consequences, he should have refused to sanction certain actions which the Axis required of him. Above all else, the prosecution taxed him for having permitted the deportation of conscripted workers, for having allowed the surrender of hostages to the Germans, and for having tolerated the merciless repression of the Resistance.

Three principal arguments emerged from the presentation of the defense. One was the argument of legality, which Pétain himself set forth in the statement he read at the opening of the trial. This reasoning held that Pétain had lawfully become Chief of State. As such, he could not be held accountable by any court of law, and those who acted in obedience to his orders were thereby relieved of personal responsibility for their actions. A second was the argument of constraint, which maintained that Pétain could not be held accountable for actions which he took under the dictate of the Germans, since he had no power to prevent them from doing whatever they wished. The third was the argument of the "double wager," which alleged that Pétain had been systematically deceiving the Germans, leading them to believe that he was cooperating with them, while actually he had been working, in agreement with the British, for their downfall. As evidence to support this contention, the defense pointed to the so-called Churchill-Rougier accord and to the Chevalier-Halifax negotiations, which seemed to indicate a common understanding between London and Vichy.

On both sides, these arguments were intended as briefs in a political debate, addressed to the opinion of the nation and the world. The verdict of the Court was never in doubt. The last of the scores of witnesses was heard on August 10, and the prosecution summed up its case on the 11th. The final pleas of the defense occupied the sessions of the 13th and 14th, coming to a close at 8 o'clock in the evening. Forthwith the Court withdrew to deliberate, returning at 4 o'clock in the morning of August 15. Finding the defendant guilty, the Court pronounced the sentence of death. But, "in view of the advanced age of the defendant," it recommended that the sentence be not executed. On the 17th, General de Gaulle commuted the punishment to imprisonment for life.

The government did its best to make sure that nothing more would be heard of Pétain. The little island of Yeu, off the coast near Bordeaux, was designated as the place of his detention. No visitors other than his wife and legal counsel were permitted. But these precautions were more than was needed. Pétain accepted his imprisonment as definitive, voicing no complaint at his treatment and making no appeal for release. Nor did he undertake to write his memoirs or otherwise prepare a defense of his name. Death came to him on July 23, 1951, when he was ninety-five years old.

Two months after the condemnation of Pétain began the trial of Laval. This was somewhat of an anticlimax. The trial of the former Chief of State amounted to a verdict on Vichy as a whole as well as upon Pétain. The case against Laval was much more personal, and the presumption against him much stronger. Nevertheless, quite as much interest attached to the case of Laval as to that of his superior, for his prosecution promised to throw new light upon what had really transpired behind the scenes at Vichy.

Yet the trial was a disappointment, whether viewed as the condemnation of the man or as a revelation of the secret history of the fallen regime. One fault was that the High Court proved quite incapable of preserving order, so that the proceedings were marred by repeated demonstrations in the courtroom, involving jurors as well as members of the audience. The other fault was that the government was in an unbecoming haste to have the trial concluded, and Laval put to death, before the national elections, which were to take place within a few weeks. Hence the High Court cut short the *instruction*—the hearing in advance of the public trial, in which the prosecution would establish the outline of its case and the counsel for the defense would be apprized of the evidence and arguments it must meet.

From the outset of the trial, therefore, the defense protested that it had not been allowed sufficient time to prepare. Laval's counsel refused even to attend the opening session, and the prisoner himself handled his own defense. The session developed into a debate between the defendant, on the one hand, and the Public Prosecutor and the Presiding Magistrate on the other. Laval proved himself the more skillful debater. As the session wore on, the interchanges waxed more and more acrimonious, until ultimately the Presiding Magistrate warned Laval to be more respectful or be removed from the room.

"Go ahead and pass sentence right away," cried Laval, "then everything will be clear!"

"Take the prisoner away!" ordered the Court.

Someone in the audience began to applaud Laval, whereupon one of the jurors shouted, "Arrest that man!"

"It's the Fifth Column!" declared another. "He deserves twelve bullets in his hide, just like Laval," shouted still another juror. In the midst of this uproar, the session was adjourned.

The next day, October 5, the session resumed in a more temperate atmosphere. Still protesting the insufficiency of time allowed them for the preparation of their case, Laval's lawyers now made an appearance. But the day's testimony, which consisted mainly of Laval's explanation of his role in inducing the National Assembly to vote *pleins pouvoirs* to Pétain, brought out little new information. Much of it was taken up by a running interchange between the defendant and one of the jurors, who had been a member of the National Assembly and thus, as Laval pointed out, now became a witness as well as a juror. The next session, on the 6th, produced an even more bitter wrangle than the first, until at last the Presiding Magistrate, in a burst of anger, ordered Laval removed from the room. Thereupon a number of the jurors rose up in their places and joined in the tumult which swept through the room.

"You provocateur!" shouted one of them, addressing Laval. "Scoundrel!" cried another; and a third, "Twelve bullets in his hide!"

An hour later, the session resumed, but Laval reappeared only to declare that he and his lawyers would take no more part in the trial, believing it impossible to gain a fair hearing. The defense remained firm in this decision. Nevertheless, the prosecution proceeded to complete its case, which took up the next two sessions. The verdict, rendered on October 9, was death. General de Gaulle refused either to commute the sentence or to grant the petition of the defense counsel for a new trial.

On the morning of October 15 the Public Prosecutor paid a visit to the prison of Fresnes, where Laval was being held, to inform him that his sentence was now irrevocable. As the guards entered his cell, it became apparent that Laval was suffering the effects of a poison, which he had taken with the intention of suicide. A physician was immediately summoned, and measures were taken to counteract the poison. But, to make sure that Laval would not succumb before his execution, it was decided to proceed at once to put the sentence into effect. So he was hurried into a van, taken to the place of execution, and shot.

In the same week as Laval, Joseph Darnand was tried and condemned to the same fate. The sentence was carried out on October 10, 1945. In February, 1946, Jean Luchaire likewise suffered death. By that time, the government announced, a total of about 110,000 cases had been listed for investigation. Of these, about one third had been referred to one or another of the courts of justice, which so far had handed down the sentence of death in about 3,000 cases and imprisonment in another 18,000. However, a large proportion of the death penalties had been commuted to imprisonment. Likewise, a substantial number of the lesser offenders had been given pardon.

Public interest in the "purge" subsided during 1946, the prosecutions slowed down, and the courts of justice showed a marked disposition to render lighter sentences. In March, Bucard, the head of Francisme, one of the minor fascist parties, was put to death. But in July, Flandin, who had been Minister of Foreign Affairs in the interval between the overthrow of Laval in December of 1940 and the accession of Darlan, was given only a nominal sentence, which was at once suspended. This decision gave rise to a loud clamor on the part of the Communists, who demanded that the High Court be reorganized so as to make sure it would be less indulgent in the future. But the other parties did not support this move, and the government withstood the pressure.

In the latter half of 1946 the High Court disposed of a number of cases of minor interest. Not until the spring of 1947 did it render decision upon other persons of large prominence. In March, the sentence of death was imposed on Brinon, and the same sentence, *in absentia*, upon Alibert. But Baudouin was given only imprisonment for five years, as was Chautemps, who had taken refuge in the United States. In June, Benoist-Méchin was sentenced to death, but the sentence was at once commuted to imprisonment for life. In December, 1947, Vallat, who made no attempt to disguise his undiminished adherence to anti-Semitism, was sentenced to ten years in prison for his role in the administration of the Statute of the Jews. Only the charge of "national unworthiness" was sustained against Adrien Marquet, in January, 1948, and in May the case against General Weygand was dismissed. In July three years' imprisonment was meted out to Bouthillier, but in December Peyrouton was acquitted, in consideration of his role in opposing Laval during December, 1940.

By the middle of 1949 the "purge" was virtually over. On July 1 the High Court cleared its docket and disbanded. In all, it had heard fifty-two cases. Sentence of death had been executed by its order upon only three persons—Laval, Darnand, and Brinon—although the supreme penalty had been imposed upon others *in absentia*. On July 21 the Tribunal Militaire of Paris condemned Otto Abetz to twenty years in prison at hard labor, and some of the other courts of justice continued to hold sessions to conclude their business. But in December, 1949, the government began to prepare a bill providing amnesty for minor offenders. This was adopted, despite the opposition of the Communists and Socialists, in December, 1950.

As the "purge" thus approached its close, it became evident that the number of persons who had suffered punishment was not large. Up to December, 1949, according to the government, the sentence of death had been imposed upon 2,700 persons present in court, and upon 4,400 others *in absentia*. But the sentence had been executed upon only 800 persons, other than those put to death by summary justice in 1944. In December, 1950, the government announced that prison sentences had been imposed upon a total of about 60,000 persons, but less than 6,000 still remained in prison at that time. About 50,000 more had been convicted of "national unworthiness" and deprived of civic rights, but not imprisoned.

The total of perhaps 3,000 persons put to death by popular vengeance, 800 executed by order of courts of justice, and not more than 6,000 imprisoned for five years or longer, is a good deal less than the number of persons shot as hostages during the occupation. Or, to make the comparison with previous instances of large-scale political justice in France, it is much less than the 20,000 persons put to death for participation in the insurrection of the Commune of Paris in 1871, and about 25,000 condemned to penal servitude or transportation when Napoleon III established his dictatorship in 1851–52.

Obviously it is impossible to make a judgment of the "purge" as a whole without passing judgment on Vichy as a whole. If Vichy was a crime against the nation, the "purge" was unquestionably too lenient. On the contrary, if Vichy was the legitimate government of France, striving to protect the interests of the nation in the face of extreme adversities, doubtless the "purge" did injustice to a number of men, who were branded with the guilt of treason for no offense but having sought to serve their country. Even in the latter view, however, it must be recognized that the "purge" was much less severe than might have been thought inevitable, considering the intense passions engendered by the occupation and the Resistance. We shall not here consider the broad question of the principle behind the "purge"—whether or not "collaboration" should have been punished as a crime—since we shall touch upon this problem in the next chapter.

Accepting, for the moment, the premises that gave sanction to the "purge," we may note that there were two practical problems involved in its implementation. One was a problem of justice—to impose the same punishment on men accused of the same crime. The other was a problem of politics—to satisfy the demand for vengeance while also conciliating those who opposed the "purge," whether because of their own incrimination or on the grounds of an impersonal opinion as to its wisdom.

On the first score, the "purge" attained but a mediocre success. Without question, there were wide disparities in the punishment allotted men whose guilt seemed of about the same degree. One reason for this was that the "purge" was administered by a number of coordinate tribunals which did not all apply the same standards. In part, this was because there were no well-established criteria of degrees of guilt, since the crime involved in "collaboration" was without precedent. Another factor was that much less public interest attached to the case of a man whose role in Vichy had been behind the scenes than to the case of one whose actions had been more conspicuous. Likewise, some men escaped with mild punishment, or none at all, because they had friends with influence in the new government. Others suffered worse, because a personal enemy made use of the "purge" as a means of settling an old account. Finally, some men met with severe punishment because their cases came to trial soon after liberation, when passions were still hot. Others, whose derelictions were no less serious, owed their better fortunes simply to the fact that their cases were not heard until a later date.

As an operation in the sphere of politics, however, the "purge" was much more successful. In the outcome, as we have noted, only a small number of persons suffered a severe punishment. Though some might feel themselves the victims of injustice, few of those who had been identified with the fallen regime could doubt but that, rightly or wrongly, they might have fared much worse. On the other hand, most parties were satisfied, by the time the "purge" died out, that it was best to let the matter drop, even though this might mean allowing a certain number of scoundrels to escape their just deserts.

Only the Communists continued to insist, after 1949, that the "purge" had not gone far enough. But by that time the Communists were once more reduced to a position of isolated and powerless political opposition. They were themselves accused, like the former advocates of "collaboration," of a wish to hand France over to the dominance of a hostile foreign power.

XIV

RETROSPECT

IN A STUDY of contemporary history, such as this, it is a hard enough task to establish the bare record of what transpired. It is still harder to draw conclusions that have more warrant than a mere personal opinion. Even if we seek to make our estimate only within the narrow bounds of an historical appraisal, endeavoring simply to determine what circumstances induced the men of Vichy to act as they did and what were the consequences of their actions, we can reach no more than tentative conclusions. Presently we may perceive some of the factors in the situation of France in the 1920s and 1930s that help explain Vichy. But not until a much longer time has passed shall we be in a position to know what will prove to be the ultimate influence of Vichy upon the later evolution of French national life.

Yet we cannot confine our attention to this kind of appraisal. Inevitably we also make a judgment of Vichy in terms of our impulses and convictions in respect to the basic political and moral problems of our generation. For example, we cannot consider the endeavor of Vichy to revise the social and political institutions of France save in terms of our view of the virtues and vices of liberalism. Nor can we discuss "collaboration" without a preconception as to whether France gained advantage from the substitution of the menace of Soviet power for that of the Axis, or without a presupposition as to whether patriotism involves a concern for national interest or for national honor, and to what extent its demands override men's other moral obligations.

We need not recapitulate the argument that Vichy was an outgrowth of the experience of France in the 1920s and 1930s as well as a response to the fact of military defeat in the spring of 1940. We have noted that, insofar as "collaboration" represented a shift in the diplomatic orientation of France away from dependence upon Britain and toward reconciliation with Germany, it gave expression to tendencies of opinion that had been gaining ground on both the Right and the Left throughout the interbellum period. And insofar as the National Revolution represented an attempt to give the nation a more decisive political leadership and to overcome the twin vices of excessive individualism and an embittered class struggle, it sought to answer a need that had become quite obvious under the Third Republic.

In 1944, it seemed indisputable that Vichy had utterly failed in both spheres of its endeavor. Within a few years, however, it became evident that this view of Vichy was too simple. It began to appear that Vichy was neither a complete failure in its time nor without consequence for the future.

Taken as an attempt to shield France from the horrors of Nazi domination, "collaboration" was not quite so vain as seemed in 1944. No one could deny that France had suffered pitiful hardships under the occupation. Some of these were the inevitable hardships of war, but some were due to systematic and ruthless exploitation by the Nazis. In particular, no one could blink the fact that the Germans had shot as hostages a large number of French men and women—perhaps the number exceeded 100,000—most of whom were innocent of any wrongdoing.

Nevertheless, the Nazis had not wreaked as much havoc in France as in some other countries under their rule. There had been no general proscription of persons known as hostile to the Nazis. Most of the leaders of the republican parties, even those conspicuous before the war as *bellicistes,* lived unmolested all through the occupation. Though Blum, Daladier, Reynaud, and some others had been imprisoned, their detention did not involve mistreatment, nor were their lives in danger. The one notable exception was Georges Mandel, who was shot by agents of the Milice while being transferred from one prison to another. But his death was an assassination rather than a political execution. The Jewish population, though terrorized and decimated, was not wiped out. The Communists bore the brunt of political persecution. Their suppression had begun under the Third Republic, however, quite without the urging of the Nazis.

Other than the hecatomb of hostages, the principal hardships due to the German occupation arose from the economic spoliation of the land, the detention of about 1,500,000 prisoners of war, and the recruitment, under threat or compulsion, of about 600,000 workers for German war industries. However, the economic distress never reached the point where it imperiled the survival of the nation. Moreover, the apologists of Vichy could point out that France had contributed a lesser quota of "slave labor," in proportion to her population, than had Belgium, and that no women had been conscripted in France.

Indeed, the Germans might well have asked themselves what advantage they had gained from their victory over the French. From a military standpoint, they had won little more benefit than came to them from the destruction of the French army, which had been accomplished before the signature of the armistice. They had made no use of the French army in the further prosecution of the war, nor taken any appreciable number of French recruits into the *Wehrmacht,* nor won control of the French navy. So their advantage came down to such matters as the use of French ports and railroads in North Africa in connection with the Axis operations in Libya and Egypt, the use of French naval bases on the Atlantic coast for the support of their submarine warfare, and the right to maintain garrisons and fortifications in France for defense against an Allied invasion of the Continent.

From an economic standpoint, the spoliation of France gave the Germans no great benefit. Even under pressure France was not capable of providing large-scale exports of either food or manufactures. To be sure, the Germans gained the services of 600,000 French workers in their factories, and ultimately of the French prisoners of war, which helped release German manpower for service in the *Wehrmacht*. But certainly the Nazis would have got no less without the belated and grudging cooperation of Vichy.

So dubious were the advantages which the Axis reaped from "collaboration" that a considerable proportion of the French remained convinced, down to the end of the war, that Pétain was really playing the "double wager"—pretending to cooperate with the Germans while actually working for their downfall. The legend long persisted that there was some kind of secret agreement between Pétain and De Gaulle, by which each recognized that they were working toward the same goal. There is no evidence to substantiate this legend.

Nevertheless, it remains true that France profited from having had two "governments" during the war, one of which was on more or less amicable terms with each of the warring camps. For Vichy gained France some of the advantage of an alignment with the Axis while the power of the Axis was at its zenith. Then, when the Axis collapsed, the Gaullists, having stood with the British in their dark hour, were in a position to demand recognition of their new French government as a partner, of equal rank with Britain, the United States, and Russia, in the alliance of the victors.

But an appraisal of "collaboration" involves more than an estimate of how effective Vichy was in withstanding or deflecting the German pressure upon France during the occupation. For, among its various meanings, this chameleonlike concept implied a recognition on the part of France that she must reconcile herself to a position in the second rank of powers and must accept the role of a satellite to one or the other of mightier nations. In the exultation of the liberation, her new government seemed determined to spurn such a role and again demand recognition of her traditional place in the inner councils of the governments which were deciding the fate of the world. Yet no one could mistake that France neither gained nor wanted the same role in 1945 as in 1918–19. De Gaulle might seek to become the heir to Clemenceau, as well as Joan of Arc, but the mass of the nation would no longer respond to the siren song of grandeur.

In another sense, too, a portion of the complex of ideas behind "collaboration" lived on after the name was anathema. For "collaboration" had been associated with the participation of France in the supranational organization of continental Europe, exclusive of Russia. Under the Nazi "New Order," this had amounted to little more than a façade for the German domination of the Continent. But soon after the close of the war, Washington took the lead in a new move to unite Europe against the Russians. As it happened, Britain chose to hold somewhat aloof, preferring to stake her fortunes upon the association of peoples once known as the British Empire, then as the Commonwealth, and ultimately as the "sterling bloc." As it happened, too, Spain remained on the margin of the new European league, as she had remained both in and out of the Axis. So the new union once more linked France, the Low Countries, Denmark, and Norway with Germany and Italy, again in opposition to Soviet Russia. Perhaps the hesitating acceptance by the French of their role in this new community was due, in part, to their previous indoctrination in the need to *faire l'Europe*.

These lingering ideas of "collaboration" were not the only vestiges of Vichy. Its prescriptions for the inner regeneration of France were not quite forgotten with the liberation. Within five years, voices were heard developing a familiar theme—that France had need of a stronger executive to afford her a more resolute leadership; that the legalized warfare among rival political parties must give way to a single, new league, embracing all parties save the Communists, which would be dedicated to "national progress" and the defense of France against the Communist threat; and that some kind of corporative institutions must be developed in order to terminate the antagonism among social classes. At the head of those demanding such reforms was to be seen the same General de Gaulle whom Vichy had once denounced as a rebel, while behind him were to be discovered a number of those who once had hailed Marshal Pétain and been denounced by the Gaullists as traitors.

Even those who became the stalwarts of the Fourth Republic were not treading quite another path. For, if we compare the pattern of political life under the Fourth Republic with that of the Third Republic before the war, we must notice a number of conspicuous changes—the Communists have been all but outlawed, the avowed fascists, such as Doriot and Déat, have disappeared from the scene, and the governing parties no longer make a cardinal principle of anticlericalism. Not a few of those "conservatives" who had designed the National Revolution would have designated these among the changes in French political life which they hoped to bring about.

It would be fatuous to suggest that France did not take a new departure in the aftermath of the liberation, representing a repudiation of both Vichy and the Third Republic. But it would be no less so to imagine that she could pass through such an experience as Vichy represented, then efface the marks without a trace. How deep those marks were and how enduring, men of this generation may never know.

The historian labors under a handicap inseparable from his vocation. He cannot hope to make a definitive appraisal of events in the past until their significance no longer matters much. But he also has an advantage in that he is under no obligation to approve or disapprove, but only to do his best to understand what happened. Perhaps in some happier age to come men will be content simply to know what happened in France under the occupation, without attempting to decide whether, or in what respect, the men in charge of her government did right or wrong. But that time has not yet arrived. We must grapple with this problem, even though—and because—it involves some of the pivotal issues of our times.

We cannot pass a single, comprehensive judgment upon Vichy, for the reason that the term "Vichy" covers a multitude of diverse sins, as well as an assortment of redeeming features and extenuating circumstances. Among those who professed themselves partisans of Marshal Pétain, as we have seen, there were two antithetical camps—the fascists and the "conservatives." The same estimate cannot hold for both. Each camp, moreover, included persons of quite different character.

Among the leading advocates of fascism, there is scarcely anyone for whom a plausible defense can be made on the ground that he came to his convictions without thought of his own interest, simply by an honest and intelligent analysis of the problems facing France. Déat seems the one who comes nearest to having a right to this defense. Even before the war, he had recognized the intellectual poverty of the orthodox Socialists, who were still mouthing the Marxian slogans of international proletarian revolution, long after they had made their peace with capitalism and nationalism. He had also begun to develop his argument in favor of a new kind of socialism, based on a frank acceptance of nationalism. But he was in such haste to gain the good graces of the Nazis, so eager to have office under any conditions—even in Sigmaringen—and so utterly subservient to the Germans that we cannot think of him as other than a man who sold himself.

Doriot requires even less consideration. No one ever made a serious argument that he was more than a professional rabble rouser, who distilled his political principles out of those slogans which he found most effective in stirring a crowd to a frenzied pitch of hatred and excitement. At the end of the spectrum is such a man as Brinon. There is little need to probe into the character of a man who became the agent of the Nazis, although his wife was Jewish, and made a fortune by selling, to Jews and others who had special need to flee from the grasp of the Nazis, the permits required to cross the line of demarcation into the unoccupied zone.

Yet the problem of guilt is never simple, even when we are dealing with fascists. What are we to think of such a man as Joseph Darnand? No one in France, with the possible exception of Pierre Laval, was more hated than the head of the Milice. As a person, however, Darnand was perhaps not the worst of his cohorts. Apparently he was a man of little intelligence or education, with a deep urge to deeds of violence and daring, and a simple-minded wish to become a patriotic hero. During the First World War, he had distinguished himself for bravery on the field of battle and had won the Médaille Militaire. After the war, he had prospered in the trucking business, but still had hankered for the thrill of fighting someone—it did not much matter whom—in the name of France. So he had drifted from one to another of the political movements that extolled authoritarian nationalism—the Camelots du Roi, the Croix de Feu, the P.P.F. of Doriot. Mobilized again in 1939, at the age of forty-two, he once more had won recognition for valor in action against the enemy. But the armistice had thrust him back into civilian life, at a time when France seemed to have need, as never before, for someone to fight for her.

Darnand might well have taken up with the Resistance and become a national hero. But he lacked the wit for a subtle examination of where lay the path of patriotic duty. So he chose, instead, to give his allegiance to the government headed by the "Victor of Verdun." And when the government had need of someone to take charge of the struggle against the "rebels" and "terrorists" of the Resistance, Darnand stepped forward, with what might well have been, by his dim lights, the same sense of patriotic duty that previously had won him the Médaille Militaire.

The men comprising the loose and diverse faction we have labeled "conservative" are much harder to appraise than the open partisans of fascism. Because the common bond among them is the ambivalence of their position—accepting "collaboration" while holding back from a firm commitment to the Axis—we can neither dismiss them out of hand as mere agents of the Nazis nor give them a clean bill.

Few of the "conservatives" are free of the suspicion of personal opportunism. Most of them showed an unbecoming eagerness to take positions of influence in the new regime, even though their tenure of office was sure to impose loathsome tasks upon them.

On the other hand, few of them showed sycophancy toward the Nazis. Nor did they present "collaboration" as the free choice of the government rather than a painful necessity consequent to the military defeat. None of them gave sign of personal or political vindic.iveness toward their adversaries, even those who had been identified with the leadership of the previous regime. Certainly the prosecution of Blum, Daladier, and Reynaud was less impassioned than the later condemnation of Pétain.

Perhaps the basic fault of the "conservatives" was a weakness of character, rather than vicious intent or personal corruption. Probably they were sincere in seeking to defend the interests of France, while accepting a "collaboration" within "narrow" bounds that seemed inescapable. But they lacked the courage to take a firm stand when the Germans, or their French agents in Paris, raised demands for a kind of "collaboration" which no honorable man should have accepted.

On the one occasion when the "conservatives" took a concerted stand —on December 13, 1940, when they insisted upon the dismissal of Laval —they won their point. Never again did they screw up their nerve to repeat the venture. From time to time, one or another might oppose a particular concession to the Axis, as when General Weygand protested at some of the provisions in the agreement which Darlan concluded with the Germans in May, 1941. But at no time after the crisis of December 13 did a considerable number of "conservatives" offer their collective resignation unless the drift toward "broad" collaboration were halted. Nor did they press Pétain to resign or force the Nazis to depose him. Most of them clung to their positions in the government or among Pétain's advisers, muttering their grievances to one another, until they were either forced out of office, one by one, or else reduced to utter complicity with those who had no scruple whatever.

Of the three men who shared the top command in Vichy, Darlan is of the least interest. It would be a bootless enterprise to discuss at length the motives of a man who had neither *politique* nor *diplomatie*. Obviously, as head of the French government, Darlan was a man who had ventured beyond his depth. His crime, which is not much less heinous than if he had better known what he was doing, was that he could not resist the lure of power or recognize his inadequacy for the task he undertook. Nevertheless, we must acknowledge that he had one simple but unshaken principle, which saved him from the final dishonor. However low he might permit the government to sink, he would not permit the navy to pass under the domination of a foreign power. Doubtless this one, obsessive principle kept him from ordering the fleet into British ports in June, 1940—but it also kept him from giving it over to the Axis.

Laval seems the simplest of all to assess. In a land like France, where public opinion is never unanimous, seldom has a man incurred such universal and unmeasured opprobrium as Laval. An outside observer would have ample warrant to presume that, since nearly forty million Frenchmen believe Laval simply sold his soul to the Germans for the sake of gaining personal political power, there is no need to bring this verdict into question.

Yet we cannot be sure this consensus proves that Laval's guilt was more obvious, or more reprehensible, than that of his accomplices. It may only mean that Laval was not a member of any faction and therefore became the foe of all. Manifestly, he earned the unremitting hatred of all those who remained loyal to the Third Republic as well as those who opposed "collaboration," whether in 1940 or not until 1944. But the fascists never regarded him as one of their own number. Though he made an alliance of sorts with Déat, he did not share Déat's convictions. He simply sought to make use of him to gain the better graces of the Nazis and to offset the antagonism of Doriot toward him. For their part, the "conservatives" detested Laval no less because he was an advocate of "broad" collaboration than because he scorned their schemes for domestic reform, which he dismissed as the mere vaporings of moss-grown reactionaries.

Laval seemed, indeed, a man quite devoid of principles. He appeared to have no ambition but to hold office. Believing German hegemony to be definitive, he was willing to stoop to any indignity, provided only that the Nazis would keep him in power as their agent. Innumerable persons who knew him well have vouched that his previous record was such as to make this a plausible interpretation of his behavior after 1940. In the politics of the Third Republic, where personal opportunism was not a rare phenomenon, Laval had earned an unenviable reputation as a man as much at home in a pool of corruption and intrigue as a fish in the sea.

His own defense, when the "purge" at last caught up with him, was that he had never had a thought but to cheat the Germans. He would give them unstinted verbal assurances of his good will, while conceding nothing of more practical importance than he could avoid. Considering how little he had to bargain with, he had accomplished a miracle, for which France owed him a debt of gratitude, in shielding her from the horrors that otherwise might have been her lot. He had had no more preference for Hitler, when he dealt with him, than earlier he had had for Stalin, when he negotiated the Franco-Soviet alliance of 1935. He would as soon have bargained with the Devil, he declared, if he had known how to reach him.

At the time, there were not many who gave credence to this plea. Everyone remembered the speech in which he had declared, "I wish to see the victory of the Axis"; the conscription and deportation of workers; the surrender of hostages; and the ruthless measures against the Resistance.

However, it is not impossible to reconcile Laval's own professions with the charges made against him. For, if he was the kind of man his enemies depict, he would have seen no harm in telling the Nazis whatever they wished to hear in order to put them in an amiable mood. What did it matter if he spat upon the Third Republic, declared his allegiance to the Fuehrer, asked French lads to work for the Germans at good wages, or even sacrificed some thousands of Communists and other troublemakers—provided France escaped the fate of Poland? After all, a woman of the town who passed a night with a German officer did not believe the flattering words she told him, nor count her fleeting favor worth the price she received. Perhaps we should think of Laval in some such terms. To give the Devil his due, we should perhaps concede that Laval made his fatal mistake when, for the first time in his life, he tried to put his talent for chicane and corruption to what he thought was the service of his fellow Frenchmen.

However severe a judgment we pass, Pétain comes off better than most of those who surrounded him. Even in the friendliest view, to be sure, his faults are obvious. He was a vain old man, who relished to the full the unrivaled prominence to which the misfortunes of France had raised him. He was self-centered, moreover, with little warmth in his relations with others, or attachment to those who gave him loyal service. He showed little or no sign of sharp insight, or deep conviction, on the basic problems of politics. This is no offense in itself. But it is a matter of reproach in a man who presumed to take a position of political leadership in such a crisis as faced France in 1940.

Yet he remained a figure of some dignity. Frenchmen might feel shame at the policies of the government to which he gave the sanction of his name but not at his personal demeanor. His public statements, with few exceptions, avoided recrimination upon France's former allies or obsequious deference toward her conquerors. The theme upon which he never tired of dwelling was that France, while recognizing the depths of her plight, must not despair of the future. Her people must dedicate themselves, with a chastened seriousness of purpose, to the task of rebuilding their greatness upon firmer foundations.

To one principle Pétain held fast—his resolution never to abandon his post as Chief of State or leave France, save as a prisoner, as long as the Germans remained on her soil. This was both his undoing and the basis of his plea for exoneration. We cannot dismiss his argument in his own defense as wholly specious. We may accuse him of poor judgment, but not of dishonor, for his original decision to accept the office of Chief of State and to undertake "collaboration" on the basis of the armistice. In the summer of 1940 he had ample reason to believe that France had no choice but to cooperate with the Axis. And we may not dismiss as mere vanity his conviction that he was the only man whose presence in France, at the head of her government, would save the nation from complete demoralization. As he later declared before the High Court, the French people saw in him the embodiment of the continuity of their history—a man who had known the humiliation of 1871, the grandeur of 1918, and then the disaster of 1940. His presence thus reminded them that neither victory nor defeat endures forever, but only France.

Nor can we deny that Pétain took up a thankless task, even though he may have relished the opportunity to become a martyr. "I made France the gift of my person," he reminded the High Court, "and at this supreme moment, let no one doubt that I made a sacrifice."

But this plea is more persuasive when we think of the summer of 1940 than the summer of 1944. It does not serve to redeem him from the opprobrium of having given France the example of mute submission, long after his government had become a sham, and "collaboration," another word for German exploitation. Because he could never bring himself to repudiate the decision he had taken at the outset, he became, instead of a symbol of unity and hope, the image of craven pusillanimity.

But it is not worth the while to pursue this problem of judging the men of Vichy. For the most part, they were men of quite an ordinary kind. Certainly none of them had qualities approaching the heroic, while the worst did not rival their Nazi masters in quintessential evil. The interest of the study of Vichy lies, rather, in the impact upon ordinary men of a crisis in which were involved factors not without parallel in other countries besides France.

So far as concerns its domestic aspect, the experience of Vichy helps throw light upon the relations between liberalism, conservatism, and fascism. In the 1930s, the supposition of outside observers was that liberalism represented the norm of French politics. This implied a government accountable to the people through the instrument of universal suffrage, which would reduce the social inequalities among them while permitting the maximum degree of personal freedom.

The crisis that developed in the summer of 1940 gave occasion to reconsider this view. First, it raised doubt as to whether liberalism did represent the norm of French political opinion. For the republican regime disappeared in favor of the autocratic rule of Marshal Pétain without any evident sign of regret on the part of the mass of the French people. We cannot help but be struck by the mere eighty votes cast against the investiture of Marshal Pétain with a personal power as absolute as that of Louis XIV, while a lone, pathetic voice cried out, "Vive la République, quand même!" We cannot help but think that, after seven decades, the Third Republic had become little more than what it had been at its inception, when Thiers dubbed it "the government that divides us least." With the passage of time, it seemed to have gained strength mainly from the force of habit.

The collapse of the Third Republic did not have the consequence that, only a short time before, would have seemed probable. The observer in the 1930s would have predicted that, should the Third Republic disappear, the arena of French politics would become the battleground of a struggle between the Extreme Right and the Extreme Left. Nothing had seemed clearer, in the period of the Popular Front, than the polarization of French opinion between these opposites and the disappearance of the middle ground.

But in point of fact, the Extreme Left did not gain ground upon the collapse of the Third Republic. Instead, the Communists virtually disappeared from the scene: their party had been outlawed before the inception of the Vichy regime, and all other parties, including the Socialists, had approved their suppression. While they still kept the allegiance of some portion of the proletariat in Paris and other cities, they had far too little popular following to make an effective protest. Nor, as a movement of the Extreme Left, did they ever regain sufficient strength to challenge the Vichy regime. After the outbreak of the Russo-German war in the summer of 1941, to be sure, they began to take a part in the Resistance. Ultimately they won wide respect as fighters against the Germans. But this did not represent popular support of the Extreme Left as against the Extreme Right. Indeed, the Communists themselves insisted that differences of opinion concerning domestic politics must be set aside in favor of a union of all parties in the struggle against the Axis. Once the Axis was destroyed, and the Communists no longer figured as the vanguard of a patriotic struggle, their influence once more receded.

On the other hand, the accession of Marshal Pétain did not mean the triumph of the Extreme Right of the 1930s—but its dissolution. As we have seen, the adversaries of the Popular Front soon split into two rival camps—the fascists, and the "conservatives." The struggle between them became no less embittered than the earlier antagonism between the Extreme Right and the Extreme Left. Moreover, it took on the character of a struggle between the Right and the Left. Not only were the principal spokesmen of fascism, Déat and Doriot, renegades from one or the other Marxian parties—Colonel de la Rocque, who had no such origin, soon passed out of the picture—but they continued to voice the slogans of the Left. Thus they denounced their adversaries in Vichy as foes of universal suffrage, pawns of the Church, and minions of the "trusts." They demanded a new government, which would draw its strength from the masses and would recognize the imperative of socialism. If we understand liberalism to mean an insistence that the government must serve the needs of the mass of the people, without regard for rank or for lesser interests than those of the nation as a whole, we must recognize fascism as an authentic expression of the Left.

On the other hand, the "conservatives" emerged in the period of Vichy as the antithesis of the fascists. Their opposition, it is true, was sharper in the realm of doctrine than in practical affairs. Likewise, it was sharper in respect to domestic issues than diplomatic ones. Yet it remains apparent that the fascists were speaking as heirs to the Revolution of 1789 when they expounded their ideal of an all-pervasive state, which would recognize no disparities or distinctions among its citizens but would "integrate" the nation into a monolithic whole. And it is no less evident that this kind of regime did not represent the vision of the "conservatives." These were dreaming of a world in which a man would attach more importance to his role as a member of a family and of an autonomous corporative association than to his role as a personless citizen of the state, a world in which the moral duties arising out of his personal relations with his fellows would take precedence over the secular demands of patriotism.

The longer we ponder the issues of this debate between the "conservatives" and the fascists, the more we are driven to a conclusion of large meaning. For the opposition between these two points of view was more than merely a phenomenon of French politics in the period of Vichy. Was it not, rather, one instance of a crisis affecting most countries of the Western world, in which "liberalism" becomes ever less distinguishable from totalitarianism and in which those who cannot reconcile themselves to "integration" are driven, willingly or not, knowingly or not, to seek some alternative to "liberalism"?

Nor is the problem involved in "collaboration" of relevance only to the situation of France under the Nazi domination. Setting aside partisanship, we cannot do other than acknowledge that "collaboration," on the basis of the armistice, was no less honorable in the summer of 1940 than the course which General de Gaulle urged. Manifestly, the whole French nation could not emigrate to London and continue the struggle against the Axis alongside the British. Yet no one could doubt but that a French government would do more than a Nazi governor to protect the interests of France after her defeat. No less obvious is it that, by the summer of 1940, "collaboration" ceased to represent any kind of advantage for France.

In an age gone by, anyone could readily distinguish between patriotism and treason; the distinction was sharp and plain. Patriotism used to mean, simply, giving one's allegiance to one's own nation; treason, giving aid to another nation at the expense of one's own. But, as the experience of France suggests, we are now living in another era. For most peoples today, the distinction between treason and patriotism has become uncertain, mobile, contingent upon a number of factors. What one deems as serving the interests of one's own nation may depend upon one's views as to which of two other powers, hostile to each other, is the stronger—if one's own nation is so weak that it must defer to the stronger—and how long the stronger power will remain superior to the other in strength. It may also depend on what views one holds on social and political issues—whether, for instance, one regards liberalism as a cancerous growth upon the nation or as its proudest heritage.

As we undertake to form a judgment as to the issues involved in "collaboration," seeking to determine whether it represented patriotism or treason, we are thus led to the problem of deciding at what moment "collaboration" ceased to be compatible with the patriotic interest of France and passed into treason. We might choose any of several crucial dates as the turning point—the failure of the German air attack upon Britain in October, 1940; the accession of Darlan in February, 1941; the outbreak of the Russo-German war in June, 1941; the entrance of the United States into the war in December, 1941; the recall of Laval in April, 1942; the invasion of North Africa in November, 1942; the Allied landing in Normandy in June, 1944. Then we might say that no man necessarily did wrong by supporting "collaboration" until the date we named, but that all who continued to endorse it thereafter were traitors to their country.

But this simple criterion will not serve. In the first place, it would force us into putting a moral premium upon sheer personal opportunism. For who can distinguish between those who changed their views at a given moment because they correctly discerned the moment when "collaboration" ceased to serve the interests of the nation and those who were intent only upon attaching their personal fortunes to the winning side? So common was this kind of opportunism, and so uninspiring, that we feel some impulse to reserve approval for only the Gaullists and the fascists, since these remained steadfast in their allegiance.

In the second place, this simple view does not recognize the tragedy of those men who accepted "collaboration" at the outset because they honestly believed it a humiliating necessity, then became prisoners of their own logic. For, as we have seen, a plausible argument could be made in favor of continuing to support Vichy at any of the successive crises in its history. In the spring of 1941, for instance, those who favored only "narrow" collaboration could see that Darlan was moving toward a "broad" partnership with the Axis. But who could say at that time that the victory of the British was close at hand, or even certain in the long run, and that France would therefore do better to have no government of her own than to acquiesce in the leadership of Darlan?

The same kind of reasoning was possible when Laval returned to office in April, 1942, or when the Allies landed in North Africa six months later. Even in the spring of 1944 no one could be sure that the Allied attempt at an invasion would prove successful, or that a general uprising of the Resistance would not bring down ruinous reprisals upon the helpless nation before the Allied armies could come to the rescue. So it was that men like Maurras, who had no wish to see the Axis maintain its rule in France, persuaded themselves that it was still too soon to turn from Pétain to the Resistance, until ultimately they wound up in the company of the mere hirelings of the Nazis.

We may dispose of the matter simply, by taking the stand that men should be wise enough to avoid such self-deception. But perhaps we thus deceive ourselves.

Is there not another lesson in this tragic experience, which we should take to heart? Is it not evident that the fault of such men was not that they were lacking in patriotism, but that patriotism was not enough? Does it not appear that they went to their undoing, not because they failed to recognize the interests of their nation or did not dedicate themselves to those interests, but because they recognized no higher obligation? In 1940 a man might well reckon that, though the price of "collaboration" included the persecution of French Jews, the hardship this put upon the Jews was less than the horror that would come upon the whole nation, if Vichy should refuse to cooperate, and Berlin should replace Pétain with a Nazi proconsul. But a man with less concern for the greatest good of the greatest number, and a keener sense of common decency and charity, would not be sure the gain was worth the price.

In 1944, to take another example, men of honor chose to risk their lives in the Resistance in order to help hasten the retribution which the Nazis had so long escaped. But a man with a duller sense of personal honor, making a cooler appraisal of the interests of France as a nation, might well have deemed it wiser for France to remain passive. Thus she could avoid the risk of horrible reprisals until the outcome of the battle between the Allies and the Germans was clear. And he could have argued that this was the course of patriotism, of service to the national interest of France.

The problem is an instance of the principle that the morality of a statesman is not the same as that of a private person. The principle is perhaps too little understood in America, perhaps too well understood in Europe.

A NOTE ON SOURCES

A SPECIAL PROBLEM arises in writing the history of contemporary events, rather than those of a more remote time. In part, this is because the historian lacks perspective on the happenings of his own time and cannot avoid viewing them in the light of his own biases on the problems of his age.

But this is not the sole handicap from which he suffers, nor the worst. By an extraordinary effort of the will, he can strive to put aside his personal predilections and animosities and seek to attain a detached point of view toward the events of which he writes. And he can make a scrupulous use of those rules of historical research which give him guidance in recognizing and compensating for both his own bias and the bias of the witnesses upon whose depositions he draws for evidence.

To be sure, he can never quite attain his goal of writing without bias. But neither can the historian who deals with events in a more remote period of the past. For in itself, a long perspective does not guarantee against bias. With the perspective of more than a century and a half, those scholars who study the history of the Revolution of 1789 are still unable to reach an un-impassioned agreement among themselves on the basic issues involved in the events which they study. The historian cannot be sure he views events in the past without personal bias until so much time has elapsed that the events no longer seem of large importance. Perhaps a hundred years hence scholars will be in a position to write the history of Vichy dispassionately— but only if no one any longer is warmly interested in the topic.

Much worse than the want of perspective or detachment on the part of the historian is the problem of materials. This arises because the scholar working on a topic in the history of his own times has too much and too little evidence. In the study of Vichy, we are seriously handicapped because we cannot make use of documents, locked up in official archives or under the control of private persons, which would answer some questions of key importance. For example, we do not have the personal papers of Pétain or Laval or Darlan, or the records of the various French ministries in the period of the Vichy regime, or the Nazi archives that would make clear the dealings of the Germans with both the French government and those persons in France that acted as German agents. This evidence will not be made available for the use of scholars within our time.

On the other hand, the mass of published materials open to our use is so vast as to discourage anyone who seeks to make an exhaustive study of the evidence. The materials at hand which are relevant to our topic include a large proportion of all the books, magazines, and newspapers published in France during the occupation—and despite the shortage of paper, the output of the printing presses in France suffered but little diminution during the war. No less extensive is the immense volume of materials published by foreign governments, during and after the war, which bear upon their relations with Vichy. The forty-odd volumes of testimony in the trials of the Nazi leaders at Nuremberg represent only a single item in this dossier. Compared with even the materials on the history of the French Revolution, for which we have a rich documentation, the evidence now available on the history of Vichy is a staggering abundance.

Historians are sometimes frank with one another when they are out of the hearing of those who are not members of their guild. On such occasions they admit that the reason they cannot cope with topics in contemporary history is that not enough of the evidence has been lost or destroyed. Not until the files of all the newspapers but half a dozen have crumbled to dust, not until the letters and diaries of nearly everyone who took part in the events have been burnt or destroyed as waste paper, can the scholar begin to work on what remains with some hope of examining "all the available evidence."

But this, of course, is not the nub of the matter. The problem is not simply that we have so much material that no one can examine it all. Rather, the crux of it is that no one can write a definitive history of Vichy until scores of scholars have worked over the evidence bearing on particular aspects of the problem, such as the activities of the Resistance, the various German policies toward Vichy, and the response of the French economy to the manifold stresses upon it. Once some considerable progress has been made in such detailed investigations, a man can hope to grasp the problem of Vichy as a whole, by drawing upon the work of other scholars to supplement and extend his own researches.

As matters stand, we have scarcely any scholarly literature on Vichy. Soon after the liberation, under the aegis of the new government, a Commission d'Histoire de l'Occupation et de la Libération was established. But this commission defined its task as involving responsibility for the collection and preservation of materials bearing upon the history of the period of Vichy. It did not undertake to sponsor particular studies.

So far, less than a dozen books have appeared, either in France or elsewhere, that even purport to provide a general survey of the period, and none of these can be regarded as scholarly. As good as any of them is Dorothy M. Pickles, *France between the Republics* (London: Contact, 1946). This is much more knowledgeable and judicious than one might suppose of a book written only a little more than a year after the liberation. It is only a brief account, however, scarcely more than an essay, and much new material, as well as new insight, has become available since it appeared.

Alexandre Zévaès, *Histoire de six ans, 1938–44* (Paris: Éditions de la Nouvelle Revue Critique, 1944), is a continuation of the author's numerous earlier studies of the history of the Third Republic and of Marxism in France. Though of some use as a manual of events, the account is superficial. The viewpoint is that of a Socialist not far removed from the Communists. The presentation is therefore sympathetic to the Resistance and hostile to Vichy. This is interesting, since the author contributed during the period of the occupation to Déat's *L'Œuvre.*

We may take note also of Louis-Dominique Girard, *La Guerre franco-française,* of which one volume, entitled *Le Maréchal républican* (Paris: André Bonne, 1950), has appeared. A second volume, announced as *La Pomme de désaccord,* is to complete the work. But this is admittedly a plea and a polemic in behalf of Vichy.

Not unlike this in tone, but opposite in point of view, are Maurice Vanino, *Le Temps de la honte: de Rethondes à l'île d'Yeu* (Paris: Éditions Créator, 1952), and Marquis d'Argenson, *Pétain et le pétinisme: essai de psychologie* (Paris: Éditions Créator, 1953). Neither attempts a chronological narrative.

Of interest is Raymond Aron, *De l'Armistice à l'insurrection nationale* (Paris: Gallimard, 1945). The author was associated with the Gaullist movement in London during the period of Vichy, and the chapters in this book were originally written as comment on the current news of France, for publication in *La Libre France.* The reportage and comment are of a much higher order than might be supposed, and the preface, written after the liberation of France, is of special interest as an indication of the author's second thoughts on the problems involved in making an unimpassioned appraisal of Vichy.

Notable among the few studies of particular aspects of the period are: Louis Baudin, *Esquisse de l'économie française sous l'occupation allemande* (Paris: Librairie Médicis, 1945); Pierre Arnoult, *Les Finances de la France et l'occupation allemande, 1940–44* (Paris: Presses Universitaires de France, 1951); Henri Michel, *Histoire de la Résistance, 1940–44* (Paris: Presses Universitaires de France, 1950); Georges Lefranc, *Les Expériences syndicales en France de 1939 à 1950* (Paris: Aubiet, 1950); Albert Kammerer, *La Vérité sur l'armistice: éphéméride de ce qui s'est réellement passé en 1940* (Paris: Éditions Médicis, 1945), and *La Passion de la Flotte française: de Mers El-Kébir à Toulon* (Paris: Arthème Fayard, 1951).

In the absence of more such studies, a work such as this cannot pretend to rest upon more than a sampling of the evidence. An effort has been made to consult the materials of outstanding importance that bear directly upon the record of the men who held positions of prominence in Vichy or Paris during the occupation. But simply to keep the task within the bounds of one man's energies, no such endeavor has been made to examine materials emanating from the Axis side or those dealing with the Gaullist movement or those bearing upon the relations of Vichy with Britain and the United States.

No documents of an archival nature are at present available for scholarly use. The Provisional Government, which took over the records of its predecessor at the time of the liberation, chose not to release any portion of these documents nor to publish an official collection designed to incriminate the men of Vichy. This reluctance to open the archives is perhaps an indication of the French sense of the continuity of the state, perhaps an indication of the desire of the Provisional Government not to give more impetus to the demand for vengeance at the time of the "purge," perhaps an indication that some of the men of Vichy were not without friends in the new government, who would preserve them from incrimination. At any event, the historian will have to rely for a long time to come exclusively upon published materials.

But these are much more nearly adequate than one might imagine. To be sure, they do not permit us to gain more than a glimpse of some portions of the history of the period. Notably, the evidence so far available does not permit us to trace a complete history of the Resistance, and no attempt to do so has been made in this study. Nor can we make out clearly what were the responses of the French economy to the pressures bearing on it. Nor do we have sufficient information to attempt a definitive biography of any of the leading figures in the regime.

Nevertheless, we can establish with a reasonable degree of assurance what were the successive crises that arose within the government, the various factions that developed and the general point of view of each, and some of the factors that helped determine the outcome of these crises.

Most of the published material relevant to the history of Vichy can be found in the Bibliothèque Nationale in Paris. This might seem a truism, since the Bibliothèque Nationale normally acquires copies of all books and periodicals published in France. But the collection was completed only with considerable trouble, after the liberation, because much of the material published in the unoccupied zone did not reach Paris during the occupation. Some items still have not been brought to that repository. Hence there is need to consult also the other principal collection, which is to be found in the Bibliothèque de Documentation Contemporaine Internationale, now administered as one of the special libraries of the University of Paris. Originally devoted to the history of the First World War, this has grown into a general library on problems of public affairs, both in France and other countries, over the entire period since 1914. For the history of Vichy, it is especially useful for its collection of works on corporatism and other issues of social and political reform.

The two official publications of basic importance that appeared in the period of the occupation were the *Journal Officiel de l'État Français,* which was the continuation of the *Journal Officiel* of the Third Republic, and the bilingual gazette containing the ordinances of the German authorities, which appeared in German as the *Verordnungsblatt für die besetzten französischen Gebiete* and in French as the *Journal Officiel contenant des ordonnances arrêtés par le Gouverneur militaire pour les territoires français occupés.* A compilation of the decrees of the German authorities was also published under the title *Législation de l'occupation: recueil des principaux textes des lois, décrets, ordonnances, arrêtés, et circulaires des autorités allemandes et françaises, promulgués depuis l'occupation* (14 vols., Paris: Imprimerie du Palais, 1940–44).

Two official publications of the Fourth Republic are of special interest for the study of Vichy. One of these is the *Enquête sur les événéments survenus en France depuis 1939 à 1945: témoignages* (6 vols., Paris: Presses Universitaires de France, n.d.). These volumes comprise testimony taken by an investigating commission, created by the Assemblée Nationale in 1947, to which was delegated the task of making a systematic inquiry into all that had transpired in France in the period leading up to the war and the armistice and throughout the era of Vichy. But most of this testimony bears on happenings before the inception of the Vichy regime. There is little that bears upon Vichy other than the testimony of Pétain himself, which he gave while in prison. And Pétain's mind had so obviously deteriorated while he was in prison that we cannot put much reliance in his deposition.

The other notable publication is France, Presidence du Conseil, Commission consultative des dommages et des reparations, *Dommages subis par la France du fait de la guerre et de l'occupation* (9 vols., Paris: Imprimerie Nationale, 1948–50). This includes a tabulation of the amount of damages, estimated in terms of francs, which France suffered as a consequence of the various spoliations which the Germans and their allies worked upon her. However, it does not indicate the evidence upon which the calculations are based.

The newspaper press is of much more help than might be presumed. The same censorship did not prevail in both zones of France. The papers appearing in occupied France were under the close surveillance of the Germans but were free to criticize what went on in Vichy, whereas those papers appearing in the unoccupied zone were not free to criticize the government of Marshal Pétain but were permitted a surprising degree of latitude in their comment on what was going on in Paris and even in their reportage of the course of the war as a whole.

Of the papers published in the unoccupied zone, the most useful for the purposes of this study is the *Action Française,* which voiced the views of those whom we have designated as "conservatives." From the beginning to the end of the Vichy regime, it remained steadfast in its support of the government of Marshal Pétain and as steadfast in its opposition to the fascist faction in Paris, of which Déat and Doriot were the leaders. It maintained a position of neutrality as between the Allies and the Axis. Even after the Allied invasion of France in June, 1944, it continued to castigate the Resistance. But at no time did it speak well of the Germans, and its columns often expressed an outspoken criticism of the Axis.

Le Figaro, like the *Action Française,* also removed from Paris after the Germans entered the capital and soon resumed publication in the unoccupied zone, at first from Clermont-Ferrand, then Lyons. It remained the voice of those elements of the upper bourgeoisie which remained loyal to the republican tradition while accepting the new regime of Marshal Pétain. It ceased to appear after the Germans moved into the unoccupied zone in November, 1942. Its suspension marked the turning point at which those conservative republicans who had accepted the Vichy regime without denouncing liberalism ceased to take an active role in public affairs.

Of some interest is *L'Effort,* also appearing in the unoccupied zone, which attempted to speak for those Socialists who accepted the new regime. Its editor, Charles Spinasse, was an associate of Léon Blum who had had some prominence during the period of the Popular Front. But, so far as can be determined, the paper never gained a large following.

The three Paris newspapers of principal importance in this period were *L'Œuvre, Le Cri du Peuple,* and *Les Nouveaux Temps. L'Œuvre,* which had been a paper of large circulation before the war, passed under the editorship of Marcel Déat. It became an advocate of "broad" collaboration and the reform of social and political institutions on much the same lines Déat had urged before the war, when he had sought to organize a "neosocialist" movement. It championed measures in the interest of the popular classes and denounced Vichy as a stronghold of the reactionaries committed to the interest of the rich. It directed most of its reproaches to the group identified with the *Action Française,* which in turn aimed numerous attacks at Déat.

Le Cri du Peuple, which became Doriot's organ, never made as much pretense at an intellectual defense of the fascist and pro-Axis position as did *L'Œuvre.* But it far outdid its rival in the virulence with which it attacked the Jews.

Les Nouveaux Temps, which Jean Luchaire edited, never attained as large circulation as the other two, nor did its editorials show as much vigor of expression or firmness of conviction. It seems probable, as has been alleged, that it could not have survived without continuous subsidies from the Germans.

Le Populaire, the official organ of the Socialist Party, suspended publication at the time of the armistice and did not resume legal publication. *L'Humanité,* the Communist organ, had been put under a legal ban before the outbreak of the active warfare on the Western Front. It reappeared after the armistice only as an illegal publication. Its attitude toward the new regime remained equivocal until the German attack upon Russia in June, 1941, whereupon it took up the cause of the Resistance.

In either zone, the newspapers which continued legal publication after the armistice are of much more value as expressions of opinion than as records of what was going on. Most of them published no more than a meager bulletin of news of national importance. American newspapers, such as the *New York Times,* published nearly as much news of France as did the French newspapers. So did some of the Swiss newspapers. In some respects, indeed, the foreign press was more informative, since its reporters could more easily circumvent the censorship of either Paris or Vichy.

For a fuller indication of what transpired behind the scenes, we must depend in large part upon the testimony given in the various trials during the "purge" of 1944–49. These are not of equal value for our purpose, and we cannot help but wish the prosecution had been more effective in developing its case. In none of the trials did the government bring forth startling new revelations from the archives of Vichy. Nor did the witnesses for the prosecution have much to offer by way of information as to what happened after July, 1940, since most of them had taken no part in the Vichy government. The evidence which the prosecution adduced bore mainly upon events leading up to the armistice. What was contributed as to later events came mostly from the testimony of the defendants or witnesses in their behalf. Seldom did the prosecution demonstrate more than mediocre skill in drawing out testimony from the defense. Nevertheless, the witnesses for the defense threw considerable light on the record of the Vichy regime, since the defendants were under a moral pressure to explain their conduct, and often one of them, in order to put himself in a favorable light, would make revelations to the discredit of another witness or the defendant in another trial.

The trial of Marshal Pétain was the most illuminating. The prosecution made a more diligent effort to develop its case in this trial than in others, and the witnesses on one side or the other included most of the surviving luminaries of both the Third Republic and Vichy. Yet even in this trial the testimony threw more light upon the events of 1939–40 than on the later period.

In principle, the trial of Laval should have shown the opposite emphasis, since the most incriminating portion of Laval's career came after his return to the government in April, 1942. But his trial soon degenerated into such tumult and disorder that the defense gave up all effort to present its case, and Laval refused even to appear in the court room. So the trial amounted to little more than a reiteration of the indictment.

For the most part, the other trials proved more interesting for what they brought out as to the background of the defendant than for what they established as to his activities during the period of the occupation. As biographical documents, some are of value.

The stenographic record of the proceedings in the trials of men of large prominence was made available soon afterwards in books issued by commercial publishers. These are unofficial versions, and some are abridged, omitting those portions of the record that involved merely legal formalities. Some were edited by the lawyers for the defense, who included *ex parte* notes of their own. In the main, however, these may be taken as a reliable record of the testimony of interest to us here.

Among the more important of these transcripts are: *Le Procès du maréchal Pétain: compte rendu sténographique* (2 vols., Paris: Albin Michel, 1945);

Le Procès Laval: compte rendu sténographique (Paris: Albin Michel, 1946); *Le Procès Flandin devant la Haute Cour de Justice* (Paris: Librairie de Médicis, 1946); *Le Procès Benoist-Méchin: compte rendu intégral des débats* (Paris: Albin Michel, 1948); *Les Procès de collaboration: Fernand de Brinon, Joseph Darnand, Jean Luchaire, compte rendu sténographique* (Paris: Albin Michel, 1948); Robert Dufourg, ed., *Adrien Marquet devant la Haute Cour: Français, jugez vous-mêmes* (Paris: Janmaray, 1948); Otto Abetz, *D'une prison: précédé du procès, vu par Jean Bernard-Derosne, les quatre témoignages principaux, et la plaidoirie de Me René Floriot* (Paris: Amiot-Dumont, 1948); Paul Buttin, ed., *Le Procès Pucheu* (Paris: Amiot-Dumont, 1948); *Le Procès Charles Maurras: compte rendu sténographique* (Paris: Albin Michel, 1946); Jacques Isorni, ed., *Le Procès Robert Brasillach* (Paris: Flammarion, 1946); *Les Procès de radio: Ferdonnet et Jean Hérold-Paquis, compte rendu sténographique* (Paris: Albin Michel, 1947); *Le Procès Xavier Vallat, présenté par ses amis* (Paris: Éditions du Conquistador, 1948).

Memoirs are of uneven value for our purpose. Pétain never published his. Nor, so far as is known, did he make an attempt to prepare materials for a posthumous defense. A poor substitute is the official biography published in the Vichy period: General Laure and others, *Pétain* (Paris: Berger-Levrault, 1941). Various editions of his public addresses were published by the Sécrétariat Général à l'Information et à la Propagande. Selections were later edited by Me Jacques Isorni, his chief counsel, under the title *Quatre Années au pouvoir* (Paris: La Couronne Littéraire, 1949), which includes a bibliography of all his writings and the more notable books dealing with the period of his government.

Nothing whatever in the nature of a memoir is available for Admiral Darlan, nor do we have even a makeshift. Amiral Docteur, *La Grande Énigme de la guerre: Darlan, amiral de la flotte* (Paris: Éditions de la Couronne, 1949), gives merely the outline of his career. Alec de Montmorency, *The Enigma of Admiral Darlan* (New York: E. P. Dutton, 1943), is of little help.

Laval provides us only slightly more accommodation. While he was awaiting his trial in 1945, he wrote an outline of his defense, which his daughter, Josée de Chambrun, caused to be published. This appeared in French under the title *Laval parle* (Geneva: Les Éditions du Cheval Ailé, 1947), and in an English translation as *The Diary of Pierre Laval* (New York: Charles Scribner's Sons, 1948). But this *apologia* is more argumentative than informative. Even as argumentation, it lacks the ring of frankness.

To supplement this, we may turn to such books as Pierre Tissier, *I Worked*

With Laval (London: George G. Harrap, 1942), and Henry Torrès, *La France trahie: Pierre Laval* (New York: Brentano's, n.d.). Both men knew Laval before the period of Vichy but had no association with him after the armistice. Of interest because they present a favorable view of him are: Julien Clermont, *L'Homme qu'il fallait tuer: Pierre Laval* (Paris: Les Actes des Apôtres, 1949); Michel Letan, *Pierre Laval: de l'armistice au poteau* (Paris: Éditions de la Couronne, 1947); and Maurice Privat, *Pierre Laval: cet inconnu* (Paris: Fournier-Valdès, 1948). Favorable views of him are also given by the lawyers who undertook to defend him at his trial in 1945: Albert Naud, *Pourquoi je n'ai pas défendu Pierre Laval* (Paris: Arthème Fayard, 1948), and Jacques Baraduc, *Dans la cellule de Pierre Laval* (Paris: Éditions Self, 1948).

Perhaps the best study of Laval, based on the scanty published materials but distinguished for its moderate judgment, is David Thomson, *Two Frenchmen: Pierre Laval and Charles de Gaulle* (London: The Cresset Press, 1951).

Otto Abetz has provided us, besides the testimony given at his trial, with a memoir which is revealing without being either perceptive or frank: *Das offene Problem: ein Rückblick auf zwei Jahrzehnte deutscher Frankreichpolitik* (Cologne: Greven Verlag, 1951). A number of his reports to Berlin were taken from the German archives after the close of the war and published as *Pétain et les Allemands* (Paris: Editions Gaucher, 1948).

A number of lesser luminaries of Vichy also published memoirs of one kind or another. Notable among them are: Paul Baudouin, *Neuf Mois au gouvernement, avril–décembre 1940* (Paris: Éditions de la Table Ronde, 1948); Yves Bouthillier, *Le Drame de Vichy* (2 vols., Paris: Plon, 1950–51); Marcel Peyrouton, *Du Service publique à la prison commune: souvenirs* (Paris: Plon, 1950); Pierre Pucheu, *Ma Vie* (Paris: Amiot-Dumont, 1948); H. du Moulin de la Barthète, *Le Temps des illusions: souvenirs, juillet 1940–avril 1942* (Geneva: Les Éditions du Cheval Ailé, 1946); Jean Tracou, *Le Máréchal aux liens: le temps de sacrifice* (Paris: André Bonne, 1948); Pierre Cathala, *Face aux réalités: la direction des finances françaises sous l'occupation* (Paris: Éditions du Triolet, 1948); Pierre Nicolle, *Cinquante Mois d'armistice: Vichy, 2 juillet 1940–26 août 1944, journal d'un témoin* (2 vols., Paris: André Bonne, 1947); Maurice Martin du Gard, *Chronique de Vichy, 1940–44* (Paris: Flammarion, 1948).

A serious shortcoming of these memoirs is that most of them emanate from men who were identified with the faction that made its headquarters in Vichy rather than the fascist camp in Paris. There is no memoir of Déat or Doriot. For what we know of their attitudes we must depend principally on their writings in the Paris press. Of the two, Déat was much the more prolific. During the Vichy period, he published a total of more than 1,200 articles, in most of which he sought to deal with the issues of the moment in the tone of a serious intellectual discussion. A number of these articles were reprinted as a collection under the title *Le Parti unique* (Paris: Aux Armes de la France, 1942). However, Déat did no more than arrange these in a logical order, rather than the order of their first appearance, and the book cannot be regarded as a treatise. Doriot made little attempt to expound his ideas systematically in his newspaper articles and did not attempt a book-length statement of his views.

For a better understanding of Déat than comes from his own writings, we may turn to Claude Varennes, *Le Destin de Marcel Déat: un témoignage de première main sur l'histoire de quatre années terribles* (Paris: Janmaray, 1948). The author was an associate of Déat, and his book is both perceptive and, to a degree, detached in viewpoint.

We lack even such help for a better understanding of Doriot. We can do little more to supplement a reading of his own articles than to consult the writings of men who were his associates, though not necessarily of quite the same mind. Among these are: Pierre Drieu La Rochelle, *Chronique politique, 1934–43* (Paris: Gallimard, 1943), *Ne plus attendre: notes à leur date* (Paris: Bernard Grasset, 1941), *Notes pour comprendre le siècle* (Paris: Gallimard, 1941), and *Le Français d'Europe* (Paris: Éditions Balzac, 1944); and Jean Hérold-Paquis, *Des Illusions . . . désillusions: 15 août 1944–15 août 1945* (Paris: Bourgoin, 1948), which deals only with the period after the downfall of Vichy, when Doriot was in exile in Sigmaringen.

Not memoirs, but of comparable interest as an indication of how the issues of the times seemed to the fascists, are: Lucien Rebatet, *Les Décombres* (Paris: Denoël, 1942); Dominique Sordet, *Les Derniers Jours de la démocratie* (Paris: Inter-France, 1944); and Francis Delaisi, *La Révolution européenne* (Paris and Brussels: publisher not indicated, 1942), and *L'Ouvrier européen* (Paris: Éditions de l'Atelier, 1942).

Some dozens of others, who were not themselves persons of large influence either in Paris or Vichy but were in a position to become better informed than the average citizen as to what was happening behind the scenes, have published narratives of what they saw and heard. Among such are: Colonel Groussard, *Chemins secrets* (Paris: Bader-Dufour, 1948); Marius Sarraz-Bournet, *Témoignage d'un silencieux: G.Q.G., Deuxième Bureau, Turin, Vichy* (Paris: Éditions Self, 1948); Georges Loustanau-Lacau, *Mémoires d'un Français rebelle, 1914–48* (Paris: Robert Laffont, 1948). Of interest for the atmosphere in Vichy is G. Saint-Bonnet, *Vichy-capitale: ce que j'ai vu et entendu* (Paris: publisher not indicated, 1941).

A number of other memoirs are available which are of much value for the events leading up to the armistice but of less help for what later transpired. Among these are: Paul Reynaud, *La France a sauvé l'Europe* (2 vols., Paris: Flammarion, 1947); M. G. Gamelin, *Servir* (3 vols., Paris: Plon, 1946–47), of which Vol. III includes a general view of military operations leading up to the Battle of France; Maxime Weygand, *Rappelé au service* (Paris: Flammarion, 1950); Jacques Weygand, *The Role of General Weygand: Conversations with His Son* (London: Eyre and Spottiswoode, 1948); Albert Lebrun, *Témoignage* (Paris: Plon, 1945); Édouard Herriot, *Épisodes, 1940–44* (Paris: Flammarion, 1950); M.-M. Tony-Révillon, *Mes Carnets, juin–octobre 1940* (Paris: Odette-Lieutier, 1945); Jean Montigny, *Heures tragiques de 1940: la défaite* (Paris: Bernard Grasset, 1941), and *Toute la vérité sur un mois dramatique de notre histoire: de l'armistice à l'Assemblée nationale, 15 juin– 15 juillet 1940* (Clermont-Ferrand: Éditions Mont-Louis, 1940); Paul Faure, *De Munich à la Cinquième République* (Paris: Les Éditions de l'Élan, n.d.); Joseph Paul-Boncour, *Entre deux guerres: souvenirs de la Troisième République,* Vol. III: *Sur les chemins de la défaite, 1935–40* (Paris: Plon, 1946); Anatole de Monzie, *Ci-devant* (Paris: Flammarion, 1941); Albert Kammerer, *La Vérité sur l'armistice,* which has been cited; Édouard Barthe, *La Ténébreuse Affaire du "Massilia": une page d'histoire, 18 juin 1940–octobre 1940* (Paris: publisher not indicated, 1945); Jean Odin, *Les Quatre-vingts* (Paris: Tallandier, 1946); F. Charles-Roux, *Cinq Mois tragiques aux Affaires Étrangères, 21 mai–1er novembre 1940* (Paris: Plon, 1949).

Of interest in this same connection are a number of journalistic narratives that appeared soon after the armistice, attempting to explain the debacle to the British and American public and placing blame upon the men who accepted the armistice. Notable among these are: André Géraud ("Pertinax"), *The Grave-Diggers of France: Gamelin, Daladier, Reynaud, Pétain, and Laval* (New York: Doubleday, Doran, 1944); André Simone, *J'Accuse: The Men Who Betrayed France* (New York: The Dial Press, 1940); Heinz Pol, *Suicide of a Democracy* (New York: Reynal and Hitchcock, 1940); and André Schwob, *L'Affaire Pétain: faits et documents* (New York: Éditions de la Maison Française, 1944), a classic statement of the charge that Pétain took power as the result of a long-standing plot to overthrow the Third Republic.

A number of books dealing with the Riom trials appeared at the time both in France and abroad, and others were published after the liberation. Among them are: Pierre Tissier, *The Riom Trial* (London: George G. Harrap, 1942), from the Gaullist point of view; Hector Ghilini, *À la barre de Riom* (Paris: Jean-Renard, 1942), from the opposite side; Pierre Mazé and Roger Génébrier, *Les Grandes Journées du procès de Riom* (Paris: La Jeune Parque, 1945); and Édouard Daladier, writing under the name of James de Coquet, *Le Procès de Riom* (Paris: Arthème Fayard, 1945).

Professor Louis Rougier has supplied his own account of his mission to London: *Mission secrète à Londres: les accords Pétain-Churchill* (Geneva: Les Éditions du Cheval Ailé, 1948), which is a revised edition of his earlier *Les Accords Pétain-Churchill: histoire d'une mission secrète* (Montreal: Éditions Beauchemin, 1945).

Of interest regarding the downfall of the regime are: J. Joubert, *La Libération de la France* (Paris: Payot, 1951); Adrien Dansette, *La Libération de Paris* (Paris: Flammarion, 1945); Pierre Taittinger, *Et Paris ne fut pas détruit* (Paris: L'Élan, 1948); and Walter Stucki, *La Fin du régime de Vichy* (Neuchâtel: Éditions de la Baconnière, n.d.). Gordon Wright, *The Reshaping of French Democracy* (New York: Reynal and Hitchcock, 1948), discusses the inception of the Provisional Government.

Another kind of memoir of value is in the nature of a personal narrative, recounting the experiences and impressions of individuals who had no role of importance in public life. Notable among these are: Alfred Fabre-Luce, *Journal de la France, 1939–44* (2 vols., Geneva: Éditions du Cheval Ailé, 1946); Jean Galtier-Boissière, *Mon Journal pendant l'occupation* (Paris: La Jeune Parque, 1944); André Baucher, *Notre Drame* (Paris: Les Éditions Internationales, 1945); Adrien Printz, *Chronique lorraine, 1940–44* (Paris: Denoël, 1945); Léon Werth, *Déposition: journal, 1940–44* (Paris: Bernard Grasset, 1946); Paul de Martigny, *L'Envers de la guerre* (2 vols., Les Éditions du Lévrier, 1946); Jean Albert-Sorel, *Le Calvaire, 1940–44* (Paris: René Juillard-Séquana, 1944); Armand Petitjean, *Combats préliminaires* (Paris: Gallimard, 1942); Roland Dorgelès, *Carte d'identité: récit de l'occupation* (Paris: Albin Michel, 1945); and Jean Guéhenno, *Journal des années noires, 1940–44* (Paris: Gallimard, 1947).

A number of foreigners who remained in France during the occupation or returned for visits have also provided notes. Among these are: Siri Rathsman, *Vichy hat das Spiel verloren: Schilderungen aus dem geschlagenen Frankreich* (Zurich: Europa Verlag, 1945); Eric Lugin, *Messieurs, la France! de la croix gammée à la croix de Lorraine* (Geneva: Les Éditions du Cheval Ailé, 1944); Walter Stucki, the Swiss minister to Vichy, whose work has been mentioned; Thomas Kernan, *France on Berlin Time* (New York and Philadelphia: J. B. Lippincott, 1941); Ray Porter, *Uncensored France: An Eye-Witness Account of France under the Occupation* (New York: The Dial Press, 1942); P. J. Philip, *France in Defeat* (London: Frederick Muller, 1940).

To understand the state of mind in France in the period of Vichy, we must also dip into some of the innumerable books, pamphlets, and tracts which private persons published, defining what seemed to them to be the crucial issues facing the nation and the proper solution. Representative of these writings are: Maurice Beauchamps, *Pour la Rénovation française* (Paris: G. Durassié et Cie., 1941); André Bellesort and others, *France 1941: la Révolution nationale —un bilan et un programme* (Paris: Éditions Alsatia, 1941); Jean Gattino, *Essai sur la Révolution nationale* (Paris: Grasset, 1941); Robert Lafitte-Laplace, *Lendemains: perspectives d'après-guerre* (Paris: Plon, 1943); Y. Urvoy, *La Révolution du XXᵉ siècle et la France* (Paris: Presses Universitaires de France, 1942); Raymond Plantier, *La Fin d'un régime: la naissance d'un ordre nouveau* (Poitiers: Imprimerie de L'Avenir de la Vienne, 1940); F. Alengry, *Principes généraux de la philosophie sociale et politique du maréchal Pétain* (Paris: Charles-Lavauzelle et Cie., 1943); Henri Marre, *Essai sur le gouvernement* (Montpellier: published by the author, 1940), and *Notre Salut* (Paris and Clermont: Fernand Sorlot, 1940); M. S. Gillet, *Réveil de l'âme française* (Paris: Flammarion, 1942); J.-J. Almira, *Thèses pour la révolution nationale: du libéralisme économique à une politique sociale* (Paris: J. Peyronnet et Cie., 1943); Jean Rivain, *Lettres au maréchal Pétain: pour l'unité française des idées et des hommes* (Paris: Éditions Alsatia, 1943); J. Picavet, *La Révolution nationale est un fait: la fin de la Troisième République, l'œuvre du maréchal* (Amiens: Imprimerie Yvert et Cie., 1941); Albert Arsac, *Retrouver la France* (Roanne: Éditions Positions, 1944); Robert Valéry-Radot, *Sources d'un doctrine nationale, de Joseph de Maistre à Charles Péguy* (Paris: Séquana, 1942); Jean de Grillet, *La France en marche* (Dijon: Imprimerie Darantière, 1941).

Representative expositions of the doctrines of corporatism in the period of Vichy include: Ernest Wattel, *Charte, corporation, révolution* (Paris: Berger-Levrault, 1943); Auguste Murat, *Le Corporatisme* (Paris: Les Publications Techniques, 1944); Max Principale, *Communauté et corporation* (Paris: Les Éditions Domat-Montchrétien, 1943); M. N. Lenormand, *Vers le régime corporatif* (Paris: Les Éditions de la Nouvelle France, 1943); Jean Luchaire, *Partage du pouvoir: patrons et salariés* (Paris: Éditions Balzac,

1943); Louis Baudin, *Le Corporatisme: Italie, Portugal, Allemagne, Espagne, France* (Paris: Librairie Générale de Droit et de Jurisprudence, 1942). The application of corporatism to agriculture is touched on in Jean Gazave, *La Terre ne ment pas: introduction à une physiocratie nouvelle* (Villefranche-de-Rouergue: C. Salingardes, 1941), and Camille Rosier, *La France agricole* (Paris: Éditions Alsatia, 1943).

In general, no endeavor has been made in this study to utilize other than French sources. Mention must be made, however, of a certain number of such sources and works which are of special interest or importance.

Notable among these is Winston Churchill, *The Second World War* (6 vols., New York: Houghton Mifflin, 1948–51). Vol. II, in particular, is of large value for what it reveals concerning the events leading up to the armistice in 1940.

Louis P. Lochner, ed., *The Goebbels Diaries, 1942–43* (New York: Doubleday, 1948), includes a number of references to personalities in Vichy and Paris. Also of marginal interest is Malcolm Muggeridge, ed., *Ciano's Diplomatic Papers* (London: Odhams Press, 1948).

Indications of value for the relations of Spain with Vichy and the Axis are to be had in: Ramon Serrano Suñer, *Entre les Pyrénées et Gibraltar: notes et réflexions sur la politique espagnole depuis 1936* (Geneva: Les Éditions du Cheval Ailé, 1947); Sir Samuel Hoare, *Complacent Dictator* (New York: Knopf, 1947); and Carlton J. H. Hayes, *Wartime Mission in Spain* (New York: Macmillan, 1945).

Admiral William D. Leahy, *I Was There: The Personal Story of the Chief of Staff to Presidents Roosevelt and Truman* (New York: Whittlesey House, 1950), includes mention of the author's services as U.S. Ambassador in Vichy.

Of special interest is William L. Langer, *Our Vichy Gamble* (New York: Knopf, 1947), which is an account of the relations of the United States with Vichy. Though he treats of Vichy only as the object of American policy, the author speaks with exceptional authority since he has had access to information in the archives of the State Department which is not yet available to other scholars. Much the same value attaches to the remarks on France which appear in *The Challenge to Isolation, 1937–40* (New York: Harper and Bros., 1952), and *The Undeclared War, 1940–41* (New York: Harper and Bros., 1953), which Professor Langer has written in collaboration with S. Everett Gleason.

INDEX